TAKING SIDES

Clashing Views in

Mass Media and Society

TAKING SIDES

Clashing Views in
Mass Media and Society

TWELFTH EDITION

Selected, Edited, and with Introductions by

Alison Alexander
University of Georgia

and

Jarice Hanson
University of Massachusetts at Amherst

McGraw-Hill

Connect
Learn
Succeed™

Connect
Learn
Succeed™

TAKING SIDES: CLASHING VIEWS IN MASS MEDIA AND SOCIETY, TWELFTH EDITION

Published by McGraw-Hill, a business unit of The McGraw-Hill Companies, Inc., 1221 Avenue of the Americas, New York, NY 10020. Copyright © 2013 by The McGraw-Hill Companies, Inc. All rights reserved. Printed in the United States of America. Previous editions © 2011, 2009, and 2007. No part of this publication may be reproduced or distributed in any form or by any means, or stored in a database or retrieval system, without the prior written consent of The McGraw-Hill Companies, Inc., including, but not limited to, in any network or other electronic storage or transmission, or broadcast for distance learning.

Some ancillaries, including electronic and print components, may not be available to customers outside the United States.

This book is printed on acid-free paper.

Taking Sides® is a registered trademark of the McGraw-Hill Companies, Inc.
Taking Sides is published by the **Contemporary Learning Series** group within the McGraw-Hill Higher Education division.

1 2 3 4 5 6 7 8 9 0 DOC/DOC 1 0 9 8 7 6 5 4 3 2

MHID: 0-07-805041-3
ISBN: 978-0-07-805041-1
ISSN: 2165-736X (print)
ISSN: 2165-7378 (online)

Managing Editor: *Larry Loeppke*
Developmental Editor: *Dave Welsh*
Permissions Coordinator: *Shirley Lanners*
Senior Marketing Communications Specialist: *Mary Klein*
Project Manager: *Erin Melloy*
Design Coordinator: *Brenda A. Rolwes*
Cover Graphics: *Rick D. Noel*
Buyer: *Nicole Baumgartner*
Media Project Manager: *Sridevi Palani*

Compositor: MPS Limited
Cover Image: © Getty Images RF

www.mhhe.com

Editors/Academic Advisory Board

Members of the Academic Advisory Board are instrumental in the final selection of articles for each edition of TAKING SIDES. Their review of articles for content, level, and appropriateness provides critical direction to the editors and staff. We think that you will find their careful consideration well reflected in this volume.

TAKING SIDES: Clashing Views in MASS MEDIA AND SOCIETY

Twelfth Edition

EDITORS

Alison Alexander
University of Georgia

and

Jarice Hanson
University of Massachusetts at Amherst

ACADEMIC ADVISORY BOARD MEMBERS

Editors/Academic Advisory Board continued

Preface

Communication is one of the most popular college majors in the country, which perhaps reflects a belief in the importance of media, as well as students' desires to work in one of the communications industries. Investigations into mass media and society have grown to incorporate the plethora of digital technologies that sometimes use the traditional media infrastructure, but also provide yet another context for exploring how media, messages, and audiences, all understand the communication process. Increasingly, people have the capacity to become producers of mediated content that can be shared online, through blogs, Web sites, social networking sites, and podcasts. Never before have we had the capacity to consume mass media, as well as produce our own forms of media and have a platform for low-cost or free distribution over the Internet. This book, which contains 36 selections presented in a pro and con format, addresses 18 controversial issues in media and society. The purpose of the volume, and indeed of any course that deals with the social impact of media, is to create a literate consumer of media—someone who can walk the fine line between a naïve acceptance of all media and a cynical disregard for any positive benefits that they may offer.

When we began this series, we concentrated on mass media that produced content for mass distribution to a large, anonymous audience. Today, we live in a world in which mass media compete with user-generated content and media that are directed to niche audiences. Today's media reflect the evolution of industries that have spread their reach to multiple types of media and, indeed, to more nations of the world than ever before. In the United States we have seen the impact of entertainment media on many forms of public discourse—news, politics, education, and more. We have also seen communication technologies rapidly enter the home in a number of ways: through the Internet and personal devices such as iPods, PDAs, and cell phones. These many forms of media extend our capacities to communicate and to consume media content, as well as to become producers of media content.

The study of media and society is very much a part of the way in which we live our lives by blending technologies and services, public and private media uses, and public and private behaviors. In the near future, many of the technologies we use today may be subsumed by yet newer technologies, or greater use of those that we already use. Film, television, music, radio, and print all come to us today over the Internet, and we expect that cell phones may soon replace laptop computers as the "all-in-one" portable technology. Since many of the issues in this volume are often in the news (or even constitute the news), you may already have opinions about them. We encourage you to read the selections and discuss the issues with an open mind. Even if you do not initially agree with a position or do not even understand how it is possible to make an opposing argument, give it a try. Remember, these problems often are not restricted to only two views; there may be many. We have expanded the introductions to each issue and have attempted to give you a "broader range" of potential ways of thinking about these issues and we encourage you to discuss these topics as broadly as possible. We believe that thinking seriously about media is an important goal.

Plan of the Book

This book is primarily designed for students in an introductory course in mass communication (sometimes called introduction to mass media, or introduction to mass media and society). We know that various instructors have found this book useful for courses in writing about communication topics, ethics, and public speaking. The issues are such that they can be easily incorporated into any media course regardless of how it is organized—thematically, chronologically, or by media form. The 36 selections have been taken from a variety of sources and were chosen because of their usefulness in defending a position and for their accessibility to students.

Each issue in this volume has an introduction, which sets the stage for the debate as it is argued in the YES and NO selections. We also pose a number of Learning Outcomes to help guide reading. Each issue concludes with a section called "Exploring the Issue" that makes some final observations about the selections and points the way to other questions related to the issue, and we indicate points of similarity in the section called "Is There Common Ground?" We also offer suggestions for further reading on the issue with additional resources.

In reading an issue and forming your own opinion, you should not feel confined to adopt one or the other of the positions presented. Some readers may see important points on both sides of an issue and may construct for themselves a new and creative approach. Such an approach might incorporate the best of both sides, or it might provide an entirely new vantage point for understanding. Relevant Internet site addresses (URLs) that may prove useful as starting points for further research are provided on the Internet References page that accompanies each unit. At the back of the book is a listing of all of the contributors to this volume, which will give you additional information on the communication scholars, practitioners, policymakers, and media critics whose views are debated here.

Changes to this edition   The twelfth edition represents a considerable revision, and the topics are perhaps more controversial than in past editions. This may be a reflection of the world in which we live, or perhaps it is the result of a greater awareness of media literacy and the ability of consumers of media now to become producers of content. Unit 1, "Media and Social Issues," includes three issues, the majority of which are new to this edition. Unit 2, "A Question of Content," addresses three key pervasive issues about the impact of content in media, with one new selection and two popular issues from Edition 11. Unit 3, "News and Politics," addresses three issues (one that is new to this edition and one with new selections) dealing with contemporary problems associated with politics and journalism. Unit 4, "Law and Policy," reflects three issues that are prominent in media today. Unit 5, "Media Business," now incorporates three issues dealing with the viability of legacy industries adapting to online models, but also addresses two of the most rapidly changing industries, music and newspapers Each of these issues has been updated with new selections. We conclude with Unit 6, "Life in the Digital Age," with three issues, all of which reflect the critical changes to the way we use media in the digital age.

A word to the instructor   An Instructor's Resource Guide with Test Questions (multiple-choice and essay) is available through the publisher for the instructor using Taking Sides in the classroom. A general guidebook, Using Taking Sides in the Classroom, which discusses methods and techniques for integrating the pro–con approach to a classroom setting, is also available. An online version of Using Taking Sides in the Classroom and a correspondence service for Taking Sides adopters can be found at www.mhhe.com/cls.

Acknowledgments   We wish to acknowledge the encouragement, support, and detail given to this project. We are particularly grateful to David Welsh, who has thoughtfully, carefully, and painstakingly worked with us to produce the best edition possible, and who has guided us through a substantial revision of this book.

We would also like to extend our appreciation to the many professors who reviewed our previous edition, and we are grateful for the advice they have provided in the preparation of this edition.

Finally, we would like to thank our families and friends (David, James, Katie, Jaime, and Torie, and Frank, Dewey, and Xena) for their patience and understanding during the period in which we prepared this book. Being cats, Dewey and Xena particularly appreciated the number of pages that were generated for this book because they provided a comfortable place for a nap.

Alison Alexander
University of Georgia

Jarice Hanson
University of Massachusetts at Amherst

Contents in Brief

Contents

Associate Professor Leigh H. Edwards examines how families are
portrayed in television and discusses how certain narrative tropes, trends,
and genres present us with real family relationships representative of
American society and culture. She raises the important point that reality
television in particular presents viewers with real conflicts to which many
families can relate, because the programs portray real cultural problems
that have no easy answers. She concludes her argument with an
assessment that public debates about family and marriage often frame the
content of the families we see on television. Sociology Professor Karen
Sternheimer cites public controversies about the real lives and on-screen
portrayals of families by celebrities who are often criticized for contributing
to demeaning family values in popular culture. She argues that these
celebrities and media figures are not to be blamed for contributing to moral
chaos, when the real-world economy provides a more powerful argument
for examining families, values, and problems in American life.

Film critic and professor Marcia Landy examines two major events in U.S.
history: the attack on Pearl Harbor in 1941 and the events of 9/11/2001 to
examine how each event has been portrayed in media and has reinforced
some values that include patriotism, destiny, and victimhood. She
examines representative issues from different forms of media to show that
all forms of media contribute to reinforcing ideas about Americanism and

American character. Noted social critic Michael Eric Dyson reflects on the August 2005 Hurricane Katrina disaster, which flooded most of the city of New Orleans and caused massive social upheaval as 90 percent of the residents of Louisiana and surrounding areas were asked to evacuate to avoid the storm. During the Katrina disaster, local media outlets were destroyed, so media elsewhere told the story of Katrina's impact. According to Dyson, the story told relied on traditional stereotypes of Blacks, rather than telling the real story of poverty, which so severely affected the lives and deaths of so many people of color.

Wajahat Ali, Eli Clifton, Matthew Duss, Lee Fang, Scott Keyes, and Faiz Shakir discuss in Fear, Inc., a special report from the Center for American Progress, how the Muslim religion is among the most maligned stereotypes in popular culture, and how these images have fueled misperceptions about the Arab world. It explores how media have been an echo chamber for misinformation created by well-funded groups dedicated to spreading fear and misinformation. These images influence politicians and citizens and contribute to public opinion. Journalist Gal Beckerman discusses how Arab bloggers from the Middle East are challenging popular stereotypes of Arab and Middle Eastern cultures. Because these bloggers are writing about their lives, the global public can read about their situations and understand them as individuals, rather than racial or ethnic group members.

UNIT 2   A QUESTION OF CONTENT   69

Shari Dworkin and Faye Wachs discuss the results of their content analysis of health magazine ads and find that the ads tell men and women that a healthy body is attainable if they buy the products and pamper themselves. Fat becomes something to be feared, and grooming practices and fashion are "sold" as imperatives for both men and women. Michael Levine and Sarah Murnen also investigate magazine ads, but find the

substance, and *The Daily Show* to be more humor than substance. The amount of substantive information between the two newscasts was about the same for both the story and for the entire half-hour program. Barry Hollander examined learning from comedy and late-night programs. National survey data were used to examine whether exposure to comedy and late-night programs actually informs viewers, focusing on recall and recognition. Some support is found for the prediction that the consumption of such programs is more associated with recognition of information than with actual recall.

In a special report *The Economist* studies "The People Formerly Known as the Audience" to argue that social media allow a wider range of people to take part in gathering, filtering, and distributing the news. A torrent of information is being posted on the Internet, creating a role for people—not limited to journalists, to evaluate, verify, and create meaning. Alex Jones describes the iron core of journalism as fact-based accountability journalism, an expensive, intensive search for information that holds those with power accountable. Opinion journalism, quasi-news programs, and even entertainment media rely on the iron core for their substance. Whether journalism that produces the iron core will continue to function as is needed is his concern.

Clay Shirky considers the ways social media have been used to organize protest and promote social change. He writes about short- and long-term consequences of social media use, but notes that the most important impact of social media use is in the promotion of a civil society and lasting change. Social media, he argues, can create shared awareness, which makes it harder for repressive regimes to maintain the status quo. Malcolm Gladwell argues that social media is unlikely to make a difference. Social change requires powerful and interpersonal ties. It is interpersonal connections that will motivate social activism, he asserts. Social media may be effective in the short term, but cannot generate the levels of commitment necessary to effect social change.

In this essay, Henry Giroux questions how and why our culture has become so mean spirited. By addressing media content in news and popular fare, he analyzes how the politics of a "pedagogy of hate" has become an exercise in power that ultimately has created a "culture of cruelty." As part of this imposed philosophy, citizens have begun to question and undermine our government's responsibility to protect their interests. Georgie Ann Weatherby and Brian Scoggins examine the content of the Web pages of four extremist groups on the Internet and discuss the persuasive techniques each uses. They find that the sites draw from traditional tactics that "soft-pedal" positions that emphasize recruiting, while downplaying the messages of hate.

Neil Swidey addresses the issue of anonymous online posters who register their opinions on the *Boston Globe* Web site, www.Boston .com. He discusses how some abusive and vitriolic postings sometimes have to be eliminated by site moderators, and how important it is to some people to have access to posting their opinions online. Unlike traditional newspapers, where comments to the editor contain a reader's name and address, the anonymous poster sometimes becomes so offensive that the nature and value of online commentary are called into question. In examining the legal relationship between privacy and anonymity, Ian Lloyd provides both a legal approach toward protecting privacy and anonymity, and provides examples of how everyday behavior challenges our expectations of anonymity and privacy when data collections violate a person's reasonable expectation of privacy. He writes that although the legal approach toward more online communication attempts to protect personal rights, good intentions often backfire, and life in the digital age comes with some possible breaches of trust.

In this selection, Siva Vaidhyanathan discusses how applications of copyright to music, film, publishing, and software companies all result in a complex system of trying to protect original ownership of intellectual property. The author gives several examples, including Google's efforts to digitize entire libraries, but reminds us that copyright also gives owners the right to say no. Stephanie Ardito examines how social networking sites have created problems for protecting copyright, because laws and enforcement of copyright law are so difficult. She believes big media companies and social networking sites will ultimately give up trying to enforce copyright, because it is too expensive and time consuming.

UNIT 5 MEDIA BUSINESS   287

Greg Kot explains the business model that dominated the recording industry throughout the 1990s and into the 2000s. In this excerpt, he identifies how rapidly the old business model crumbled and how record executives feared the evolving technological changes that foretold of an economic model that would revolutionize the corporate music structure. Panos Panay examines specific changes to the live music scene, and the growth of niche markets that contributed to the evolution of several new models for the music business. Despite a poor economy in 2010, fans are becoming more active and involved in the production of a successful band and/or record. Along with a new model of entrepreneurship, Panay offers insights to how the recording industry is evolving.

Clay Shirky argues that the old economies of newspapers are destroyed in the digital age. This is a revolution similar to that which occurred with the invention of the printing press. No one knows what the future will hold, but we can only hope that journalism is not lost with the demise of newspapers. All news media are facing challenges in these difficult economic times. Paul Farhi, a *Washington Post* staff writer, argues that newspapers have unique competitive advantages that should assure that the worst case won't happen.

Chris Anderson, an editor of *Wired* magazine, writes of the decline of the mass market and the rise of niche markets. He claims that the future of business, particularly in book, music, and DVD sales, will shift toward selling a wider range of media to audiences that have much broader interests. Professor Kathryn Montgomery looks at the cooperative relationships between social interest groups and media content providers, to better understand how themes with social objectives permeate media content.

UNIT 6   LIFE IN THE DIGITAL AGE   349

Author and professor David T. Z. Mindich addresses the sobering facts of why youth do not follow the news. He links this with low voter turnout, a widening knowledge gap between younger and older citizens, and a lack of trust in news media. The author of *Tuned Out: Why Americans Under 40 Don't Follow the News*, Mindich explores the essential link between news and information and being an informed and engaged citizen. The Pew Internet & American Life Project released *The Internet and Civic Engagement* in 2009. This report examined whether the Internet could change long-established patterns of civic and political involvement. Based on a sample of more than 2,000 adults, the project found that new forms of civic engagement based on the Internet, blogs, and social media have the potential to alter long-standing patterns of information and engagement of younger voters.

Penny Leisring discusses negative effects of using online technology to cyberstalk or harass someone. Use of social networking, e-mail, GPS systems, cell phone spamming, and caller ID all can be used to create a threatening or hostile environment for those people who use them for antisocial purposes. The author also addresses the situations that lend themselves most often to these undesirable uses of communication technology, such as in the break-up of romantic relationships, abusive relationships, or just plain hostile behaviors and interactions. Amanda Lenhart reports the findings of a Pew Internet & American Life Project that investigated the likelihood of teen harassment and cyberbullying and finds that the most likely candidates to experience online abuse are girls between the ages of 15 and 17, though the reported statistics for all teens of both genders are disturbing. However, Amanda Lenhart reports that, still, more teens report being bullied offline than online.

Linda Jackson et al. conducted a 16-month survey of Internet use by youth age 10–18 in low-income homes. They found that youth who used the Internet more had higher scores on standardized tests of reading achievement and higher GPAs. This work supports the optimism surrounding the Internet as a tool to level the educational playing field. Mark Bauerlein finds the hopes for better-educated youth in the digital age to be an empty promise. Youth spend much of their leisure time in front of computer and television screens, but the information age has failed to produce a well-informed, thoughtful public. Instead we have a nation of know-nothings who don't read, follow politics, or vote—and who can't compete internationally.

Correlation Guide

The *Taking Sides* series presents current issues in a debate-style format designed to stimulate student interest and develop critical thinking skills. Each issue is thoughtfully framed with an issue summary, an issue introduction, and an Exploring the Issue section. The pro and con essays—selected for their liveliness and substance—represent the arguments of leading scholars and commentators in their fields.

Taking Sides: Clashing Views in Mass Media and Society, 12/e is an easy-to-use reader that presents issues on important topics such as *the future of newspapers, video violence,* and *social media and bullying.* For more information on *Taking Sides* and other *McGraw-Hill Contemporary Learning Series* titles, visit www.mhhe.com/cls.

This convenient guide matches the issues in **Taking Sides: Clashing Views in Mass Media and Society, 12/e** with the corresponding chapters in three of our best-selling McGraw-Hill Mass Media textbooks by Dominick and Baran.

Taking Sides: Mass Media and Society, 12/e	Dynamics of Mass Communication: Media in Transition, 12/e by Dominick	Introduction to Mass Communication: Media Literacy and Culture, 7/e by Baran	Introduction to Mass Communication: Media Literacy and Culture, Updated Edition, 7/e by Baran
Issue 1: Are Family Values Shaped by the Mass Media?	**Chapter 3:** Historical and Cultural Context	**Chapter 1:** Mass Communication, Culture, and Media Literacy **Chapter 13:** Theories and Effects of Mass Communication	**Chapter 1:** Mass Communication, Culture, and Media Literacy **Chapter 13:** Theories and Effects of Mass Communication
Issue 2: Do Media Unite the Population in Times of Crisis?	**Chapter 18:** Social Effects of Mass Communication	**Chapter 13:** Theories and Effects of Mass Communication	**Chapter 13:** Theories and Effects of Mass Communication
Issue 3: Do Media Distort Representations of Islam and Arab Cultures?	**Chapter 3:** Historical and Cultural Context **Chapter 17:** Ethics and Other Informal Controls	**Chapter 1:** Mass Communication, Culture, and Media Literacy	**Chapter 1:** Mass Communication, Culture, and Media Literacy
Issue 4: Do Media Cause Individuals to Develop Negative Body Images?	**Chapter 15:** Advertising **Chapter 18:** Social Effects of Mass Communication	**Chapter 12:** Advertising **Chapter 13:** Theories and Effects of Mass Communication	**Chapter 12:** Advertising **Chapter 13:** Theories and Effects of Mass Communication
Issue 5: Do Video Games Encourage Violent Behavior?	**Chapter 12:** The Internet and the World Wide Web	**Chapter 9:** Video Games	**Chapter 9:** Video Games

Taking Sides: Mass Media and Society, 12/e	Dynamics of Mass Communication: Media in Transition, 12/e by Dominick	Introduction to Mass Communication: Media Literacy and Culture, 7/e by Baran	Introduction to Mass Communication: Media Literacy and Culture, Updated Edition, 7/e by Baran
Issue 6: Is Advertising Good for Society?	**Chapter 15:** Advertising	**Chapter 12:** Advertising **Chapter 14:** Media Freedom, Regulation, and Ethics	**Chapter 12:** Advertising **Chapter 14:** Media Freedom, Regulation, and Ethics
Issue 7: Does Fake News Mislead the Public?	**Chapter 13:** News Gathering and Reporting	**Chapter 8:** Television, Cable, and Mobile Video **Chapter 14:** Media Freedom, Regulation, and Ethics	**Chapter 8:** Television, Cable, and Mobile Video **Chapter 14:** Media Freedom, Regulation, and Ethics
Issue 8: Will Evolving Forms of Journalism Be an Improvement?	**Chapter 5:** Newspapers **Chapter 13:** News Gathering and Reporting	**Chapter 10:** The Internet and the World Wide Web	**Chapter 10:** The Internet and the World Wide Web
Issue 9: Do Social Media Encourage Revolution?	**Chapter 4:** The Internet and Social Media **Chapter 13:** News Gathering and Reporting **Chapter 18:** Social Effects of Mass Communication	**Chapter 10:** The Internet and the World Wide Web	**Chapter 10:** The Internet and the World Wide Web
Issue 10: Is Hate Speech in the Media Directly Affecting Our Culture?	**Chapter 5:** Newspapers **Chapter 13:** News Gathering and Reporting	**Chapter 10:** The Internet and the World Wide Web **Chapter 14:** Media Freedom, Regulation, and Ethics	**Chapter 10:** The Internet and the World Wide Web **Chapter 14:** Media Freedom, Regulation, and Ethics
Issue 11: Does Online Communication Compromise the Rights of an Individual When Information Is "Anonymous?"	**Chapter 4:** The Internet and Social Media	**Chapter 10:** The Internet and the World Wide Web **Chapter 14:** Media Freedom, Regulation, and Ethics	**Chapter 10:** The Internet and the World Wide Web **Chapter 14:** Media Freedom, Regulation, and Ethics
Issue 12: Do Copyright Laws Protect Ownership of Intellectual Property?	**Chapter 16:** Formal Controls: Laws, Rules, Regulations	**Chapter 10:** The Internet and the World Wide Web **Chapter 14:** Media Freedom, Regulation, and Ethics	**Chapter 10:** The Internet and the World Wide Web **Chapter 14:** Media Freedom, Regulation, and Ethics
Issue 13: Did Consolidation of the Music Industry Hurt Music Distribution?	**Chapter 9:** Sound Recording	**Chapter 7:** Radio, Recording, and Popular Music **Chapter 14:** Media Freedom, Regulation, and Ethics	**Chapter 7:** Radio, Recording, and Popular Music **Chapter 14:** Media Freedom, Regulation, and Ethics

(Continued)

Taking Sides: Mass Media and Society, 12/e	Dynamics of Mass Communication: Media in Transition, 12/e by Dominick	Introduction to Mass Communication: Media Literacy and Culture, 7/e by Baran	Introduction to Mass Communication: Media Literacy and Culture, Updated Edition, 7/e by Baran
Issue 14: Should Newspapers Shut Down Their Presses?	**Chapter 4:** Newspapers	**Chapter 7:** Radio, Recording, and Popular Music **Chapter 14:** Media Freedom, Regulation, and Ethics	**Chapter 7:** Radio, Recording, and Popular Music **Chapter 14:** Media Freedom, Regulation, and Ethics
Issue 15: Do New Business Models Result in Greater Consumer Choice of Products and Ideas?	**Chapter 2:** Perspectives on Mass Communication	**Chapter 2:** Convergence and the Reshaping of Mass Communication	**Chapter 2:** Convergence and the Reshaping of Mass Communication
Issue 16: Are Youth Indifferent to News and Politics?	**Chapter 18:** Social Effects of Mass Communication	**Chapter 2:** Convergence and the Reshaping of Mass Communication	**Chapter 2:** Convergence and the Reshaping of Mass Communication
Issue 17: Are Online Services Responsible for an Increase in Bullying and Harassment?	**Chapter 18:** Social Effects of Mass Communication	**Chapter 10:** The Internet and the World Wide Web **Chapter 13:** Theories and Effects of Mass Communication	**Chapter 10:** The Internet and the World Wide Web **Chapter 13:** Theories and Effects of Mass Communication
Issue 18: Are People Better Informed in the Information Society?	**Chapter 13:** News Gathering and Reporting **Chapter 18:** Social Effects of Mass Communication	**Chapter 2:** Convergence and Reshaping of Mass Communication **Chapter 10:** The Internet and the World Wide Web **Chapter 13:** Theories and Effects of Mass Communication	**Chapter 2:** Convergence and Reshaping of Mass Communication **Chapter 10:** The Internet and the World Wide Web **Chapter 13:** Theories and Effects of Mass Communication

Topic Guide

This topic guide suggests how the selections in this book relate to the subjects covered in your course. You may want to use the topics listed on these pages to search the Web more easily. They are arranged to reflect the issues of this Taking Sides reader. You can link to these sites by going to www.mhhe.com/cls. All the articles that relate to each topic are listed below the bold-faced term.

Advertising

6. Is Advertising Good for Society?

Body Image

4. Do Media Cause Individuals to Develop Negative Body Images?

Consumer Generated Content

3. Do Media Distort Representations of Islam and Arab Cultures?
8. Will Evolving Forms of Journalism Be an Improvement?

Crisis Communication

2. Do Media Unite the Population in Times of Crisis?

Cultural Images

1. Are Family Values Shaped by the Mass Media?
2. Do Media Unite the Population in Times of Crisis?
3. Do Media Distort Representations of Islam and Arab Cultures?
4. Do Media Cause Individuals to Develop Negative Body Images?

Cyberbullying

17. Are Online Services Responsible for an Increase in Bullying and Harassment?

Digital Rights/Intellectual Property

12. Do Copyright Laws Protect Ownership of Intellectual Property?
13. Did Consolidation of the Music Industry Hurt Music Distribution?

Family Values

1. Are Family Values Shaped by the Mass Media?

First Amendment

10. Is Hate Speech in the Media Directly Affecting Our Culture?
11. Does Online Communication Compromise the Rights of an Individual When Information Is "Anonymous?"

Information Age

11. Does Online Communication Compromise the Rights of an Individual When Information Is "Anonymous?"
18. Are People Better Informed in the Information Society?

Internet

10. Is Hate Speech in the Media Directly Affecting Our Culture?
11. Does Online Communication Compromise the Rights of an Individual When Information Is "Anonymous?"
17. Are Online Services Responsible for an Increase in Bullying and Harassment?
18. Are People Better Informed in the Information Society?

Journalism

2. Do Media Unite the Population in Times of Crisis?
7. Does Fake News Mislead the Public?
8. Will Evolving Forms of Journalism Be an Improvement?
14. Should Newspapers Shut Down Their Presses?
16. Are Youth Indifferent to News and Politics?

(Continued)

Introduction

Ways of Thinking about Mass Media and Society

Alison Alexander and Jarice Hanson

Media are everywhere in the industrialized world today. It is likely that anyone reading this book has access to more forms of media than their grandparents could have ever dreamed of. Many readers are probably adept at multitasking—a term unheard of when this book series began in 1987. Many readers are probably adept at using so many technologies that deliver content over the Internet or cell phones that it almost seems strange to think that broadcast TV, cable TV, film, radio, newspapers, books and magazines, and the recording industry all once were thought of as different forms of media, all delivered in different ways, and all with different economic structures. The convergence of these media over wired and wireless distribution forms now presents us with words, sounds, and images that often blur former distinctions among media forms and industries.

Media are also often scapegoats for the problems of society. Sometimes the relationship of social issues and media seems too obvious *not* to have some connection. For example, violence in the media may be a reflection of society, or, as some critics claim, violence in the media makes it seem that violence in society is the norm. But in reality, one important reason that the media are so often blamed for social problems is that the media are so pervasive. Their very ubiquity gives them the status that makes them seem more influential than they actually are. If one were to look at the statistics on violence in the United States, it would be possible to see that there are fewer violent acts today than in recent history—but the presence of this violence in the media, through reportage or fictional representation, makes it appear more prevalent.

There are many approaches to investigating the relationships that are suggested by media and society. From an organizational perspective, the producers of media must find content and distribution forms that will be profitable, and therefore, they have a unique outlook on the audience as consumers. From the perspective of the creative artist, the profit motive may be important, but the exploration of the unique communicative power of the media may be paramount. The audience, too, has different use patterns, desires for information or entertainment, and demonstrates a variety of choices in content offered to them, as well as what they take from the media. Whether the media reflect society or shape society has a lot to do with the dynamic interaction of many of these different components.

To complicate matters, the "mass" media have changed in recent years. Not long ago, "mass" media referred to messages that were created by large organizations for broad, heterogeneous audiences. This concept no longer suffices for the contemporary media environments. While the "mass" media still exist in the forms of radio, television, film, and general interest newspapers and magazines, many media forms today are hybrids of "mass" and "personal" media technologies that open a new realm of understanding about how audiences process the meaning of the messages. Audiences may be smaller and more diverse, but the phenomenon of using media to form a picture of the world and our place in it is still the fundamental reason for studying the relationship of media and society.

As we look at U.S. history, we can see that almost every form of media was first subject to some type of regulation by the government or by the media industry itself. This has changed over the years so that we now have a media environment in which the responsibility for the content of media no longer rests entirely in the hands of the FCC or the major corporations. We, as consumers, are asked to be critical of that media which we consume. This requires that we become educated consumers, rather than relying on standards and practices of industry or government intervention into questionable content. While this may not seem like a big problem for adult consumers, the questions and answers become more difficult when we consider how children use the media to form judgments, form opinions, or seek information.

Our habits are changing as the media landscape grows. The average American still spends over three hours a day viewing television, which is on in the average home over seven hours a day, but recent statistics indicate that the "average" American actually spends about 10 hours a day facing a screen of some sort—whether that is a TV screen, computer screen, or cell phone screen. That interaction with media clearly warrants some understanding of what happens in the process of the person/media interaction and relationship.

Politics and political processes have changed, in part, due to the way politicians use the media to reach voters. A proliferation of television channels has resulted from the popularity of cable, but does cable offer anything different from broadcast television? Videocassettes deliver feature-length films to the home, changing the traditional practice of viewing film in a public place, and video distribution via the Internet is now a practical option for anyone with transmission lines large enough to download large files. The recording industry is still reeling over the impact of MP3 and free software that allows consumers to sample, buy, or steal music online. Communications is a multibillion-dollar industry and the third fastest-growing industry in America. From these and other simple examples, it is clear that the media have changed American society, but our understanding of how and why remains incomplete.

Dynamics of Interaction

In recent years, the proliferation and availability of new media forms have changed on a global scale. In the United States, 98 percent of the homes have at least one telephone, but in 2008 the number of cell phones outnumbered land phones. On a global scale, about half of the world's people now have access to a cell phone. In the United States, over 98 percent of the population has access to at least one television set, but in some parts of the world, televisions are still viewed communally or viewed only at certain hours of the day. The use of broadband connections continues to grow in the United States, while some other countries (usually smaller countries, with high GNP) are reaching saturation with broadband technologies, and other countries still have limited dial-up services for the Internet.

But apart from questions of access and available content, many fundamental questions about the power of media in any given society remain the same. How do audiences use the media available to them? How do message senders produce meaning? How much of the meaning of any message is produced by the audience? And increasingly important for discussion is, How do additional uses of media change our interpersonal environments and human interactions?

Progress in Media Research

Much of media research has been in search of theory. Theory is an organized, commonsense refinement of everyday thinking; it is an attempt to establish a systematic view of a phenomenon in order to better understand that phenomenon. Theory is tested against reality to establish whether or not it is a good explanation; so, for example, a researcher might notice that what is covered by news outlets is very similar to what citizens say are the important issues of the day. From such observations came agenda setting (the notion that the media confer importance on the topics they cover, directing public attention to what is considered important).

Much of the early media research was produced to answer questions of print media because print has long been regarded a permanent record of history and events. The ability of newspapers and books to shape and influence public opinion was regarded as a necessity to the founding of new forms of governments—including the U.S. government; and a good number of our laws and regulations were originally written to favor print (like copyright and freedom of the press). But the bias of the medium carried certain restrictions. Print media necessarily were limited to those individuals who could read. The principles that emerged from this relationship were addressed in an often-quoted statement attributed to Thomas Jefferson, who wrote, "Were it left to me to decide whether we should have a government without newspapers, or newspapers without a government, I should not hesitate a moment to prefer the latter." But the next sentence in Jefferson's statement is equally important and often omitted from quotations: "But I should mean that every man should receive those papers and be capable of reading them." Today, however, the newspaper is no longer the primary distribution form for information that is critical to living in a democracy.

Today, media research on the relationships of media senders, the channels of communication, and the receivers of messages is not enough. Consumers must realize that "media literacy" and maybe even "technological literacy" are important concepts too. People can no longer take for granted that the media exist primarily to provide news, information, and entertainment. They must be more attuned to what media content says about them as individuals and as members of a society, and they need to be aware of how the ability for almost everyone to create media (like blogging, or social networking) challenges traditional ownership and privacy laws and regulations. By integrating these various cultural components, the public can better criticize the regulation or lack of regulation that permits media industries to function the way they do.

The use of social science data to explore the effects of media on audiences strongly emphasized psychological and sociological schools of thought. It did not take long to move from the "magic bullet theory"—which proposed that media had a direct and immediate effect on the receivers of the message, and the same message intended by the senders was the same when it was "shot" into the receiver—to other ideas of limited, or even indirect, means of influencing the audience.

Media research has shifted from addressing specifically effects-oriented paradigms to exploring the nature of the institutions of media production themselves, as well as examining the unique characteristics of each form of media and the ability of the media user to also produce media products. What most researchers agree upon today is that the best way to understand the power and impact of media is to look at context-specific situations to better understand the dynamics involved in the use of media and the importance of the content.

Still, there are many approaches to media research from a variety of interdisciplinary fields: psychology, sociology, linguistics, art, comparative literature, economics, political science, and more. What these avenues of inquiry have in common is that they all tend to focus attention on individuals, families or other social groups, society in general, and culture in the broad sense. All of the interpretations frame meaning and investigate their subjects within institutional frameworks that are specific to any nation and/or culture.

Many of the questions for media researchers in the twenty-first century deal with the continued fragmentation of the audience, caused by greater choice of channels and technologies for traditional and new communication purposes. The power of some of these technologies to reach virtually any place on the globe within fractions of a second will continue to pose questions of access to media and the meaning of the messages transmitted. As individuals become more dependent upon the Internet for communication purposes, the sense of audience will further be changed as individual users choose what they want to receive, pay for, and keep. For all of these reasons, the field of media research is rich, growing, and challenging.

Questions for Consideration

In addressing the issues in this book, it is important to consider some recurring questions:

   1. Are the media unifying or fragmenting? Does media content help
      the socialization process, or does it create anxiety or inaccurate portrayals of the world? Do people understand what they are doing

when they post personal information online or open themselves to immediate criticism and feedback?

2. How are our basic institutions changing as we use media in new and different ways? Do media support or undermine our political processes? Do they change what we think of when we claim to live in a "democracy"? Do media operate in the public interest, or do media serve the rich and powerful corporations' quest for profit? Can the media do both simultaneously?

3. Whose interests do the media represent? Do audiences actively work toward integrating media messages with their own experiences? How do new media technologies change our traditional ways of communicating? Are they leading us to a world in which interpersonal communication is radically altered because we rely on information systems to replace many traditional behaviors?

Summary

We live in a media-rich environment where almost everybody has access to some forms of media and some choices in content. As new technologies and services are developed, are they responding to the problems that previous media researchers and the public have detected? Over time, individuals have improved their ability to unravel the complex set of interactions that tie the media and society together, but they need to continue to question past results, new practices and technologies, and their own evaluative measures. When people critically examine the world around them—a world often presented by the media—they can more fully understand and enjoy the way they relate as individuals, as members of groups, and as members of a society.

Internet References . . .

Communication Studies: General Communication Resources

An encyclopedic resource related to a host of mass communication issues, this site is maintained by the University of Iowa's Department of Communication Studies. It provides excellent links covering advertising, cultural studies, digital media, film, gender, and media studies.

www.uiowa.edu/commstud/resources/general.html

About.com: Secondary Education

A useful article for understanding the process by which book complaints are brought to school systems, the variety of reasons why, and the possible outcomes. Extensive links to additional sources.

http://712educators.about.com/cs/bannedbooks/a/bookbanning.htm

Arab Media & Society

Arab Media & Society is an online journal about all forms of media and their interaction with society in the Muslim world. The site is multimedia and contains archival material as well as real-time excerpts of articles from the Arab media.

www.arabmediasociety.com/about_the_journal.php

Nielsen Media Glossary of Terms

A handy compendium of terms used within the media industries.

www.nielsenmedia.com/glossary/

Media Awareness Network

The Media Awareness Network is a Canadian site dedicated to promoting critical thinking in youth about the media. Media issues discussed include violence, stereotyping, online hate, and information privacy.

www.media-awareness.ca

Media and Social Issues

Do media reflect the social attitudes and concerns of our times, or are they also able to construct, legitimate, and reinforce the social realities, behaviors, attitudes, and images of others? Do they operate to maintain existing power structures, or are they symbolic communication central to our culture? The ways media help us to shape a sense of reality are complex. How much do media influence us, versus how we use media to fit our already preconceived ideas? Should concern be directed toward vulnerable populations like children? If we truly have a variety of information sources and content to choose from, perhaps we can assume that distorted images are balanced with realistic ones—but is this a likely scenario in our society? Questions about the place of media within society, and within what many people call the "information age," are important for us to understand, whether we use media, or whether media use us.

- Are Family Values Shaped by the Mass Media?
- Do Media Unite the Population in Times of Crisis?
- Do Media Distort Representations of Islam and Arab Cultures?

ISSUE 1

Are Family Values Shaped by the Mass Media?

YES: **Leigh H. Edwards**, from "Reality TV and the American Family," in Julie Anne Taddeo and Ken Devorak, eds., *The Tube Has Spoken* (The University Press of Kentucky, 2010), pp. 123–141

NO: **Karen Sternheimer**, from "Hollywood Doesn't Threaten Family Values," *Contexts* (2008)

Learning Outcomes

After reading this issue, you should be able to:

- These selections should help students understand the range of issues related to the portrayal of families in the media and in society.
- Students should better understand the role of reality television as one aspect of communicating social values to the public.
- Students should be able to cite the range of sociological concepts that influence our understanding of the relationship of mass media and society.
- Students should be able to reflect on the relationship of media content and the social impact of the media.

ISSUE SUMMARY

YES: Associate Professor Leigh H. Edwards examines how families are portrayed in television and discusses how certain narrative tropes, trends, and genres present us with real family relationships representative of American society and culture. She raises the important point that reality television in particular presents viewers with real conflicts to which many families can relate, because the programs portray real cultural problems that have no easy answers. She concludes her argument with an assessment that public debates about family and marriage often frame the content of the families we see on television.

NO: Sociology Professor Karen Sternheimer cites public controversies about the real lives and on-screen portrayals of families by celebrities who are often criticized for contributing to demeaning family values in popular culture. She argues that these celebrities and media figures are not to be blamed for contributing to moral chaos, when the real-world economy provides a more powerful argument for examining families, values, and problems in American life.

Do media reflect social reality as though we were looking into a mirror, or do they frame the issues within social life so that we see them in a different way? These basic questions support all studies that focus on the relationship of media and society. From early studies that suggested that the values portrayed in media would be immediately seized by the public, to models of limited and indirect effects, scholars, citizens, and students have grappled with the way media and society inform and relate to each other. Today we no longer question whether the media do affect our values—the question is now, *how* media affects our values?

Since television's early days, families have been represented as the focus of many genres and formats. The assumption that "everyone" can relate to domestic conflict and the roles family members play in their social lives seems to be a basic construct for drama as well as for comedy. Some theories support the idea that a "family structure" is such a basic social group with such universal understanding and appeal that every cast member in a show—whether representing members of a family or not—actually represents an archetype of some member of a family unit.

Television has often been criticized for the way it portrays *family values*. The term itself has become politicized in recent years as television has become a focus for secular and religious debate over morality. Members of some conservative political parties have questioned representations of individuals and families that they feel do not adequately represent the "typical" American family. Others claim that the typical "nuclear" family, which is represented by a female mother, male father, and children, all of whom constitute a primary social group, is no longer the exclusive norm in American society. In this issue, you will undoubtedly have to consider what you feel is a "family" in society today, as well as in popular culture. As you examine your own beliefs, you may have to "take a side."

The authors of these selections approach the topic of family representations in media with particular viewpoints. Professor Leigh H. Edwards' selection gives some history of the representations of the American family in television over the years, but she examines the genre of reality programming to suggest that four narrative structures have evolved: a nostalgia for the traditional nuclear family; representations of a new, modified nuclear family norm in which the husband and wife both work outside the home; an ideal of family pluralism; and a questioning of norms that give us a different sense

3

of family diversity. She cites many contemporary reality television shows in which some semblance of "family" is represented, but claims that what unites all of these diverse family structures is the sense that people have to deal with cultural conflicts.

Karen Sternheimer takes a broader view of the relationship of cultural icons, celebrity, and representations of family issues and values by juxtaposing celebrity culture with mainstream American values. Her viewpoint is that what really contributes to family relationships, structures, and family conflict has much more to do with contemporary social, economic, and political realities than any idolizing of celebrity culture or media content.

In addition to examining the changing family in America and representations of families, this issue addresses bigger questions about the relationship of media and social values in our lives today. We know media are powerful, but their power is not always easy to understand. From ideas such as the "agenda setting theory" of communication, which posits that media do not tell us what to think, but rather tell us what to think *about*, to studies of parasocial interactions (the relationships we form with people whom we see in the media), and ideas of *resonance*, which describes how we relate to the images we see in the media, there are several assumptions and theories to guide an inquiry into the relationship of media content and its relationship to social values.

In general, however, the many representations of family roles and family relationships as portrayed in the media suggest one of the most fundamental themes in all of media today. From fictionalized portrayals to shows that emulate "reality," we interpret media content according to our own experiences, beliefs, assumptions, and values. At the same time, we think of media portrayals as either "believable" or "unbelievable." The tension between these two terms and the thought the "in between" area provides for us gives us a sense of how similar or different our experiences are to the media portrayals of family life, but they may also provide a yardstick by which we gauge our own sense of "normal" or "abnormal." All in all, these media representations of families and family values provide a context to which we measure our own lives and experiences.

YES

Leigh H. Edwards

Reality TV and the American Family

Reality television shows are reframing ideas of the family in U.S. culture. The genre titillates by putting cultural anxieties about the family on display, hawking images of wife swapping, spouse shopping, and date hopping. Its TV landscape is dotted with programs about mating rituals, onscreen weddings, unions arranged by audiences, partners testing their bonds on fantasy dates with others, family switching, home and family improvement, peeks into celebrity households, parents and children marrying each other off on national television, and families pitching their lives as sitcom pilots. Though obviously not the only recurring theme pictured, family is one of the genre's obsessions. Scholars have begun to draw attention to certain questions surrounding family, gender, and sexuality, but we have yet to address fully how the genre debates . . . reshapes the family or to account for the centrality of that theme in reality programming. This discussion of the family is important, since TV has always played such a vital role in both shaping and reflecting fantasies of the American family.

Using historicized textual analysis, this essay demonstrates how the reality TV genre both reflects and helps shape changing "American family" ideals. A significant number of reality shows picture a seemingly newfound family diversity. For every traditional "modern nuclear family," with its wage-earning father, stay-at-home mother, and dependent children, we see a panoply of newer arrangements, such as post-divorce, single-parent, blended, and gay and lesbian families. What is the significance of this family diversity as a recurring theme in factual programming? Concurrent with images of demographic change, we also see a familiar rhetoric of the "family in crisis." Witness the emergency framework of *Nanny 911* (a British nanny must save inept American parents who are at their breaking point) or *Extreme Makeover: Home Edition* (a design team must renovate the home of a family otherwise facing disaster). Their premise is that the American family is in trouble. Many scholars have noted how the family has constantly been described as being in crisis throughout its historical development—with the calamity of the moment always reflecting contemporaneous sociopolitical tensions. The idea of crisis has been used to justify "family values" debates, which usually involve public policy and political rhetoric that uses moral discourses to define what counts as a healthy family.

I would argue that reality programs focused on the familial settings and themes implicitly make their own arguments about the state of the American family, entering long-running family values debates. In their representation of family diversity (which different series laud or decry) and in their use of family crisis motifs, reality narratives capture a sense of anxiety and ambivalence about evolving family life in the United States. Reality TV market themes about our current period of momentous social change: the shift from what sociologists term the "modern family," the nuclear model that reached its full expression in the context of Victorianera industrialization and peaked in the postwar 1950s, to the "postmodern family," a diversity of forms that have emerged since then. Indeed, a key theme in reality TV depictions is that family is now perpetually in process or in flux, open to debate. Social historians define the modern family as a nuclear unit with a male breadwinner, female homemaker, and dependent children; its gendered division of labor was largely only an option historically for the white middle class whose male heads of household had access to the "family wage." This form was naturalized as universal but was never the reality for a majority of people, even though it was upheld as a dominant cultural ideal. Diverse arrangements have appeared since the 1960s and 1970s, constituting what the historian Edward Shorter termed "the postmodern family." New familial forms have emerged, spurred by increases in divorce rates and single-parent households, women's entrance into the labor force in large numbers after 1960, the decline of the "family wage," and the pressures on labor caused by postindustrialism and by globalization.

Taken as a whole, reality series about the family alter some conventional familial norms while reinforcing others. I would agree with critics such as Tania Modleski and Sherrie A. Inness, who argue that popular culture texts that address issues such as gendered roles and the real contradictions in women's lives often both challenge and reaffirm traditional values. These reality programs picture some updated norms (frequently, the edited narratives validate wider definitions of familial relations or urge men to do more domestic labor). The genre's meditation on the shift in norms is not radical, however, because it occurs within TV's liberal pluralism framework. Various programs construct their own sense of the contradictions of family life, such as tensions involving women juggling work and child care, gender role renegotiations, further blurring of public and the private "separate sphere" ideologies, racialized family ideals, and fights about gay marriage. Such shows celebrate conflict, spectacularizing fraught kinship issues as a family circus in order to draw more viewers and advertising, but they most often resolve the strife into a liberal pluralist message by episode's end (for example, using the liberal discourse of individualism to represent racism as an interpersonal conflict that can be resolved between individuals through commonsense appeals rather than as a structural social issue).

I would contextualize these themes both in terms of television's long history as a domestic medium and in reference to ongoing family values battles. The new household models and demographic changes, such as increased divorce rates, sparked a political backlash beginning in the 1970s: the family values media debates that have intensified since the 1990s. These skirmishes, such as Dan Quayle's attack on the sitcom character Murphy Brown as a symbol of unwed motherhood in the 1992 presidential debates, are an important sociohistorical context for the current reality programming trend. For my purposes here, I date the full advent of the current genre to the premiere of MTV's *The Real World* in 1992, although related forerunners like police and emergency nonfiction series emerged in the late 1980s, and factual programming has, of course, been around since the medium's origins. Though critics debate the looseness of the term *reality TV* as a genre, I use it to refer to factual programming with key recurring generic and marketing characteristics (such as unscripted, low-cost, edited formats featuring a mix of documentary and fiction genres, often to great ratings success).

The links between TV and the family are foundational, as long-running research on television and the family has established. The television historian Lynn Spigel has shown how early TV developed coextensively with the postwar suburban middle-class families that the medium made into its favored topic and target audience. The historian Stephanie Coontz has noted how current nostalgia for the nuclear family ideal is filtered through 1950s domestic sitcoms like *Leave It to Beaver*. As critics have illustrated, family shows comment not only on society's basic organizing unit but also on demographic transformations by tracing their influence on the family. Ella Taylor traces a family crisis motif in 1970s series such as *All in the Family*, *The Jeffersons*, and *One Day at a Time*, noting network efforts to generate socially "relevant" programming to grab a targeted middle-class demographic as well as to respond to social changes prompted by the women's and civil rights movements. Herman Gray, likewise, in *Watching Race*, has detailed assimilationist messages, reflecting prevailing social discourses, in portraits of black families in the 1980s, like *The Cosby Show*. I demonstrate how reality TV opens a fresh chapter in TV's long-running love affair with the family—the medium has birthed a new genre that grapples with the postmodern family condition.

Reality TV mines quarrels about family life, producing, for example, gay dating shows (such as *Boy Meets Boy*, 2003) at the precise moment of national deliberations over gay marriage. The genre sinks its formidable teeth into these controversies. Much as domestic sitcoms did in the 1950s, it gives us new ways of thinking about familial forms in relationship to identity categories like gender and sexuality or to larger concepts like citizenship and national identity. It does so in part by illuminating the cultural tensions underlying family values debates, such as the family's contested nature as a U.S. institution that legitimates social identities, confers legal and property rights, and models the nation imagined as a family, whether a "house united" or a "house divided."

Tracing recurring tropes in reality programs about the family, I would argue for four key narrative stances toward social change: nostalgia for the traditional modern nuclear family; promotion of a new, modified nuclear family norm in which husband and wife both work outside the home; a tentative, superficial embrace of family pluralism in the context of liberal pluralism; and an open-ended questioning of norms that might include a more extensive sense of family diversity. These narrative trends are particularly evident in some specific reality subgenres: family-switching shows (*Trading Spouses*,

Wife Swap, Black. White, Meet Mister Mom); observations of family life (*The Real Housewives of Orange County; Little People, Big World*); celebrity family series (*The Osbournes, Run's House, Meet the Barkers, Being Bobby Brown, Breaking Bonaduce, Hogan Knows Best*); home and family makeover programs (*Extreme Makeover: Home Edition, Renovate My Family*); family workplace series (*Dog the Bounty Hunter, Family Plots, Family Business*); family gamedocs (*Things I Hate about You, Race to the Altar, Married by America, The Will, The Family*); parenting series (*Nanny 911, Supernanny, Showbiz Moms and Dads*); and historical reenactment programs with family settings (*Colonial House, Frontier House*).

These programs watch middle-class "average joes," perhaps the viewer's friends and neighbors, navigate the shoals of domesticity, grappling with cultural problems such as the tension between kinship and chosen bonds, the effect of the media on the family, and the state's efforts to define "family" as a matter of national concern and to legislate access to marriage rights. Ultimately, these shows convey a kind of emotional engagement, what Ien Ang would term "emotional realism," regarding changes in family structures in the United States, capturing a recent shift in middle-class attitudes toward the American family, a change in what Raymond Williams would call that group's "structure of feeling."

Narrative Tropes

Reality TV spectacularizes such issues as a family circus in order to draw viewers and sell advertising. Part of its vast ratings appeal stems from the fact that it portrays real people struggling with long-running cultural problems that have no easy answers: tensions in the ties that bind, between kinship and chosen bonds, between tradition and change; personal versus social identity; and competing moralities. The genre explores angst about what "the American family" is in the first place. Such widespread worries are not surprising, given that this unit is a social construction that is notoriously difficult to define, particularly since it has historically encoded gendered roles and hierarchies of class, race, and sexuality that define ideas of social acceptance, a crucible for selfhood and nationhood. Critics have noted the regulatory nature of the modern nuclear family model, and official discourse has traditionally framed that unit as a white, middle-class heterosexual norm to which citizens should aspire.

Reality TV does not explicitly solve those family values disputes. Instead, it concentrates on mining the conflict between the two familial forms, one residual and one emergent. Rather than answering questions about what the postmodern family will become, it rehearses sundry arguments about how the familial unit is getting exposed, built up, torn down, and redefined. Some programs offer wish-fulfillment fantasies, smoothing over rancorous public squabbles and social changes but not resolving those tensions.

For example, Bravo's *Things I Hate about You* (2004), reflecting this panoply, turns domesticity into a sport in which snarky judges determine which member of a couple is more annoying to live with and partners happily air their dirty laundry on TV (sometimes literally). One week we see an unmarried heterosexual couple with no children, the next a gay domestic partnership. No one model dominates. The series fits all these groupings into the same narrative framework: a story about family and the daily irritations of domesticity. . . .

Trends in Reality TV's Textual Representations of the Family

Drawing on the sociopolitical and media history of the family values debates, reality TV offers viewers the voyeuristic chance to peer into other people's households to see how all this cultural ruckus is affecting actual families. As the genre takes up the modern and postmodern family in various ways, it often explicitly engages with public policy and media discussions. The way reality serials address familial life illuminates an uneasy shift from modern nuclear family ideals to the postmodern reality of diverse practices.

One main trend in reality programming is for series to look backward with a nostalgia for the modern nuclear family that reveals the instability of that model. Some series revert to older concepts, such as the sociologist Talcott Parsons's mid-twentieth-century theories of functional and dysfunctional family forms. He argued that the modern nuclear family's function under industrialized capitalism was to reproduce and socialize children into dominant moral codes, as well as to define and promote norms of sexual behavior and ideas of affective bonds associated with companionate marriage. Dysfunctional families that deviated from norms were functionalism's defining "Other," and some critics argue that this paradigm still influences sociological research on family life (Stacey, *In the Name of the Family*). Pop psychology concepts of functionalism and dysfunctionalism certainly circulate widely in today's mass media, and we see their influence in reality shows.

A particularly apt example is the spouse-swapping subgenre, which includes shows like ABC's *Wife Swap*. The titillating title implies it will follow the wild exploits of swingers, but the show instead documents strangers who switch households and parenting duties for a short period. Similarly, on Fox's *Trading Spouses: Meet Your New Mommy* (the copycat show that beat ABC's to the air), two parents each occupy the other's home for several days. Both series focus on the conflict between households, revealing a fierce debate among participants as to whose family is healthier, more "normal," or more "functional." On *Trading Spouses*, one two-part episode swaps mothers from white suburban nuclear families, each comprising a husband, a wife, two kids, and a dog ("Bowers/Pilek"). Both clans want to claim modern nuclear family functionality for themselves, but economic tensions ensue, even though each woman describes her family as middle class. A California mom with an opulent beach house judges her Massachusetts hosts, with their modest home and verbal fisticuffs, as unkempt, whereas her outspoken counterpart deems the beach household materialistic and emotionally disconnected. Each woman characterizes the other family as dysfunctional. Their conflict reveals not only the degree to which many people still use these older ideals as their own measuring sticks, here staged as issues such as tidiness or appropriate levels of emotional closeness, but also the tenuousness of those ideals, given the intense contradictions between two supposedly functional families.

Through the premise of swapping households or roles for several days, these programs explore Otherness by having participants step into someone else's performance of kinship behaviors. In so doing, they illuminate identity categories that are performed through the family. This dynamic was perhaps most notably executed on the series *Black. White*, which used makeup to switch a white and black family for several weeks and staged racial tensions between them. In this subgenre more generally, participants reproduce a version of their counterparts' social identity. Thus, the switch highlights the arbitrariness of such identity performances. Since the shows allow the participants to judge each other, family appears as a topic of open-ended debate.

These programs depend on conflict generated by social hierarchies of race, class, gender, and sexuality, and they privilege white male heteronormativity. Their narratives often focus on gender, encouraging men to take on more child care and domestic chores. Yet they still rely on ideologies of gender difference to explain household units and to reaffirm the mother's role as nurturer-caregiver. By absenting the mother, the wife-swap series imply that husbands and kids will learn to appreciate the woman of the house more.

These series encourage a liberal pluralist resolution to conflicts, one that upholds an easy humanist consensus, or what critics term "corporate multiculturalism," which markets diversity as another product rather than picturing and validating substantive cultural differences. The framing narratives resolve competing ideas, most often by defining as normal a modified modern nuclear family (two working parents). In shows about alternative households, for example, the narratives sympathize with the single mom or the lesbian couple but uphold the intact nuclear family as more rational and functional. Yet the narratives also often critique participants' overly intense nostalgia for the bygone modern nuclear ideal, and they sometimes allow for some validation of alternative models, such as an African American extended family. They depend on sensationalism and conflict over values to spark ratings.

This open warfare over functional and dysfunctional families includes a huge helping of nostalgia, as epitomized by a series like MTV's *The Osbournes*. This hit show supports the sense that if the modern nuclear ideal has been replaced by a diversity of family forms, U.S. culture still has an intense nostalgia for the older norm. Is nostalgia for the fantasy nuclear unit actually a defining characteristic of the postmodern family? It is for *The Osbournes*. Viewers flocked to the show because it juxtaposes a famously hard-living, heavy-metal family with classic sitcom family plotlines, edited to emphasize the irony of seeing the cursing, drug-abusing rock star Ozzy and his brood hilariously butchering *Ozzie and Harriet*–style narratives.

The entertainment press dubbed them "America's favorite family," and a series of high-profile magazine cover stories tried to explain the show's wild popularity by pointing to how the Osbournes "put the fun in dysfunctional." The show garnered MTV's highest-rated debut at that time and enjoyed some of the strongest ratings in the channel's history during its run from 2002 until 2005. Part of the appeal lies in how the Osbournes seem to capture on videotape a more accurate sense of the pressures of family life, ranging from sibling rivalry to teen sex and drug use to a serious illness (such as Sharon's cancer diagnosis and treatment). Even though their fame and fortune make them unlike home viewers, the family can be related to because of the struggles they confront openly. Likewise, they reflect current family diversity because they are a blended family; their brood includes their son and two daughters (one of whom declined to appear on the series), Ozzy's son from his first marriage, and their children's teen friend whom they adopted during the show after his mother died of cancer. Ozzy himself suggested that he did the series in order to expand understandings of the family: "What is a functional family? I know I'm dysfunctional by a long shot, but what guidelines do we all have to go by? *The Waltons?*" Ozzy here is both arbiter and agent; he notes TV's power to define a range of meanings for the family, whether through the Waltons or the Osbournes.

Yet even while the program's narrative meditates on entertaining dysfunctionality and new family realities, it also continuously tries to recuperate the Osbournes as a functional nuclear family. Story arcs are edited to frame them as dysfunctional (cursing parents, wild fights, teenage drug use), but also to rescue them as functional; there are sentimental shots of the family gathered together in their kitchen or clips of them expressing their love and loyalty despite the titillating fights. Even though Ozzy tells his family they are "all f—ing mad," in the same breath he says he "loves them more than life itself" ("A House Divided"). The edited narrative purposefully emphasizes the bonds of hearth and home, sometimes trying to establish functionality by cutting out serious family events that would have made Parsons blanch: Ozzy's drug relapse, severe mental illness, and nervous breakdown during taping; trips to rehab by Jack and Kelly, the son and daughter; and Sharon's temporary separation from Ozzy over these issues. Press coverage of the show and fan response likewise emphasized a recuperative dynamic, both looking for the loveable, reassuring nuclear family beneath the rough exterior. As an *Entertainment Weekly* cover story noted, Ozzy Osbourne went from being boycotted by parents' groups in the 1980s for bat biting and supposedly Satanic lyrics to being asked for parenting advice from men's magazines. Thus, even while registering the limitations of Parsons's model, the series still tries to rehabilitate this celebrity family as functional. As a result, this program and others like it explore the postmodern family, but at the same time they look back wistfully on the old modern nuclear paradigm.

The Osbournes is also a prime example of a program that explicitly comments on the influence of television on family ideals. Part of the show's insight comes from registering how much the media, whether the popular music industry or television, have shaped this family unit. Brian Graden, then president of MTV Entertainment, described the program's draw as "the juxtaposition of the fantastical rock-star life with the ordinary and the everyday"; summarizing one episode, he laughed, "Am I really seeing Ozzy Osbourne trying to turn on the vacuum cleaner?" Graden noted that after they collected footage on the Osbournes, producers realized that "a lot of these story lines mirrored classic domestic sitcom story lines, yet with a twist of outrageousness that you wouldn't believe." Watching footage of their daily experiences, Graden immediately views them through the lens of earlier TV sitcoms; everywhere he looks, he sees the Cleavers on speed. And the show Graden's company makes of this family's life might one day comprise the plotlines other viewers use to interpret their own experiences in some way. After their smash first season, the Osbournes were feted at the White House Correspondents' dinner and managed to parlay such national attention into more entertainment career opportunities, with a new MTV show, *Battle for Ozzfest* (2004–), hosted by Sharon and Ozzy and featuring bands competing to join their summer tour; Sharon's syndicated talk show that ran for one season (2003–2004); and their children's slew of TV, movie, and music ventures growing out of their exposure from the reality program.

Though most families could not follow the Osbournes into celebrity, what many do share with the rockers is the knowledge that TV significantly shapes familial ideals. This media awareness marks a parenting trend. In their recent audience study of family television-viewing practices, Stewart M. Hoover, Lynn Schofield Clark, and Diane F. Alters found that parents had a highly self-reflexive attitude toward the media. They were well conscious of how the mass media both reflect and shape social beliefs, and they worried about the daily influence of television in their children's lives. Hoover et al. identified this media anxiety as part of what they term "self-reflexive parenting" behaviors stemming from increased concerns about child rearing since the 1960s. They see this model of parenting as part of what Anthony Giddens calls the project of self-reflexivity in modernity, in which people are reflective about their interaction with the social world as they continually incorporate mediated experiences into their sense of self. . . .

Cultural Histories and Family Values Media Debates

I would argue that reality TV is the popular media form with the most to say about the current status of the American family. The television historian Lynn Spigel has shown that early TV developed coextensively with the post–World War II suburban middle-class family—a specific kind of modern nuclear family model the medium made into its favored subject and audience. As Spigel notes, while sociologists like Talcott Parsons were arguing in the 1940s and 1950s that the modern nuclear family is the social form best suited to capitalist progress, the new electronic TV medium targeted the postwar white, middle-class families flocking to the suburbs, encouraging the development of the modern family as a consumer unit.

As a new genre now exploring the self-conscious imbrication of family and the media as one of its main themes, reality TV raises vital issues of marketing and consumerism. If television enters the home to become, as Cecelia Tichi has shown, "the electronic hearth" around which the family gathers, so too does the family envision itself through the tube. TV addresses the family as ideal viewer, imagined community, and the basis for democracy mediated through mass communication; the nation is figured as a collective of families all watching their television sets (a collective that can now exercise its democratic rights by calling in to vote for a favorite singer on *American Idol*). If the domestic sitcom was like an electronic media version of a station wagon trundling the modern family along in the 1950s, reality TV is the hybrid gas-electric car of the postmodern family today. . . .

Not surprisingly, recent public arguments about family and marriage often turn reality TV into prime fodder. Conservative groups frequently protest reality fare. Most spectacularly, complaints made by conservative activists from the Parents Television Council prompted the Federal Communications Commission (FCC) to threaten Fox with a fine of $1.2 million, the largest to date, for *Married by America* when it was on the air. The show had audiences pick mates for couples who could have gotten married on air (though none did and all the arranged couples stopped dating after the show). The protestors found it a vulgar trivialization of the institution of marriage.

On the flip side of the coin, progressive thinkers have used reality TV to make public arguments advocating a greater diversity of marriage and household arrangements. The cultural theorist Lisa Duggan, in a 2004 *Nation* article, explores public policy about state-sanctioned marriage in the context of the debates over gay marriage, critiquing, for example, "marriage promotion" by both the Clinton and the Bush administrations as a way to privatize social welfare. Duggan calls for a diversification of democratically accessible forms of state recognition for households and partnerships, a "flexible menu of choices" that would dethrone the privileged civic status of sanctified marriage and "threaten the normative status of the nuclear family, undermining state endorsement of heterosexual privilege, the male 'headed' household and 'family values' moralism as social welfare policy." She uses reality TV as an example of current dissatisfaction with gendered, "traditional" marriage and a marker of its decline, describing "the competitive gold-digging sucker punch on TV's *Joe Millionaire*" (which tricked eager women into believing they were competing to marry a millionaire) as an entertainment culture indicator of the statistical flux in marriage and kinship arrangements. She argues that the franchise confirms social anxiety that "marriage is less stable and central to the organization of American life than ever." Notably, Duggan pairs her *Joe Millionaire* example with the pop singer Britney Spears's rapidly annulled 2004 Las Vegas wedding (to a high school friend, Jason Alexander) as similar social indexes; the celebrity life and the reality show plot represent similar kinds of evidence, both equally real (or equally fake) in current entertainment media culture.

Regardless of the different ways the genre enters into existing political discussions, what is striking is that it continually becomes a site for family values debates. A case in point is how a couple competing on the sixth season of CBS's *The Amazing Race* (2005) made headlines because critics accused the husband of exhibiting abusive behavior toward his wife in the series footage. The couple, Jonathan Baker and Victoria Fuller, made the rounds of talk shows to protest that characterization, but the main dynamic of press coverage has been to turn them into a teaching moment. Both went on the entertainment TV newsmagazine *The Insider* and were asked to watch footage of themselves fighting and answer the charge that it looked abusive; Baker responded: "I'm a better person than that. I have to say I had a temper tantrum, you know, I pushed her, I never should have, and you know, I regret every moment of it and you know what, hopefully that experience will make me a better person. That's our story line, you know, that's who we were on television. That's not who we are in real life."

Such a framing of that reality TV footage is emblematic: the show is perceived as somewhat mediated and constructed but still real enough to warrant a press debate. Through a bit of internal network marketing, Dr. Phil actually made them the topic of one of his CBS prime-time specials on relationships. Noting that the show sparked reams of hate mail and even death threats toward the couple, Dr. Phil explicitly argues that America was watching the couple and wants to debate them in TV's public sphere. At the outset of the interview, he invokes and calls into being an imagined national public, saying, "America was outraged and appalled by what they've seen." After he exhorts the husband to correct his behavior, he concludes, "So America doesn't need to worry about you?" (*Dr. Phil Primetime Special*). Dr. Phil does not completely buy Baker's argument that he was only acting aggressively for the camera or that the editing heightened his behavior, and he admonishes the man for exhibiting bad behavior in any context, mediated or not. Dr. Phil is well aware of the construction of images that he himself perpetuates, and he even draws attention to how Baker tries to manipulate this on-camera interview by coaching his wife, yet he insists on a substantial component of actuality in all these depictions. In the press and popular response, the gamedoc show couple becomes a paradigmatic reality TV family example that can be used to analyze the state of the American family more generally.

Ultimately, reality programs add a new wrinkle to television's family ideas. The genre illuminates how the current definition of the family is up for grabs, and reality TV enters the debate arena in force. Instead of having nostalgia for the Cleavers as a model of the modern American family, viewers might one day have nostalgia for the Osbournes as a model of the postmodern American family. The amplified truth claims of reality TV comment on the social role of television itself as an electronic medium offering "public scripts" that, as the medium evolves, viewers increasingly want to interact with on the screen and participate in themselves.

Karen Sternheimer

 **NO**

Hollywood Doesn't Threaten Family Values

In 1992, then-Vice President Dan Quayle charged that Murphy Brown, a fictional character on the CBS sitcom of the same name, glamorized single motherhood by having a child outside marriage. His comment ignited a national debate about not just single parenthood, but the influence Hollywood and celebrities have over the choices Americans make in their lives. In a speech about civil unrest in Los Angeles, Quayle charged that characters like Brown indirectly contribute to central city problems by "mocking the importance of fathers."

The *Murphy Brown* controversy gave voice to concerns that changes in family structure, particularly the rise in rates of single parenthood, were in some part caused by popular culture. This debate found its way to the front page of *The New York Times* and marked the beginning of serious discussion about the influence Hollywood has on families.

Writing in *Atlantic Monthly* one year later, Barbara Dafoe Whitehead's article "Dan Quayle was Right" argued that children in single-parent families face a host of challenges. As for the cause of the rise in single-parent led households, Whitehead also focused on Hollywood, arguing it characterizes divorce and single parenthood as liberating and marriage as dysfunctional. In similar fashion, conservative film critic Michael Medved's 1992 book *Hollywood vs. America* contended that movies and sitcoms portray families in a negative light and celebrities who have children outside marriage promote "illegitimacy chic."

Fast forward more than 15 years, and the seemingly ubiquitous coverage of celebrities' personal lives has led critics to question whether or not stars are bad role models. Bloggers dissect the personal choices of celebrities from Britney Spears to Angelina Jolie, debating amongst themselves what effect their choices might have on the non-famous. In their *New York Times* best-selling book about celebrities' private lives, *Hollywood, Interrupted: Insanity Chic in Babylon*, journalists Andrew Breitbart and Mark Ebner claim that "Hollywood . . . is on a mission to obliterate the ideal of the nuclear family and to undermine traditional childrearing practices." Jonathan Last, a writer for the conservative *Weekly Standard,* has even offered a formula to explain how Hollywood and its celebrities have altered the American family landscape: "radical family values + infinite financial resources + cultural idol worship = moral chaos."

Obviously families and relationships have undergone significant changes over the past few decades. But neither Hollywood nor its celebrities are responsible for them.

The Popularity of Culture

Although sociologists have documented the serious challenges facing single parents, particularly single mothers living in poverty, conservative commentators often attribute the heart of the problem to culture, rather than broader social forces. Focusing on the idea that changes in social norms make divorce and having children outside marriage seem less taboo, the media seem to be obvious sources that normalize what were previously deviant life choices.

In our celebrity-saturated environment, Hollywood seems to be a reasonable target; stars' relationships are increasingly fodder for cable news networks, especially if their lifestyles appear outrageous and unconventional. As media scholar Neal Gabler describes, celebrities aren't simply famous for their performances, but are now stars in their own "lifies" that perhaps draw larger audiences than their movies, television shows, or music. As objects of fascination, their private lives are sources of public interest—and often public derision.

Interest in celebrities' private lives is by no means new, of course. When movie magazines were first published in the 1910s, readers clamored for more information about the "picture players." The movie industry's growth can in some part be credited with audience curiosity about the "real" lives of stars, which seemed more wholesome than the stars' lives of today. But this illusion was the result of both revisionist history and the studios' information control.

During the first half of the 20th century, at the height of the Hollywood studio system's power, studio publicity machines exercised tremendous control over what the public knew about stars' personal lives. With the threat of powerful studio bosses cutting off access to their entire stable of stars, magazines felt pressure to publish only stories that studios approved. "Gentlemen's agreements" with the studios kept sensitive information secret, Rock Hudson's homosexuality being a famous example. This did not, however, stop the press from gathering potentially damaging information about the stars—information the studios themselves used as a means to control their stars, particularly during contract negotiations.

At the same time, stars were under contracts that contained "morality" clauses, so news that an unmarried celebrity was pregnant could easily end a career if it wasn't quickly covered up. Operating as monopolies, the studios could prevent a celebrity from appearing in movies indefinitely, suspending both their income and potentially their fame.

Starting in the 1950s, the studio system began to erode. Actors became independent contractors, had much more say about what projects they participated in, and could negotiate higher salaries. Perhaps the one downside to creative independence, however, was the absence of a powerful institution to prevent embarrassing stories from being published. Today, though, the gloves are off, and so are most "gentlemen's agreements." The proliferation of rumor-laden gossip magazines and websites, many of which report on celebrities hourly, fuel the belief that Hollywood's inhabitants are morally bankrupt.

Politicians have played on this apparent disconnect between Hollywood celebrities and mainstream American values. From Bob Dole to Al Gore and George W. Bush to Hillary Clinton, politicians from both the right and left have chastised Hollywood in order to demonstrate their support for "family values." The bipartisan focus on culture as a key problem reinforces the view that Hollywood and its celebrities hold an inordinate amount of power over the choices millions of Americans make.

While culture is by nature visible and easy for observers to point to as a cause of social change, elements of social structure, such as policies, laws, and economic shifts, are more difficult to see. Thus, social and institutional arguments are often ignored in favor of simpler cultural arguments. Although we shouldn't deny the importance of culture (or the questionable choices some celebrities make), it's problematic to completely ignore how other societal changes have altered marriage and families in recent decades. Hollywood may provide multiple examples of people who have children without being married or seem to be less-than-committed spouses, but the real causes of these changes are far less glamorous.

Illegitimacy Chic

It's not hard to come up with examples of Hollywood celebrities whose children were born or adopted outside marriages. Unmarried parents Angelina Jolie and Brad Pitt have a growing clan who frequently appear in celebrity news. And when Tom Cruise and Katie Holmes had their daughter before getting married it was anything but scandalous. So do they, as Medved suggested, make illegitimacy chic?

Until the 1968 U.S. Supreme Court ruling in *Levy v. Louisiana,* "illegitimate" births could have serious legal and economic consequences. Mothers could lose custody of children born outside of marriage and courts rarely held fathers economically responsible. Once parents and children gained custodial and financial protections, however, illegitimacy lost its legal status.

In the United States today, approximately one in three births are to unmarried parents. Between 1990 and 2004, births to unmarried teen mothers fell, but rose slightly for unmarried women over 20. Notably, the number of babies born to unmarried women over 40 more than doubled during this time, although the vast majority of unmarried mothers are in their 20s and 30s.

While celebrities may appear to be leading this trend, it's both the improved ability of single parents to support children on their own and the instability of working-class men's wages that fuel single parenthood. Since the 1970s, men's real wages have declined, making marriage less economically viable for many. While more upper-income women choose to become single mothers, as some celebrities have, the vast majority of mothers who never marry are low earners. Of course, women of all income levels sometimes become single mothers by chance, not choice. Fans of Murphy Brown might recall that the baby's father, Brown's ex-husband, left upon hearing she was pregnant.

As Kathryn Edin found in her study of low-income single mothers, many unmarried women hope to wed someday, but would only consider marriage with an economically stable partner. For many women barely surviving, the fear of having a spouse with an unstable job history to support in addition to their children makes going it alone seem like a better choice. This trend is likely to continue, particularly as a larger proportion of women attend college than men and industrial jobs get outsourced overseas.

Obliterating the Nuclear Family

In *Hollywood, Interrupted,* Breitbart and Ebner describe the poor parenting practices of many people within the entertainment industry in great detail and argue that "the pathological behavior of celebrities . . . (has) demeaned family values." While certainly numerous examples of unstable celebrity families are exposed in gossip pages and tell-all books like this one, the so-called nuclear family faces a much bigger foe than Hollywood: the economy.

The idealized family form of the mid-20th century—a household with a biological father and stay-at-home mother—was itself an anomaly. Prior to that time, many recombinant families formed due to the death of a parent. Following World War II, the vast expansion of suburbs coupled with GI Bill benefits (predominantly available only to white men) made housing very affordable. Many of these men had financial opportunities their parents didn't (and their grandchildren wouldn't). The economic boom meant wages were high enough for a single earner, even a working-class worker, to support a household.

This changed in the 1970s with the rise in inflation. Workers' real wages started to decline, making a second income more of a necessity. Women's labor force participation had been rising throughout the 20th century, but between 1970 and 1990 jumped from 43 percent to 58 percent and continued to creep up through the 1990s. Divorce rates also increased significantly between 1970 and 1980, from 3.5 divorces per thousand to 5.2 per thousand.

But we shouldn't presume "intact" families were necessarily stable or happy. Before this time other constraints kept families together. Women who sought divorce risked losing not only their economic security but their children as well. Until the Progressive Era, custody after divorce was almost universally granted to fathers, as children were regarded as property of their father except in cases of proven cruelty. Further, until no-fault divorce laws became more common in the 1970s, divorces had to be granted by a judge after just cause was proven in court. Ironically, the first no-fault divorce statute was signed into law in 1969 by then-California governor (and "family values" champion) Ronald Reagan.

Remaining in an unhappy marriage was all but a given for women until they had more opportunities to support themselves. Most women had difficulty obtaining credit in their own name until 1975, when creditors no longer required a male cosigner. In 1970, women earned approximately 60 cents for every dollar men earned; by 2005 that rate had increased to 82 cents (mostly due to declines in men's wages). Thus, marriage provides less economic incentive for women to remain in otherwise unhappy relationships today.

Acceptance of divorce also became more common in American culture following these legal changes, changes that are often depicted within popular culture. But culture itself wasn't necessarily the engine driving the train; if anything, it was the caboose. In spite of the fact that divorce rates started their climb shortly after World War II, movies and television programs mostly shied away from the topic. It is telling that television's most popular blended family of the 1970s, The Brady Bunch, was the product of the death of spouses, not divorce.

In spite of our tendency to view marriages in the past as idyllic, many ended through desertion or separation, although a legal divorce may not have been sought. Estimates suggest that in 1940, 1.5 million couples lived apart without being legally divorced.

As historian Stephanie Coontz points out, marriage has mutated to become a source of emotional fulfillment rather than an economic arrangement. Consequently, marriages can become unstable as expectations for having a high-quality partnership rise. Coontz argues that "love conquered marriage" when it became less tied to inheritance or crafting family allegiances. As romantic love, something inherently unstable, became the ideal for creating unions, it also became inevitable that they would sometimes falter. Yet, despite the prevalence of divorce, marriage still matters. A 2006 *Washington Post* poll found that 76 percent of respondents felt that being married was somewhat or very important to them.

Interest v. Admiration

It's important not to confuse the continual news coverage of celebrities' relationships with "idol worship." Rather than simply a reflection of public demand, Hollywood "news" has become easy filler for networks on 24-hour news cycles. Gathering such information is cheaper and easier than reporting and writing on other topics of more depth.

Celebrity stories don't require much of audiences either—viewers need little background information to follow the drama, in comparison with political news, which often requires more of an understanding of both foreign and domestic policy issues. In short, relationship sagas are useful diversions for both producers and viewers.

It's too simple to say that audiences use these stories as cues for their own lives; viewer *interest* shouldn't be mistaken for *admiration* of celebrity relationships. As Joshua Gamson found in his study of celebrity audiences, even the most ardent fans are often quite critical of those whose lives they follow. Some of his informants noted they had little respect for celebrities, and enjoyed learning that famous people had problems, too.

At a time when families and relationships continue to be redefined, celebrities are easier for critics to blame than the host of economic, political, and social changes behind the shifts in families we've witnessed in recent decades. Rather than the decline of "family values," cultural norms have changed to adapt to structural shifts in American society.

Despite the many challenges families face in the 21st century, we aren't experiencing moral chaos. Although many families might not look as they did during the middle of the last century, one key indicator of chaos, violent crime rates, has exhibited national declines during the past 15 years (especially in Los Angeles, the basis for Dan Quayle's complaint). And according to census data, the divorce rate actually fell between 1990 and 2004, from 4.7 divorces per thousand to 3.7 per thousand. Trends like this actually suggest growing stability, rather than calamity.

EXPLORING THE ISSUE

Are Family Values Shaped by the Mass Media?

Critical Thinking and Reflection

1. What family portrayals in media do you most experience *resonance*? By that, we mean, which portrayals seem most similar to your own experiences?
2. How much of reality television do you think is real? How have these individuals or family units been chosen to participate in the reality program, and what do they bring to the televised experience of representing the real world?
3. How significant are the real sociological, economic, and political issues that the "typical" media family represents? Do these families represent real class, gender, race, and ethnic realities in our society?
4. Do you see the families portrayed in media as a "reflection of reality" or a "window on the world?" In what way(s) do these family portrayals tell us what it is like to be a member of American society and culture?

Is There Common Ground?

Both of the authors of these selections ground their approach in a different way of seeing the world. Professor Edwards is searching for the themes that media families portray, and Professor Sternheimer approaches the argument from the perspective of contrasting celebrity culture with sociological data. However, there is some common ground that the two authors describe, and that involves how essential family life is to the way each of us defines our value system. Undoubtedly, media gives us some reference to our own lives, and to the broader world beyond our own experiences. It is up to each of us to try to evaluate, measure, and critically consider media images that represent family life and "family values."

Over decades, our society changes, but different people within our society judge these changes according to different criteria. In the early part of the twentieth century, divorce was often scandalous. Today, divorced couples may seem normal. Only 50 years ago, it might seem odd for a single person to adopt a child, but today that seems like a natural option to consider. By examining these questions and the authors' perspectives, you should gain a better sense of your own perspectives on families in society, families in the media, and how the two types of families reflect or distort your sense of reality and social values.

Additional Resources

Richard M. Huff, ed., *Reality Television* (Praeger, 2006)

This collection of essays includes additional perspectives on family portrayals in the media, reality television, and celebrity culture.

Marc Andrejevic, *Reality TV: The Work of Being Watched* (Rowman & Littlefield, 2004)

This collection of essays focuses on how reality television got started, and the themes that have evolved in the genre.

Henry Jenkins, "Buying into *American Idol*: How We Are Being Sold on Reality TV," in *Convergence Culture* (New York University Press, 2006)

Jenkins is an astute critic of popular culture, and in this essay, he specifically addresses the commodification of *American Idol* as a theme in reality TV.

The first family-based reality TV show was *An American Family*, which aired in 1973. PBS has produced a documentary to chronicle the importance of the program and to focus on the story of Lance Loud's coming out publicly on television as a gay man.

www.pbs.org/lanceloud/american/

A Web site listing reality TV shows that have family themes can be found at:

www.realitytvlinks.com/

ISSUE 2

Do Media Unite the Population in Times of Crisis?

YES: Marcia Landy, from "'America Under Attack': Pearl Harbor, 9/11, and History in the Media," in Wheeler Winston Dixon, ed., *Film and Television After 9/11* (Southern Illinois University Press, 2004), pp. 79–100

NO: Michael Eric Dyson, from "Unnatural Disasters: Race and Poverty," *Come Hell or High Water: Hurricane Katrina and the Color of Disaster* (Basic Books, 2006)

Learning Outcomes

After reading this issue, you should be able to:

- Understand the range of issues that shape media messages.
- Evaluate the underlying social problems and realities that may influence media coverage of events and the way representations become reflections of reality.
- Analyze stereotypes and apply a critical framework to understanding how inclusion and omission in media forms influence our knowledge of society and social justice.

ISSUE SUMMARY

YES: Film critic and professor Marcia Landy examines two major events in U.S. history: the attack on Pearl Harbor in 1941 and the events of 9/11/2001 to examine how each event has been portrayed in media and has reinforced some values that include patriotism, destiny, and victimhood. She examines representative issues from different forms of media to show that all forms of media contribute to reinforcing ideas about Americanism and American character.

NO: Noted social critic Michael Eric Dyson reflects on the August 2005 Hurricane Katrina disaster, which flooded most of the city of New Orleans and caused massive social upheaval as 90 percent of the residents of Louisiana and surrounding areas were asked to evacuate to avoid the storm. During the Katrina disaster, local media outlets were destroyed, so media elsewhere told the story of Katrina's impact. According to Dyson, the story told relied on traditional stereotypes of Blacks, rather than telling the real story of poverty, which so severely affected the lives and deaths of so many people of color.

In some of the earliest research on the relationship of media and society, communication pioneer Harold Lasswell wrote that part of the function of communication included "(1) the surveillance of the environment; (2) the correlation of the parts of society in responding to the environment; (3) the transmission of the social heritage from one generation to the next (Lasswell, "The Structure and Function of Communication in Society," in Wilbur Schramm and Donald F. Roberts, eds., *The Process and Effects of Mass Communication*, rev. ed., 1977). Lasswell's ideas have often been quoted when we think about the uniting factor of mass media and how we know about the world in which we live. For example, many of us collectively watched television to see the destruction of the World Trade Towers in New York City on September 11, 2001. Media helped us understand what was going on, and helped us collectively grieve as we learned about the acts of terrorism, and the act of the First Responders' heroism. Many of us collectively felt a struggle with our ideas of patriotism, as well as loss, being stunned, and wondering what all of this meant.

We also often feel a connection to others when we experience the power of mass media to help us understand other events that may be far from our own communities, including the loss of a cultural icon, the devastation of natural forces, like hurricanes, tornados, and floods, or perhaps even a national celebration, like the SuperBowl, the Olympics, or the marriage of British Prince William and Kate Middleton. Because mass media do have the power to unite us and show us real events from other places in the world, Lasswell's concepts underlying the power of the "structure and function" of communication—or mass media, in particular—have always been an important feature of examining the relationship between media and society.

The authors of the selections in this issue examine the idea of whether media unite us in a time of crisis, or not. Film critic and professor Marcia Landy examines two American experiences: the Japanese bombing of the American fleet in World War II, and the terrorist bombing of the World Trade Towers and the Pentagon on 9/11/2001. She cites the similarities of each major catastrophe, and discusses how Americans, and particularly viewers of the events, have remembered the events and how these remembrances affect our ideas of patriotism and "Americanism."

Social critic and professor Michael Eric Dyson contrasts this idea of "uniting" us as a country, with the events that occurred after one of the most deadly hurricanes in U.S. history, Hurricane Katrina, flooded a huge section of New Orleans and surrounding areas, in 2005. In this case, many of the mainstream media outlets were unable to function. The electrical power grid, radio transmitters, and cell phone towers were destroyed, and communication in and around the affected areas was destroyed. In this disaster, the poorest members of the affected area had the least opportunity to be evacuated, and as a result, many of the poor, and particularly Black residents, were killed, or their homes destroyed by the Hurricane's force. The stories and news reports that made it out of the region reinforced traditional racial stereotypes of Blacks as thieves and miscreants, as they looted stores, and otherwise acted like uncivilized people. Rather than uniting us, the media in the Katrina situation actually divided us as a nation by identifying the poorest members of the community as subhuman and missing the real story behind the problems of racism, poverty, and destitution in the United States. Furthermore, it was determined that the lack of the U.S. government's concern with these victims of the storm reflected an uncaring, unconcerned government.

This issue and the selections within it ask us to think about the role of the media in times of crisis. What if we had no media to provide sound and images to give us the experiences of the people undergoing trauma? How do media, when there are no visuals or audio sources available, tell us what's going on? We often rely on the media to help us understand the environment at these key moments, but perhaps we need to evaluate whether the media is actually giving us a well-researched, authentic experience while the disaster is in progress.

There have been many natural disasters in which the population has been mobilized to help, not only in the 9/11 situation, but in the 2010 earthquake in Haiti, and the subsequent fund-raising by celebrities like musician Wyclef Jean and actor George Clooney. Without some of the real images and sound cues, it is almost impossible to feel the emotional pull of disasters over which we have no control. This issue allows us to consider how important media are to helping us understand our environment, and even more so, how the images and representations that are constructed affect our emotions and our call to action.

YES

Marcia Landy

"America Under Attack": Pearl Harbor, 9/11, and History in the Media

September 11 and Remembering Pearl Harbor

On September, 11, 2001, CBS News anchorman Dan Rather referred to the aircraft-missile attacks on the World Trade Center and the Pentagon, and the crashing of a plane near Pittsburgh, as "the Pearl Harbor of terrorism." The visuals that accompanied this pronouncement, emphasizing the crashing of the planes and the images of people leaping to their deaths from the windows of the World Trade Center, were described as "unimaginable. But part of today's reality." The constant news reports and television specials that emanated from CNN, NBC, ABC, CBS, and Fox on September 12 inundated the public with images of the disaster, and commentaries by anchors such as Dan Rather, Peter Jennings, and Tom Brokaw and interviews with government officials, historians, and even psychiatrists were quick to locate an historical analogy in December 7, 1941.

Repeatedly, images of the New York skyline minus the twin towers were interspersed with references to Pearl Harbor and "the day of infamy." Rather talked of how that earlier event "brought the United States of America together and propelled it to victory." On the same program, Rather interviewed the Israeli foreign minister, Shimon Perez, in Jerusalem, who commented, "The most important consequence today is to develop a strategy against terror." When asked whether there was a connection between the attacks and the U.S. support of Israel, Perez responded, "Terror is a new phenomenon, and Israel is not the only target." This interview was interrupted by Karen Hughes, who reported on the whereabouts of the president and other high officials, also a matter of confusion and concern in the first media responses to the day. The program ended with Bob Schieffer interviewing Chuck Hagel, Republican senator from Nebraska, about the setting in place of security precautions at airports and other strategic sites. Hagel described the attack as a direct assault on the freedom of every American and, indeed, on the freedom of anyone who has it around the world.

On CNBC the following day, September 12, historian Doris Kearns Goodwin was interviewed by anchor Chris Matthews about the historical import of September 11. Matthews questioned her about the pertinence of the comparisons of September 11 to December 7. She replied that the assault at Pearl Harbor was on a military base where people felt vulnerable after the attack but that the September 11 bombings were on "people in their everyday lives and offices, walking on the streets." Unwilling to relinquish the analogy with Pearl Harbor and the retaliation by the United States, however, she stated, "It's high time now" for all the countries in the world to whom we have provided World War II support in the form of Lend-Lease, the Marshall Plan, NATO, and foreign aid to show their support for our nation. Recalling war efforts during World War II, she asserted that there is again a need for trained air marshals, the creation of war bonds, and more recruitment of competent individuals into intelligence agencies. She described the enemy as exemplifying how "the fire of anti-Americanism . . . has been bred into their system." The interview ended with her exhortation, "We have to allow our commensurate power as a superpower to be mobilized . . . now . . . and unto twenty years from now." Her interpretation of history is consonant with the other media events described above—selective in its choice of analogy and combative.

On September 13, Peter Jennings anchored "Special News Report: America under Attack," in which he joined with a number of reporters and specialists to evaluate the events to date. He, too, had on hand an historian to assess the events of September 11. Michael Beschloss described the attack as unique, not to be compared with earlier events such as Pearl Harbor, but he presented an ahistorical view that inevitably includes Pearl Harbor, since according to him, Americans are the same now as they were then: the American character has not changed. America is and has been "compassionate," with a great respect for civil liberties, thanks to a "national character" that is "woven into our genetic code." Thus he directly invoked biology as inherent to national character, responsible for compassion and benevolence, and presumably available as justification for war and violence. In terms that echo the numerous allusions to Pearl Harbor, Beschloss asserted that September 11 has "unified the nation." In talking about the effect of the casualties, Beschloss added another strand to the genetic character of the American—resilience.

Maintaining this optimistic and sociobiologic view of Americans, the program introduced reporter Dan Harris in an interview with a woman on the street who talked of the bravery exhibited by the New York firefighters and her appreciation of their work. Heroizing of the firefighters, as well as of Mayor Giuliani, began to emerge and would approach veneration in the following months. The next segment of the special was an interview with a spokesman for the National Football League, which had decided to cancel the weekend games to allow opportunity to "pause, grieve, and reflect." The baseball commissioner and several baseball team owners concurred with this decision. These instances, in Beschloss's terms, provided yet more proof of the "compassion" and "resilience" of the "American character."

After a report about the security precautions being instituted at airports, Jennings lauded "the unity and patriotism we have seen in the country today."

However, the invocation of trauma was not neglected, as the story of Sheila Wood was presented. She told of her escape from death in the World Trade Center, her attempts to get air; her entrapment, her praying, and the appearance "of a man with a fire extinguisher" who was sent by an "angel to get me out of there." Immediately after this segment, psychiatrist Alvin Poussaint was asked by Jennings to comment on the woman's narrative. He described her as having suffered a great deal of "trauma, and it's likely that this may stay with her for the rest of her life." Comparing the attacks to a rape, Poussaint portrayed the victims in terms of similar feelings of violation. He described the "towers as phallic symbols" and the attack as "a kind of symbolic or attempted symbolic castration," thus reducing the public event to a subjective experience, completely unaware of the reductiveness of his analysis that fit in well with the popular psychologizing characteristic of this historical event.

On December 7, 2001, the sixtieth anniversary of Pearl Harbor, comparisons of September 11 to December 7, 1941, were again prominent in the television news as the president sought to legitimize the "war on terrorism." In a speech that day to veterans and survivors of Pearl Harbor, President Bush referred to the Taliban as fascists who cannot be "appeased" and echoed Roosevelt's position of unconditional surrender in flatly stating that "they must be defeated. This struggle will not end in a truce or treaty." The President's language was again steeped in references to "our mission" and to a "great calling" as he told the grandchildren of the Pearl Harbor survivors, "[N]ow your calling has come." At the Citadel on December 11, the president again commemorated Pearl Harbor with a speech broadcast on *Talk of the Nation*, during which he again linked Pearl Harbor and September 11 and, in militant terms, stated, "No cave is deep enough to escape the political justice of the United States." Challenging the terrorists, he promised "new tactics, new weapons, informed intelligence experts" who "know the Taliban and who understand the local culture." After the speech and commentary by various news analysts, *Talk of the Nation* climaxed with the words of Theodore Olson, solicitor general of the United States, whose wife died in the plane that crashed near Pittsburgh. Olson charged angrily that "the atrocities of September 11th cannot prevail" and called the perpetrators of the attack "bigots, zealots, and persecutors" who hate "American's freedom, tolerance, and respect for all people." CNN's *Mornings with Paula Zahn* reproduced images of patriotism from December 7 newsreels, then from September 11.

Similarly patriotic, Tom Brokaw, in a December 8, 2001, interview on the Tim Russert CNBC show, reiterated comments from the *National Geographic* program about Pearl Harbor he had narrated, stressing the "determination to defend all we believe in." An excerpt from his own TV show was shown, in which he commented on the lessons to be learned from September 11. He described Ground Zero as a "holy place to be enshrined" in the same fashion as the *Arizona* at Pearl Harbor. In another expression of patriotism linked to World War II, the *NBC Nightly News,* focusing on the dedication of the D-Day Museum, featured a reading by Tom Hanks of Roosevelt's speech after the attack on Pearl Harbor: "With confidence in our armed forces, with unbounded determination, we will gain the inevitable triumph. So help us God." . . .

Pearl Harbor, the Film, and Documentaries

In the entertainment section of the *Pittsburgh Post-Gazette* on December 7, 2001, Barbara Vancheri commented on the "timeliness and profits" of the Jerry Bruckheimer and Michael Bay film *Pearl Harbor* (2001). She quoted producer Bruckheimer on the patriotism of that earlier era: "We're seeing a lot of it again. The military is looking much differently since September." The film had been released months before the attacks on the World Trade Center and the Pentagon, and the plane crash near Pittsburgh. It was scheduled to commemorate the sixtieth anniversary of the Japanese attack of Pearl Harbor. The year 2001 also saw the appearance of two television programs about Pearl Harbor, one produced by the History Channel and the other by *National Geographic*. These three productions deserve examination for their resurrection of a traditional mode of narrating America history that, in the aftermath of the September 11, became all the more poignant.

The Pearl Harbor productions illuminating December 7, 1941, dramatize American exceptionalism and its sense of destiny in strikingly similar terms— a narrative of adversity and triumph exemplary for how much it reveals as well as for how much it elides. The main lines of this narrative involve a dramatization of the violation of innocence, a portrait of U.S. victimhood and of Japanese perfidy. The texts are constructed in elegiac fashion as a lament for the victims. While the survivors' accounts are replete with their detailed descriptions of horror accompanied by repeated images and reconstructions of the catastrophe, they are balanced by descriptions of extraordinary acts of heroism. The narrative of Pearl Harbor also focuses on the changes and the trauma wrought by the catastrophe on "the people" both at Pearl Harbor and at home, accentuating the patriotism that emerges from the event. The overriding insistence, in all of these productions, on national unity, the need for retaliation, the belief in a "mission," and the absolute necessity of "remembrance" are abundantly evident in the newspapers and television coverage of September 11.

Pearl Harbor is a genre film, a war movie in the spirit of such films as *So Proudly We Hail* (1943), *From Here to Eternity* (1953), and *Tora! Tora! Tora!* (1970), with added and updated elements derived from the technology of the later twentieth and early twenty-first centuries—the "realism" of loud Dolby sound, underwater cinematography, and digital effects to augment and intensify the battle scenes. In fact, this union of contemporary technology with 1940s genre conventions parallels the union of earlier World War II heroism with concessions to contemporary audiences in the toned-down treatment of the Japanese and the inclusion of an African American character. Also, in the conventions of contemporary mixed-genre production, the film seeks to anastomose three different narratives—romantic melodrama, action drama, and historical docudrama.

The melodrama features a romance between Rafe McCawley (Ben Affleck) and Evelyn Johnson (Kate Beckinsale) that begins with love at first sight, the promise of undying love, the belief in the virtue of chastity, and of course, an inevitable rupture that involves Rafe's best friend, Danny Walker (Josh Hartnett) in a not-so-chaste relationship with Evelyn after Rafe has been assumed dead. This triangle serves the discourse of the film well, invoking the familiar conventions of the action genre in which neither the conflict nor even the romance are between the man and the woman but between the men in their initial bonding, later antagonism, and finally reunion, if only through the death of Danny. One of the dominant themes of the romance is, in familiar generic terms, the transformation of the protagonist from a stage of innocence into knowledge of "a world forever changed" but a reconstituted one of national unity, family, and restoration of a belief in the future. . .

The second line of narrative in the film, paralleling the romance, entails a portrait of the peaceful and idyllic world of Pearl Harbor before the attack, a world of camaraderie and innocence that is violated. To reinforce the element of surprise, the film contrasts scenes of military personnel and nurses enjoying the Hawaiian milieu—dancing, drinking, lovemaking, and images of an empty hospital ward as a contrast to the frenzied action that takes place there after the Japanese strike. The disintegration of Rafe and Danny's relationship over Evelyn, culminating in a barroom brawl between the two men, anticipates the "betrayal" by the Japanese (then suing for peace) of the United States. The action scenes dramatically reconstruct the disaster wrought on land and sea, the strafing of civilians, the explosion of Red Cross ambulances, the devastating attacks on the ships in the harbor, and the desperate struggles of sailors to escape from the burning and sinking ship. As the relationship between the two men is restored through the unity engendered by means of combat with a common enemy, so their reconciliation serves as a prolepsis for the collective overcoming of national defeat. In the spirit of the war film, this dimension of the narrative anticipates victory by including the two men's volunteering for a dangerous mission organized by Jimmy Doolittle (Alec Baldwin) to bomb Tokyo. In the dramatization of the successful attack, the vicissitudes of the romance narrative are paralleled in the action sequences that stress the romance of heroism, sacrifice, bonding, and remembrance in the harrowing but exhilarating experiences of danger in fighting the enemy and inflicting losses on him in the air strike over Tokyo. Danny's death also serves as a parallel to the martyrdom of the sailors entombed in the *Arizona,* sunk by the Japanese.

The third trajectory of the film involves historical reconstruction of the events leading up to the attack, conflicts in intelligence, and refusals to interpret signs properly. This narrative line especially involves President Franklin Delano Roosevelt, played by Jon Voight, portrayed as lamenting U.S. lack of involvement in the European war. Other historical episodes in the film involve the reconstructed roles of admirals Kimmel and Short; Doolittle; Admiral Yamamoto, played by Mako; and a black sailor, Doris "Dorie" Miller, played by Cuba Gooding Jr. These portraits are largely drawn from Pearl Harbor archives, interviews with survivors, and reconstructions of Roosevelt's response to the attack and pleas for preparedness: "We're building refrigerators, while our enemies build bombs." Roosevelt's concern for impending war is reinforced by the images of Admiral Yamamoto and other Japanese military and government officials as they draft, train, and execute their plan "to annihilate . . . [the] Pacific fleet in a single blow at Pearl Harbor," the motivation articulated as a response to the U.S.

embargo, shortages of fuel, and control of the Pacific. Intercut with these scenes are those involving the role of intelligence agencies, the deciphering of codes, the relay of messages, and instances of belated or intercepted messages. Several portents of the impending disaster do not rouse admirals Kimmel and Short.

This historical segment of the narrative film makes the most use of newsreel footage, and where that was not available or feasible, animation or computer simulation fills the gaps. The film does not evade documentation, providing newsreel footage of Hitler and his conquest of the masses along with images of the Japanese incursion into Manchuria and the massacre of Nanking. Other than this footage, the treatment of the Japanese from Yamamoto to the pilots and submarines is, in the film, concentrated on the stages of the planning and the attack itself. The two-hour-long attack by the Japanese is presented in great detail, if only with the help of exquisite computer animation, producing a vivid sense of the devastation wrought on the people and naval fleet. The film laboriously reconstructs the destruction of the *Arizona* and the images of the many men who tried to escape but were entombed in the sinking ship or drowned in the sea.

But the film does not end on a note of defeat. Proleptically, Yamamoto is shown to say, "I only fear that we have awakened a sleeping giant." And Roosevelt, as if reinforcing Yamamoto's words, is presented in a meeting with his cabinet, saying, "We have been trained to think we are invincible. . . . We have to strike back now." The element of U.S. indomitability and invincibility is reinforced in a scene reminiscent of Peter Sellers's role in *Dr. Strangelove, or, How I Learned to Stop Worrying and Love the Bomb* (1964). Struggling from his wheel-chair laboriously to stand without aid, Voight's Roosevelt challenges the "defeatists" who say a quick response is impossible, explaining to them that he now realizes that he has been "brought low," for a higher purpose—the salvation of the United States.

Images from newsreel footage of sped-up production to "avenge" Pearl Harbor are conjoined to the development of the Doolittle mission to bomb Tokyo, signs of the rousement of the "sleeping giant." "Let them repeat that we are a nation of weaklings and playboys," Roosevelt intones. The Doolittle episode will show otherwise, and the ending of the film centers on reflections concerning the "war that changed America." Thus the film has orchestrated the themes of blamelessness, the profundity of the trauma that transformed the United States, the element of "surprise" necessary to reinforce the sense of innocence unprotected, and the coming of age of the nation in the resurrection of national honor. In a sense, *Pearl Harbor* suggests the oft-repeated phrase associated with the Holocaust—"never again." At the end, the unity of the family is conjoined to revitalized images of manifest destiny and American uniqueness, themes that have resonated loudly since the Reagan years but have their source in a history and literature that far precedes the present.

The film was not reviewed kindly. In commentaries on *Pearl Harbor* before September 11, one reviewer for *Variety* described the film as exemplary of "the anti-historical approach that Hollywood seems to think the modern public prefers." In line with this assessment, an anonymous article in *Time International* quoted the comments of a contributor to an Internet chat room as saying, "They'll probably make a movie called *Hiroshima* next in which the heroic American soldiers bomb those evil Japanese and save the world." A major share of the complaints against the film involved the view that, though "it gets a lot of things right," it does not "finally paint a clear picture of the attack or the political events leading to it," which seems naïve both in relation to commercial war cinema and as an assessment of what is problematic about the representation of the past: not its fidelity to fact but its failure to be critical of cultural politics.

The most strident criticism came from Rand Richards Cooper in a review in *Commonweal* that linked the film's point of view to Reagan conservatism and to its backlash against contemporary opposition to U.S. foreign policy. For Cooper, the film is an anachronism: "It's startling to see an essentially nineteenth-century romantic vision assembled so faithfully in a twenty-first-century movie. And discouraging, too." Also in a critical vein, Stanley Kauffmann in the *New Republic* of June 18, 2001, concluded that "the film compel[s] the viewer to look not for the truth of that hour but for the schemings of today," though the nature of these "schemings" was not detailed. The initially negative critical reviews of *Pearl Harbor* disappeared with the post–September 11 media responses to the attacks on the United States. Whereas. before September 11, *Variety* had claimed that the film exhibited a *"Classics Illustrated* fifth-grade approach to one of the most literally explosive moments" in United States history, such responses were no longer in evidence after the attack.

A brief excursion into the History Channel's production *Pearl Harbor* echoes the theatrical film's "romance of nation," drawing on similar newsreel footage, the same moments from the archive, and repetitive statement. As befits a television documentary, the program relies on conventions of the form: the use of narrator (in this case, *History Channel* host Roger Mudd) to set the stage and offer wisdom and counsel to the viewer, and the reliance on words of the survivors intercut with images of the disasters they describe. Once again is conveyed the idea that Pearl Harbor was a "turning point in history" when "the era of confidence" was "forever lost." In predictable fashion, the program rehearses, with the aid of "documentation" obtained through newsreel footage, the tension between the growing power of Hitler and the dominant "isolationist" sentiments as uttered by Charles Lindbergh. Also central to the unfolding of the narrative is the image of Hirohito, who is introduced with a voice-over explanation of the concept of Bushido, a Japanese belief in the sense of duty and patriotism owed to the nation on the part of its warriors. This concept is presented as something alien, marking "differences" between Japanese imperialism and the U.S. notion of patriotism. The documentaries, like the film, also present the event of Pearl Harbor as "a turning point of history" that "changed the world."

In the spirit of reinforcing an image of U.S. victimhood, the History Channel program begins its recounting of the events of December 7 with an invocation of the sunken *Arizona*, "a ship of destiny," a synecdoche for the nation, and the victim of Japanese aggression. This memorializing moment is a prelude to a breakdown of events, moment by moment, that interweaves the political elements that were slow to recognize the impending danger; the images of Pearl Harbor as "a paradise on earth"; accounts of survivors who validate the news-reel footage, albeit with personal accounts; and the images of the attacks themselves. In search of a reassuring closure, the program adopts two strategies: One entails an emotional treatment of the memorial built above the *Arizona*, as well as one in Japan, involving survivors and tourists. Keeping with the commemorative spirit of the documentary, Roger Mudd comments that survivors and their families are determined to "keep the memory of Pearl Harbor alive for all eternity." The other strategy that the program conveys to avoid defeatism and pessimism is "never again"—by invoking images of great men that saved the country from defeat—in particular, Admiral Chester Nimitz, who assumed control after Kimmel was disgraced and engineered victories in the Pacific Theater, and Roosevelt, whose leadership is credited with uniting the nation morally and militarily. The documentary parallels the Bruckheimer and Bay film in its emphasis on destiny, invincibility, betrayal, and ultimately, victory.

The *National Geographic* program, although cast very much in the mold of memorializing and the importance of "history" to that process, includes a narrative thread that highlights the concrete attempts to document December 7 by Bob Ballard (of *Titanic* fame through his underwater explorations). His mission, for which he is granted only two weeks, is to locate the remains of the Japanese minisub that was attacked by the U.S. Navy but never considered as a warning before the arrival of the planes. The narrator for this production is Brokaw, author of *The Greatest Generation*. The question animating the program as articulated by Brokaw is "what happened that fateful day?" Also drawing on accounts by U.S. and Japanese survivors, historians, newsreel footage from U.S. and Japanese archives, as well as maps and animation, the program presents Pearl Harbor as a place of pilgrimage and as a museum, emphasizing especially the memorial to the USS *Arizona* and the sailors interred in it. To reinforce survivors' accounts, the program provides the familiar blow-by-blow description of the day's events intercut with Ballard's ultimately futile attempt to locate the downed Japanese minisub. Ballard remains convinced, however, that "history tells us what you need to know," thus strengthening the film's claims to monumental history. Unlike the History Channel's explanation of Japanese militarism in the context of Bushido, however, this program describes the attack as a "suicide" mission.

In the spirit of memorializing, the documentary especially highlights one survivor, Carl Carson, who now has a fatal illness and is determined to finally tell his story after many years of silence, recounting his involvement in the gruesome nature of the events of that December 7 morning, his own wounding, and sense of helplessness before the wounded and dying. The program climaxes with a service on the memorial for the *Arizona* and camera shots of the names inscribed on a large tablet, as well as underwater shots of the various quarters and their remains on the ship.

In the documentaries, the question of conspiracy, incompetence, and disbelief are evident as they describe the several events that could have tipped off the United States to an impending attack. In line with the film, however, they seek to enact the event "as it really was" and end with an emphasis on

U.S. victory. In a sense, the three productions are cast in an elegiac form, a memorial for the dead, especially in the case of the documentaries in that they rely on survivors to tell their stories of that day, on their memories, on their pain and inability to forget, and on the hope for a better future.

These three productions, while exhibiting some formal differences in their reconstructive modes, uses of documentation, treatment of the politics, and questions of failed intelligence processes, are emblematic of the process of what Friedrich Nietzsche terms "the uses and disadvantages of the past for the present moment." In their styles, they are faithful to the conventions of historical representation as exemplified by media—radio, film, and television. They all invoke a sense of national tradition and an implied sense of abiding national virtue. They are narratives of innocence and experience, coming-of-age rituals, and melodramas of betrayal based on the perfidy of the Japanese Other. They express a belief in American uniqueness, democracy, justice at home, righteous imperial power globally in the name of civilization and the injunction to "remember."

Epilogue

Television and newspaper reportage has seized on the event of Pearl Harbor to name and situate the events of September 11 and even when they claim that the 2001 event dwarfs Pearl Harbor, they recapitulate traditional forms of explanation and forms of response to confront the two events, reaching backward into American history rather than confronting critically the exigencies of profound global changes in which the United States plays a predominant role. In this sense, the film *Pearl Harbor* and the two commemorative documentaries produced before September 11 set the stage for this retrospective and regressive view of U.S. history and politics. . . .

The film and the manifold reports in newspapers and on television do not rely directly on the film, but the film in its style and discursive strategies embodies strikingly similar assumptions about the American nation, its people, and its mission in the world. It is insufficient to describe its conventions as clichéd, because they address a way of organizing and aestheticizing knowledge and politics that requires tracing in terms of antecedents and conceptions of history. The very notion of historicizing demands examination. The film *Pearl Harbor* relies on a form of historicizing that could be described as monumental and antiquarian, relying on approximations and generalities, making "what is dissimilar look similar," and ignoring causes. Monumental history thus "tends naturally toward the universal," considering effects in themselves, and "the only causes that it understands are simple duels opposing individuals."

Thus the narratives of Pearl Harbor that filter through most of the commentaries on September 11, emphasizing a sense of uniqueness, manifest destiny, paradise lost and regained, and the righteousness granted by divine mandate to set wrongs aright, are inherent to all these accounts but are not deeply indebted to Hollywood; rather Hollywood is indebted to these visions of American exceptionality. Hence conceptions of America's role as policeman of the world not only are divinely sanctioned but thrive on creating a melodrama of good and evil that cannot tolerate ambiguity or contradiction. Therefore, despite contemporary concessions to political correctness through multiculturalism, as updating notions of the American melting pot and versions of populism, these narratives must be built on an edifice of Truth based on the essential goodness of the American character and its mission and calling. Moreover, in relation to internationalism and to the current moment described in terms of globality, this monumental and antiquarian vision of history must be adapted to current economic and political realities. This vision must be augmented and accounted for in relation to media representations of December 7, 1941, and September 11, 2002—namely, the uses of popular psychology under the rubric of "trauma" to reinforce the "infamy," "surprise," and "horror" of violations to American sovereignty.

The injunction to remember is allied to biological and psychological conceptions of the permanent damage to the individual and national psyche and the need to rehearse and mitigate the conditions of the shock attendant on the unexpected and inexplicable events. Thus, though the film *Pearl Harbor* and the two television programs preceded September 11, they exemplify a way of thinking that allows the continuity of religious notions of the sacred sense of place and of the sense that Americans have an ordained destiny in the world, which may involve the uses of war and violence to stop those forces that seek to impede this "progress."

While the documentaries and the film *Pearl Harbor*, like numerous reports and editorials about September 11, justify war and violence in the name of democracy, and while they rely on selective versions of history to underpin U.S. sovereignty, they reflect little on the terms of another aspect of history—namely, the transformations that have taken place in the United States from early founding conceptions of constitutional democracy to its present role as the world's policeman, a mantle inherited from the legacy of European sovereignty. Of this transformation, Hannah Arendt wrote,

> The American government, for better or worse, has entered into the heritage of Europe as though it were its patrimony—unaware, alas, of the fact that Europe's declining power was preceded and accompanied by political bankruptcy of the nation-state (and its concept of sovereignty). . . . [W]ar is still the *ultima ratio*, the old continuation of politics by means of violence. It is a secret from nobody that the famous random event is more likely to arise from those parts of the world where the old adage "There is no alternative to victory" retains a high degree of plausibility.

These statements describe what the Pearl Harbor productions expose but do not regard it critically, mired as they are in the language of an earlier mythology of America. Speaking specifically of a tradition of organic thought that underpins the justification of politics by means of violence, Arendt identifies it as the tendency to think in biological terms, particularly of the sick body and its correlative, the "sick society," which she believes "enables the glorification of violence . . . [to] appeal to the undeniable fact that in the household of nature destruction and creation are but two sides of the creative process . . . as a continuing prerequisite for continuing life in the animal kingdom."

The trope of disease relies on a conception of crisis, catastrophe, and rupture from a previous balanced state. One can see this in the frequent recourse after September 11 to the language of injury and trauma, and the quest for restitution or compensation endemic to many of the pronouncements by the government and the media in relation to World War II and the "war on terrorism." In relation to traditional and dominant expressions of the American reliance on a form of historicism based on biological, organic, and teleological thinking, the monumental narratives that link December 7, 1941, to September 11, 2001, raise important questions concerning the means and ends, the strategic uses of traditional modes of historical representation as expressed through media.

Unnatural Disasters: Race and Poverty

The barrage of images in newspapers and on television tested the nation's collective sense of reality. There were men and women wading chest-deep in water—when they weren't floating or drowning in the toxic whirlpool the streets of New Orleans had become. When the waters subsided, there were dead bodies strewn on curbsides and wrapped in blankets by fellow sufferers, who provided the perished their only dignity. There were unseemly collages of people silently dying from hunger and thirst—and of folk writhing in pain, or quickly collapsing under the weight of missed medicine for diabetes, high blood pressure, or heart trouble. Photo snaps and film shots captured legions of men and women huddling in groups or hugging corners, crying in wild-eyed desperation for help, for any help, from somebody, anybody, who would listen to their unanswered pleas. The filth and squalor of their confinement—defecating where they stood or sat, or, more likely, dropped, bathed in a brutal wash of dredge and sickening pollutants that choked the air with ungodly stench—grieved the camera lenses that recorded their plight.

Men, women, and children tore through deserted streets lined with empty stores, hunting for food and water and clothing for their bodies. They were hurried along by the steadily diminishing prospect of rescue by the government, by *their* government, whose only visible representatives were the police who came after them for looting. There were wailing infants clasping crying mothers who mouthed prayers for someone to please just save their babies. There were folk stuffed in attics pleading for the cavalry to come. Many colors were present in this multicultural stew of suffering, but the dominant color was black. From the sight of it, this was the third world—a misnomer, to be sure, since people of color are two-thirds of the world's population. The suffering on screen created cognitive dissonance; it suggested that this must be somewhere in India, or the outskirts of Biafra. This surely couldn't be the United States of America—and how cruelly that term seemed to mock those poor citizens who felt disunited and disconnected and just plain dissed by their government. This couldn't be the richest and most powerful nation on the globe, leaving behind some of its poorest citizens to fend for themselves.

And yet it was. It was bad enough to witness the government's failure to respond to desperate cries of help scrawled on the tattered roofs of flooded homes. But Hurricane Katrina's violent winds and killing waters swept into

From *Come Hell or High Water: Hurrican Katrina and the Color of Disaster* by Michael Eric Dyson (Basic Civitas Books, 2006). Copyright © 2006 by Michael Eric Dyson. Reprinted by permission of Basic Civitas, a member of Perseus Books Group, LLC via Rightslink.

the mainstream a stark realization: the poor had been abandoned by society and its institutions, and sometimes by their well-off brothers and sisters, long before the storm. We are immediately confronted with another unsavory truth: it is the exposure of the extremes, not their existence, that stumps our national sense of decency. We can abide the ugly presence of poverty so long as it doesn't interrupt the natural flow of things, doesn't rudely impinge on our daily lives or awareness. As long as poverty is a latent reality, a solemn social fact suppressed from prominence on our moral compass, we can find our bearings without fretting too much about its awkward persistence. . . .

Our being surprised, and disgusted, by the poverty that Katrina revealed is a way of remaining deliberately naive about the poor while dodging the responsibility that knowledge of their lives would entail. We remain blissfully ignorant of their circumstances to avoid the brutal indictment of our consciences. When a disaster like Katrina strikes—a *natural* disaster not directly caused by human failure—it frees us to be aware of, and angered by, the catastrophe. After all, it doesn't directly implicate us; it was an act of God. Even when human hands get involved, our fingerprints are nowhere to be found. We're not responsible for the poor and black being left behind; the local, state, or federal government is at fault.

We are thus able to decry the circumstances of the poor while assuring ourselves that we had nothing to do with their plight. We can even take special delight in lambasting the source of their suffering—a source that is safely external to us. We are fine as long as we place time limits on the origins of the poor's plight—the moments we all spied on television after the storm, but not the numbing years during which we all looked the other way. Thus we fail to confront our complicity in their long-term suffering. By being outraged, we appear compassionate. This permits us to continue to ignore the true roots of their condition, roots that branch into our worlds and are nourished on our political and religious beliefs.

There are 37 million people in poverty in our nation, 1.1 million of whom fell below the poverty line in 2004. Some of the poorest folk in the nation, people in the Delta, have been largely ignored, rendered invisible, officially forgotten. FEMA left them dangling precipitously on rooftops and in attics because of bureaucratic bumbling. Homeland Security failed miserably in mobilizing resources to rescue Katrina survivors without food, water, or shelter. President Bush lighted on New Orleans only after Mayor Ray Nagin's profanity-laced radio-show diatribe blasting the federal government for its lethal inertia. Because the government took its time getting into New Orleans, Katrina took many lives. Hundreds of folk, especially the elderly, died while waiting for help. But the government and society had been failing to pay attention to the poor since long before one of the worst natural disasters in the nation's history swallowed the poor and spit them back up. The world saw just how much we hadn't seen; it witnessed our negligence up close in frightfully full color.

The hardest-hit regions in the Gulf States had already been drowning in extreme poverty: Mississippi is the poorest state in the nation, with Louisiana just behind it. More than 90,000 people in each of the areas stormed by Katrina in Louisiana, Mississippi, and Alabama made less than $10,000 a year. Black folk in these areas were strapped by incomes that were 40 percent less than those earned by whites. Before the storm, New Orleans, with a 67.9 percent black population, had more than 103,000 poor people. That means the Crescent City had a poverty rate of 23 percent, 76 percent higher than the national average of 13.1 percent. New Orleans's poverty rate ranked it seventh out of 290 large U.S. counties.

Although black folk make up 31.5 percent of Louisiana's population, their offspring account for 69 percent of the children in poverty. Though the national average for elders with disabilities is 39.6 percent, New Orleans hovers near 57 percent. The New Orleans median household income is $31,369, far beneath the national median of $44,684. A full 9 percent of households in New Orleans didn't own or have access to a vehicle. That means that nearly one in four citizens in New Orleans, and one in seven in the greater New Orleans metropolitan area, had no access to a car.

In fact, New Orleans ranks fourth out of 297 metropolitan areas in the country in the proportion of households lacking access to cars. The top three metropolitan spots are in the greater New York area, which has the most extensive public transportation system in the country. New Orleans ranks ninth among 140 big cities for the same category, a far higher ranking than cities with similar demographic profiles such as Detroit and Memphis. Black households nationwide generally have far less access to cars than white households, a trend mirrored in New Orleans, where only 5 percent of non-Latino whites were without car access, while 27 percent of blacks in New Orleans were without cars. Nationwide, 19 percent of blacks lack access to cars.

And children and elderly folk are even more likely to live in households without access to cars. Children and the elderly made up 38 percent of the population in New Orleans, but they accounted for 48 percent of the households without access to cars in the city. The poor and the near-poor made up the vast majority of those without car access in New Orleans, accounting for nearly 80 percent of the city's car-less population. These facts make it painfully clear just why so many folk could not evacuate before Katrina struck. They weren't shiftless, stupid, or stubborn, as some have suggested (FEMA's Michael Brown blamed the poor for staying behind and drowning while discounting or ignoring the many obstacles to their successful exodus). They simply couldn't muster the resources to escape destruction, and, for many, death.

The most glaring feature of their circumstance suggests that Katrina's survivors lived in concentrated poverty—they lived in poor neighborhoods, attended poor schools, and had poorly paying jobs that reflected and reinforced a distressing pattern of rigid segregation. Nearly 50,000 poor folk in New Orleans lived in areas where the poverty rate approached 40 percent. In fact, among the nation's fifty largest cities with poor black families jammed into extremely poor neighborhoods, New Orleans ranked second. Those households living in concentrated poverty often earn barely more than $20,000 a year. In neighborhoods with concentrated poverty, only one in twelve adults has a college degree, most children are reared in single-parent families, and four in ten working-age adults, many of whom are disabled, have no jobs. Nearly every major American city has several neighborhoods that are desperately poor and severely segregated. Cities like Cleveland, New York, Atlanta, and Los Angeles have economically distressed neighborhoods where more than 30 percent of their population's poor black live. . . .

Frames of Reference: Class, Caste, Culture, and Cameras

If race grabbed the biggest headlines in the aftermath of Katrina because of poverty and politics, its force was also felt in other dimensions of the cultural and personal response to the hurricane. The media became a big part of the story. Reporters' anger at the government's tragic delay leaped off allegedly neutral pages and TV screens even as the stories also reinforced stereotypes of black behavior in exaggerated reports of looting and social anarchy. The black elite stepped up to express support for the poor and outrage at their treatment, putting aside, perhaps even denying, elements of its own recent assaults on poor blacks. And despite its embattled status as the purveyor of perversity, patriarchy, and pornography, quarters of hip-hop responded admirably, reminding us that they have been one of the few dependable sources of commentary on the black poor all along. The disaster also sparked renewed interest in the "race or class" debate as to what element of the dyad accounted more reliably for the fate of the black poor.

But one of the untold stories of Katrina is how the hurricane impacted racial and ethnic minorities other than blacks. For instance, nearly 40,000 Mexican citizens who lived (mostly in trailers) and worked in New Orleans were displaced. Altogether, nearly 145,000 Mexicans in the entire Gulf Coast region were scattered by Katrina. Latinos make up 3 percent of Louisiana's population, 124,222 people of the state's 4,515,770 residents. Many Latinos who live in the South are foreign born and are undocumented laborers on farms or in hotels, restaurants, and other service industry jobs. . . .

Thousands of Native Americans on the Gulf Coast were hard hit by the storm as well. According to the National Congress of American Indians (NCAI), several Native American tribes were in harm's away across the damaged region, although early on there was little contact with affected members. In the immediate aftermath of Katrina, there was little information about the death tolls among the six federally recognized Native American tribes in Alabama, Louisiana, and Mississippi, including the Parch Band Creek Indian Tribe in Alabama; the Coushatta Indian Tribe, Jena Band of Choctaw, and Tunica-Biloxi Tribe in Louisiana; and the Chitimacha Tribe and the Choctaw Indians in Mississippi. For one tribe near Chalmette, Louisiana, the local high school served as a tribal morgue, holding the bodies of Native American workers, including shrimpers and other fishermen, who were drowned in the flooding near New Orleans. The Mississippi Band of Choctaw Indians experienced power outages on their reservation and sought shelter at tribal hotels. The NCAI partnered with the National Indian Gaming Association (NIGA) to raise relief funds for Native Americans in the Gulf States.

There were also nearly 50,000 Vietnamese fishermen who labored on the Louisiana coast—while others worked in the service and manufacturing industries—along with a large contingent of Filipino American shrimpers, part of the oldest Filipino community in North America. A community of Vietnamese shrimpers also lived and worked near Mississippi; many of them were displaced, while others died in the horrible pounding of Katrina. There were nearly 30,000 Vietnamese evacuees dispersed to Houston, although many of them were denied entry into the Astrodome, finding shelter instead at Houston's Hong Kong City Mall.

The oversight of Latino, Native American, and Vietnamese and Filipino suffering in the catastrophe not only reinforces for the latter three groups their relative invisibility in American culture, and for Latinos their relative marginalization in the region. It shows as well that our analysis of minorities must constantly be revised to accommodate a broader view of how race and ethnicity function in the culture. As important as it is, the black-white racial paradigm simply does not exhaust the complex realities and complicated interactions among various minority groups and the broader society.

The black-white racial paradigm was also pressured by an enduring question among social analysts that was revived in the face of Katrina: is it race or class that determines the fate of poor blacks? Critics came down on either side during the crisis, but in this case, that might equate to six in one hand, half a dozen in the other. It is true that class is often overlooked to explain social reality. Ironically, it is often a subject broached by the acid conservatives who want to avoid confronting race, and who become raging parodies of Marxists in the bargain. They are only concerned about class to deflect race; they have little interest in unpacking the dynamics of class or engaging its deforming influence in the social scene. In this instance, race becomes a marker for class, a proxy, blurring and bending the boundaries that segregate them.

Class certainly loomed large in Katrina's aftermath. Blacks of means escaped the tragedy; blacks without them suffered and died. In reality, it is how race and class interact that made the situation for the poor so horrible on the Gulf Coast. The rigid caste system that punishes poor blacks and other minorities also targets poor whites. Even among the oppressed, however, there are stark differences. Concentrated poverty doesn't victimize poor whites in the same way it does poor blacks. For instance, the racial divide in car ownership discussed earlier partially reflects income differences between the races. However, as if to prove that not all inequalities are equal, even poor whites are far more likely to have access to cars than are poor blacks. In New Orleans, 53 percent of poor blacks were without cars while just 17 percent of poor whites lacked access to cars. The racial disparity in class effects shows up in education as well. Even poor white children are far less likely to live in, or to attend school in, neighborhoods where poverty is highly concentrated.

Moreover, one must also account for how the privileges of whiteness that transcend class open up opportunities for poor whites that are off limits to the black poor, whether it is a job offer at a restaurant wary of blacks or a schoolroom slot in a largely white, stable community. This is not to deny the vicious caste tensions that separate poor and working class whites from their middle-class and upper-class peers. Such tensions result in a dramatically different quality of life for the well-off and the have-nots. I simply aim to underscore the pull of racial familiarity that is often an unspoken variable, and sometimes the crucial difference, in the lives of the white and non-white poor. It is bad enough to be white and poor; it is worse still to be black, or brown, and female, and young, and poor. Simply said, race makes class hurt more.

In African American life, class and caste differences show up most dramatically in the chasms between the black fortunate and the black poor. As I watched Hurricane Katrina sweep waves of mostly poor and black folk into global view, I thought of the controversy stirred by Bill Cosby's assault on the black poor—that they are detrimentally promiscuous, disinclined to education, unappreciative of good speech, determined to saddle their kids with weird names, and bent on blaming the white man for all their ills. Cosby's views were widely celebrated in the press, and in many quarters of black America, especially among the black elite—the *Afristocracy*. Those few who were publicly critical of Cosby were said to be making excuses for the black poor while denying their need to be responsible for their own destinies. Others agreed with Cosby that the poor hampered their own progress because they were either too lazy or too ignorant to do better. In any case, Cosby, and a slew of critics, believed that the black poor suffered because they desired or deserved to be poor.

In the aftermath of Katrina, some of the same black critics who had previously sided with Cosby suddenly decried conservative visions of the black poor that, interestingly enough, accord quite well with the comedian's views. For instance, *Atlanta Journal-Constitution* editorial page editor Cynthia Tucker penned a column, "Katrina Exposes Our Callous Treatment of the Poor," nearly a week after the storm struck. She began dramatically—"Here in America, the land of opportunity, we gave up on the poor more than two decades ago." She writes that under Ronald Reagan "we learned that the poor were simply too lazy to improve their prospects and their misery was their own fault." Tucker argues that we "not only gave up trying to help the poor, but we also bought the argument that trying to assist them, especially through government programs, would just make matters worse."

The right-wingers, she says, convinced us that the poor are illiterate, sick, and unemployed because of welfare, and because they choose to be. "So we turned our backs on the impoverished and tuned them out, leaving them stranded in the worst neighborhoods, worst schools and the worst geography." Tucker writes that the images of the poor in the wake of Katrina shouldn't surprise us, since it is the outgrowth of a culture that has left the poor to their own devices. Tucker concludes her column with a rousing portrayal of the insular attitudes that deny the privileges of the well to do, blame the poor for their ills, and sweep the plight of the poor under our collective social carpet.

> In fact, it's easy for all of us who live in relative prosperity to forget that most of us are here because we had the good sense to be born to the

right parents. While a few impoverished young adults can still scratch and claw their way into the mainstream, it is getting harder and harder to do so as the industrial jobs that created the great middle class are disappearing. (Why do you think so many working-class sons and daughters volunteer for the armed forces?) Income inequality is increasing in this country; the latest census shows that the number of people living in poverty is rising. Still, a few predictable voices on the far-right fringe are already thinking up ways to blame Hurricane Katrina's victims for their plight. Some are playing up the lawlessness of a few thugs; others are casting responsibility for the crisis solely on local authorities. Haven't we listened to those callous self-promoters long enough? Hurricane Katrina overwhelmed levees and exploded the conventional wisdom about a shared American prosperity, exposing a group of people so poor they didn't have $50 for a bus ticket out of town. If we want to learn something from this disaster, the lesson ought to be: America's poor deserve better than this.

But less than a year before Tucker's heroic defense of the vulnerable, she had heartily endorsed Cosby's equally callous condemnation of the black poor. In a column entitled "Bill Cosby's Pointed Remarks May Spark Much-Needed Debate," Tucker lauded the comedian—cum—social critic for his willingness to address the black poor's "self-inflicted wounds" in his "pointedly politically incorrect" diatribe against the black poor. After briefly acknowledging that American society "still bears some responsibility for the failure of so many black Americans to join the economic and cultural mainstream," Tucker asked if black Americans shouldn't "acknowledge that, at the dawn of the 21st century, personal responsibility has at least as much to do with success in modern America as race, especially since the Supreme Court decision in *Brown v. Board* rolled back much of systemic racism?"

A few months later, in a column entitled "Bill Cosby's Plain-Spokenness Comes Not a Moment Too Soon," Tucker affirmed the need for the Afristocracy to bear down on their less-fortunate kin by favorably citing the earlier example of black elites doing just that. "Throughout the first half of the 20th century, accomplished blacks routinely policed the behavior of their less polished brethren, urging thrift, moderation, tidiness." Such policing of black behavior gave way to a black leadership class during the civil rights movement that was loath to admit black failure for fear that it "would damage the movement," while black power advocates "denounced any black critic of black failure as a race traitor." Tucker concludes her column comparing American blacks to their kin throughout the diaspora who come to this country and succeed against the odds. She draws the lesson from their success that race simply isn't that big a barrier to black achievement.

But black parents ought to note this, as well: The success of black immigrants strongly suggests that race is no great barrier to achievement. While many black activists contend that there is still a grave disadvantage in being the descendant of slaves, it is hard to see what that could be. (Note, too, that black West Indians are also the descendants of slaves.) Yes, our ancestors suffered. But the 21st-century racist aims his hate at the color of our skin—not at where we came from or who our grandparents were. . . .

It seems that Tucker only opposes assaults on the poor when they originate from white society. She can only detect the heinous disregard for the social conditions that plague the poor when they emerge outside the race. But when the flag of attack waves broadly in black culture, especially under the leadership of an embittered Afristocrat such as Bill Cosby—an attack that is often joined by figures like talk show host Larry Elder or writer Shelby Steele—Tucker can only join the cavalry and ride roughshod over the nuanced and complex positions she otherwise upholds. As Tucker well knows, Cosby's words count even more because he is a celebrated comic whose race-neutral politics have endeared him to a white audience that he has never tested, or turned against, in the way he has the black poor. . . .

Of course, it is a marvelous sight to see so many black folk rally around the poor after Katrina. The press noted how Katrina was a "generation-defining catastrophe" that galvanized black generosity and solidarity throughout the nation. Black churches around the country raised millions of dollars for relief efforts. Several artists held or participated in fund-raisers. There was the S.O.S. (Saving OurSelves) Relief Telethon broadcast on BET and cosponsored by the National Urban League, the American Red Cross, the Hip-Hop Summit Action Network, and Essence Communications, which raised $10 million. The Jazz at Lincoln Center's "Higher Ground" relief benefit was spearheaded by New Orleans native and the center's artistic director Wynton Marsalis. There were several fund-raisers hosted by hip-hop artists, including Mississippi native David Banner's Heal the Hood Hurricane Relief Concert. There were also extensive fund-raising efforts made by New Orleans natives Master P and Juvenile, Chicago's Twista, and Brooklyn writer and activist Kevin Powell—joined by Common, Kanye West, Mos Def, and Talib Kweli. Many black professional athletes also visited the Gulf Coast and contributed money and time to relief efforts.

We should be reminded, however, that the black poor are flooded daily by material misery; they are routinely buffeted by harsh racial winds. The obvious absence of the black blessed at times of ongoing difficulty—to defend and protect the poor in principled fashion—underscores the woefully episodic character of black social regard. Lots of well-to-do black folk are doing a lot to help, but too many of us have left the black poor stranded on islands of social isolation and class alienation. Episodes of goodwill and compassion are no replacement for structural change. As Martin Luther King, Jr., said at Riverside Church exactly a year before he was murdered:

> On the one hand we are called to play the good Samaritan on life's roadside; but that will be only an initial act. One day we must come to see that the whole Jericho road must be transformed so that men and women will not be constantly beaten and robbed as they make their journey on life's highway. True compassion is more than flinging a coin to a beggar; it is not haphazard and superficial. It comes to see that an edifice which produces beggars needs restructuring.

Charity is no substitute for justice. If we never challenge a social order that allows some to accumulate wealth—even if they decide to help the less fortunate—while others are shortchanged, then even acts of kindness end up supporting unjust arrangements. We must never ignore the injustices that make charity necessary, or the inequalities that make it possible. . . .

EXPLORING THE ISSUE

Do Media Unite the Population in Times of Crisis?

Critical Thinking and Reflection

1. How are stories changed over time? For example, Landy discusses how different media representations reinforce and change our value system? How do fictional representations reflect real-world events?
2. To which forms of media do you turn when you need confirmation of a breaking story? Are some forms of media more trustworthy?
3. How are our impressions of events changed over time? Does memorializing, or telling stories in narrative form, change the experience of the disaster and our relationship to it?
4. Do our media sources fall into traditional interpretations that exemplify a stereotypical response to unfolding events? How much interpretation do media give us, especially in times of crisis?

Is There Common Ground?

Both of the authors of these selections situate their perspectives with a different relationship to events as they occur. Landy discusses how time and storytelling in the media shape values over a long period of time, while Dyson specifically focuses on a disaster and the reports that emanated from it. Does time play an important factor in helping us, as well as media producers, sort out the issues that result from moments of crisis?

One thing that both authors would agree is that media are essential to storytelling about our environment, and as Lasswell predicted, media may provide some of the most important ways in which we communicate in and among ourselves with relationship to our environment. Whether the media unite us or divide us may result in the uniqueness of each disaster in our lives.

Additional Resources

Wheeler Winston Dixon, ed., *Film and Television After 9/11* (Southern Illinois University Press, 2004) (a collection of essays)

The above reference is an interesting source for further information on this topic, from which Landy's essay has been edited. This collection suggests many more media representations of the 9/11 disaster and its aftermath, as represented by media.

Michael Eric Dyson, *Come Hell or High Water* (Basic Books, 2006)

This book includes a much more in-depth analysis of the politics resulting from the Hurricane Katrina disaster and its aftermath.

A Web site that focuses on global issues identifies a number of global natural disasters and discusses how they were handled:

www.globalissues.org/article/568/media-and-natural-disasters

The British newspaper, *The Independent*, printed an interesting story on how media cover natural disasters:

www.independent.co.uk/news/media/tv-radio/catastrophe-on-camera-why-media-coverage-of-natural-disasters-is-flawed-2189032.html

ISSUE 3

Do Media Distort Representations of Islam and Arab Cultures?

YES: Wajahat Ali, Eli Clifton, Matthew Duss, Lee Fang, Scott Keyes, and Faiz Shakir, from "Fear, Inc.: The Roots of the Islamophobia Network in America," Center for American Progress (August 2011), selections from 1–152

NO: Gal Beckerman, from "The New Arab Conversation," *Columbia Journalism Review* (January/February, 2007)

Learning Outcomes

After reading this issue, you should be able to:

- Discuss the misrepresentation of Arab culture.
- Evaluate the possibility of blogs and other social media to combat stereotypes.
- Describe the ways in which journalistic practices promote stereotypes.
- Apply these concepts to stereotyping in society.

ISSUE SUMMARY

YES: Wajahat Ali, Eli Clifton, Matthew Duss, Lee Fang, Scott Keyes, and Faiz Shakir discuss in Fear, Inc., a special report from the Center for American Progress, how the Muslim religion is among the most maligned stereotypes in popular culture, and how these images have fueled misperceptions about the Arab world. It explores how media have been an echo chamber for misinformation created by well-funded groups dedicated to spreading fear and misinformation. These images influence politicians and citizens and contribute to public opinion.

NO: Journalist Gal Beckerman discusses how Arab bloggers from the Middle East are challenging popular stereotypes of Arab and Middle Eastern cultures. Because these bloggers are writing about their lives, the global public can read about their situations and understand them as individuals, rather than racial or ethnic group members.

Stereotypes and distorted images of racial, ethnic, and gender groups abound in the media, but can these images distract the public so severely that they influence political ideology? Our history of understanding the impact of racial profiling, based on stereotypes that distort what is commonly called "the Other," indicates that these stereotypes can have multiple harmful effects. Throughout American popular culture, we have seen how different groups portrayed in the media contribute to public opinion of groups for whom we have little or no firsthand understanding.

It has been said that despite recent sensitivity to multiculturalism and a growing call for respect for people of other races and ethnicities, the image of the Arab still represents evil. No doubt our multiyear wars with people in Iraq and Afghanistan have contributed to a misunderstanding of who or what our military troops are fighting, and for what purpose, but the conflation of the people of the Middle East with "the enemy" is an example of how powerful stereotypes can be.

Journalist Gal Beckerman focuses on the impact of bloggers and the ability of these individuals to get personal messages out to others beyond geographic borders. Despite the Arab world's limited Internet access, Beckerman finds blogs represent humane voices in a sea of confusion. The contrast of the individual bloggers' messages compared to the mainstream Arab media provides one point of departure for getting to know "the Other" in a more intimate way, but at the same time, as Beckerman writes, "the Middle East is a region where the historical and the personal slam up against each other daily in a way they do only once a decade or so in America." In the voices of bloggers, we get to know the daily beliefs, frustrations, and humanity of "the Other." In knowing "the Other," simplistic stereotypes become harder to maintain.

If stereotypes could be managed by simply coming to know the people behind the image, perhaps social media could erase the misperceptions. The Center for American Progress fears that powerful forces are at work that will prevent that resolution. Fear, Inc. argues that misrepresentations and stereotypes are encouraged in the United States by a small group of anti-Muslim organizations and individuals. Quoted elsewhere in the article is a report on the organization Stop Islamization of America, which the Anti-Defamation League concluded "promotes a conspiratorial anti-Muslim agenda under the guise of fighting radical Islam." Much of the power of these groups comes from what Fear, Inc. describes as a well-developed right-wing media echo chamber that amplifies a few marginal voices. Explicitly, this report names *The Rush Limbaugh Show*, *The Sean Hannity Show*, and the Fox Network among others.

In evaluating this claim, it is important to understand some of the internal practices of news organizations. Classically, *balance* in news stories is achieved by representing both sides of an issue. To display balance in a newspaper story, stories on controversial issues may often be represented by quotes from both supporters and dissenters. Fairness can also be achieved by presenting both sides in a news story. This is a traditional journalistic practice. Editorials are a different matter in that they typically state an opinion and build an argument for that opinion's validity. Currently, television and radio are full of talk shows that highlight certain points of view or focus on bringing opposing voices together. Why are there so many of these types of shows? Quoted elsewhere in this volume is a telling phrase, "News is expensive, opinion is cheap." Shows that bring in politicians and pundits are not expensive. In addition, they function to allow those with a point of view to build their argument for the American public. To promote robust and hard-hitting debate, hosts look for individuals with controversial points of view. When the show itself has a point of view, hosts again look to controversial figures to challenge prevailing opinion and to perhaps shape it in their direction. These are the conditions under which a few voices promote anti-Muslim sentiment in America.

This issue brings up more than the question of the power of stereotyping in the media: It asks us to determine the underlying intent that is creating these stereotypes. It makes us ask whether the images in media really matter to us, where these images come from, and whether different types of media can communicate more effectively than others depending upon the content. Anytime we are challenged to question our own beliefs, and how those beliefs may be influenced by media, we get one step closer to understanding the complexity of media images, media forms, and how we, individually and collectively, understand our place and role in society.

Whenever we deal with issues of stereotypes and whether they do or do not influence our perceptions of people in society, we broach the uncomfortable area of human biases and prejudices. We know that media do indeed shape our sense of self and how we "fit" our own culture, but what if you are a person who does not see images of people who look like you, or who share your traditions, heritage, race, ethnicity, gender, or religion in media? The people who are not portrayed and the images we don't see are just as important as the distorted images that we do see. Absence of accurate images can be as harmful as the presence of distorted images. Gaye Tuchman, a sociologist of media, called it "symbolic annihilation."

The most insidious thing about stereotypes is that we seldom question whether they are accurate or not, and yet questioning the images we see in media is one of the most important features of understanding media's relationship to society. There is evidence that U.S. media have improved in terms of portrayals of African Americans, Hispanics, and Asians, and images of gays and lesbians are starting to improve; but as these selections show, accurate representations of Arabs in the mainstream media still have a long way to go.

Perhaps blogging or alternative media will lead the way.

YES

Wajahat Ali et al.

Fear, Inc.: The Roots of the Islamophobia Network in America

Introduction and Summary

On July 22, a man planted a bomb in an Oslo government building that killed eight people. A few hours after the explosion, he shot and killed 68 people, mostly teenagers, at a Labor Party youth camp on Norway's Utoya Island.

By midday, pundits were speculating as to who had perpetrated the greatest massacre in Norwegian history since World War II. Numerous mainstream media outlets, including *The New York Times*, *The Washington Post*, and *The Atlantic*, speculated about an Al Qaeda connection and a "jihadist" motivation behind the attacks. But by the next morning it was clear that the attacker was a 32-year-old, white, blond-haired and blue-eyed Norwegian named Anders Breivik. He was not a Muslim, but rather a self-described Christian conservative.

According to his attorney, Breivik claimed responsibility for his self-described "gruesome but necessary" actions. On July 26, Breivik told the court that violence was "necessary" to save Europe from Marxism and "Muslimi-zation." In his 1,500-page manifesto, which meticulously details his attack methods and aims to inspire others to extremist violence, Breivik vows "brutal and breathtaking operations which will result in casualties" to fight the alleged "ongoing Islamic Colonization of Europe."

Breivik's manifesto contains numerous footnotes and in-text citations to American bloggers and pundits, quoting them as experts on Islam's "war against the West." This small group of anti-Muslim organizations and individuals in our nation is obscure to most Americans but wields great influence in shaping the national and international political debate. Their names are heralded within communities that are actively organizing against Islam and targeting Muslims in the United States. . . .

While these bloggers and pundits were not responsible for Breivik's deadly attacks, their writings on Islam and multiculturalism appear to have helped create a world view, held by this lone Norwegian gunman, that sees Islam as at war with the West and the West needing to be defended. According to former CIA officer and terrorism consultant Marc Sageman, just as religious extremism "is the infrastructure from which Al Qaeda emerged," the writings of these anti-Muslim misinformation experts are "the infrastructure from which Breivik emerged." Sageman adds that their rhetoric "is not cost-free." . . .

This network of hate is not a new presence in the United States. Indeed, its ability to organize, coordinate, and disseminate its ideology through grass-roots organizations increased dramatically over the past 10 years. Further-more, its ability to influence politicians' talking points and wedge issues for the upcoming 2012 elections has mainstreamed what was once considered fringe, extremist rhetoric.

And it all starts with the money flowing from a select group of founda-tions. A small group of foundations and wealthy donors are the lifeblood of the Islamophobia network in America, providing critical funding to a clutch of right-wing think tanks that peddle hate and fear of Muslims and Islam—in the form of books, reports, websites, blogs, and carefully crafted talking points that anti-Islam grassroots organizations and some right-wing religious groups use as propaganda for their constituency.

The Right-Wing Media Enablers of Anti-Islam Propaganda

Spreading anti-Muslim hate in America depends on a well-developed right-wing media echo chamber to amplify a few marginal voices. The think tank misinformation experts and grassroots and religious-right organizations profiled in this report boast a symbiotic relationship with a loosely aligned, ideologically-akin group of right-wing blogs, magazines, radio stations, news-papers, and television news shows to spread their anti-Islam messages and myths. The media outlets, in turn, give members of this network the expo-sure needed to amplify their message, reach larger audiences, drive fundraising numbers, and grow their membership base.

Some well-established conservative media outlets are a key part of this echo chamber, mixing coverage of alarmist threats posed by the mere existence of Muslims in America with other news stories. Chief among the media part-ners are the Fox News empire, the influential conservative magazine National Review and its website, a host of right-wing radio hosts, *The Washington Times* newspaper and website, and the Christian Broadcasting Network and website.

Members of the Islamophobia network published articles or hit the air-waves this year and in 2010 to misinform our nation about Muslim American congregations. Here's a sampling.

- David Yerushalmi in *Middle East Quarterly* misinforms America that more than 80 percent of U.S. mosques advocate or promote violence.
- Frank Gaffney of the Center for Security Policy writes in *The Washing-ton Times*:

"Most mosques in the United States are actually engaged in—or at least supportive of—a totalitarian, seditious agenda they call Shariah. Its express purpose is undermining and ultimately forcibly replacing the U.S. government and its founding documents. In their place would be a "caliph" governing in accordance with Shariah's political-military-legal code."

- Islamophobia grassroots organizer Pamela Geller says that "4 out of 5 mosques preach hate" on CNN Sunday Morning.
- Fox News commentator Bill O'Reilly, in an interview with Rep. Keith Ellison (D-MN) on the O'Reilly Factor, cites Frank Gaffney to charge that "violent extremism and sharia law is being condoned in 75 percent of the American Muslim mosques."
- Rep. Peter King (R-NY) says that "over 80 percent of the mosques in this country are controlled by radical Imams" on the Laura Ingraham Show. . . .

Let's look at each in turn.

Hate Radio

Anti-Muslim websites work in tandem with popular radio talk-show hosts who repeat and amplify the alarmist threats and conspiracy theories promoted by the blogs and their supporters. The industry of "hate radio" includes nationally known personalities such as Rush Limbaugh, Michael Savage, Glenn Beck, and others. Together, they use their programs as bully pulpits to preach anti-Muslim messages of intolerance and hate.

'The Rush Limbaugh Show'

Rush Limbaugh hosts the most popular radio talk show in America. "The Rush Limbaugh Show" is carried by more than 600 radio stations nationwide and is broadcast to more than 15 million listeners a week. Limbaugh, age 60, calls himself "America's anchorman" and "America's truth detector." He uses his highly influential radio pulpit to spread the word, and one of his favorite messages is casting suspicion on President Obama's religious identity. Limbaugh has called Obama "Imam Obamadinejad," said the president is into caliphate building, and that he might think of himself as the 12th imam.

Such claims have an effect. In 2010, nearly 18 percent of Americans incorrectly believed that President Obama was a Muslim, due in no small part to the media orchestration of such claims.

Limbaugh joins Pamela Geller and others as a vociferous critic of the Park51 community center in New York City. During the protests last summer, he compared Muslims building the community center to the Klu Klux Klan establishing a "memorial at Gettsyburg." Limbaugh also charged that the community center was a "recruiting tool for foreign extremists," and repeated the talking point that organizers want the center to be a "victory monument at Ground Zero." Unfortunately Limbaugh's microphone will stay on for years to come. In 2008, he signed an eight-year, $400 million renewal contract with Clear Channel.

'The Sean Hannity Show'

The nation's second most popular talk show is "The Sean Hannity Show," a nationally syndicated talk-radio show that airs on Premiere Radio Networks and is hosted by Sean Hannity. Hannity, age 49, also hosts a cable-TV news show, "Hannity," on Fox News. Nearly 14 million listeners tune into Hannity's radio show each week to hear guests repeat the same talking points and conspiracy theories that can be heard on Limbaugh, Fox News, and other places. Questions abound about President Obama's religious affiliation, the Muslim Brotherhood infiltrating the Conservative Political Action Committee, and threats of homegrown terrorism in our midst. Listening to Hannity, one could hear Rep. Peter King (R-NY) agree with his host that 85 percent of mosques in America are run by Islamic fundamentalists after Hannity cited Steven Emerson and Daniel Pipes to prove his point.

'The Savage Nation'

Mike Savage hosts "The Savage Nation," another top-rated national radio program, which is syndicated through Talk Radio Network. More than 350 radio stations broadcast his show to nearly 9 million weekly listeners, putting him just behind Rush Limbaugh and Sean Hannity in ratings. Savage, 69, is known for his angry diatribes against minorities, including Muslims. On April 17, 2006, for example, he told listeners that Americans should "kill 100 million" Muslims. In October 2007 he said, "I don't wanna hear one more word about Islam. Take your religion and shove it up your behind. I'm sick of you." He then suggested that American Muslims be deported.

Along with Limbaugh, Savage promotes the myth that President Obama could be a secret Muslim. Before Obama was elected, Savage called him "Senator Barack Madrassas Obama." During the 2008 campaign, Savage said, "Now we have an unknown stealth candidate who went to a madrassa in Indonesia and, in fact, was a Muslim." Seeking to get "the facts," Savage insisted that "[w]e have a right to know if he's a so-called friendly Muslim or one who aspires to more radical teachings."

'The Glenn Beck Program'

Glenn Beck also has a popular radio show that is broadcast by more than 400 stations and syndicated by Premiere Radio Networks. Beck's show ties with Savage's show for third place for national radio talk shows with more than 9 million listeners weekly. Beck, 47, conjures fears equating Muslims with terrorists and brings religion into the mix. Last December, he speculated on his show about the number of American Muslims who might be terrorists, saying: "Let's say it's half a percent of the U.S. population. That's being generous. What's that number? What is the number of Islamic terrorists, 1 percent? I think it's closer to 10 percent."

In February, one of Beck's guests was Joel Richardson, the apocalyptic author of the book *The Islamic Antichrist*. Richardson was on the show to discuss "Islam's Mahdi, the Antichrist, the Middle East and Bible prophecy." According to Richardson, the "Antichrist" will be a Muslim and Islam will be Satan's "primary vehicle" to usher the end of times. . . .

The Right-Wing Mainstream News Enablers of Islamophobia

Fox News has one of the biggest and most influential megaphones in TV news. It uses this megaphone to amplify anti-Muslim alarmist threats and conspiracy theories on a regular basis. Virtually all the leading Islamophobia players have made recurring appearances on popular Fox News programs, such as "Hannity," "The O'Reilly Factor," and "Fox & Friends." The cable news network also featured former Speaker of the House of Representatives Newt Gingrich as a commentator, which he uses to promote his increasingly Islamophobic opinions, such as his call for curbs on freedom of speech to keep terrorists from spreading their message after six imams were mistakenly removed from a Minneapolis flight in 2006.

On these shows, players echo one another's warnings and repeat with serious certainty the same threats they warned about on radio shows and in blogs, newspapers, online magazines, and more. Their staple threats include: Muslims imposing Sharia in America, Muslims establishing a global caliphate, Muslims engaging in homegrown jihad, and Muslims infiltrating President Obama's administration to promote dangerous Islamist agendas.

Gingrich in particular has made Sharia law his hobby horse. In September last year, for example, he told the audience at a Value Voters Summit in Washington, D.C., "We should have a federal law that says sharia law cannot be recognized by any court in the United States." Such a law will let judges know, Gingrich went on, that "no judge will remain in office that tried to use sharia law." These words prompted a standing ovation from the crowd.

Gingrich, age 68, is helping shift this once-fringe conspiracy about Sharia into the mainstream. He's doing so not just by spouting the network's talking points but also by endorsing their products: For instance, Gingrich narrated the fearmongering documentary "America at Risk," produced by the conservative Citizens United Productions, which warns of the threat of Sharia and Islamic extremism infiltrating America. Unsurprisingly, the documentary features Center for Security Policy's Frank Gaffney. Gingrich screened the movie at David Horowitz's Restoration Weekend in November 2010.

Gingrich's rhetoric has escalated to levels to where it is no longer logically consistent. In March, Gingrich bizarrely worried aloud that his two children would grow up in a "secular atheist country, potentially dominated by radical Islamists," suggesting that the country would be simultaneously run by Islamists and atheists.

Sadly, these scare tactics are working. It is not surprising that when alarmist threats are repeated with enough frequency through multiple outlets to millions of people with no rebuttal by like-minded leaders, that those threats become conventional wisdom. And so, the nonpartisan Public Religion Research Institute found in a recent poll that there was a strong correlation between holding erroneous views about Muslims and Islam and watching Fox News. These are correlative, not necessarily causative findings, but they are striking.

Specifically, the poll found that:

- Americans who most trust Fox News are more likely to believe that Muslims want to establish Sharia law, have not done enough to oppose extremism, and believe investigating Muslim extremism is a good idea.
- Nearly twice as many Republicans as Democrats believe that Muslims want to establish Sharia law in America, 31 percent to 15 percent. One-third of white evangelical Christians believe this compared to 20 percent of white protestants and 22 percent of white Catholics.
- More than three-quarters of those who most trust Fox News believe that Rep. Peter King's congressional hearings on Muslim radicalization were a good idea, compared to just 45 percent of those who most trust CNN, and 28 percent of those who most trust public television. . . .

National Review

National Review is a biweekly magazine founded in 1955 by influential conservative William F. Buckley Jr. It calls itself "America's most widely read and influential magazine and website for conservative news, commentary, and opinion." While *National Review* speaks to a more mainstream conservative audience than many of the media outlets described in this chapter, it also features writers and articles that raise alarmist warnings and threats about Muslims and Islam, though often in less apocalyptic language. . . .

   National Review publishes pieces by Daniel Pipes in the magazine and on the website. In 1990 Pipes wrote: "Western European societies are unprepared for the massive immigration of brown-skinned peoples cooking strange foods and maintaining different standards of hygiene . . . All immigrants bring exotic customs and attitudes, but Muslim customs are more troublesome than most."

The Washington Times and the Clarion Fund

Then there is *The Washington Times*—a conservative daily newspaper and website created by Sun Myung Moon, founder of the Unification Church. *The Washington Times* promotes socially and politically conservative views and often features members of the Islamophobia network profiled in this report. Despite its small readership, *The Washington Times* punches well above its weight in the national media because many of the views it raises and voices it carries are picked up by media outlets with powerful megaphones, such as Fox News and conservative talk-radio shows, helping spread anti-Muslim messages into the larger public sphere. *The Washington Times*, for example, helped promote a flawed study about U.S. mosques written by David Yerushalmi. The newspaper's editorial page added to attacks against Park51 in August of 2010. And columnists from *The Washington Times* have contributed to the myth that President Obama is a Muslim.

   The Clarion Fund is a New York City-based nonprofit organization that aims "to educate Americans about issues of national security" by focusing on "the threats of Radical Islam." The organization was founded by Canadian-Israeli film producer and Rabbi Raphael Shore. Although very little is known about its funding sources, evidence suggests that Chicago businessman Barre Seid may have contributed $17 million to the Clarion Fund to help bankroll the production and dissemination of the inflammatory anti-Muslim movie, "Obsession: Radical Islam's War on the West." The film "reveals an 'insider's view' of the hatred the Radicals are teaching, their incitement of global jihad, and their goal of world domination," according to the movie's own website. During the 2008 presidential campaign, 28 million DVDs of the movie were sent to 28 swing states. In addition, the film was cited in Breivik's manifesto.

The Clarion Fund also produced a documentary, "The Third Jihad," narrated by Zudhi Jasser and briefly used to train NYPD officers on counterterrorism. After seeing the video, a police officer said, "It was so ridiculously one-sided. It just made Muslims look like the enemy. It was straight propaganda."

How the Anti-Muslim Media Work Together

These right-wing media outlets play a major role in pushing out a playlist of nonexistent Sharia threats, Islamic takeovers of the world, extremist Muslim infiltration into society and government, and more. As we demonstrate in the next chapter of this report, politicians at the national, state, and local levels rely on these media enablers to spread their anti-Muslim messages to conservative grassroots and religious-right groups, helping them to raise campaign funds and get voters to the polls.

By taking extreme anti-Islam views from fringe blogs to radio shows all the way to national television shows, anti-Muslim voices and views gain legitimacy and credibility. [A] network of anti-Muslim forces created a set of false facts to raise a national controversy over the establishment of a Muslim community center in lower New York City—the so-called Ground Zero mosque. [T]he Islamophobia network's media outlets successfully manufactured hysteria surrounding the community center in the summer of 2010.

Pamela Geller introduced the controversy on December 8, 2009, in her blog, Atlas Shrugs. Within two weeks Geller was calling the community center the "mosque at Ground Zero," even though it was not a mosque and was not located at Ground Zero.

Interestingly, Fox News was not initially opposed to the project. On Dec. 21, 2009, Fox News host Laura Ingraham invited Daisy Khan, the wife of Imam Feisal Abdul Rauf, one of the center's lead organizers, to discuss the proposed community center. Ingraham said, "I can't find many people who really have a problem with it." She added, "I like what you're trying to do."

Even so, Geller continued to manufacture hysteria around the center and its alleged proximity to Ground Zero. At a May 2010 Tea Party convention in Tennessee, Geller called the center "the ultimate flag of conquest" and "a shrine to the very ideology that inspired the jihadist attacks at Ground Zero." A few days later, she posted "Vote on Mega Mosque at Ground Zero" on her blog.

Geller claimed the Park51 organizers planned to "leverage" the mosque's proximity to Ground Zero to proselytize and "grow the Muslim community."

She also said that Imam Rauf "embraced" Sharia, which she described as "brutal policies that discriminate against women, gays, and religious minorities."

Throughout the summer, the Islamophobia network was amplifying Geller's accusations and pushing them out via radio shows and other outlets. On his radio show in August, Glenn Beck called the Park51 center "the 9-11 mosque." That same month, Rush Limbaugh told millions of listeners that the community center was a "recruiting tool for foreign extremists," and a "victory monument at Ground Zero." And Geller went on Hannity's Fox News show to declare the center a "provocative mega mosque" that aimed to "trample on the grief of 9–11 families and all Americans.

Islamophobia leaders added to the frenzy, appearing on mainstream TV news channels to hold forth about the community center. Brigitte Gabriel, founder of ACT! for America, did her part when she appeared on Sean Hannity's Fox News show and said the center was a "project to advance Islam" and a "slap in the face." Gabriel also claimed that the "Muslim world operates on symbols, everything has to be symbolic. And this—they chose this place in particular because of the symbol it represents to the Arabic world."

In December 2010, well after the summer had ended and plans for the community center were being revised, Frank Gaffney went on Fox News and scolded the network for underestimating the threat of "stealth jihad" that mosques were introducing in America. Gaffney linked the "Ground Zero Mosque" to his favorite threat, Sharia, claiming that "a mosque that is used to promote a seditious program, which is what Sharia is . . . that is not a protected religious practice, that is in fact sedition."

This example of how the Islamophobia network's leaders and media enablers turned a local zoning case into a national controversy provides a reason as to why many right-wing politicians are so eager to parrot anti-Muslim attacks: They raise funds and get conservative voters to the polls. . . .

The New Arab Conversation

Bombs don't discriminate between combatants and children. This sad fact became an inconvenient one last summer [2006] for Israel, which had maintained that its bombing of Lebanon was solely an attack on Hezbollah, the Shiite militia that had kidnapped two Israeli soldiers and menaced the Jewish state's northern border. To an anxious Lebanese population who'd seen most of their country's south reduced to a parking lot, Israel's persistent message— We are doing this for your own good—rang increasingly hollow.

By the beginning of August, the French and American ambassadors to the United Nations had finally hammered out a cease-fire resolution. But as the Security Council prepared to vote, the Lebanese government and the Arab League declared that the agreement was too favorable to Israel. A tense and edgy delegation arrived in New York on August 8 to plead the Arab case.

Dan Gillerman, the Israeli ambassador to the UN, didn't have to do much at those deliberations—simply listen to the complaints, appear to be the least obstructionist in the room, and restate his country's position, as absurd as it may have sounded by that point, that Israel's bombs were in fact helping the Lebanese people to free themselves from the "cancer" of Hezbollah that had metastasized in their midst. In this last task, he had an unusual ally: "I believe that one courageous Lebanese youngster was speaking for many when he wrote in his Internet blog, and I quote, 'It is not only Israeli soldiers that the Hezbollah has taken hostage. It is us, the people of Lebanon.'"

This "Lebanese youngster" was, of course, a blogger, and maybe the first to have his words bounce off the solemn walls of the United Nations. And though he probably would not have appreciated being deployed as a weapon in Israel's public-relations war, the presence of his independent voice, a counterintuitive opinion not filtered through any official source, said a lot about the power of Middle Eastern Web logs to expose a hidden trove of multiple perspectives in a world that the West often imagines as having only one perspective—that of the "Arab Street," a place of conformity, of mass acquiescence to singular passions, be they blind support for a dictator or seething hatred of Israel.

Last summer was, in fact, a watershed moment for the Middle Eastern blogosphere. The conflict between Israel and Hezbollah not only brought attention to the many different Arab conversations that had taken place on homemade Web sites in the past two or three years, but also launched thousands more of them. And they were more than just a handful of aberrant

From *Columbia Journalism Review,* January/February 2007, pp. 17–19, 20, 21, 22–23 (excerpts). Copyright © 2007 by Columbia Journalism Review. Reprinted by permission.

voices. They reflected a new culture of openness, dialogue, and questioning. And unlike the neoconservative notion that these ideals can be dropped on a foreign population like so many bomblets, the push for change here is coming from within. Whether it is a Jordanian student discussing the taboo subject of the monarchy's viability or a Saudi woman writing about her sexual experiences or an Egyptian commenting with sadness at an Israeli blogger's description of a suicide bombing, each of these unprecedented acts is one small move toward opening up these societies.

The Arab blogosphere has been growing for a few years now, though not at a particularly quick pace. Only 10 percent of the Arab world has Internet access, yet that is a five-fold increase from 2000. Of course, not all Arab blogs are about liberalizing Arab society. Some use the technology as another front in the jihad against the West being waged by groups like Al Qaeda. One, Irhabi 007, who was recently profiled in *The Atlantic Monthly*, created Web sites to disseminate videos of beheadings and insurgent attacks on U.S. forces in Iraq. Most analysts and bloggers put the number of Arab bloggers at fewer than 25,000. Of those, a majority blog in Arabic. And though there are surely interesting discussions happening on those sites, Arab bloggers themselves say that a particularly interesting alternative space is being formed on the sites composed in English. Now aggregated on blogging portals like iToot.net and enhanced by the YouTube-like Web site Ikbis, it is in this community of people who are self-consciously half-turned toward the West that one can feel the breathing becoming easier.

Those bloggers are people like Roba Al-Assi, a twenty-one-year-old design student in Amman, Jordan, who recently wrote about her opposition to the death penalty for Saddam Hussein:

> It is the premeditated and cold-blooded killing of a human being by the state in the name of justice (I know he killed thousands, but it is in my moral fabric to be better than others. Throw him in jail for the rest of his life, that's a lot worse than death).

Or the Egyptian blogger who calls himself Big Pharaoh, a twenty-seven-year-old graduate of the American University in Cairo, who expressed his support for the Egyptian culture minister who was criticized for stating that he thought the hijab, the traditional woman's head covering worn by some Muslim women, was "regressive":

> There are numerous things that make me proud of this country. How the country descended into such stupidity, ignorance, and darkness is definitely not among them. I feel like vomiting every time I think about how this man was virulently attacked for merely stating his opinion on a thing as stupid as the hair cover.

Or Laila El-Haddad, who, on her blog, "Unplugged: Diary of a Palestinian Mother," describes herself as a "journalist, mom, occupied Palestinian—all packed into one," and posted this account of crossing at Rafah from Egypt back into Gaza, after waiting in limbo for weeks for the border to open:

Some wailed in exhaustion, others fainted; still others cracked dry humor, trying to pass the time. We stood, thousands of us, packed together elbow to elbow like cattle, penned in between steel barriers on one end, and riot-geared Egyptian security guards on the perimeter, who were given orders not to allow anyone through until they hear otherwise from the Israelis—and to respond with force if anyone dared.

In the American blogosphere, opinions and life tales blossom a million-fold every day. But against the background of a largely party-line mainstream local Arab media, and the absence of avenues for national conversation, these Arab bloggers, most of whom are anonymous for their own safety, commit small acts of bravery simply by speaking their minds. It should be said that most of the people maintaining blogs do come out of the highest strata of society, economically and educationally, so their opinions can seem at times to represent no wider a circle than the upper crust of any given country. But, as Ammar Abdulhamid, a Syrian blogger who was forced into exile in September 2005 for his democracy activism, which included blogging about his eight-month interrogation by Syrian security services, put it: "There is nothing wrong with admitting that we represent a certain elite. It's not exclusively an economic elite, though economics surely plays a large factor. These are people who are comfortable, who have more time to blog. But in itself this is not the problem. The importance of this technology at this stage is to connect the elites better, to network the elites, to make them able to share more ideas and organize." The power of the medium, Abdulhamid says, will come when those bloggers find a way to "cross the bridge between the elite and the grass roots"—a process that is already beginning, through a few organized demonstrations coordinated by bloggers, online campaigns, and the posting of information about police brutality or sexual harassment.

Blogs can serve two functions: they are diaries, where the minutiae of a life are spelled out in 500-word posts, and they are a personal op-ed page, in which a writer comments at will about news articles and daily political developments, rambles in anger or appreciation, or promotes ideas. All of this happens every day on American blogs. But the context in the Arab blogosphere is different. For one thing, it is so much smaller. In the U.S., political blogs tend to split off into separate spheres of left and right that rarely touch—call them Huffingtonville and Hewittland—each with its predictable response to any political event. But the small size of the Arab blogosphere forces people with contrary opinions, or even more mildly divergent viewpoints, to engage each other. As one Arab blogger said, "We're not big enough to preach to the choir yet. There is no choir."

But the more compelling reason for the singularity of the Arab blogosphere is that the Middle East is a region where the historical and the personal slam up against each other daily in a way they do only once a decade or so in America. This gives even mundane musings elevated significance. Bloggers are writing about their lives. But those lives are taking place in environments in which politics and history cannot be perceived as mere elements on the margins. For the twentysomething growing up in Riyadh, writing resentfully about the power of the religious authorities, the questions are fundamental ones about the state of her society. For the Egyptian blogger, the brutal suppression of a demonstration can make the difference in whether he chooses to stay in the country or leave. This urgency makes the commentary more complex and interesting than the us-versus-them combat of so many American blogs. "We see it's the whole country at stake," said a well-known Lebanese blogger who goes by the nom de blog Abu Kais. "For us, watching politics is not like watching a football game. It's existential."

◦◈◦

Salam Pax is widely acknowledged as the Adam of Middle East bloggers. The blogging revolution that first began to spread through America in the late 1990s (the first "online diary," as a blog was then known, was created by a Swarthmore student in January 1994) reached the Middle East three or four years ago, and it was only with Pax's quirky and insightful dispatches in 2003 from a prewar and then postwar Iraq that Americans were made aware that the phenomenon had arrived there, too.

His blog, "Where is Raed?" had all the hallmarks of those that would follow in its wake. A twenty-nine-year-old recently graduated architecture student who had spent time in the West, Pax wrote in fluent English, observing the chaos that was quickly accumulating around him. At first, he was writing for himself, using the blog as a diary, but then he became aware of the scarcity of Arab bloggers writing in English about anything other than religious matters. As he told *The Guardian* in 2003, "I was saying, 'Come on, look, the Arabs here: sex, alcohol, belly dancers, TV shows, where are they?' All you saw was people talking about God and Allah. There was nothing about what was happening here." Then the war began, and that impulse to expose the parts of his world that the West was not seeing took on an even greater urgency. By the time of the invasion, 20,000 people were reading Pax regularly. His posts captured an emotional, lived experience of the war, one that evaded most journalists covering the conflict. . . .

The dynamism of the blog posts, as well as the string of comments that usually follow each of them, can best be appreciated when viewed against a backdrop of the mainstream Arab media. With the exception of a few papers in Lebanon (notably, the English-language *Daily Star*) and a handful of publications in Egypt and Jordan, most local media in the Arab world are still either directly state-controlled or subject to such intimidation by the government that journalists and editors rarely challenge authority. Each country's media have their red lines that cannot be crossed. In Jordan, it is the monarchy. In Egypt, it's the Mubarak regime. Any criticism of fundamentalist Islam's growing role in Arab society is off limits to everyone. And in much of the Arab local media Israel is portrayed as the ultimate evil. Israel, in fact, can be a tool of state control in Arab media. A high level of anti-Israel rhetoric serves the purpose of directing anger and scrutiny away from the regimes in power.

That was mitigated somewhat by the advent in recent years of satellite channels like Al-Jazeera and Al-Arabiya, which offer at least the potential of a more independent analysis and criticism of Arab governments. But by some accounts, both channels, though Al-Jazeera more so, have taken on a tone and a content that plays, as one Syrian blogger put it, "to the largest common denominator, drawing on the same language of victimhood, the tired Arab nationalist line. It is Fox news. Many people compare it to CNN. I think it has to be compared to Fox." (The Israeli media, for their part, though certainly free and open to criticizing the government and not averse by any means to plastering the country's problems on the front page, also resort most often to simple narratives and well-known generalizations when it comes to depicting the Arab enemy, not giving serious attention to the aspiration of the Palestinians, for example.)

The bloggers have stood out against this background. Some of them have even used the Web for political action. Bloggers led an Arab movement to support products from Denmark in the aftermath of the Danish cartoon riots and the Arab boycott that followed. They have also organized demonstrations and, much like American bloggers, used their Web sites as forums to expose injustices. Egyptian bloggers recently circulated video of men wilding in the streets of Cairo, sexually assaulting women at random, eventually bringing the incident to the world's attention. Jordanian bloggers, angry that the government regulators had decided to block access to Skype, a phone service that allows users to communicate freely over the Internet, started a campaign that led to the decision's reversal. And then there was the war, in which bloggers organized donations for the displaced of Lebanon.

Still, there are good reasons why most of the Arab blogosphere remains anonymous. Just this past year, several bloggers were jailed in Egypt, including Abdel Karim Sulaiman Amer, who was arrested in November and charged with "spreading information disruptive of public order," "incitement to hate Muslims," and "defaming the President of the Republic." Earlier last year, another Egyptian blogger, Alaa Ahmed Seif al-Islam, was arrested and given three consecutive fifteen-day detentions in prison, largely for his blogging activity. Other countries, like Bahrain and Saudi Arabia, don't arrest bloggers, but they aggressively block blogs they find subversive.

The Committee to Protect Bloggers, a now defunct U.S. organization that monitored bloggers who found themselves in danger, kept track of the various forms of intimidation and suppression. Curt Hopkins, who was the group's director, says there are three basic methods that countries employ to suppress bloggers: technical filtering, the law, and direct intimidation. Though it is fairly easy to track down bloggers using IP addresses, bloggers have an easier time evading the authorities than do journalists working for a newspaper. "When it comes to shutting down a publication, it's pretty easy," says Hopkins. "You just send some goons with baseball bats and suddenly you don't have a publication. It's that simple. Also it's easier to find people because they are in the offices when you come to arrest them. And though it's true that if you have enough money and time, you can find almost anyone, you've got to remember that most governments don't have enough money and enough time." Abdulhamid, the Syrian blogger who continued to update his blog every day, even while the state police were interrogating him, also noticed such limitations. "During my interrogation, I saw that, one, most security apparatus really don't have access to the Internet; two, they don't know how to use that technology very well to begin with, even if they did have access." Still, enough bloggers have either been arrested or, as in Abdulhamid's case, had their lives threatened, for the fear to be well founded. . . .

Maybe the most dramatic way in which this blogosphere is affecting the Arab world is by breaking down that ultimate taboo. Even in a place like Lebanon, with a large portion of the population striving to create a liberal, modern society, Israel is the last barrier. That is rooted in Lebanon's history, including recent history. Yet there is so much investment in seeing Israel as the source of all its problems that it has become a mindless reflex for many.

There are, of course, plenty of bloggers who use the Internet as a way to disseminate more hate and misunderstanding, many of whom also gained attention last summer during the war. One case, infamous among Arab and Israeli bloggers, is Perpetual Refugee, a Lebanese businessman who had occasion to visit Israel a few times, socialized with Israelis . . . and subsequently wrote friendly posts about making peace. As soon as the war came, he made what was described as a "360-degree turn," becoming virulently hateful about Jews, about how Israel "massacred innocent souls to fulfill its biblical destiny." But Perpetual Refugee was something of a high-profile anomaly among the English-language bloggers.

"I always say there are two kinds of arguments," says Sandmonkey. "There are the arguments in which you hope to find the truth and the arguments in which you want to defend an established truth." It's the first type of argument that seems to be prevailing. Take this post by Charles Malik (also a pseudonym), a Lebanese blogger, who found himself exploring the Israeli blogosphere last April, by chance on Holocaust Remembrance Day. He asks questions that would seem almost blasphemous considering the climate in the Middle East:

> Think about what Israelis deal with on a daily basis: frequent suicide bombs, support for such attacks by the popularly elected Palestinian government, threats of annihilation from a country arming itself with nuclear weapons, constant words of hate from the Arabic speaking world, and remembrances of the Holocaust. . . . Not knowing about "them" is the worst crime we can commit. It invalidates them as humans, as if they don't even matter. They are Stalin's faceless enemy, the rabid dog, the evil bloodsuckers whom it is righteous to kill. Our papers definitely need to start covering more than major political events in Israel. We should remember their tragedies.

If the Arab bloggers tend to be those who have been exposed to the West, many of the Israelis interacting with them are recent immigrants like Lisa Goldman, who arrived six years ago, and Lirun Rabinowitz, who has been living in Israel for a year and a half. Rabinowitz shares his blog with a Lebanese woman and was recently invited to be a co-author on the United Arab Emirates community blog and, even more surprisingly, on an annual Ramadan blog, in which various bloggers write about how the Muslim holiday is celebrated in their countries. Recently, on the UAE blog, he was accused in the comments section of being needlessly provocative for putting the words "Tel Aviv" after his name at the end of his posts. To his surprise, a number of Arab readers rushed to his defense in the comments section.

Rabinowitz says that perusing the Arab blogosphere has deepened his understanding of what is happening inside Arab society. "When I go to them, I see what are they worrying about, what are they wondering, how they are feeling, what level of analysis they are putting on things, how keen they are to see my side, and when they are only prepared to see their own. Is there room for bridging? And I learn a lot about what their knee-jerk reaction looks like, what their analysis looks like, what their fears look like." And to him, that added layer of knowledge is a rebuke to the other forces in Israeli society that he feels are trying to define the "enemy" for him. "You want to tell me that these people are stupid? Well, they're not," says Rabinowitz. "You want to tell me that these people want to live in a dictatorship? Well, they don't. You want to tell me that they can't be Muslim and tolerant and friendly at the same time? Well, it's wrong. You want to tell me that they hate me just because they're Muslim and I'm Jewish? Well that's wrong, too. And they prove that to me every day. And I get this amazing opportunity to dispel every demonic myth and every stupid stereotype that I could have ever thought of, and that's amazingly liberating."

Is this hopeful? Yes, as long as one keeps in mind, once again, what a small segment of the population, both Arab and Israeli, is sitting in front of glowing screens and reaching out to the "other." The bloggers will say, universally, that revolutions almost always start with a tiny elite. But we are a long way from this revolution's doorstep. Instead, this blogosphere feels more like a small community of open-minded young people who have discovered pathways that were previously closed.

Still, seeds do grow. The grass-roots student wing of the civil rights movement, born at Shaw University in Raleigh, North Carolina, in 1960, in what evolved into the Student Nonviolent Coordinating Committee (or SNCC), was made up of young people, privileged enough to be attending college but not content with the pace of integration in America. They made themselves into a vanguard, tearing holes in walls so that others could then pass through after them. Someone had to take the first step, and who better than they—young, educated, and sensitive to the restrictions that were going to be placed on their personal and communal advancement.

The young insider-outsiders of the Middle East, blogging openly about their frustrations with the Arab world, about its persistent prejudices and limitations, as a way of liberalizing their societies, are doing what the front line of any social movement does—they say the unspeakable, they form the bonds that were previously unthinkable, they stand in the places that they are not supposed to stand. The Arab world will reform only when mindsets begin to change and a culture of dissent burgeons where it has never been allowed to exist openly before. If there is a way to kick-start this process, it is surely in the post of a twentysomething blogger wondering out loud why things can't be more open, more transparent—more different.

EXPLORING THE ISSUE

Do Media Distort Representations of Islam and Arab Cultures?

Critical Thinking and Reflection

1. What are the possibilities for social media to create more balanced perceptions of others? Are there other ways in which the Internet could foster better relationships globally?
2. How are stereotypes created and maintained, particularly where there is little ability to interact with others directly? What part do the media play? And, how is the media influenced by the agendas of different groups?
3. Do journalistic practices of balance encourage oppositional thinking and enhance the power of marginal groups?
4. How can these concepts be applied to issues of stereotyping overall in the media and in society?

Is There Common Ground?

Over the years both media and society in general have become more aware of stereotyping. Groups who feel they have been stereotyped have sought more realistic portrayals, the limitations of roles in entertainment programming, and a recognition that one attribute does not define the individual. Progress has been made; more is needed. Yet when a group or a country is defined as the enemy, it is hard to remember that it still is composed of a diverse set of people and attitudes. It was a humorous sidebar when French Fries were renamed Freedom Fries in the House of Representatives cafeteria, as a result of anti-French sentiment when France protested the 2003 invasion of Iraq. It was much less humorous when friends were denied service at a D.C. fast food restaurant because they had been overheard speaking French.

Anti-Muslim sentiment is widespread as indicated by the chilling attack in Norway recounted in Fear, Inc. The tragedy of 9/11 made it all too easy to conflate Muslim and terrorism. Yet, there were many voices after 9/11 that urged us to not overgeneralize to an entire religion the actions of a few. We have many examples of where common ground has been found among previous disparate groups; we have other examples of great tragedies when relegating a group to "the Other" status has contributed to repression and even genocide. In all cases, common ground is found in ethical and thoughtful responses to overgeneralized stereotypes.

Additional Resources

Brigitte Lebens Nacos and Oscar Torres-Reyna, *Fueling Our Fears: Stereotyping, Media Coverage, and Public Opinion of Muslim Americans* (Rowman & Littlefield, 2007)

This book discusses the Arab/Muslim controversy, particularly for Muslims born in America, and considers how Americans look at Arabs and Muslims at home and abroad.

Edward Schiappa, *Beyond Representational Correctness: Rethinking Criticism of Popular Media* (State University of New York Press, 2008)

The book addresses the role of stereotyping in general in the media, and the parasocial relationships we have with people in the media.

The Journal of Arab and Muslim Media

An online source that often focuses on content and images within media and can be accessed through most academic libraries.

Peter Morey and Amina Yagin, *Framing Muslims: Stereotyping and Representation after 9/11* (Harvard University Press, 2011)

In this volume, the authors display the ways in which stereotypes that depict Muslims as an inherently problematic presence in the West are constructed and create a gulf between representations and reality.

Edward Said, *Covering Islam: How the Media and the Experts Determine How We See the Rest of the World* (Vintage Books, 1997)

In this seminar work, Edward Said, an influential professor and a cultural critic, looked at how American popular media have used and perpetuated a narrow and unfavorable image of Islamic peoples, and how this has prevented understanding while providing a fictitious common enemy for the diverse American populace.

Internet References . . .

Advertising Age

The Web site of *Advertising Age* magazine provides access to articles and features about media advertising, such as the history of television advertising.

http://adage.com

Entertainment Software Association

ESA serves the business and public affairs needs of video game publishers. Its sections on public policy and games in life provide extensive information about the benefits of video games.

www.theesa.com

The U.S. Department of Health and Human Services

The Web site by U.S. Department of Health and Human Services helps women with issues of body image, nutrition.

www.womenshealth.gov/body-image/

Center for Media and Public Affairs

This site offers information about ongoing debates concerning media fairness and impact, with particular attention to political campaigns and political journalism.

www.cmpa.com

The Center for Media and Democracy

The Center for Media and Democracy regularly posts interesting items on the interface between politics and advertising.

www.prwatch.org/

Project Censored

Project Censored often reports on attempts by the ad industry to control information.

www.projectcensored.org/

A Question of Content

*W*e *no longer live in a world in which all of our media are directed toward mass audiences. Today we have both mass media and personal media, like video games, iPods, and cell phones. Because people use media content in very different ways, and so much of how we make sense of media depends on our own ages and life experiences, the issue of media content that is appropriate for certain audiences takes on a new importance. In this section, we deal with issues that often influence people from all ages, ethnic groups, and all walks of life—but the questions for discussion become more pointed when we consider that different audiences may perceive different things in the content of some forms of media. In this section, we examine some specific aspects of using media for a sense of identity and belonging.*

We conclude with an issue that addresses some of the most fundamental questions about this industry, and this is sure to spark debate.

- Do Media Cause Individuals to Develop Negative Body Images?

- Do Video Games Encourage Violent Behavior?

- Is Advertising Good for Society?

ISSUE 4

Do Media Cause Individuals to Develop Negative Body Images?

YES: Shari L. Dworkin and Faye Linda Wachs, from "What Kinds of Subjects and Objects? Gender, Consumer Culture, and Convergence," in *Body Panic: Gender, Health, and the Selling of Fitness* (New York University, 2009)

NO: Michael P. Levine and Sarah K. Murnen, from "Everybody Knows That Mass Media Are/Are Not [*pick one*] a Cause of Eating Disorders: A Critical Review of Evidence for a Causal Link Between Media, Negative Body Image, and Disordered Eating in Females," *Journal of Social and Clinical Psychology* (2009)

Learning Outcomes

After reading this issue, you should be able to:

- Evaluate the media messages about body image in a better way.
- Analyze how the images influence children and people who may have a particular viewpoint about standards of beauty and attractiveness.
- Understand the power of advertising and marketing lifestyle to a range of age groups.
- Apply the critical skills to other aspects of your lives.

ISSUE SUMMARY

YES: Shari Dworkin and Faye Wachs discuss the results of their content analysis of health magazine ads and find that the ads tell men and women that a healthy body is attainable if they buy the products and pamper themselves. Fat becomes something to be feared, and grooming practices and fashion are "sold" as imperatives for both men and women.

NO: Michael Levine and Sarah Murnen also investigate magazine ads, but find the assumption that media cause eating disorders to be too limited. Instead, they cite a wide range of social, behavioral, and cultural issues over time to understand the complex conditions under which girls begin to adopt negative body issues that result in eating disorders.

Often media are accused of representing images that result in people's negative behaviors. Sometimes, media are so present in our lives that it seems apparent that there is, or should be, a direct link between media images and real-life manifestations of those images. We know that media have *some* influence over the way *some* people construct their ideas of reality, but the most difficult considerations have to do with *who* is affected, and under *what* conditions. The authors of these two selections look specifically at magazines and how ideas of health and body image are constructed, with two different conclusions.

In their investigation, Professors Shari Dworkin and Faye Wachs find that men and women are increasingly being represented in similar ways in popular health and fitness magazine advertising. They discuss the way a healthy body image is constructed in ads, promising that if people consume these products, they can turn their negative body image around and be as fit, healthy, and happy as the people in the ads. They remark on how similar lifestyle ads are in targeting both men and women and representing a "healthy body" ideal. The result then is the consumers, feeling that if they don't consume these products, they will feel worse about their bodies.

We also know that in extreme cases, some people develop eating disorders, based on the ideal body image as super thin, that are unhealthy and harmful to their bodies. Professors Michael Levine and Sarah Murnen evaluate the literature on what causes girls to develop eating disorders, and find that media may play a limited role in contributing to one's negative body image, but that other cultural, social, and psychological issues play a much larger role in causing girls to actually harm themselves by extreme behaviors. Their perspective examines how behavior and self-image are formed over time, and in a world that has several competing causes for why someone psychologically succumbs to extreme eating behavior.

The complexities between media images and self-image are many indeed, and we know that not everyone is influenced by media in the same way. Socialization, family pressures and expectations, the type of media one consumes, and how peers talk about media images all have the potential to influence us in different ways, and, still, probably all of us at some time know that something we saw in media made us feel a certain way or think about something in a special way. When it comes to internalizing those images, our minds often register reactions in ways of which we may not be aware.

Advertisers often seek to understand the underlying motivations that cause us to respond—especially to buy products, but sometimes we look for support from other people to confirm what we want to believe. Celebrities also tend to project body images that are often significantly underweight, thereby providing role models that may influence conscious or unconscious desires to be "like them." American culture is rife with stories about the perils of obesity and unhealthy lifestyles. As a result, it is difficult to seek one particular cause that could be the definitive answer to why anyone develops the self-image he or she does. But the process of trying to understand the range of psychological processes that come part-and-parcel with media images is fascinating, and sometimes, frightening.

Many critics have praised Dove soap's "Campaign for Real Beauty," which premiered in 2004 and featured girls and women who did not have the ideal media body type. The campaign used real people and identified them as beautiful for being who and what they were, but in 2008, Unilever (Dove's parent company) and Ogilvy and Mather, the product's advertising company, came under fire for retouching the pictures of the real people. In May 12, 2008, article in *Advertising Age*, it was reported that the alleged retouching had created a "ruckus" that was one of the largest scandals in the history of advertising.

This issue is closely related to the question of whether advertising is good for society (Issue 6). The social role of advertising suggests that consumers are suggestible, and that they are motivated to improve themselves, their lifestyles, and their attitudes about their self-work by consuming "newer" and "better" products. Often people make assumptions that ads reflecting body type are primarily a female-only issue, but as these authors indicate, there are increasing similarities to female and male advertising, especially when it comes to body image and health.

In many ways, we could expand this issue to reflect other representations of beauty and health in the media. Do athletes suggest a certain standard of physical attractiveness, and can that power and ability be naturally cultivated, or do steroids enter the picture as an alternative way to achieve the appearance of power and mastery over one's body? Do actresses on television and in films have healthy bodies? In her influential work, *The Beauty Myth*, Naomi Wolf identifies that most actresses weigh significantly less than what is considered the healthy norm for an active person.

Right now, in American life, we constantly hear about how Americans are becoming obese. This is particularly problematic for children who may not get the type of physical fitness they need in school, and who often sit at a computer rather than playing active games or doing exercise outside of the house. These cultural realities are difficult to reconcile with the idea that the products we buy actually can help us look or feel in a certain way, but advertisers know that by praying on our weaknesses, we are often tempted to buy more.

YES

Shari L. Dworkin and Faye Linda Wachs

What Kinds of Subjects and Objects? Gender, Consumer Culture, and Convergence

[Women] are said to be accounted for by these theories—and yet they barely make an appearance. On the other hand, if and when they do appear . . . they surface only as objects of various different agencies . . . which are seen to act upon them and force them into a particular range of roles. The question of how individuals make certain modes of behavior their own, how they learn to develop one particular set of needs as opposed to certain others, is never addressed.

Women are not only objects of male desire: they themselves play a part in their creation as such. To see femininity in this way is to identify a subjective aspect within being-as-object, and thus effectively to recognize the inadequacy of the subject-object metaphor.

Consumer culture had discovered and begun to develop the untapped resources of the male body.

How then is the idealized body constructed in consumer culture today? Examining mainstream health and fitness magazines provides insight into dominant cultural constructions of "health" and by extension allows researchers to examine what constitutes a privileged body. Given the importance of sex assignment in Western culture, this body is always already a gendered body. However, what the assignment of sex means for bodies is changing and evolving in consumer culture. Instead of reiterating long held subject/object dichotomies that tend to analyze the situation from the position that men are given the status of subjects while women are objects, we rely on Frigga Haug's concept of the "subjective-aspects-within-being-as-object" (defined below) and apply it to the case of women's fitness media texts. For an analysis of men's fitness media texts, we introduce a concept we term the "objective-aspects-within-being-as-subject" and therefore extend Haug's work to consider the case of men, bodies, and consumer culture. Indeed, looking at the two terms side by side suggests greater possibility for overlap between subjective and objective status than has typically been offered in previous analyses of gender and the body.

Frigga Haug et al. coined and first used the phrase the "subjective-aspects-within-being-as-object" to refer to how women experience identity, subject-hood, and pleasure in the process of bodily objectification. In her book, *Female Sexualization: Questions for Feminism,* Haug described and analyzed cultural materials (newspaper articles, art, film) and women's own stories about what she calls "body projects"—for example, doing one's hair, shaving one's legs, choosing fashion trends, etc. Such an approach allowed Haug to structure an analysis of the relationship between subjectivity and objectivity in the process of female sexualization. A main part of her argument is that there is an extensive *process of subjectivity* (not necessarily harm and force) that goes unrecognized in the arguments on this topic. Previous arguments generally assumed that women were having something "done to them" by media images, texts, and larger cultural norms. Haug's work demonstrates the agency of the subject in the creation of objecthood. This does not diminish previous analysis, but adds a critical dimension to understanding relations of power and privilege.

Adding subjectivity to an analysis of gender and the body was a much needed corrective to feminists who had long noted that in Western culture, there is an imperative toward the sexual objectification of women—and this was conceived of as wholly negative. To a large degree, according to this position, women's power and experience of self is based on the ability to meet current cultural ideals. Women and girls come to experience themselves as if someone were looking at them (as an object) and evaluate themselves based on appearance and their successful presentation of self as an object. Some argue that this lack of subjecthood is not simply about the surface of the body but is linked to sexuality and the expression of desire. That is, the way in which subjecthood is constructed for young girls leads to a lack of female desire in heterosexuality, where girls and women are centrally concerned about making themselves into an attractive object of desire instead of "owning" or knowing desire for themselves. One might suspect that this more passive view of the body contrasts with what is found within sport coverage of female athletes, for example, that when female subjects are viewed as engaging in some type of action, the presentation of self is usually paramount to performance rather than some other standards.

Despite sport as a realm of action, researchers frequently note that women's performances are "offset" by depictions of feminine aesthetics and beauty standards. By contrast, male subjecthood has often been linked directly to status, societal position, or power, while male appearance historically has been considered far less important (until recently). Certainly, the history of fashion and its current state demonstrate that men too have taken great care in the presentation of self. However, the links between attractiveness, status, and bodily ideals have had a long and complicated racialized, classed, gendered history. Indeed, for men, it is generally the characteristics of the powerful that come to be imbued with attractiveness.

The subject/object distinction around gender and the body needs to be understood in the context of Western philosophy more generally. The choice between subject and object reflects traditional Western cultural dualisms, or the tendency to present people, domains, and/or groups as categorical opposites. Feminist epistemology problematized traditional Western dualisms, such as nature/culture, male/female, and subject/object and how these dualisms have come into play in gender relations. This means that over time, femininity was associated with being an object and linked to emotion and nature. By contrast, masculinity was associated with subjecthood and was tied to Enlightenment principles such as knowledge and reason. Feminist theorists have long critiqued the exclusion of women's subjecthood, ways of knowing, and experiences from the production of knowledge and the limitations imposed on women as a result of these presumptions. Certainly, it could be argued that women have effectively been denied a philosophical experience of subjecthood that does not center on the self as object.

It is certain that both men and women have been objectified; however, male power and privilege have been maintained by partly limiting women's source of power to their ability to be the "right" kind of object. Specific researchers argue that women's consent to being a valued object seals the deal, as Connell notes in his 1987 work *Gender and Power*. Connell defines "emphasized femininity" as the most valued form of femininity, and contrasts it to hegemonic masculinity, the most privileged form of masculinity. In these definitions, there is a difference between male privilege and female value, indicating a patriarchal gender order. The subject/object dichotomy further underscores the difference between these two terms. . . .

As has been noted by Kimmel, at the turn of the millennium, men's and women's lives are becoming "more similar," at least for the most advantaged. For the privileged, most professions are gender-neutral, and women and men are routinely employed in the same professions, enjoy the same leisure activities, and engage in similar rituals of self-care. Women's increased earning power can also mean that some couples and single women are able to "buy off" the second shift of household labor and childcare. The growing importance of women as consumers has been linked to women's greater social power, especially in the world of sports and fitness. These tendencies combine with the objectifying propensities of consumer culture (for all bodies) to narrow the gap in how gender is defined, constructed in image, and practiced. This is revealed in the convergence of men's and women's bodily displays and practices in health and fitness magazines—the focus of this chapter.

Converging Bodies: Gender and Consumer Culture

Men's and women's bodily practices converge in several notable ways. First, fat is a powerfully feared cultural transgression for both women and men. Second, men and women are coming to be presented in a more similar manner, as objects (here, we analyze body positioning, smiles, head shots, and active/passive imagery). Third, what is marketed to male and female bodies is converging. Grooming practices and fashion expand, as it is framed as "imperative" for both women and men to be up to date in fashion. In addition, leisure practices are expanding as they converge for both women and men (manscaping, manicures, spa treatments, personal training, massages).

In the first case, fat is now a powerfully feared cultural transgression. For both men and women, any visible body fat is presented as problematic. "Are you fat?" asks *Men's Health* (January/February 1999). The article includes a test to determine this with certainty, followed by ratings of different diet and exercise plans. Given this trend, it may not be surprising that 38 percent of dieters in the United States are now male within a diet industry that is now worth $58.7 billion. The obesity crisis has been much touted in the mass media. Although we don't dispute the negative health consequences of being overweight, the link between (a relatively homogeneous) appearance and health is dubious at best. Moreover, there is an ongoing tendency to frame the overweight body as a threat to the self and to the general populace. Maintaining a fit body is no longer viewed as a personal choice, but as an obligation to the public good and a requirement for good citizenry. The once narcissistic body obsession has not only become a marker of individual health, but a form of social responsibility and civic participation. Over time, body weight has taken on the aura of a broader social problem related to public health. This obscures the relationship between social privilege and the development and maintenance of a fit body, and reinforces the stigmatization of "othered" bodies.

Despite evidence that suggests a totally fat-free form can be unrealistic and unhealthy, this form is idealized and venerated. Analyses of consumer culture suggest that this constructs a culture of "bodily lack" that requires constant maintenance. A key set of fundamental assumptions that shape the content and tone of the magazine center on the negative aspects of *any* body fat. Fat is unhealthy. Unaesthetic. Prevents you from being everything you can be. Leads to public ridicule, especially at the hands of the opposite sex. Is a sign of one's failure to demonstrate a proper "work ethic." The reification/ deification of the fat-free form is visually reinforced almost continuously with the imagery in magazines. Idealized bodies with no body fat are featured on the covers and throughout the magazines.

It is not just imagery that offers this impression, but the tendency for magazines to blur the boundaries between the purpose of text, image, expert advice, and ads increases over time in our ten-year sample. In fact, the difference between advertising and content imagery can become largely irrelevant, and indeed, one cannot meaningfully separate magazine content from ads in many places. This is most notable when examining the ubiquitous short "snippet" that promotes new products, practices, or services, and the photo essay, usually a magazine-prepared advertisement. The images merge seamlessly in the magazine from article to ad and back again. They reinforce messages of idealized physical forms and undermine text that might speak in a bold or trite way of self-acceptance. An analysis of the covers demonstrates that only a few models, whose photographed bodies have been trimmed and touched up, meet these ideals. Mainstream newspaper articles that interview athletes, fitness experts, or trainers highlight that the athletes themselves are surprised at how their photographs have been altered in fitness imagery, underscoring that even professional athletes rarely measure up.

Advertisements also usually feature very slim or cut models, and similarly computer-altered, airbrushed, and trimmed photos of models. When taken together, they create the impression that the ideal body is *necessarily* fat-free. This is reinforced because more realistic but still presumably healthy bodies rarely appear. Heavier bodies appear only as "before" photos in "success stories." The paucity of a range of healthy fit images literally denies their existence, and refutes the possibility that a person can be larger and still be fit and healthy. The symbolic annihilation of the wide range of healthy bodies operates to conflate fat-free with "healthy" and undermines any textual references to the existence of this range. The assumptions that emerge in the text further vilify fat while extolling the moral virtue of the fat-free form. (Our own students exalt the value of the fat-free form as inherently right and healthy; we frequently compare notes about how to discuss the lack of a continuum of body fat in imagery—much of which could be conceived of as quite far from "fat," but also rather healthy and plenty attractive.) The obliteration of this continuum leaves the impression that the range of fit bodies is far narrower than it is in reality.

The preponderance of articles on diets, health, nutrition, and workouts included a discussion of cutting body fat for both men and women. While men were encouraged to "eat to grow," cutting body fat was the second most common diet proscription for men, and was frequently referenced in conjunction with gains in muscle size. *EMO* encourages men to "Torch Your Bodyfat! New Supplements Do the Trick." *Exercise & Health* offers "25 Ways to Shed Fat." Because historically, reducing body fat had feminine connotations, it is necessary to masculinize men's fat reduction. Cutting fat is masculinized by linking it to the revelation of manly striations and cuts. Abdominals are specifically noted as visible signs of masculinity that can only be revealed when body fat is exorcised. While *all* men should spend their time attempting to reveal a minimum of six-pack abdominals, the "eight-pack" is appearing with increasing frequency. The diet industry is attempting to further masculinize weight loss; even the weight-loss giant Nutrisystem recently hired its first male spokesperson, former quarterback Dan Marino.

For women, decreasing fat (without mention of the striations or cuts underneath) was the most common diet recommendation, coupled with recipes and hints. For women, fitness and dieting are critical to attaining a slim, toned, and cellulite-free form. *Shape* provides "7 Sneaky Reasons Dining Out Is Making You Fat." *Fitness* promises to "Speed Up Your Metabolism in Just 10 Minutes." The magazines do not present any obvious benefits to a faster metabolism, except weight loss.

The majority of workouts further highlighted a fat-free form, even when many explicitly acknowledged in the text that one cannot spot reduce, or that toning will not be visible without removing fat, and that the only way to reduce fat is to consume less. Workouts for women focused on toning and tightening muscles that could only be revealed with a modified and rather Spartan diet. *Fitness* exhorts women to "Lose Your Ab Flab" with a workout that combines aerobics and pilates that "Not only will you get your heart pumping and burn 420 calories per hour (about 17 percent more than in a traditional mat class), but you'll experience total-body conditioning through balance challenges and see the ab-sculpting benefits." Workouts like "The

No-Fat Back" promise a reduction in body fat with diet and exercise. Notice that despite textual references to the impossibility of spot reduction, the titles of workouts clearly suggest fat will be removed from a specific area of the body. For men, workouts also often emphasized lower fat intake to reveal cuts or to trim fat from the waist.

Success stories in women's magazines almost exclusively highlighted people who lost weight, with only a few that covered those who strove to gain weight or battled eating disorders. Weight loss was noted in pounds lost, inches lost, and accompanied by ab-baring before and after photos. *Shape* features "Success Stories: A Special Guide—How 5 Women Got in Shape! You can too with our sure-fire plan." This piece features a diet, followed by success stories of five women who followed the diet. For each woman, inches and pounds lost are the first statistics provided with their pictures. The focus on these types of measures sends a clear message about the primary meaning of success in fitness. Though many articles on being satisfied with oneself at a larger size appear, the almost complete exclusion of alternative imagery contradicts the messages of acceptance.

Control of the body remains a central organizing principle in postindustrial society. The need to control the unruly body emerges in the postindustrial world as a marker of the self. Linked to personal displays that demonstrate success or failure, the presentation of the body in the twenty-first century signifies a variety of meanings, not the least of which is one's moral worth. While the fat body remains stigmatized as lazy, undisciplined, or as a poor member of the social body, the fit body becomes a metaphor for success, morality, and good citizenship. Just as wealth marked morality for the Calvinists, the "fit" body marks a moral and disciplined self that demonstrates sufficient participation in the regimes of bodywork necessary to support consumer capitalism. As argued by Gimlin, "The body is fundamental to the self because it serves to indicate who an individual is internally, what habits the person has, and even what social value the individual merits." Hence, the fit body simultaneously validates the individual and legitimates the value of such a body.

Further, the normalization of the completely fat-free form operates to stigmatize bodies left out of the frame. Spitzack in 1990 and later on, Duncan, in 1994, employ Foucauldian thought to demonstrate how the confessional process centered on fitness and the body ultimately results in the disempowerment of the subject. While Duncan was studying the content of women's magazines and Spitzack studied women's narratives of "confessional excess" about their bodies, both of their arguments can be extended to men's experiences given trends of convergence. Here, we mean that all readers lose the ability to define the image of a healthy body as based on critical measures of health (cholesterol, pulse rate, blood pressure, cardiovascular fitness, pulmonary function, and so forth). Instead, an image of health becomes paramount and as Duncan suggests, "panoptic mechanisms" lead the reader to internalize self-surveillance of the surface of the body, conflating body image with morality, success, and good citizenship. The fat-free fit form also serves as a marker of class status to some degree, as the bodywork required to maintain this form requires a significant amount of time and money.

While body fat is one area where there is overlap across men's and women's magazines, there were other ways in which the presentation of male and female bodies converged. . . .

The results of the initial sample are consistent with Duncan's analysis of sports media texts which revealed that mainstream media construct men as active and women as inactive. In this view, women are often shown as "being visually perfect" and "passive, immobile, and unchanging." The initial sample reflects this tendency. Men are more often featured as active or with action implied. The presence of action implies subjecthood, that one is an active subject. In the initial sample, men are depicted actively engaging in sports or fitness with over 80 percent of the covers featuring them either directly engaged in action, or with action implied through the use of props. By contrast, women are far more often presented as objects, with just over 85 percent of covers featuring women engaging only in the act of posing, experiencing the subjective aspects of being as object. Further, the action-implied covers are almost exclusively from one publication, *Women's Sports & Fitness*. . . .

We coded covers according to models' facial expressions, gaze, and body positioning. These studies indicate that dominance and submission are transmitted through the body using nonverbal communication, reflective of one's status in society. Body language as expressed through body positioning, eye contact, head tilts, and facial expression (smiling, etc.) also provides culturally recognizable cues that media have used to produce and reflect gendered bodies. . . .

Duncan, in her examination of how sports photographers use corporeal cues to embody sexual difference, found that women were often portrayed with direct eye contact to the camera, accompanied by a sideways tilt of the head and/or slightly parted lips. Duncan labels these bodily cues as nonverbal heterosexual "come-ons" linked to those found in men's soft-core pornography. Head-on poses are generally less submissive than head-tilted shots. The tilt usually involves the model looking up at the camera, giving the viewer a "come hither gaze." Similarly, body positioning that is straight toward the camera is less submissive than bodies that are tilted up toward the camera. Hip thrusts further indicate a provocative pose designed to please and entice the viewer. Finally, facial expressions indicate status. Inviting smiles versus serious expression indicate one's status. . . .

While over 85 percent of the original men's sample featured shots that were taken head-on, only 50 percent of the second sample reveals the same tendency. For women, two-thirds of the original sample was shot head-on, while 37.9 percent of the new sample is shot this way. The shift to the "come hither look" for both men and women indicates a shift toward men as deploying self-presentation as object. As previously noted, the tilt usually indicates submission or enticement. This is further demonstrated in hand positioning. The hand on the self in the manner of most of these magazines connotes a "look at me" presentation, further enhancing the subjective aspects within being-as-object.

Trends toward bodily convergence by gender are evident in the models' facial expressions. The type of smile displayed reveals something about the status of the individual. An inviting smile is the most common facial expression in both codes. In the initial sample, 81.0 percent of women have full smiles, and the remaining 19 percent displayed partial smiles. In the full coding, 63.6 percent sport full smiles, 33.4 percent exhibit partial smiles, and 3.0 percent appear serious. Of the men's cover models in the original sample, 52.4 percent have a full smile, an additional 14.3 percent feature partial smiles, and 28.6 percent are serious. In the updated sample, 36.7 percent of men wear full smiles, but 21.7 percent present partial smiles, and almost the same percentage, 28.3 percent, have serious facial expressions. Though gender differences remain in terms of who can display a serious face and still be deemed desirable, Henley's work is particularly instructive, as she argues that women are often publicly responsible for a continuous display of pleasantness and amiability. We view the decrease in full smiles in favor of partial smiles for men and women as reflecting a shift. The partial smile also creates a more knowing look. We suggest the ironic presentation of the self as object is becoming more common. In other words, the model displays a realization of the self as object and the consciousness of display.

Researchers argue that women's smiles reify gender ideals of agreeableness or vulnerability, while men's smiles might be indicative of the fact that privileged and powerful men are allowed a wider range of emotional displays than subordinated men. In our original sample, there are only three men of color featured on the men's covers, and it is striking that all of these men had partial or full smiles. This seems consistent with researchers who argue that smiles are often used to represent men of color so as to undercut prevalent (racist) associations of potential threat or danger. In the original sample, boxer Oscar De La Hoya is shown boxing with his cocked fists aiming playfully at the reader. Boxing is a blood sport that has been widely contested as violent. Therefore, De La Hoya's smile might be employed to make him seem less threatening and aggressive. In the new sample, only two nonwhite men appear on the covers. Both are smiling. One is an NBA all-star, the other, an unknown model. We will return to more comments on the racialized dimensions of the findings at the end of the chapter. . . .

Third, what is advertised to men and women shows considerable overlap. For example, compare *Men's Health* from May 2004 with *Shape* from May 2004. *Men's Health* is 218 pages total (including front and back covers) and has 111 full pages devoted to advertising (though some ads were several pages, and others only half a page). Thus, 50.9 percent of the issue is devoted solely to advertising. (Additional ads sometimes shared pages with content, but in the interest of clarity, we focused on full-page ads only.) Twenty ads are for cars or motorcycles (18.0 percent), ten are for food or meal replacements (9.1 percent), nineteen are for clothing or accessories (17.1 percent), six are for grooming products of various types (5.4 percent), and four are for medications or pain killers (3.6 percent). *Shape* is 324 pages, of which 156 pages are devoted entirely to advertising (48.1 percent). Nine ads are for automobiles (5.8 percent), twenty-six are for food or meal replacements (16.7 percent), thirteen are for clothing or accessories (8.3 percent), thirty-three are for grooming products (21.2 percent), thirteen are for medications or pain killers (8.3 percent).

Increasingly, men and women are encouraged to use a wide range of hair, skin, hygiene, and grooming products. While *Men's Health* features more advertisements for automobiles than *Shape* (18.0 percent compared to 5.8 percent) and *Shape* features more advertisements for food than *Men's Health* (16.7 percent to 9.1 percent) and grooming products (21.2 percent to 5.4 percent), there is a great deal of overlap in what is being advertised to male and female consumers. Body products, such as skin care and hair care products, are increasingly being offered to both male and female consumers.

In addition to the direct ads, regular columns often provide coverage of products. These products are presented with the same excited aplomb as significant information regarding health, making a "new way to make hair shine" or a "new fragrance" appear to be as significant as a new way to combat breast or prostate cancer. While this may sound like a strange characterization, it is easier to explain with examples. For example, *Fit* mixed information about strokes, jump ropes, aquaphor healing ointment, osteoporosis, pony tails, growing longer nails, and new floral scents in snippets on different pages. *Men's Health* combined information on martial arts, Mr. Rogers, healthy meals, prostate cancer tests, pajamas, exercise bands, flashlights, sports drinks, digital voice recorders, airline tickets, how to shoot a basketball, microbrews, and more in just one "Malegrams" column. Mixing together different types of information, products, and expert advice creates the impression that all these topics should receive similar consideration.

The convergence of grooming products offered to both men and women is particularly noteworthy. Most of the men's magazines featured regular columns on grooming that cover such topics as alpha-hydroxy, hair care products, and potent scents. Though men and women may use products that smell different, are packaged in different colored bottles, and are described with different adjectives, the range of products offered overlapped considerably. Men's grooming products are expected to be a $10 billion market by 2008, compared to the $15 billion expected for women's grooming products in the same year. In 2006, the top-selling fragrance for 9 of 12 months was a man's fragrance. Not surprisingly, men's products were masculinized by linking them to sports stars and celebrities. For example, in 2006, Yankees' shortstop Derek Jeter began marketing a line of men's grooming products and a signature fragrance with Avon. Clive Owen, the ruggedly handsome Academy Award–nominated actor, is on the Lancôme payroll.

Additionally, leisure time activities were also de-gendered, having overlapped across women's and men's magazines. A key example is the repackaging of spa treatments and body services such as manicures and pedicures for male consumers. All of the magazines highlighted body treatments of various types for men. *EMO* included spa reports regularly, for example, in one issue they ranked body services such as the "Detoxifying Algae Wrap," "Holistic Back, Face and Scalp Session," and "Balneotherapy" (a combo tub soak, seaweed wrap, and massage) provided by Tethra Spa in Dublin, Ireland. *Prime* compared two spas and offered tips on finding a spa near you. One chain of spas reported that now, 15–20 percent of its clients are men, a new and growing trend. Manicures and pedicures are becoming regular recommendations for men in the magazines we studied and in popular culture in general.

Again, athletes and actors were used to market and masculinize such treatments. Just as men were encouraged to try services traditionally marketed exclusively to women, women were encouraged to try activities and experiences once thought of as more appropriate for men. For example, women were urged to try three North Spas that offer kayaking and other sport activities in addition to more traditional spa treatments. While privileged men have long been "pampered," modern conceptions of the hegemonic man have tended to exclude anything that carried the taint of femininity. By the same token, more adventurous activities for women are also normalized as gender-appropriate for either men or women.

Michael P. Levine and
Sarah K. Murnen

"Everybody Knows That Mass Media Are/Are Not [*pick one*] a Cause of Eating Disorders": A Critical Review of Evidence for a Causal Link Between Media, Negative Body Image, and Disordered Eating in Females

Numerous professionals, parents, and adolescents find the media's status as a cause of body dissatisfaction, drive for thinness, and eating disorders to be self-evident: *"Of course,* mass media contribute to unhealthy beauty ideals, body dissatisfaction, and disordered eating—haven't you seen the magazine covers in the supermarket newsstands lately? No wonder so many girls have body image issues and eating disorders." On the contrary, a growing number of parents, biopsychiatric researchers, clinicians, and cynical adolescents find proclamations about media as a *cause* of any disorder to be an irritating distraction. Their contention is, in effect: *"Of course,* we know now that eating disorders, like mood disorders and schizophrenia, are severe, self-sustaining psychiatric illnesses with a genetic and biochemical basis. So, *of course,* no scientist seriously thinks that mass media and the escapades of actors, models, and celebrities have anything to do with causing them." . . .

The relationships between mass media, negative body image, and unhealthy behaviors (e.g., use and abuse of steroids and food supplements) in males are receiving increasing attention. The gender differences (conservatively, 6 to 8 females for each male) in the prevalence of anorexia nervosa, bulimia nervosa, and eating disorder not otherwise specified (EDNOS) other than Binge Eating Disorder are among the largest reported for mental disorders.

Although the matter of dimensions and/or categories is complex and unresolved, substantial evidence suggests that the serious and frequently chronic conditions recognized as the "Eating Disorders" are composite expressions of a set of dimensions, such as negative emotionality, binge eating, and unhealthy forms of weight and shape management. The latter includes restric-

From *Journal of Social and Clinical Psychology,* vol. 28, no. 1, January 2009, pp. 9–16, 19–26, 30–34 (excerpted, refs. omitted). Copyright © 2009 by Guilford Publications. Reprinted by permission via Copyright Clearance Center.

tive dieting, self-induced vomiting after eating, and abuse of laxatives, diuretics, diet pills, and exercise.

The adhesive drawing together and framing these intertwined continua is negative body image. In most media effects research the multidimensional construct of body image is represented by various measures of what are essentially perceptual-emotional conclusions (e.g., "I look too fat to myself and others" + "I am disgusted by and ashamed of this" = "I hate how fat I look and feel"). For females "body dissatisfaction" results from—and feeds—a schema that integrates three fundamental components: idealization of slenderness and leanness; an irrational fear of fat; and a conviction that weight and shape are central determinants of one's identity. . . .

Researchers in many fields have stopped thinking about "the" cause of a disorder as "the agent" that directly brings about the undesirable outcome. Instead, there is an emphasis on variables that are reliably and usefully associated with an increase over time in the probability of a subsequent outcome. Such variables are called risk factors.

Thinking in terms of risk factors has two major implications for investigating mass media as a "cause" of eating disorders. The first concerns the oft-heard "relative rarity" argument: How could mass media be a cause when the vast majority of girls and young women are exposed to ostensibly toxic influences, but only a small percentage develop eating disorders? This critique dissolves when one considers multiple risk factors as multiplicative probabilities. Assume, conservatively, that 35% of adolescent girls are engaged with those mass media containing various unhealthy messages. Assume also that three other risk factors—such as peer preoccupation with weight and shape; family history of overweight/obesity; and being socialized by parents and older siblings to believe firmly that a female's identity and worth are shaped primarily by appearance—each have a probability of .35 of occurring in the population. . . .

Second, if mass media constitute a *causal risk factor* for the spectrum of negative body image and disordered eating, then the following will be the case. *Cross-sectional studies* will show that the extent of exposure to mass media, or to various specific forms of mass media, is a correlate of that spectrum. *Longitudinal studies* will demonstrate that exposure to mass media precedes and predicts development of negative body image and disordered eating. *Laboratory experiments* should show that well-controlled manipulation of the media risk factor (independent variable) causes the hypothesized changes in "state" body satisfaction and other relevant dependent variables, while *controlled analog (laboratory) or field experiments* should demonstrate that prevention programs designed to combat known risk factors do indeed reduce or delay the onset of disordered eating.

These criteria are demanding in and of themselves. Nevertheless, it is also important to incorporate the contributions to knowledge of two further sources: common sense and people's "lived experience." Specifically, if mass media are a causal risk factor, then *content analyses* should document that media provide the raw material from which children and adolescents could *readily* extract and construct the information, affective valences, and behavioral cues necessary to develop the components of disordered eating. Similarly, *surveys and ecological analyses* will reveal that engagement with mass media is frequent and intensive enough to provide multiple opportunities for this type of social-cognitive learning. Finally, *surveys and qualitative studies* should find that, beginning at the age where they can think critically about themselves in relation to personal and outside influences, children and adolescents will report that mass media are sources of influence, and even pressure, on themselves, their peers, and others. . . .

Appearance, status, sexuality, and buying and consuming are, for many reasons (including the power of mass media), very important aspects of life throughout many countries. Consequently, the content of mass media provides daily, multiple, overlapping, and, all too often, unhealthy messages about gender, attractiveness, ideal body sizes and shapes, self-control, desire, food, and weight *management*. These messages sometimes intentionally, sometimes incidentally indoctrinate developing girls and boys with the following easily extracted themes: (a) being sexually attractive is of paramount importance; (b) the sources of ideals about attractiveness ("being 'hot'!"), style, and the best, most competitive practices for becoming and staying beautiful are obviously located outside the self; and (c) mass media are the most important and inherently enjoyable "external" source of the information, motivation, and products necessary to be attractive and fashionable.

Mass Media and the Thinness Schema

Thus, with respect to the cultural foundations of negative body image and disordered eating, even girls (and boys) as young as 4 or 5 have no trouble finding in mass media the raw materials for various maladaptive but *entirely normative* media-based *schemata* concerning gender and attractiveness. The *"thinness schema"* for females is a set of assumptions, "facts," and strong feelings that are organized so as to establish a readiness to think and respond in terms of, for example, the following themes: (1) Women are "naturally" invested in their beauty assets and thus beauty is a woman's principal project in life; (2) a slender, youthful attractive "image" is really something substantive, because it is pleasing to males and it demonstrates to females that one is in control of one's life; and (3) learning to perceive, monitor, and indeed experience yourself as the object of an essentially masculine gaze is an important part of being feminine and beautiful.

Transnational Idol: The Exaltation of Thinness and the Vilification of Fat

There is a wealth of evidence from content analyses that the ideal female body showcased on television, in movies, in magazines, and on the internet reflects, indeed embodies, the proposition that "thin is normative and attractive." While (because?) American girls and women are becoming heavier, the current body *ideal* (idol) for women has become and remains unrealistically thin.

In fact, mass media are one of many sociocultural sources for the normative prejudice that fat is "horrible and ugly," and that "getting fatter" is a sign of at least 4 of the classic "7 deadly sins"—extravagance, gluttony, greed, sloth, and, maybe, pride. . . .

The presence of a positive correlation between level of exposure to mass media, or to certain types of mass media, and the spectrum of disordered eating is a necessary but not sufficient condition for determination of causal agency. However, absence of a positive correlation negates the argument for causality. . . .

Longitudinal Correlates of Exposure to Mass Media

. . . Compared to cross-sectional studies, longitudinal research linking media exposure with body image is sparse. The few published studies do suggest that early exposure to thin-ideal television predicts a subsequent increase in body-image problems. For a sample of Australian girls aged 5 to 8, viewing of appearance-focused television programs (but not magazines) predicted a decrease in appearance satisfaction 1 year later. For European American and African American girls ages 7 through 12 greater overall television exposure predicted both a thinner ideal *adult* body shape and a higher level of disordered eating 1 year later. The results of both studies were valid regardless of whether the children were heavy, or perceived themselves to be thin or heavy, at the outset of the research. The thrust of these two studies is consistent with Sinton and Birch's finding that, among the 11-year-old American girls they studied, awareness of media messages about thinness was related to the strength of appearance schemas a year later.

The importance of a longitudinal design is revealed in recent studies of older children and young adolescents conducted by Tiggemann and by Field and colleagues. In a sample of 214 Australian high school girls (mean age = 14), Tiggemann found that the only measure of television exposure, including total hours of exposure, to produce meaningful cross-sectional and longitudinal correlations was the self-reported extent of watching soap operas. Cross-lagged correlational analyses showed that Time 1 exposure to soap operas predicted, to a small but significant degree, internalization of the slender ideal and level of appearance schema at 1-year follow up (Time 2). Time spent reading appearance-oriented magazines, but not other magazines, at Time 1 predicted, also to a small but significant degree, Time 2 levels of internalization, appearance schema, and drive for thinness. However, none of the media exposure variables was a significant longitudinal predictor of body dissatisfaction. Moreover, hierarchical regressions controlling for Time 1 level of each of the four criterion variables (e.g., internalization) found that none of the media exposure measures added significantly to prediction of the Time 2 criteria.

Although Field and colleagues used only single-variable measures of media exposure, their longitudinal research also casts doubt on exposure as a causal risk factor for older children and younger adolescents. Field et al. investigated a sample of over 6900 girls who were ages 9 through 15 at the 1996 baseline. Preliminary cross-sectional work did produce the expected positive linear association between frequency of reading women's fashion magazines and intensity of weight concerns. However, subsequent longitudinal research revealed that over a 1-year period the key predictor of the *development* of weight concerns and frequent dieting was "making a lot of effort to look like same-sex figures in the media." A 7-year follow-up showed that initiation of binge-eating, but not purging, in (now) adolescent and young adult females was predicted independently by frequent dieting and by Time 2 level of attempting to look like persons in the media.

The only longitudinal investigation of young adult women we could locate was Aubrey's 2-year panel study of college-age women. In support of Criterion 4, the extent of exposure to sexually objectifying media at Time 1 predicted level of self-objectification at Time 2, especially in women with low self-esteem. Measures of the tendency to self-objectify are positively correlated with eating disorder symptoms such as misperceptions of weight and shape, body shame, drive for thinness, and restrictive dieting.

Conclusion

Evidence from a very small number of longitudinal studies indicates that for children and very young adolescents, extent of media exposure does appear to predict increases in negative body image and disordered eating. Tiggemann's suggests that by early adolescence the causal risk factor is not media exposure, or even internalization of the slender beauty ideal, but rather the intensity and extent of "core beliefs and assumptions about the importance, meaning, and effect of appearance in an individual's life." . . .

Multimethod studies by Hargreaves and Tiggemann in Australia produced compelling evidence for the contention that mass media have negative and cumulative effects on body image in girls and young women. The adolescent girls whose body image was most negatively affected by experimental exposure to 20 television commercials featuring the thin ideal tended to have greater levels of body dissatisfaction and drive for thinness 2 years later, even when initial level of body dissatisfaction was controlled statistically.

The most vulnerable girls may well have a self-schema dominated by the core importance of physical appearance. In a study of girls ages 15 through 18 Hargreaves and Tiggemann found that appearance-focused TV commercials did activate an appearance-related self-schema, as reflected in several measures of cognitive set. Moreover, as predicted, appearance-focused commercials generated greater appearance dissatisfaction for those girls who began the study with a more extensive, emotionally charged, self-schema for appearance. Interestingly, the negative impact of the thin-beauty ideal in television commercials was, unlike previous findings with magazine images, unaffected by either the girls' initial level of body dissatisfaction or whether their viewing style was more personal (self-focused) or more detached (image-focused).

Positive (Assimilation) Effects. Durkin and Paxton found that 32% of the 7th grade girls and 22% of the 10th grade Australian girls who were exposed to images of attractive models from magazines exhibited an *increase* in state body satisfaction. Similarly, two studies of Canadian college students found that restrained eaters showed moderate to large increases in body satisfaction following exposure to similar magazine images, whereas unrestrained eaters had very large decreases in body satisfaction.

Two studies in the United States by Wilcox and Laird suggest that young women who focus on the slender models in magazines while defocusing attention on themselves are more likely to identify with the models and thus to feel better about their own bodies. Conversely, women who self-consciously divide their attention between the models and themselves are more likely to evaluate themselves and reach a conclusion that leaves them feeling inferior and worse. This finding is supported by research showing that self-evaluative processes, as opposed to self-improvement motives, are more likely to reflect and activate "upward" social comparison processes, which themselves tend to generate negative feelings about one's body.

Pro-Ana Web Sites. The internet offers many pro-anorexia (pro-ana) and pro-bulimia (pro-mia) web sites. Some of the most prominent pro-ana sites defiantly and zealously promote AN as a sacred lifestyle rather than a debilitating psychiatric disorder. Their "thinspirational" images of emaciation and their explicit behavioral instructions for attaining and sustaining the thin ideal are intended to reinforce the identity and practices of those already entrenched in AN or BN.

If concentrated exposure to typical images of slender models have negative experimental effects, then we might well expect the images and messages from pro-anorexia web sites to have even more negative effects. Two recent experiments by Bardone-Cone and Cass examined the effects of a web site that they constructed to feature the prototypical content of pro-ana sites. As predicted, exposure to this site had a large number of negative effects on young women, independent of their dispositional levels of thin ideal internalization and disordered eating. At present, we do not know what effects pro-ana and pro-mia sites have on the adolescent girls and young women who avidly seek them out because they already have a full-blown eating disorder. . . .

Media Literacy: Laboratory Investigations

. . . Media literacy (ML) is a set of knowledge, attitudes, and skills that enable people to work together to understand, appreciate, and critically analyze the nature of mass media and one's relationships with them. Systematic investigations of ML can be categorized into analog laboratory studies, brief interventions, and longer, more intensive programs.

. . . Several controlled experiments show that very brief written or video interventions can inoculate college-age women, including those who already have a negative body image, against the general tendency to feel worse about their bodies and themselves after viewing slides or video containing media-based images of the slender beauty ideal. The most effective ML "inoculation" highlights the clash between the artificial, constructed nature of the slender, flawless, "model look" versus two stark realities: (1) the actual shapes and weights of females (and males) naturally vary a great deal across a population; and (2) dieting to attain an "ideal" and "glamorous" weight/shape that is unnatural for a given individual has many negative effects, including risk for an eating disorder. . . .

Several programs for high-school and college-age females used slide presentations or Jean Kilbourne's video *Slim Hopes* (www.mediaed.org/videos/MediaAndHealth/SlimHopes) to help participants consider the history of changing, but consistently restrictive, beauty ideals and then to answer some fundamental questions: Do *real* women look like the models in advertising? Will buying the product being advertised make me look like this model? These programs emphasize how fashion models, working with the production staffs of magazines and movies, use "cosmetic" surgery, computer graphics, and other technologies to *construct* idealized *images*. Participants are encouraged to explore how these manipulations are carefully orchestrated to stir up the desire to purchase products, many of which will supposedly reduce the discrepancy between such unreal, "perfect" images versus the body shapes and weights of normal, healthy females.

These ML programs are brief, so positive effects are necessarily limited. Nevertheless, it is noteworthy that they tend to reduce, at least in the short run, one important risk factor for disordered eating: internalization of the slender beauty ideal.

Well-controlled studies of multi-lesson, multifaceted media literacy programs that unfold over 1 to 2 months have shown that media literacy training can help girls *and* boys ages 10 through 14 to reduce risk factors such as internalization of the slender or muscular ideal, while increasing the potentially protective factors of self-acceptance, self-confidence in friendships, and confidence in their ability to be activists and thus affect weight-related social norms. In addition to spending considerable time working on the same components as those in the analog and brief interventions, intensive ML programs address the process and costs of social comparison. They also get participants involved in working within their ML groups, their school, and their larger community to translate their increasing literacy into peer education, consumer activism, and creating and promoting new, healthier media.

Recent investigations with college students also show ML to be a promising form of prevention. For example, Watson and Vaughn developed a 4-week, 6-hour intervention consisting of psychoeducation about the nature and sources of body dissatisfaction; group-based content analysis of beauty ideals in popular women's magazines; discussion of media ideals and beauty enhancement techniques; and a brief cognitive intervention designed to help participants dispute negative beliefs and feelings activated by media images of the thin ideal. Compared to a 1-day, 90-min version of this intervention, a one-time viewing of a 34-min media literacy film, and a no-intervention control, the extended intervention was the most successful in reducing the following risk factors for disordered eating: unhealthy social attitudes, internalization of the slender ideal, and body dissatisfaction. . . .

Presumed Influences on Others

In thinking about the subjective experiences of media pressures and influences, it is worth examining more closely the construct of "awareness" of the thin ideal. The perception that peers and people in general (e.g., employers) are influenced by thin-ideal media can itself be a form of subjective pressure that motivates young people to diet in an attempt to meet that ideal. In fact, it appears that the mere presumption of media effects on others may exert its own effect, at least on older females. Park's analytic study of over 400 undergraduates found that the more issues of beauty and fashion magazines a young woman reads per month, the greater the perceived prevalence of the thin ideal in those magazines. The greater this perceived prevalence, the greater the presumed influence of that ideal on *other women;* and in turn the greater the perceived influence on *self,* which predicted the desire to be thin. More research of this type with younger samples is needed to test this "cultivation of perceived social norms" hypothesis: Greater consumption of beauty and fashion magazines or of appearance-focused TV and internet content will foster stronger, more influential beliefs that the slender ideal is ubiquitous and normative for peers. This logic will, in turn, be a source of pressure and inspiration for the person's own desire to be thin(ner). . . .

And, yet, in light of the important research by Tiggemann and by Field et al. there remains a need to demonstrate more conclusively that either (1) direct engagement with mass media or (2) media effects that are mediated by parents and/or peers *precede* development of the more proximal risk factors such as negative body image. Similarly, despite the preliminary but encouraging evidence from media literacy interventions of varying intensities, to date no studies have tested the deceptively simple proposition that prevention programs can increase media literacy and thereby reduce or eliminate negative media influences—and in turn reduce or delay development of proximal risk factors (e.g., internalization of the thin ideal, social comparison tendencies) *and* attendant outcomes such as EDNOS.

What We Need to Know but Don't Know Yet

This review suggests five principal gaps in our knowledge about mass media as a potential causal risk factor for the spectrum of disordered eating. The first three are derived from the conclusion immediately above. First, there is a need for longitudinal research that examines the predictive validity of media exposure, motives for media use, and the subjective experience of media influences. Second, as noted by an anonymous reviewer of this manuscript, there remains a dearth of information about whether it is the thinness-depicting aspects of magazine, TV, and other media content that exert negative effects. Thus, survey-based longitudinal investigations of media exposure should strive to determine as precisely as possible not only frequency and intensity of consumption, but also the nature of the images, articles, programs, and such to which participants are exposed. Third, there is a need for prevention research that capitalizes on and extends the promising findings of extended media literacy interventions.

The fourth research direction concerns the relationship, particularly from a developmental perspective, between engagement with mass media and other causal risk factors. We need to learn much more about the ways in which body image disturbance and disordered eating are influenced by perceived social norms, by the confluence of media, family, and peer messages about weight and *shape,* and by *indirect* media exposure, such as acquisition of body ideals and eating behaviors via interactions with family, peers, and significant adults (e.g., coaches) who learned them directly from television and magazines. Direct media effects may be small to modest, but the combination of direct and indirect effects, that is, the cumulative media effect, may be substantial.

Finally, the transactions between the developing child (or adolescent) and media constitute another set of important research questions to address. A cross-sectional study by Gralen, Levine, Smolak, and Murnen (1990) indicated that the correlates of negative body image and disordered eating in young adolescents tended to be more concrete and behavioral (e.g., onset of dating, pubertal development, teasing about weight and shape), whereas the predictors in middle to later adolescence were more psychological, such as the experience of a discrepancy between perception of one's own shape versus an internalized ideal shape. More recently, a longitudinal study by Harrison found that the number of hours that children ages 6 through 8 watched television per week predicted an increase in disordered eating without predicting idealization of a slender body. This raises the interesting and testable proposition that exposure to various salient media messages, including those contained in the onslaught of advertisements for diet-, fitness-, and weight-related products, might have little effect on the "thinness beliefs" of young children, while leading them to vilify fat, glamorize dieting as a grown-up practice, and yet still think of fattening, non-nutritious foods as desirable in general and useful for assuaging negative feelings.

With respect to the transformation of relevant psychological processes over late childhood, early adolescence, and later adolescence, Thompson and colleagues have developed and validated various features of the Tripartite Model in which media, family, and peers influence directly internalization of the slender beauty ideal and social comparison processes. This valuable model reminds us that, after nearly 25 years of research on media and body image, we still know relatively little about the automatic, intentional, and motivational processes involved in the role of *social comparison* in media effects. Basic questions remain: What dispositional and situational factors determine when people will make upward social comparisons with highly dissimilar fashion models whose "image" has been constructed by cosmetic surgeons, photographers, and computer experts? And under what circumstances will such comparisons result in negative effects (contrast) or positive effects (assimilation)?

Multidimensional models such as Thompson's also emphasize the need to determine when and how in the developmental process a number of important mechanisms such as appearance schematicity, thin-ideal internalization, social comparison processes, and self-objectification begin to play key roles. Further experimental and longitudinal studies of these mediators will be a very positive step toward understanding the emergence, particularly around puberty, of attentiveness and vulnerability to thin-ideal media images *and* to the many other potentially negative influences that emanate from family, peers, and influential adults such as coaches.

EXPLORING THE ISSUE

Do Media Cause Individuals to Develop Negative Body Images?

Critical Thinking and Reflection

1. What media celebrities or personalities do you emulate? What type of body image do they portray? Do you see your own sense of self influenced by the standards media people exemplify?
2. How are stories about eating disorders framed in the media? Are we told that eating disorders are a choice or that they are detrimental to our health?
3. How would you identify a healthy lifestyle for children and adults?
4. What evaluative measures do you have to assess beauty, health, or eating disorders? How do you describe each? What does your description say about your own views on each of these topics?
5. How do you form standards of what is "appropriate" and what do you do to measure your own behaviors? For example, do you have a weak self-image because you feel you can't measure up to mediated standards of health or beauty? What types of control do you exercise (if you do exercise control) to make you feel that you have a healthy attitude about body image?

Is There Common Ground?

It is very interesting that Shari Dworkin and Faye Wachs have found a similarity to the way both women and men are portrayed in magazines, and it is also surprising to see that Miachel P. Levine and Sarah K. Murnen can see "two sides of the same coin" in examining research on the causal links between media images and eating disorders. The common ground these authors discuss shows how broad a range of topics self-image has, in a world saturated with media images.

The psychology of one's body image is a subject worthy of thought and contemplation. Many books and articles have been written to untangle the many possible threads that lead to self-image, and often these books become best sellers, indicating that the subject of self-reflection and self-understanding is important to many.

Additional Resources

Naomi Wolf, *The Beauty Myth: How Images of Beauty Are Used Against Women* (William Morrow and Company, 1991)

This book crafted a persuasive argument that the concept of beauty was a political issue that kept women stuck in a patriarchal system. By media and social issues preying on women's insecurities about their bodies, women's ability to fully participate in the labor force and in the social world was undermined. In 2002, Wolf published the second edition of the book with a new introduction, and in reviewing the new version, critic Emily Wilson, writing for *The Guardian* in the U.K., noted, "The world has changed—a bit—over the past decade and a half, but not enough."

Vickie Rutledge Shields and Dawn Heinecken, *Measuring Up: How Advertising Affects Self-Image* (University of Pennsylvania Press, 2002), or Ellen Cole and Jessica Henderson Daniel, eds., *Featuring Females: Feminist Analyses of Media* (Washington, DC: American Psychological Association, 2005)

For more reading on images of ideal bodies in the media and the impact on consumers who may find their own bodies lacking, check out the above-mentioned books.

Arnold E. Andersen, *Making Weight: Men's Conflicts with Food, Weight, Shape & Appearance* (Gurze Books, 2000)

For a study of body image from the male perspective, the above-mentioned book is a helpful analysis of men's increasing sensitivity to issues of weight and appearance.

The U.S. Department of Health and Human Services has posted a Healthy Weight Chart on the Internet:

www.nhlbisupport.com/bmi

The popular magazine, *Psychology Today* occasionally writes about self-esteem issues. One such article that can be helpful to consult is

www.psychologytoday.com/basics/self-esteem

ISSUE 5

Do Video Games Encourage Violent Behavior?

YES: Craig A. Anderson, from "FAQs on Violent Video Games and Other Media Violence," www.CraigAnderson.org

NO: Henry Jenkins, from "Reality Bytes: Eight Myths About Video Games Debunked," www.pbs.org/kcts/videogamerevolution/impact/myths.html

---

Learning Outcomes

After reading this issue, you should be able to:

- Describe the differences between Craig Anderson's and Henry Jenkins' perspectives on violent video games.
- Gain an understanding of the potential consequences of video gaming.
- Discuss the ways in which virtual worlds can shape understanding and behavior.
- Apply these concepts to parental and regulatory reactions.

ISSUE SUMMARY

YES: Craig A. Anderson is an expert on the effect of violence in television and film. Based on extensive research, he holds the position that video games prompt young people toward even more aggression and violence than do other media content.

NO: Henry Jenkins tackles a broad array of misconceptions about the place and impact of video games on society. He argues that the primary audience is not children, that violence is not increasing in society, and that concerns about isolation, desensitization, and violence are overblown.

In recent years, the subject of the effect of video games has joined television, films, and recorded music as a topic that provokes strong reactions among individuals who feel that some content may encourage violent, or at least aggressive behavior, among young people. There is less concern about how any type of content affects adults, so most of the attention is focused on how children, adolescents, and young adults use controversial media content. The underlying reason for this is that younger users are assumed to have a lesser sense of moral responsibility and judgment about the relationship of media content and reality, and thus be more vulnerable to its effects. Even though the video game industry voluntarily rates the content of video games (as do the motion picture, television, and recording industries), many parents and critics of media violence feel that video games are a unique form of entertainment that warrants special consideration. Since the games are often played alone, on personal devices, consoles, or computers, the video game user's interaction with the game is engaged and direct. The sophistication of computer graphics has produced images that look even more realistic than ever before. Linkages drawn between the Columbine shootings and the perpetrators obsession with the game "Doom" in 1999 frightened the general public. The controversy became heated during the summer of 2005 when "Grand Theft Auto" was released and found to contain some hidden sex scenes. In 2011, the Supreme Court struck down Californian law that banned the sale of violent video games to minors on the grounds of freedom of expression. See www.nytimes.com/2011/06/29/arts/video-games/what-supreme-court-ruling-on-video-games-means.html for a spirited discussion of video games and freedom of expression.

Both selections chosen to represent controversial views for this issue cite evidence of research studies that have different conclusions. This raises important problems for us, as readers. How do we decide which studies to believe? How do we weigh the evidence and the credibility of the authors of differing studies? How much of our own experience informs the way we think about some of these types of issues?

As you will see, both Dr. Craig Anderson and Dr. Henry Jenkins offer a series of questions about the effects of video games and purport to debunk them. In the process, they come to opposite conclusions. Dr. Craig Anderson's FAQ list evolves from his years of studying the relationship of media content and violence/aggression. He references decades of research that finds a link between violence and aggression, a conclusion that he has testified to before congressional committees. Less research has examined the concern about the violent content of video games, because most violent games only came to the market in the 1990s. Yet the amount of time spent with games and the high levels of engagement by players lead Craig Anderson, program head of psychology at Iowa State University, to fear that the relationship between violent content and aggressive/violent behavior may be enhanced.

Dr. Henry Jenkins, professor at the University of Southern California and previously head of the comparative media studies program at MIT, offers eight myths about video games. He describes his desire to "challenge the dominant media effects paradigm and call for a more complex understanding of teens' relationship to popular culture." Whether speaking and writing about Columbine or about video games and violence, he argues that the fantasies of children's culture are an important arena to understand how we as a culture are constructing our future.

It may be true that there are few long-term studies of the effect of playing video games now, but this will change in time. There are many longitudinal studies of the way violence and aggression are portrayed in other forms of media. In all of these cases, it is important to consider who sponsors the research and what agenda the sponsoring agency may have. In this edition of *Taking Sides*, you will see several cases for which the attitudes or biases of the authors of certain studies should suggest a critical framework for evaluating their position.

This type of controversy also takes into consideration whether a media industry can adequately control access to questionable material through ratings systems. While ratings on the packages of many games and other content may be somewhat effective as a measure of who may have access to media content, how are those ratings enforced? Is it possible for an industry to monitor use when the bottom line is selling their product? How much regulation should be exercised from outside? Should the government take a stronger role in creating guidelines, or should the bulk of the responsibility be placed on the shoulders of parents and guardians?

As mentioned in the preface to this book, the distribution and appearance of media content has changed dramatically over the years. As mediated images become more realistic through computer enhancement or computer generation, studies of perception will undoubtedly change too. And, as individuals continue to use interactive media, we can expect to see more sophistication in future studies about the effects of media content on audiences of different ages, and in different circumstances.

When asked about the effects of video games on teens, a colleague of mine who studies video games quipped, "They'll have great eye-hand coordination and terrible social skills." Although violence gets much of the attention, his comment reminds us that there are uses and consequences of video game playing other than violent ones. An extensive area of research is emerging on the development of cognitive skills from interactive games. Influence on the development of visual spatial skills, multitasking ability, and attentional skills is being observed. Ironically, finding academic benefits of playing educational games has been more elusive. See Subrahmanyam and Greenfield, referenced in Postscript, for more on these issues. An interesting study detailed in that chapter (p. 81) discusses how action video game skills along with past video game experience predicted laparoscopic surgical skills. It describes the "moral panics" that have erupted during the introduction of almost all new media into society. Parental concerns and media hype have often contributed to concerns about massive negative effects that have ultimately proved to be unwarranted. As you consider the evidence provided by the two positions on this issue, how do you formulate your own position? If you were a parent, would you see things differently? Are video games different from any other form of traditional media content?

YES

Craig A. Anderson

FAQs on Violent Video Games and Other Media Violence

1. For your 2003 article on *The Influence of Media Violence on Youth* you and a distinguished group of media scholars selected by the National Institute of Mental Health reviewed 50 years of research on media violence and aggression. What have been the main research steps, and what are the main conclusions?

Most of the early research focused on two questions:

1. Is there a significant association between exposure to media violence and aggressive behavior?
2. Is this association causal? (That is, can we say that violent television, video games, and other media are directly causing aggressive behavior in our kids?)

The results, overall, have been fairly consistent across types of studies (experimental, cross-sectional, and longitudinal) and across visual media type (television, films, video games). *There is a significant relation between exposure to media violence and aggressive behavior.* Exposing children and adolescents (or "youth") to violent visual media increases the likelihood that they will engage in physical aggression against another person. By "physical aggression" we mean behavior that is intended to harm another person physically, such as hitting with a fist or some object. A single brief exposure to violent media can increase aggression in the immediate situation. Repeated exposure leads to general increases in aggressiveness over time. *This relation between media violence and aggressive behavior is causal.*

2. What have researchers focused on in more recent years? How does exposure to media violence increase later aggressive behavior?

Early aggression researchers were interested in discovering how youth learn to be aggressive. Once they discovered observational learning takes place not only when youth see how people behave in the real world but also when they see characters in films and on television, many began to focus on exactly how watching such violent stories increases later aggression. In other words, more recent research really focused on the underlying psychological mechanisms.

In the last 10 years there also has been a huge increase in research on violent video games. Based on five decades of research on television and film violence and one decade of research on video games, we now have a pretty clear picture of how exposure to media violence can increase aggression in both the immediate situation as well as in long term contexts. Immediately after consuming some media violence, there is an increase in aggressive behavior tendencies because of several factors.

1. Aggressive thoughts increase, which in turn increase the likelihood that a mild or ambiguous provocation will be interpreted in a hostile fashion.
2. Aggressive (or hostile) emotion increases.
3. General arousal (e.g., heart rate) increases, which tends to increase the dominant behavioral tendency.
4. Youth learn new forms of aggressive behaviors by observing them, and will reenact them almost immediately afterwards if the situational context is sufficiently similar.

Repeated consumption of media violence over time increases aggression across a range to situations and across time because of several related factors.

1. It creates more positive attitudes, beliefs, and expectations regarding aggressive solutions to interpersonal problems. In other words, youth come to believe that aggression is normal, appropriate, and likely to succeed.
2. It also leads to the development of aggressive scripts, which are basically ways of thinking about how the social world works. Heavy media violence consumers tend to view the world in a more hostile fashion.
3. It decreases the cognitive accessibility of nonviolent ways to handle conflict. That is, it becomes harder to even think about nonviolent solutions.
4. It produces an emotional desensitization to aggression and violence. Normally, people have a pretty negative emotional reaction to conflict, aggression, and violence, and this can be seen in their physiological reactions to observation of violence (real or fictional, as in entertainment media). For example, viewing physical violence normally leads to increases in heart rate and blood pressure, as well as to certain brain wave patterns. Such normal negative emotional reactions tend to inhibit aggressive behavior, and can inspire helping behavior. Repeated consumption of media violence reduces these normal negative emotional reactions.
5. Repetition increases learning of any type of skill or way of thinking, to the point where that skill or way of thinking becomes fairly automatic.

3. Is there a difference between the effects of TV/film violence versus video-games violence?

Most of the research has focused on TV/film violence (so-called "passive" media), mainly because they have been around so much longer than video games. However, the existing research literature on violent video games has yielded the same general types of effects as the TV and Cinema research. At a theoretical level, *there are reasons to believe that violent video games may have a larger harmful effect than violent TV and film effects.* This is a very difficult research question, and there currently is no definite answer. But, recent studies that directly compare passive screen media to video games tend to find bigger effects of violent video games.

4. Is that why there have been so many school shootings by kids who play lots of violent video games? Can such games turn a normal, well-adjusted child or adolescent into a school shooter?

No, that would be an overstatement, one that mainstream media violence researchers do not make. The best way to think about this is the risk factor approach. There are three important points to keep in mind.

First, there are many causal risk factors involved in the development of a person who frequently behaves in an aggressive or violent manner. There are biological factors, family factors, neighborhood factors, and so on. Media violence is only one of the top dozen or so risk factors.

Second, extreme aggression, such as aggravated assault and homicide, typically occurs only when there are a number of risk factors present. In other words, none of the causal risk factors are "necessary and sufficient" causes of extreme aggression. Of course, cigarette smoking is not a necessary and sufficient cause of lung cancer, even though it is a major cause of it. People with only one risk factor seldom (I'm tempted to say "never") commit murder.

Third, consumption of media violence is the most common of all of the major risk factors for aggression in most modern societies. It also is the least expensive and easiest risk factor for parents to change. In sum, playing a lot of violent games is unlikely to turn a normal youth with zero or one or even two other risk factors into a killer. But regardless of how many other risk factors are present in a youth's life, playing a lot of violent games is likely to increase the frequency and the seriousness of his or her physical aggression, both in the short term and over time as the youth grows up.

5. Are some social groups more susceptible to the negative effects of violent video games than others? Are some groups immune to these effects?

There is some research suggesting that individuals who are already fairly aggressive may be more affected by consumption of violent video games, but it is not yet conclusive. Similarly, video game effects occasionally appear to be larger for males than females, but such findings are rare. Most studies find that males and females are equally affected, and that high and low aggressive individuals are equally affected. One additional point is worth remembering: Scientists have not been able to find any group of people who consistently appear immune to the negative effects of media violence or video game violence.

6. How important is the distinction between realistic violence versus fantasy violence?

This is an extremely important question because it is so frequently misunderstood. Many people, including psychiatrists and psychologists, tend to think: "Well, it is just a game, this boy (girl) is able to understand the difference between it and reality. Let us not worry about it." *One of the great myths surrounding media violence is this notion that if the individual can distinguish between media violence and reality, then it can't have an adverse effect on that individual.* Of course, the conclusion does not logically follow from the premise. And in fact, most of the studies that have demonstrated a causal link between exposure to media violence and subsequent aggressive behavior have been done with individuals who were fully aware that the observed media violence was not reality. For instance, many studies have used young adult participants who knew that the TV show, the movie clip, or the video game to which they were exposed was not "real." These studies still yielded the typical media violence effect on subsequent aggressive behavior.

7. Aren't there studies of violent video games that have found no significant effects on aggression?

Yes, such studies do exist. *In any field of science, some studies will produce effects that differ from what most studies of that type find.* If this weren't true, then one would need to perform only one study on a particular issue and we would have the "true" answer. Unfortunately, science is not that simple.

As an example, consider the hypothesis that a particular coin is "fair," by which I mean that upon tossing it in the air it is equally likely to come up "heads" as "tails." To test this hypothesis, you toss it 4 times, and it comes up heads 3 times (75% heads). I toss it 4 times and get 2 heads (50%). My two graduate students toss it 4 times each, getting 4 tails and 2 heads (0% heads, 50% heads, respectively). Is the coin fair? Why have different people gotten different results? Well, part of the problem is that each of us has conducted a "study" with a sample size that is much too small to produce consistent results. We each should have tossed the coin at least 100 times. Had we done so, each of us would have had about 50% heads (if the coin was truly a "fair" coin). But we still wouldn't have gotten the exact same results. Chance plays some role in the outcome of any experiment. So even if all the conditions of the test are exactly the same, the results will differ to some extent. Of course, in the real world of science, the situation is much more complex. Each study differs somewhat from every other study, usually in several ways.

Given that scientific studies of the same question will yield somewhat different results, purely on the basis of chance, how should we go about summarizing the results of a set of studies? One way is to look at the average outcome across studies. This is essentially what a meta-analysis does. And when one does a meta-analysis on the video game violence research literature, the clear conclusion is that the results are quite consistent. On average there is a clear effect: exposure to violent video games increases subsequent aggression. This has been found for each of the three major research designs (experimental, cross-sectional, and longitudinal), for youth and for young adults, and for youth in North American, Japan, and Western Europe.

Some of the few contradictory studies can be explained as being the result of poor methods. For example, one frequently cited study that failed to find a video game effect did not actually measure aggressive behavior; instead, it measured arguments with a friend or spouse. That same study also failed to show that participants in the "high video game violence" condition actually played more violent games than participants in the "low video game violence" condition. In fact, when you separate studies into those that were well conducted versus those that had major flaws, you find that the well conducted studies found bigger average effects of violent video games on aggression than did the poorly conducted studies. Some well-conducted and some poorly-conducted studies suffer from a too small sample size. But the main point is that even well con- ducted studies with appropriate sample sizes will not yield identical results. For this reason, any general statements about a research domain must focus on the pooled results, not on individual studies.

8. But what about the claims made by the media industries and by some other media violence experts, who say that the existing research evidence shows no effects of violent media?

The various entertainment media industries have lots of money to spend on trying to convince the general public and political leaders that there is noth- ing to worry about. And they do spend large sums on this. Unlike the research community, which has no vested interest in the topic, *the media industry is very concerned about profits* and will do almost anything to protect those profits. A recent book by James Steyer titled "The Other Parent: The Inside Story of the Media's Effect on Our Children," reveals much about how this works in the U.S. I suspect that most people would be shocked by many of the revelations contained in this book. I personally have witnessed media industry lobbyists lie about a factual issue, watched them get caught in that lie, and then seen the same lobbyist deliver the same lie to a different group a year later. So, one must distinguish between real vs. industry supported experts.

9. But haven't other media violence experts also claimed that there is no valid scientific evidence linking media violence to aggression?

Yes, and no. The media industries seek out, promote, and support "experts" who will make such claims. There are several such "experts" who have made their careers by bashing legitimate research. Examining their credentials is quite revealing. Many do not have any research training in an appropri- ate discipline. Of those who do have advanced degrees in an appropriate discipline (for example, social psychology), almost none of them have ever conducted and published original media violence research in a top-quality peer-reviewed scientific journal. That is, they have never designed, carried out, and published a study in which they gathered new data to test scien- tific hypotheses about potential media violence effects. In other words, they are not truly experts on media violence research. Again, to get at the truth, one must distinguish between actual vs. self-proclaimed (and often industry-backed) experts.

10. Are there any evaluations of the media violence research literature done by groups who have the appropriate expertise but who are not themselves media violence researchers?

Interestingly, a number of professional organizations have asked their own experts to evaluate the media violence research literature. One of the most recent products of such an evaluation was a "Joint Statement on the Impact of Entertainment Violence on Children," issued by six medical and public health professional organizations at a Congressional Public Health Summit on July 26, 2000. This statement noted that ". . . entertainment violence can lead to increases in aggressive attitudes, values, and behavior, particularly in children." The statement also noted that the research points ". . . overwhelmingly to a causal connection between media violence and aggressive behavior in some children." The six signatory organizations were: American Academy of Pediatrics, American Academy of Child & Adolescent Psychiatry, American Medical Association, American Psychological Association, American Academy of Family Physicians, and the American Psychiatric Association. Along the same line, several reports by the U.S. Surgeon General have concluded that exposure to media violence is a significant risk factor for later aggression and violence. Both the American Academy of Pediatrics and the American Psychological Association have specifically addressed the violent video game issue; both concluded that playing violent video games is a causal risk factor for later aggression against others, and called for a reduction in exposure of youth to this risk factor.

11. The claim has been made that in terms of the general public's beliefs about media violence effects, we are currently in a situation that is very similar to where the public was some 30 years ago in the tobacco/lung cancer issue. In what ways are these two cases similar? Dissimilar?

The medical research community knew that cigarette smoking causes lung cancer long before the general public came to hold such beliefs. In fact, there are still sizable numbers of smokers who don't really believe this to be true. The tobacco industry was quite effective keeping the public confused regarding the true causal effect of tobacco on lung cancer. Among other tactics, they promoted "experts" who claimed that the research was badly done, or was inconsistent, or was largely irrelevant to lung cancer in humans. The media industries have been doing much the same thing, seeking out, promoting, and supporting "experts" willing to bash media violence research.

The tobacco industry successfully defended itself against lawsuits for many years. There have been several lawsuits filed in the U.S. against various video game companies in recent years. As far as I know, none have been successful yet. One big difference between the tobacco industry case and the violent media case is that the main sources of information to the public (e.g., TV news shows, newspapers, magazines) are now largely owned by conglomerates that have a vested interest in denying the validity of any research suggesting that there might be harmful effects of repeated exposure to media violence.

The tobacco industry certainly had some influence on the media, because of their advertising revenues, but the violent media industries are essentially a part of the same companies that own and control the news media. Thus, it is likely to be much more difficult for the general public to get an accurate portrayal of the scientific state of knowledge about media violence effects than it was to get an accurate portrayal of the tobacco/lung cancer state of scientific knowledge. Given that it took 30-some years for the public to learn and accept the tobacco/lung cancer findings, it seems unlikely that we'll see a major shift in the public's understanding of media violence effects. Indeed, a study that my colleague Brad Bushman and I published in 2001 suggests that the media violence/aggression link was firmly established scientifically by 1975, and that news reports on this research have gotten less accurate over time. Another big difference is in the proportion of people who were hooked on these risk factors as children. The vast majority of youth repeatedly consume violent media, well before they turn 18; this was never true of tobacco products. This is important in part because of the "third person effect," a psychological phenomenon in which people tend to **think** that they personally are immune to risk factors that can affect others.

12. The U.S. Senate invited you to deliver an expert's opinion on violent video games in March, 2000. Has anything changed in the video game research literature since then?

Yes, since that time a large number of new video game studies have been published. One of the most important developments is that now there have been several major longitudinal studies of violent video game effects on youth. In such studies, the research gathers information about a child's video game habits and their typical level of aggressiveness at two separate points in time. The two time points may be separated by months or years. Sophisticated statistical techniques are used to answer a simple question: Do those who played lots of violent video games at the first measurement time show larger increases in aggression over time than those who played few violent video games? Such longitudinal studies from North America, Europe, and Japan have all found the same answer: Yes.

In addition, my colleagues and I have done several meta-analyses of all of the video game studies. It is even clearer today than it was at that earlier date that violent video games should be of concern to the general public. That is, even stronger statements can now be made on the basis of the scientific literature.

13. What is your advice concerning public policy towards violent entertainment media, particularly violent video games violence managing?

My colleagues and I try very hard to restrict our role in public policy debate to that of an expert media violence researcher. After all, that's what our training is in, and what we have devoted our careers to doing. So, when the U.S. Senate (or anyone else) asks what the current scientific research literature shows, I tell them as plainly and clearly as possible. There is a "correct" answer to such a question, and I do my best to convey that answer. When asked what society should do about it, well, that's a political question that should (in my view) be publicly debated. There is no single "correct" answer to this public policy question because a host of personal values are relevant to the debate, in addition to the relevant scientific facts. In addition, there are legal issues that differ for different countries.

Nonetheless, I am willing to give a vague answer to the public policy question. Given the scientific evidence that exposure to media violence (and video game violence) increases aggression in both the short-term and the long-term, and given my belief that the level of aggression in modern society could and should be reduced, I believe that we need to reduce the exposure of youth to media violence. My preference for action is to somehow convince parents to do a better job of screening inappropriate materials from their children. It is not always an easy task for parents—in part because of poor ratings systems— and perhaps there are appropriate steps that legislative bodies as well as the media industries could take to make it easier for parents to control their children's media diet. But of course, as long as the media industries persist in denying the scientific facts and persist in keeping the general public confused about those facts, many parents won't see a need to screen some violent materials from their children. Ironically, the industry's success in keeping parents confused and in making parental control difficult is precisely what makes many citizens and legislators willing to consider legislation designed to reign in what they perceive to be an industry totally lacking in ethical values. . . .

14. Does violence sell?

Clearly, violence does sell, at least in the video game market. But it is not clear whether the dominance of violent video games is due to an inherent desire for such games, or whether this is merely the result of the fact that most marketing dollars are spent on promoting violent games instead of nonviolent ones. One great irony in all of this is the industry belief that violence is necessary in their product in order to make a profit. One result of that belief is that most of marketing efforts go into marketing violence. In fact, the media has seemingly convinced many people in the U.S. that they like only violent media products. But nonviolent and low violent products can be exciting, fun, and sell well. *Myst* is a good example of an early nonviolent video game that sold extremely well for quite some time. More recent examples include *The Sims,* many sports and racing games, and many simulation games. Interestingly, in some of our studies college students have to play nonviolent video games. Some of the these students report that they have never played nonviolent games, and are surprised to learn that they like some of the nonviolent ones as much as their violent games.

Even more intriguing is recent research on the psychological motivations that underlie judgments about which games are the most fun and worthy of repeat business. Scholars at the University of Rochester conducted six studies on game players' ratings of game enjoyment, value, and desire for future play. They found that games that give the player a lot of autonomy (lots of choices within the game) and feelings of competence (for example, success in overcoming difficulties with practice) were rated much more positively than games without these characteristics, regardless of whether or not the games included violence. In other words, violent games are so popular mainly because such games tend to satisfy both autonomy needs and competence needs, not because they contain violence.

15. So are video games basically bad for youth?

No, a better summary statement is that a well-designed video game is an excellent teaching tool. But what it teaches depends upon its content. Some games teach thinking skills. Some teach math. Some teach reading, or puzzle solving, or history. Some have been designed to teach kids how to manage specific illnesses, such as diabetes, asthma, and cancer. But all games teach something, and that "something" depends on what they require the player to practice. In short, there are many nonviolent games that are fun, exciting, and challenging. Children and adolescents (and adults) like them and can learn positive things from them. Some even get you to exercise muscles other than those in your hands. *In moderation, such games are good for youth.* But parents and educators need to check the content of the games they are considering for the youth in their care. You can't simply use the game ratings, because many games rated by the industry as appropriate for children and for teens contain lots of violence. But with a bit of parental effort, and some household rules about game-playing, the youth's gaming experience can be fun and positive.

 **NO**

Reality Bytes: Eight Myths About Video Games Debunked

A large gap exists between the public's perception of video games and what the research actually shows. The following is an attempt to separate fact from fiction.

1. The Availability of Video Games Has Led to an Epidemic of Youth Violence.

According to federal crime statistics, the rate of juvenile violent crime in the United States is at a 30-year low. Researchers find that people serving time for violent crimes typically consume less media before committing their crimes than the average person in the general population. It's true that young offenders who have committed school shootings in America have also been game players. But young people in general are more likely to be gamers—90 percent of boys and 40 percent of girls play. The overwhelming majority of kids who play do NOT commit antisocial acts. According to a 2001 U.S. Surgeon General's report, the strongest risk factors for school shootings centered on mental stability and the quality of home life, not media exposure. The moral panic over violent video games is doubly harmful. It has led adult authorities to be more suspicious and hostile to many kids who already feel cut off from the system. It also misdirects energy away from eliminating the actual causes of youth violence and allows problems to continue to fester.

2. Scientific Evidence Links Violent Game Play with Youth Aggression.

Claims like this are based on the work of researchers who represent one relatively narrow school of research, "media effects." This research includes some 300 studies of media violence. But most of those studies are inconclusive and many have been criticized on methodological grounds. In these studies, media images are removed from any narrative context. Subjects are asked to engage with content that they would not normally consume and may not understand.

Finally, the laboratory context is radically different from the environments where games would normally be played. Most studies found a correlation, not a causal relationship, which means the research could simply show that aggressive people like aggressive entertainment. That's why the vague term "links" is used here. If there is a consensus emerging around this research, it is that violent video games may be one risk factor—when coupled with other more immediate, real-world influences—which can contribute to anti-social behavior. But no research has found that video games are a primary factor or that violent video game play could turn an otherwise normal person into a killer.

3. Children Are the Primary Market for Video Games.

While most American kids do play video games, the center of the video game market has shifted older as the first generation of gamers continues to play into adulthood. Already 62 percent of the console market and 66 percent of the PC market is age 18 or older. The game industry caters to adult tastes. Meanwhile, a sizable number of parents ignore game ratings because they assume that games are for kids. One quarter of children ages 11 to 16 identify an M-Rated (Mature Content) game as among their favorites. Clearly, more should be done to restrict advertising and marketing that targets young consumers with mature content, and to educate parents about the media choices they are facing. But parents need to share some of the responsibility for making decisions about what is appropriate for their children. The news on this front is not all bad. The Federal Trade Commission has found that 83 percent of game purchases for underage consumers are made by parents or by parents and children together.

4. Almost No Girls Play Computer Games.

Historically, the video game market has been predominantly male. However, the percentage of women playing games has steadily increased over the past decade. Women now slightly outnumber men playing Web-based games. Spurred by the belief that games were an important gateway into other kinds of digital literacy, efforts were made in the mid-90s to build games that appealed to girls. More recent games such as *The Sims* were huge crossover successes that attracted many women who had never played games before. Given the historic imbalance in the game market (and among people working inside the game industry), the presence of sexist stereotyping in games is hardly surprising. Yet it's also important to note that female game characters are often portrayed as powerful and independent. In his book *Killing Monsters,* Gerard Jones argues that young girls often build upon these representations of strong women warriors as a means of building up their self confidence in confronting challenges in their everyday lives.

5. Because Games Are Used to Train Soldiers to Kill, They Have the Same Impact on the Kids Who Play Them.

Former military psychologist and moral reformer David Grossman argues that because the military uses games in training (including, he claims, training soldiers to shoot and kill), the generation of young people who play such games are similarly being brutalized and conditioned to be aggressive in their everyday social interactions.

Grossman's model only works if:

- we remove training and education from a meaningful cultural context.
- we assume learners have no conscious goals and that they show no resistance to what they are being taught.
- we assume that they unwittingly apply what they learn in a fantasy environment to real world spaces.

The military uses games as part of a specific curriculum, with clearly defined goals, in a context where students actively want to learn and have a need for the information being transmitted. There are consequences for not mastering those skills. That being said, a growing body of research does suggest that games can enhance learning. In his recent book, *What Video Games Have to Teach Us about Learning and Literacy,* James Gee describes game players as active problem solvers who do not see mistakes as errors, but as opportunities for improvement. Players search for newer, better solutions to problems and challenges, he says. And they are encouraged to constantly form and test hypotheses. This research points to a fundamentally different model of how and what players learn from games.

6. Video Games Are Not a Meaningful Form of Expression.

On April 19, 2002, U.S. District Judge Stephen N. Limbaugh Sr. ruled that video games do not convey ideas and thus enjoy no constitutional protection. As evidence, Saint Louis County presented the judge with videotaped excerpts from four games, all within a narrow range of genres, and all the subject of previous controversy. Overturning a similar decision in Indianapolis, federal Court of Appeals Judge Richard Posner noted: "Violence has always been and remains a central interest of humankind and a recurrent, even obsessive theme of culture both high and low. It engages the interest of children from an early age, as anyone familiar with the classic fairy tales collected by Grimm, Andersen, and Perrault are aware." Posner adds, "To shield children right up to the age of 18 from exposure to violent descriptions and images would not only be quixotic, but deforming; it would leave them unequipped to cope with the world as we know it." Many early games were little more than shooting galleries where players were encouraged to blast everything that moved. Many current games are designed to be ethical testing grounds. They allow players to navigate an expansive and open-ended world, make their own choices and witness their consequences. *The Sims* designer Will Wright argues that games are perhaps the only medium that allows us to experience guilt over the actions of fictional characters. In a movie, one can always pull back and condemn the character or the artist when they cross certain social boundaries. But in playing a game, we choose what happens to the characters. In the right circumstances, we can be encouraged to examine our own values by seeing how we behave within virtual space.

7. Video Game Play Is Socially Isolating.

Much video game play is social. Almost 60 percent of frequent gamers play with friends. Thirty-three percent play with siblings and 25 percent play with spouses or parents. Even games designed for single players are often played socially, with one person giving advice to another holding a joystick. A growing number of games are designed for multiple players—for either cooperative play in the same space or online play with distributed players. Sociologist Talmadge Wright has logged many hours observing online communities interact with and react to violent video games, concluding that meta-gaming (conversation about game content) provides a context for thinking about rules and rule-breaking. In this way there are really two games taking place simultaneously: one, the explicit conflict and combat on the screen; the other, the implicit cooperation and comradeship between the players. Two players may be fighting to death on screen and growing closer as friends off screen. Social expectations are reaffirmed through the social contract governing play, even as they are symbolically cast aside within the transgressive fantasies represented onscreen.

8. Video Game Play Is Desensitizing.

Classic studies of play behavior among primates suggest that apes make basic distinctions between play fighting and actual combat. In some circumstances, they seem to take pleasure wrestling and tousling with each other. In others, they might rip each other apart in mortal combat. Game designer and play theorist Eric Zimmerman describes the ways we understand play as distinctive from reality as entering the "magic circle." The same action—say, sweeping a floor—may take on different meanings in play (as in playing house) than in reality (housework). Play allows kids to express feelings and impulses that have to be carefully held in check in their real-world interactions. Media reformers argue that playing violent video games can cause a lack of empathy for real-world victims. Yet, a child who responds to a video game the same way he or she responds to a real-world tragedy could be showing symptoms of being severely emotionally disturbed. Here's where the media effects research, which often uses punching rubber dolls as a marker of real-world aggression, becomes problematic. The kid who is punching a toy designed for this purpose is still within the "magic circle" of play and understands her actions on those terms. Such research shows us only that violent play leads to more violent play.

EXPLORING THE ISSUE

Do Video Games Encourage Violent Behavior?

Critical Thinking and Reflection

1. How are the effects of video games suggested in the YES and NO selections different from one another? Do they share any similarities?
2. How can the virtual world influence behaviors and thoughts in the real world? Do games shape values? Are video games different from other types of media content?
3. What are some of the assumptions that underlie social science research? How do they differ from the assumptions that underlie the cultural approach of Jenkins?
4. As a future parent, what rules would you set regarding your teens' use of violent video games?
5. Currently video games are rated. What, if any, other public policy regulations would be appropriate?

Is There Common Ground?

Anderson argues for negative effects on individuals. Jenkins points to a lack of change in the social order due to video games. Can both be true? Dr. Anderson et al. in a 2003 study says "The 14-year-old boy arguing that he has played violent video games for years and has not ever killed anybody is absolutely correct in rejecting the extreme 'necessary and sufficient' position, as is the 45-year-old two-pack-a-day cigarette smoker who notes that he still does not have lung cancer. But both are wrong in inferring that their exposure to their respective risk factors (violent media, cigarettes) has not causally increased the likelihood that they and people around them will one day suffer the consequences of that risky behavior." Perhaps it is in rejecting the extremes of both sides that common ground will be found.

Dramatic anecdotes abound concerning the violent consequences of video games. Yet history shows that moral panics abate as new media or other social changes emerge in the social world and become the target of public concern. Perhaps time gives context and perspective; perhaps it just diverts attention. But issues of importance, such as the impact of media on behavior should not be forgotten.

Additional Resources

Craig A. Anderson, Douglas A. Gentile, and Katherine E. Buckley, *Violent Video Game Effects on Children and Adolescents: Theory, Research, and Public Policy* (Oxford University Press, 2007)

> An edited volume that offers additional studies of violent video game effects. Studies test theories to explain these consequences and then consider public policy.

Peter Vorderer and Jennings Bryant (eds). *Playing Video Games: Motives, Responses, and Consequences* (Wiley, 2006)

> This volume offers a multidisciplinary approach to the media psychology of video games.

Bernard Perron and Mark J. P. Wolf (eds). *The Video Game Theory Reader 2* (Routledge, 2008)

> These articles address the many ways in which video games are shaping entertainment with a focus on the theories that may help us to understand their importance.

Thomas A. Hemphill. "The Entertainment Industry, Marketing Practices, and Violent Content: Who's Minding the Children?" *Business and Society Review* (vol. 108, pp. 263–277, 2003)

> Hemphill examines the way the entertainment industry targets young audiences.

Kaveri Subrahmanyam and Patricia Greenfield, "Digital Media and Youth: Games, Internet and Development," in Singer and Singer (eds), *Handbook of Children and the Media* (Sage, 2011).

> The Handbook offers extensive coverage of a variety of issues concerning children. Subrahmanyam and Greenfield offer a balanced review of existing issues concerning video games.

ISSUE 6

Is Advertising Good for Society?

YES: John E. Calfee, from "How Advertising Informs to Our Benefit," *Consumers' Research* (April 1998)

NO: Dinyar Godrej, from "How the Ad Industry Pins Us Down," *New Internationalist* (September 2006)

Learning Outcomes

After reading this issue, you should be able to:

- Become more aware of the positive and negative aspects of advertising.
- Develop a critical framework for evaluating ads, and consider whether they help inform a consumer, or raise unreasonable expectations about what consumption can do to, and for you.
- Analyze ads more easily and consider how they function in our media environment.
- Raise the question about emotional media content; and understand the various techniques of advertising, and how they appeal to our emotions.

ISSUE SUMMARY

YES: John Calfee takes the position that advertising is very useful to people and that the information that advertising imparts helps consumers make better decisions. He maintains that the benefits of advertising far outweigh the negative criticisms.

NO: Dinyar Godrej makes the claim that advertising doesn't really tell us anything new about products, but instead, it acts upon our emotions to create anxiety if we don't buy products. The result, then, is a culture in which we consume more than we need to, and still feel bad about ourselves. This type of consumer culture then permeates our lifestyles.

Professor Dallas Smythe first described commercial media as a system for delivering audiences to advertisers. This perception of the viewing public as a "market" for products as well as an audience for advertising—a main source of media revenue—reflects the economic orientation of the current media system in America. The unplanned side effects of advertising, however, concern many critics. The creation of a consumer society, materialism, and high expectations are one set of concerns, but these issues also conflict with many cultural expectations, histories, and social systems in many countries where advertising is considered a Western, capitalist construct.

John Calfee addresses many of these issues but also focuses on how the information in ads benefits consumers. He takes the position that advertising functions in the public's interest, and that even the controversies about ads can be beneficial because they can result in competitive pricing for consumers. Citing some specific cases, he states that individuals can learn about important issues (such as health) through ads. He even considers what he calls "less bad" ads, which give consumers important negative information that can be useful to their well-being.

In the NO selection, Dinyar Godrej takes the perspective that advertising creates an assault on our senses, that advertising can act as a "compulsive liar," and that the clutter that advertising creates bombards us with images and ideas that result in a subtle cultural shift that creates desires that only the wealthy can actually attain. This author takes the point of view that there is really nothing positive that advertising contributes to a society, and that just about everything about advertising is negative.

These views illustrate the extreme polarities in positions that people often take when it comes to the topic of advertising. There are also other, more neutral views, such as those held by people who don't mind advertising, and see it as an economic engine to deliver "free" programs to people, or the idea that advertising is an art form in itself, that, if viewed critically, can make a social comment on the styles, consumer culture, and artifacts of different social groups. Yet others focus on the creative aspects of advertising and revere the way it can stimulate, motivate, or resonate with viewers. Whatever the perspective, one thing is true: Advertising can have both manifest and latent impact. It can be defended on solid ground and criticized on solid ground.

Many students today don't seem to mind advertising. A typical comment is that they just don't let the messages "get" to them, but it is important to think about one's own critical faculties and those of others. Do you think of advertising as one of today's most persuasive forms of communication or just a by-product of something else? It might be interesting to try to think about how a person's environment would be different if there were no ads.

A thorough understanding of how advertising functions in society, and as an industry that is responsible for billions of dollars annually, helps form a person's views on the impact of advertising in their lives, and in the lives of others. It also helps to think about what products are advertised and to whom: Should tobacco and alcohol ads be targeted to children and teens? Do advertising costs actually raise the price of goods, rather than stimulate the circulation of goods in society? Is advertising the engine that runs a consumer society, or does capitalism create industries, like advertising, to continue to support its operation within a society? Furthermore, as Godrej points out, what impact does advertising (particularly from Western societies) have on traditional cultures?

It should also be noted that there are many forms of advertising. We often first think of product advertising, but what of corporate sponsorship or indirect advertising through product placement (referred to in the industry as "product enhancement")? Dinyar Godrej does an excellent job of reminding us that there are many subtle styles of influence that go beyond the initial knee-jerk reaction to advertising as a harmless by-product of industry in the twenty-first century.

Since the development of the advertising industry, the question of advertising ethics has periodically resurfaced. Advertising was once considered a way to keep the cost of newspapers down, to help deliver "free" TV and radio to the public, and to help consumers understand what issues were important in society. Many defenses of advertising relied on helping consumers make more informed decisions about how to spend their money. But over the years, the real impact of advertising has been more critically considered. Today, issues of corporate power, mind-control, deceptive advertising, and cultivating desires in children and people who can't afford to buy products are considered to be more pressing social problems.

The ad industry has responded to criticism in many ways. Traditional defenses of tobacco and alcohol advertising have resulted in the creation of industry-supported projects to "prevent" misuse, but the purpose of these projects must also be carefully considered. Do industries attempt to fight regulation by doing "something" about a problem—like establishing programs to prevent underage drinking, or placing warning labels on cigarettes—or do they exercise "good neighbor" practices because they feel that they have a moral obligation to do so? In most cases, the real reason is that the industries would prefer to demonstrate that they can police their own industries, rather than accept regulation from outside.

Since the growth of technologies that are more individually used, like the Internet, the advertising industry has responded with a far more complicated structure to attract attention, and a far more complicated system of appealing to audiences they consider are most easily persuaded. Use of pop-up ads, banners, and promises of easy consumption permeate Internet sites. Advertisers don't seem to mind spam, or links that lead to new products or services, or cookies that unobtrusively collect consumer data about computer users. Digital video recorders have the technological capability of screening out commercials, but advertisers have created ways to insert ads into programs so that the eye catches them, even if the conscious brain does not. Even some television programming has become a substitute for ads, when products used in shows like *Extreme Make-Over* and *Queer Eye for the Straight Guy* are mentioned and highlighted.

Finally, the impact of advertising to children has long been a topic for concern. You might say it is one thing to advertise to an adult who is expected to have developed a critical eye, and who should be responsible for their actions, but children have not yet developed enough of a world view to put advertising into perspective.

The Disney Corporation, for example, has made a concerted effort to glorify Disney products and cultivate consumers for life. Young children today are barraged with Disney videos, products, clothing, and other ideas—including the notion that every little girl should be a "princess." Before the Disney Corporation realized that it would pay to develop life-long consumers, the idea of being a "princess" was something that, though not unheard of, was much less obvious in our culture. Similarly, occasional re-releases of Disney visual products (new and remastered!) give the impression that today's child grows up with Disney images, characters, values, and most of all, products.

Parents' groups have been attempting to curb the amount of advertising geared to children for decades. One of the first activist groups, Action for Children's Television (ACT), founded in 1968, effectively lobbied the FCC to mandate a clear separation of program content from commercials for children's television programming. Other attempts have included adding nutritional information to food advertising for kids, and pro-social messages. If children learn a good deal about what is appropriate in the world from media content, doesn't it stand to reason that adults might make some of the same decisions, or expeience a "suggestability" for advertising too?

Finally, it should be acknowledged that most of our media industries use advertising to help them make a profit. Without a profit, they won't survive—but what other models might be there, other than advertising?

In some cases, the amount of advertising is kept to a minimum so the user might not be as aware of the presence of this type of financial underwriting. An online service, like Pandora, for example, plays music, but bunches ads together in a short time frame. Rather than punctuating the music content, as is done on radio or TV, some of the online services can still use advertising support without capitulating to earlier time frames or program formats. Could other models of supporting media content be found? The Corporation for Public Broadcasting relies on corporate sponsorship and individual donors but does not break up many programs with announcements of these sponsors. Subscriptions are another way of financing a media system, but this too has its drawbacks.

Advertising is likely to continue to be a mainstay of financial support for media content, but it will be interesting to see how new advertising applications (like banner ads, contextual ads, and advergames) on the Internet change traditional financial support. Similarly, what we consider "free" content on the Internet is really not so free when you start noticing the amount of advertising to which you are subjected.

Are you one of the people who says ads don't bother them? Why not consider the perspectives in this issue and begin to become a more critical media consumer of programs and ads.

YES

John E. Calfee

How Advertising Informs
to Our Benefit

A great truth about advertising is that it is a tool for communicating information and shaping markets. It is one of the forces that compel sellers to cater to the desires of consumers. Almost everyone knows this because consumers use advertising every day, and they miss advertising when they cannot get it. This fact does not keep politicians and opinion leaders from routinely dismissing the value of advertising. But the truth is that people find advertising very useful indeed.

Of course, advertising primarily seeks to persuade and everyone knows this, too. The typical ad tries to induce a consumer to do one particular thing—usually, buy a product—instead of a thousand other things. There is nothing obscure about this purpose or what it means for buyers. Decades of data and centuries of intuition reveal that all consumers everywhere are deeply suspicious of what advertisers say and why they say it. This skepticism is in fact the driving force that makes advertising so effective. The persuasive purpose of advertising and the skepticism with which it is met are two sides of a single process. Persuasion and skepticism work in tandem so advertising can do its job in competitive markets. Hence, ads represent the seller's self interest, consumers know this, and sellers know that consumers know it.

By understanding this process more fully, we can sort out much of the popular confusion surrounding advertising and how it benefits consumers.

How useful is advertising?   Just how useful is the connection between advertising and information? At first blush, the process sounds rather limited. Volvo ads tell consumers that Volvos have side-impact air bags, people learn a little about the importance of air bags, and Volvo sells a few more cars. This seems to help hardly anyone except Volvo and its customers.

But advertising does much more. It routinely provides immense amounts of information that benefits primarily parties other than the advertiser. This may sound odd, but it is a logical result of market forces and the nature of information itself.

The ability to use information to sell products is an incentive to create new information through research. Whether the topic is nutrition, safety, or more mundane matters like how to measure amplifier power, the necessity of achieving credibility with consumers and critics requires much of this research to be placed in the public domain, and that it rest upon some academic credentials. That kind of research typically produces results that apply to more than just the brands sold by the firm sponsoring the research. The lack of property rights to such "pure" information ensures that this extra information is available at no charge. Both consumers and competitors may borrow the new information for their own purposes.

Advertising also elicits additional information from other sources. Claims that are striking, original, forceful or even merely obnoxious will generate news stories about the claims, the controversies they cause, the reactions of competitors (A price war? A splurge of comparison ads?), the reactions of consumers and the remarks of governments and independent authorities.

Probably the most concrete, pervasive, and persistent example of competitive advertising that works for the public good is price advertising. Its effect is invariably to heighten competition and reduce prices, even the prices of firms that assiduously avoid mentioning prices in their own advertising.

There is another area where the public benefits of advertising are less obvious but equally important. The unremitting nature of consumer interest in health, and the eagerness of sellers to cater to consumer desires, guarantee that advertising related to health will provide a storehouse of telling observations on the ways in which the benefits of advertising extend beyond the interests of advertisers to include the interests of the public at large.

A cascade of information   Here is probably the best documented example of why advertising is necessary for consumer welfare. In the 1970s, public health experts described compelling evidence that people who eat more fiber are less likely to get cancer, especially cancer of the colon, which happens to be the second leading cause of deaths from cancer in the United States. By 1979, the U.S. Surgeon General was recommending that people eat more fiber in order to prevent cancer.

Consumers appeared to take little notice of these recommendations, however. The National Cancer Institute decided that more action was needed. NCI's cancer prevention division undertook to communicate the new information about fiber and cancer to the general public. Their goal was to change consumer diets and reduce the risk of cancer, but they had little hope of success given the tiny advertising budgets of federal agencies like NCI.

Their prospects unexpectedly brightened in 1984. NCI received a call from the Kellogg Corporation, whose All-Bran cereal held a commanding market share of the high-fiber segment. Kellogg proposed to use All-Bran advertising as a vehicle for NCI's public service messages. NCI thought that was an excellent idea. Soon, an agreement was reached in which NCI would review Kellogg's ads and labels for accuracy and value before Kellogg began running their fiber-cancer ads.

The new Kellogg All-Bran campaign opened in October 1984. A typical ad began with the headline, "At last some news about cancer you can live with." The ad continued: "The National Cancer Institute believes a high fiber, low fat diet may reduce your risk of some kinds of cancer. The National Cancer

Institute reports some very good health news. There is growing evidence that may link a high fiber, low fat diet to lower incidence of some kinds of cancer. That's why one of their strongest recommendations is to eat high-fiber foods. If you compare, you'll find Kellogg's All-Bran has nine grams of fiber per serving. No other cereal has more. So start your day with a bowl of Kellogg's All-Bran or mix it with your regular cereal."

The campaign quickly achieved two things. One was to create a regulatory crisis between two agencies. The Food and Drug Administration thought that if a food was advertised as a way to prevent cancer, it was being marketed as a drug. Then the FDA's regulations for drug labeling would kick in. The food would be reclassified as a drug and would be removed from the market until the seller either stopped making the health claims or put the product through the clinical testing necessary to obtain formal approval as a drug.

But food advertising is regulated by the Federal Trade Commission, not the FDA. The FTC thought Kellogg's ads were non-deceptive and were therefore perfectly legal. In fact, it thought the ads should be encouraged. The Director of the FTC's Bureau of Consumer Protection declared that "the [Kellogg] ad has presented important public health recommendations in an accurate, useful, and substantiated way. It informs the members of the public that there is a body of data suggesting certain relationships between cancer and diet that they may find important." The FTC won this political battle, and the ads continued.

The second instant effect of the All-Bran campaign was to unleash a flood of health claims. Vegetable oil manufacturers advertised that cholesterol was associated with coronary heart disease, and that vegetable oil does not contain cholesterol. Margarine ads did the same, and added that vitamin A is essential for good vision. Ads for calcium products (such as certain antacids) provided vivid demonstrations of the effects of osteoporosis (which weakens bones in old age), and recounted the advice of experts to increase dietary calcium as a way to prevent osteoporosis. Kellogg's competitors joined in citing the National Cancer Institute dietary recommendations.

Nor did things stop there. In the face of consumer demand for better and fuller information, health claims quickly evolved from a blunt tool to a surprisingly refined mechanism. Cereals were advertised as high in fiber and low in sugar or fat or sodium. Ads for an upscale brand of bread noted: "Well, most high-fiber bran cereals may be high in fiber, but often only one kind: insoluble. It's this kind of fiber that helps promote regularity. But there's also a kind of fiber known as soluble, which most high-fiber bran cereals have in very small amounts, if at all. Yet diets high in this kind of fiber may actually lower your serum cholesterol, a risk factor for some heart diseases." Cereal boxes became convenient sources for a summary of what made for a good diet.

Increased independent information   The ads also brought powerful secondary effects. These may have been even more useful than the information that actually appeared in the ads themselves.

One effect was an increase in media coverage of diet and health. *Consumer Reports*, a venerable and hugely influential magazine that carries no advertising, revamped its reports on cereals to emphasize fiber and other ingredients (rather than testing the foods to see how well they did at providing a complete diet for laboratory rats). The health-claims phenomenon generated its own press coverage, with articles like "What Has All-Bran Wrought?" and "The Fiber Furor." These stories recounted the ads and scientific information that prompted the ads; and articles on food and health proliferated. Anyone who lived through these years in the United States can probably remember the unending media attention to health claims and to diet and health generally.

Much of the information on diet and health was new. This was no coincidence. Firms were sponsoring research on their products in the hope of finding results that could provide a basis for persuasive advertising claims. Oat bran manufacturers, for example, funded research on the impact of soluble fiber on blood cholesterol. When the results came out "wrong," as they did in a 1990 study published with great fanfare in *The New England Journal of Medicine*, the headline in *Advertising Age* was "Oat Bran Popularity Hitting the Skids," and it did indeed tumble. The manufacturers kept at the research, however, and eventually the best research supported the efficacy of oat bran in reducing cholesterol (even to the satisfaction of the FDA). Thus did pure advertising claims spill over to benefit the information environment at large.

The shift to higher fiber cereals encompassed brands that had never undertaken the effort necessary to construct believable ads about fiber and disease. Two consumer researchers at the FDA reviewed these data and concluded they were "consistent with the successful educational impact of the Kellogg diet and health campaign: consumers seemed to be making an apparently thoughtful discrimination between high- and low-fiber cereals," and that the increased market shares for high-fiber non-advertised products represented "the clearest evidence of a successful consumer education campaign."

Perhaps most dramatic were the changes in consumer awareness of diet and health. An FTC analysis of government surveys showed that when consumers were asked about how they could prevent cancer through their diet, the percentage who mentioned fiber increased from 4% before the 1979 Surgeon General's report to 8.5% in 1984 (after the report but before the All-Bran campaign) to 32% in 1986 after a year and a half or so of health claims (the figure in 1988 was 28%). By far the greatest increases in awareness were among women (who do most of the grocery shopping) and the less educated: up from 0% for women without a high school education in 1984 to 31% for the same group in 1986. For women with incomes of less than $15,000, the increase was from 6% to 28%.

The health-claims advertising phenomenon achieved what years of effort by government agencies had failed to achieve. With its mastery of the art of brevity, its ability to command attention, and its use of television, brand advertising touched precisely the people the public health community was most desperate to reach. The health claims expanded consumer information along a broad front. The benefits clearly extended far beyond the interests of the relatively few manufacturers who made vigorous use of health claims in advertising.

A pervasive phenomenon   Health claims for foods are only one example, however, of a pervasive phenomenon—the use of advertising to provide essential health information with benefits extending beyond the interests of the advertisers themselves.

Advertising for soap and detergents, for example, once improved private hygiene and therefore, public health (hygiene being one of the under-appreciated triumphs in twentieth century public health). Toothpaste advertising helped to do the same for teeth. When mass advertising for toothpaste and tooth powder began early in this century, tooth brushing was rare. It was common by the 1930s, after which toothpaste sales leveled off even though the advertising, of course, continued. When fluoride toothpastes became available, advertising generated interest in better teeth and professional dental care. Later, a "plaque reduction war" (which first involved mouthwashes, and later toothpastes) brought a new awareness of gum disease and how to prevent it. The financial gains to the toothpaste industry were surely dwarfed by the benefits to consumers in the form of fewer cavities and fewer lost teeth.

Health claims induced changes in foods, in non-foods such as toothpaste, in publications ranging from university health letters to mainstream newspapers and magazines, and of course, consumer knowledge of diet and health.

These rippling effects from health claims in ads demonstrated the most basic propositions in the economics of information. Useful information initially failed to reach people who needed it because information producers could not charge a price to cover the costs of creating and disseminating pure information. And this problem was alleviated by advertising, sometimes in a most vivid manner.

Other examples of spillover benefits from advertising are far more common than most people realize. Even the much-maligned promotion of expensive new drugs can bring profound health benefits to patients and families, far exceeding what is actually charged for the products themselves.

The market processes that produce these benefits bear all the classic features of competitive advertising. We are not analyzing public service announcements here, but old-fashioned profit-seeking brand advertising. Sellers focused on the information that favored their own products. They advertised it in ways that provided a close link with their own brand. It was a purely competitive enterprise, and the benefits to consumers arose from the imperatives of the competitive process.

One might see all this as simply an extended example of the economics of information and greed. And indeed it is, if by greed one means the effort to earn a profit by providing what people are willing to pay for, even if what they want most is information rather than a tangible product. The point is that there is overwhelming evidence that unregulated economic forces dictate that much useful information will be provided by brand advertising, and *only* by brand advertising.

Of course, there is much more to the story. There is the question of how competition does the good I have described without doing even more harm elsewhere. After all, firms want to tell people only what is good about their brands, and people often want to know what is wrong with the brands. It turns out that competition takes care of this problem, too.

Advertising and context   It is often said that most advertising does not contain very much information. In a way, this is true. Research on the contents of advertising typically finds just a few pieces of concrete information per ad. That's an average, of course. Some ads obviously contain a great deal of information. Still, a lot of ads are mainly images and pleasant talk, with little in the way of what most people would consider hard information. On the whole, information in advertising comes in tiny bits and pieces.

Cost is only one reason. To be sure, cramming more information into ads is expensive. But more to the point is the fact that advertising plays off the information available from outside sources. Hardly anything about advertising is more important than the interplay between what the ad contains and what surrounds it. Sometimes this interplay is a burden for the advertiser because it is beyond his control. But the interchange between advertising and environment is also an invaluable tool for sellers. Ads that work in collaboration with outside information can communicate far more than they ever could on their own.

The upshot is advertising's astonishing ability to communicate a great deal of information in a few words. Economy and vividness of expression almost always rely upon what is in the information environment. The famously concise "Think Small" and "Lemon" ads for the VW "Beetle" in the 1960s and 1970s were highly effective with buyers concerned about fuel economy, repair costs, and extravagant styling in American cars. This was a case where the less said, the better. The ads were more powerful when consumers were free to bring their own ideas about the issues to bear.

The same process is repeated over again for all sorts of products. Ads for computer modems once explained what they could be used for. Now a simple reference to the Internet is sufficient to conjure an elaborate mix of equipment and applications. These matters are better left vague so each potential customer can bring to the ad his own idea of what the Internet is really for.

Leaning on information from other sources is also a way to enhance credibility, without which advertising must fail. Much of the most important information in advertising—think of cholesterol and heart disease, antilock brakes and automobile safety—acquires its force from highly credible sources *other* than the advertiser. To build up this kind of credibility through material actually contained in ads would be cumbersome and inefficient. Far more effective, and far more economical, is the technique of making challenges, raising questions and otherwise making it perfectly clear to the audience that the seller invites comparisons and welcomes the tough questions. Hence the classic slogan, "If you can find a better whisky, buy it."

Finally, there is the most important point of all. Informational sparseness facilitates competition. It is easier to challenge a competitor through pungent slogans—"Where's the beef?", "Where's the big saving?"—than through a step-by-step recapitulation of what has gone on before. The bits-and-pieces approach makes for quick, unerring attacks and equally quick responses, all under the watchful eye of the consumer over whom the battle is being fought. This is an ideal recipe for competition.

It also brings the competitive market's fabled self-correcting forces into play. Sellers are less likely to stretch the truth, whether it involves prices or subtleties about safety and performance, when they know they may arouse a merciless response from injured competitors. That is one reason the FTC once worked to get comparative ads on television, and has sought for decades to dismantle government or voluntary bans on comparative ads.

"Less-bad" advertising   There is a troubling possibility, however. Is it not possible that in their selective and carefully calculated use of outside information, advertisers have the power to focus consumer attention exclusively on the positive, i.e., on what is good about the brand or even the entire product class? Won't automobile ads talk up style, comfort, and extra safety, while food ads do taste and convenience, cigarette ads do flavor and lifestyle, and airlines do comfort and frequency of departure, all the while leaving consumers to search through other sources to find all the things that are wrong with products?

In fact, this is not at all what happens. Here is why: Everything for sale has something wrong with it, if only the fact that you have to pay for it. Some products, of course, are notable for their faults. The most obvious examples involve tobacco and health, but there are also food and heart disease, drugs and side effects, vacations and bad weather, automobiles and accidents, airlines and delay, among others.

Products and their problems bring into play one of the most important ways in which the competitive market induces sellers to serve the interests of buyers. No matter what the product, there are usually a few brands that are "less bad" than the others. The natural impulse is to advertise that advantage—"less cholesterol," "less fat," "less dangerous," and so on. Such provocative claims tend to have an immediate impact. The targets often retaliate; maybe their brands are less bad in a different respect (less salt?). The ensuing struggle brings better information, more informed choices, and improved products.

Perhaps the most riveting episode of "less-bad" advertising ever seen occurred, amazingly enough, in the industry that most people assume is the master of avoiding saying anything bad about its product.

Less-bad cigarette ads   Cigarette advertising was once very different from what it is today. Cigarettes first became popular around the time of World War I, and they came to dominate the tobacco market in the 1920s. Steady and often dramatic sales increases continued into the 1950s, always with vigorous support from advertising. Tobacco advertising was duly celebrated as an outstanding example of the power and creativity of advertising. Yet amazingly, much of the advertising focused on what was wrong with smoking, rather than what people liked about smoking.

The very first ad for the very first mass-marketed American cigarette brand (Camel, the same brand recently under attack for its use of a cartoon character) said, "Camel Cigarettes will not sting the tongue and will not parch the throat." When Old Gold broke into the market in the mid-1920s, it did so with an ad campaign about coughs and throats and harsh cigarette smoke. It settled on the slogan, "Not a cough in a carload."

Competitors responded in kind. Soon, advertising left no doubt about what was wrong with smoking. Lucky Strike ads said, "No Throat Irritation— No Cough . . . we . . . removed . . . harmful corrosive acids," and later on, "Do you inhale? What's there to be afraid of? . . . famous purifying process removes certain impurities." Camel's famous tag line, "more doctors smoke Camels than any other brand," carried a punch precisely because many authorities thought smoking was unhealthy (cigarettes were called "coffin nails" back then), and smokers were eager for reassurance in the form of smoking by doctors themselves. This particular ad, which was based on surveys of physicians, ran in one form or another from 1933 to 1955. It achieved prominence partly because physicians practically never endorsed non-therapeutic products.

Things really got interesting in the early 1950s, when the first persuasive medical reports on smoking and lung cancer reached the public. These reports created a phenomenal stir among smokers and the public generally. People who do not understand how advertising works would probably assume that cigarette manufacturers used advertising to divert attention away from the cancer reports. In fact, they did the opposite.

Small brands could not resist the temptation to use advertising to scare smokers into switching brands. They inaugurated several spectacular years of "fear advertising" that sought to gain competitive advantage by exploiting smokers' new fear of cancer. Lorillard, the beleaguered seller of Old Gold, introduced Kent, a new filter brand supported by ad claims like these: "Sensitive smokers get real health protection with new Kent," "Do you love a good smoke but not what the smoke does to you?" and "Takes out more nicotine and tars than any other leading cigarette—*the difference in protection is priceless*," illustrated by television ads showing the black tar trapped by Kent's filters.

Other manufacturers came out with their own filter brands, and raised the stakes with claims like, "Nose, throat, and accessory organs not adversely affected by smoking Chesterfields. First such report ever published about any cigarette," "Takes the fear out of smoking," and "Stop worrying . . . Philip Morris and only Philip Morris is entirely free of irritation used [sic] in all other leading cigarettes."

These ads threatened to demolish the industry. Cigarette sales plummeted by 3% in 1953 and a remarkable 6% in 1954. Never again, not even in the face of the most impassioned anti-smoking publicity by the Surgeon General or the FDA, would cigarette consumption decline as rapidly as it did during these years of entirely market-driven anti-smoking ad claims by the cigarette industry itself.

Thus advertising traveled full circle. Devised to bolster brands, it denigrated the product so much that overall market demand actually declined. Everyone understood what was happening, but the fear ads continued because they helped the brands that used them. The new filter brands (all from smaller manufacturers) gained a foothold even as their ads amplified the medical reports on the dangers of smoking. It was only after the FTC stopped the fear ads in 1955 (on the grounds that the implied health claims had no proof) that sales resumed their customary annual increases.

Fear advertising has never quite left the tobacco market despite the regulatory straight jacket that governs cigarette advertising. In 1957, when leading cancer experts advised smokers to ingest less tar, the industry responded by cutting tar and citing tar content figures compiled by independent sources. A stunning "tar derby" reduced the tar and nicotine content of cigarettes by 40% in four years, a far more rapid decline than would be achieved by years of government urging in later decades. This episode, too, was halted by the FTC. In February 1960 the FTC engineered a "voluntary" ban on tar and nicotine claims.

Further episodes continue to this day. In 1993, for example, Liggett planned an advertising campaign to emphasize that its Chesterfield brand did not use the stems and less desirable parts of the tobacco plant. This continuing saga, extending through eight decades, is perhaps the best documented case of how "less-bad" advertising completely offsets any desires by sellers to accentuate the positive while ignoring the negative. *Consumer Reports* magazine's 1955 assessment of the new fear of smoking still rings true:

> ". . . companies themselves are largely to blame. Long before the current medical attacks, the companies were building up suspicion in the consumer by the discredited 'health claims' in their ads. . . . Such medicine-show claims may have given the smoker temporary confidence in one brand, but they also implied that cigarettes in general were distasteful, probably harmful, and certainly a 'problem.' When the scientists came along with their charges against cigarettes, the smoker was ready to accept them."

And that is how information works in competitive advertising.

Less-bad can be found wherever competitive advertising is allowed. I already described the health-claims-for-foods saga, which featured fat and cholesterol and the dangers of cancer and heart disease. Price advertising is another example. Prices are the most stubbornly negative product feature of all, because they represent the simple fact that the buyer must give up something else. There is no riper target for comparative advertising. When sellers advertise lower prices, competitors reduce their prices and advertise that, and soon a price war is in the works. This process so strongly favors consumers over the industry that one of the first things competitors do when they form a trade group is to propose an agreement to restrict or ban price advertising (if not ban all advertising). When that fails, they try to get advertising regulators to stop price ads, an attempt that unfortunately often succeeds.

Someone is always trying to scare customers into switching brands out of fear of the product itself. The usual effect is to impress upon consumers what they do not like about the product. In 1991, when Americans were worried about insurance companies going broke, a few insurance firms advertised that they were more solvent than their competitors. In May 1997, United Airlines began a new ad campaign that started out by reminding fliers of all the inconveniences that seem to crop up during air travel.

Health information is a fixture in "less-bad" advertising. Ads for sleeping aids sometimes focus on the issue of whether they are habit-forming. In March 1996, a medical journal reported that the pain reliever acetaminophen, the active ingredient in Tylenol, can cause liver damage in heavy drinkers. This fact immediately became the focus of ads for Advil, a competing product. A public debate ensued, conducted through advertising, talk shows, news reports and pronouncements from medical authorities. The result: consumers learned a lot more than they had known before about the fact that all drugs have side effects. The press noted that this dispute may have helped consumers, but it hurt the pain reliever industry. Similar examples abound.

We have, then, a general rule: sellers will use comparative advertising when permitted to do so, even if it means spreading bad information about a product instead of favorable information. The mechanism usually takes the form of less-bad claims. One can hardly imagine a strategy more likely to give consumers the upper hand in the give and take of the marketplace. Less-bad claims are a primary means by which advertising serves markets and consumers rather than sellers. They completely refute the naive idea that competitive advertising will emphasize only the sellers' virtues while obscuring their problems.

 **NO**

How the Ad Industry Pins Us Down

Buddhism and Hinduism recommend it. A retreat from clamour, a wondrous detachment that allows the material world to float up, like a sloughed-off skin, for one's dispassionate consideration. Whether they offer useful advice on re-engaging after this revelation, I don't know. The first astronauts saw a floating world, too. It provoked suitably joined-up thoughts about its (and our) fragility and essential unity.

But there are other worlds. And the one that elbows itself to the front of our attention's queue painstakingly creates surface and whips up froth. It's the one that the 125 residents of Clark, Texas, signed up to in 2005 when they changed the name of their township to Dish in return for a decade's free cable TV from the DISH Network. Hey, what's in a name except a wacky corporate PR opportunity, right?

The bubbly, dazzling world of which Dish has become an emblem shows little sign of floating up for our inspection. If we inspect it nonetheless, it reveals itself to be firmly riveted down by that old culprit—disproportionate corporate power.

Advertising is a bit of a compulsive liar. In the early days it was quite barefaced—the beverage giant, Dewar's, claiming in the 1930s that their Scotch whiskey repelled colds and flu; cigarette brands claiming that they soothed the throat and helped asthma. Some of this still goes on. Quack cures are advertised in numerous Majority World countries. The half of all Mexican citizens who are overweight are pummelled daily on TV by products that promise to melt 10 centimetres off the waistline in two hours.

Repeat After Me

Nowadays, regulatory bodies will see off many of the more obviously fraudulent claims.

But advertising is involved in soul fraud instead. If that sounds a bit deep, just stay with me a while.

Advertising today has little to do with introducing a new product or describing an existing one's virtues. It has everything to do with images, dreams and emotions; stuff we are evolutionarily programmed to engage with but which is, almost without exception in the ad biz, fake. Imagine how much attention you would pay if there were just text and no images. When ads for Sprite (owned by Coca-Cola) proclaimed: 'Image is nothing, thirst is

From *New Internationalist,* September 2006, pp. 3–5. Copyright © 2006 by New Internationalist. Reprinted by permission.

everything', they were reassuring people that they were right to be distrustful, while building up images of honesty and straight talk, using professional basketball players to push the product: Sprite jumped several notches up the soft-drink rankings; moolah was minted. Image was everything, even if it was purporting to be an anti-image.

Amid the visual clutter, advertising—the chief agent of the mess—has to jump out at us. It must trigger off associations, however tangential, that will keep our attention. Endless repetition through media channels should build up a handy cloud of associations. According to one industry executive: 'In the context of most advertising, particularly passively consumed media like television and cinema, learning is incidental, not deliberate. This is why people tell you they are not influenced by advertising. They are not actively trying to take anything away from the experience, and therefore are not influenced at that time; but the effects will show up later, long after a particular viewing experience is forgotten.

Much effort is expended upon trying to sink boreholes into the vast iceberg of the subconscious mind, probably because the products being flogged are in reality just variations on the same old same old. A recent buzzword is 'neuromarketing'. Neuroscientists and psychiatrists are searching for the buy-button in the brain. This involves putting subjects into brain-scanning machinery and pitching concepts and images at them to see which ones make the lights flash. In one experiment, subjects were made to blind-taste Pepsi and Coke. Pepsi scored higher in terms of response in the ventral putamen, the part of the brain associated with feelings of reward—ie, most thought Pepsi tasted better. But when the subjects were informed which drink was Coke before they tried it, their medial prefrontal cortexes lit up. This is an area of the brain believed to control cognition. Most now said they preferred Coke. So just the name had prompted memories and brand nostalgia which influenced the taste of the stuff. One might question the validity of using expensive hospital equipment and highly trained medical professionals to explain choices of fizzy drinks with no nutritional value whatsoever—but that would be to get a bit real.

The good news is that all this dubious effort is just as likely to fail as it is to succeed. If an ad can latch on to the emotion of a winning goal in a football match or the tears and triumphs of Pop Idol, then there's a good chance it will do the trick. Much else is trial and error. Focus groups assembled to pretest the vibe are notoriously unreliable as they can be suggestible and become dominated by loudmouths.

Anxieties of Influence

One might well ask: so what? So what if silly money . . . pushes the usual goods/junk, if I can still make an informed choice about what I buy?

Well, maybe. . . . But how would you react if all this were seeping into the very pores of the culture you're part of—and changing it? Mass advertising is about brands with the most money behind them pushing to the top. Smaller companies with less of this fluff-muscle don't always survive.

More perniciously, corporate giants try every trick in the book to control our media channels. Much of the mainstream media exists to sell audiences to advertisers. Newspapers aren't profitable based on sales alone. The missing factor is ad money. It's their lifeblood. Teen magazines (especially those aimed at girls) are little more than catalogues for products—and that's the content. The profile of the chubby hero who saved a life is usually tucked away at the end.

Here's what an agency representing Coca-Cola demanded in a letter to magazines: 'We believe that positive and upbeat editorial provides a compatible environment in which to communicate the brand's message. . . . We consider the following subjects to be inappropriate and require that our ads are not placed adjacent to articles discussing the following issues: Hard News; Sex related issues; Drugs (Prescription or Illegal); Medicine (eg chronic illnesses such as cancer, diabetes, AIDS, etc); Health (eg mental or physical conditions); Negative Diet Information (eg bulimia, anorexia, quick weight loss, etc); Food; Political issues; Environmental issues; Articles containing vulgar language; Religion'. So, not much chance of a mention of the intimidation of union workers in Coke's Colombian plant, or of the charges of water pollution in India, then (read more at www.killercoke.org).

If anyone still thought they were watching 'the news' on CNN, anchor Jack Cafferty's on-air views might disabuse them: 'We are not here as a public service. We're here to make money. We sell advertising, and we do it on the premise that people are going to watch. If you don't cover the miners because you want to do a story about a debt crisis in Brazil at the time everybody else is covering the miners, then Citibank calls up and says, "You know what? We're not renewing the commercial contract." I mean, it's a business'. In the US, one study found that 40 percent of the 'news' content of a typical newspaper originated in press releases, story memos and suggestions from PR companies.

Hungry for Cool

More subtle is the cultural shift wrought in the media—light, non-political television programming that contributes to a 'buying mood'; magazines filled with little nuggets of 'instant gratification'; serious newspapers that insert lengthy travel and fashion sections for no obvious reason. So much happiness, so unbearable.

Advertising consistently portrays 'lifestyles' that are beyond the reach of all but the wealthy. This is somehow viewed as 'apolitical'. Yet charities' ads calling for dropping Southern debt or opposing cruelty to animals often fall foul of regulators or media ad-sales teams for being 'too political'.

As a child I loved the ads before the movie. They were zippy and bright. I found the varied angles they took before the 'Ta-dahhh!' moment when the product was plugged ingenious. I still find the creative energy that goes into them intriguing, but feel tired by their consistently conservative values and know better about the social, economic and environmental issues behind the products they push. I also feel fed up by the sheer volume of the glitzy deluge. Corporate advertisers know this fed up feeling all too well and have responded with marketing moves that look less like traditional advertising but seep more than ever into our lives. The upshot is that everything gets branded, logoed or sponsored. Supermarkets that shaft farmers sponsor children's play areas and school computers. Children are employed to hand out freebies to other kids and talk them up ('peer marketing'). Conspicuous charity abounds, trying to make the brand look more benign—for example, Ronald McDonald House offers accommodation to families with sick children. Product placement sneaks into movies, TV shows, computer games and even novels. Our email and cell phones are bombarded. Most websites would collapse without revenue from ads that get ever more lively and mysterious.

With traditional advertising showing diminishing returns, corporations get into all sorts of contortions. The apparel company Diesel ran a multimillion-dollar campaign contrasting clothing ads with scenes of hardship in North Korea; Benetton notoriously used the image of a man dying of AIDS to push its duds. Wow, just feel that edge!

A certain amount of advertising is probably unavoidable—indeed, countries that curb it often flood mental spaces with political propaganda instead. But the worldview the ad biz pushes is so out of touch with real life that it can mess up our heads. Ever wondered where that urge to shop when you're feeling a bit down comes from? Or how our desire for social change or rebellion gets transformed into speed, sex, indulgence and living for the moment? Why is so much of our culture about dictating taste (the tyrannies of 'cool') and transforming it into want? Why are disadvantaged groups (be they dark-skinned, sexual minorities, people with disabilities, you name it) so absent from this trendy world, unless they are being fetishized by niche marketing?

With the deluge comes avoidance. Ungrateful wretches that we are, we try to block out as much as we can. TV advertising is in crisis. Ad guru Lord Saatchi thinks young people nowadays have 'continual partial attention—the kind of brain that's constantly sifting but records little. His answer is for companies to strive for 'one-word equity' to fit this goldfish attention span—Be™, Live™, Buy™, anyone?

This dizziness is reflected in the philosophical musings of Maurice Levy, top honcho of advertising giant Publicis: 'Consumers do not want only to be given an astonishingly wide-ranging choice. They want that choice to be renewed at intervals that are always shorter. This is the reason why we have to redefine our very notion of time. What we have to deal with is not only change, but an acceleration of change itself. Not only transformations, but the transformation of transformations: it will be a real challenge to make fidelity out of inconstancy.'

He doesn't stop to ponder how his work is all about creating this blur of inconstancy. Advertising's influence is being implicated in eating, compulsive and attention-deficit disorders. In the Majority World the big brand steamroller is intent on creating Westernized aspirational cultures often at odds with local cultures.

If we are to free identity from consumerism, reality checks are our strongest weapon. If struck by an ad, it's useful to measure how much of it is actually telling you something about the product and how much is image. Brands are eager that you identify with them, make them a part of your lives—deny them that privilege. Independent media (like the NI and, yes, this is a shameless plug) can give us all the dirt we need to chuck at corporate ad lies. Thinking before we buy, and buying nothing—especially when irrational urges prompt us to do otherwise—are bound to punch a few holes. The idea of our world and its public spaces as shared commons is becoming increasingly visible. Streets are being reclaimed by 'citizen artists' redrawing ads to reveal their subterfuges, and by social movements gathering to protest government by corporations.

There's quite a bit of ad-industry nervousness as brands come under attack and marketing tactics backfire. Could the industry one day start to tell us things we actually want to know? The distorting mirror will need to shatter first before a floating world comes into view.

EXPLORING THE ISSUE

Is Advertising Good for Society?

Critical Thinking and Reflection

1. Are the positive and negative aspects of advertising equal, or are there different aspects to trying to understand how advertising can both introduce new concepts and create an imbalance in desire for new products and items?
2. Examine the ads that go along with your favorite television programming. What do these ads tell you about the target audience for this show? Do the ads use particular appeals (such as an appeal to fear, insecurity or self-image?).
3. Give some thought to the alternatives to advertising for the funding of media content. Do you understand how expensive it is to produce media and what role advertising plays in this type of support?
4. How are our emotions manipulated by advertisers? Do you see ads that make you laugh or cry? How do they make you feel?

Is There Common Ground?

Alternative financing models might suggest a different way for industries to turn a profit, but advertising in America is big business, and the ad industry has a vested interest in maintaining the status quo. Do new communication technologies suggest other ways of sharing or distributing content? How expensive is it to produce media content? Where does the money for that process come from? Financial support is critical for the media, and if the industries are not going to be able to advertise, how likely are they to survive?

Ultimately, as the authors of the YES and NO selections indicate, advertising does infiltrate society on a number of levels. Fortunately, we have many wonderful sources to consider to help us understand advertising's social impact.

Additional Resources

Jean Kilbourne, *Can't Buy My Love* (Touchstone, 1999)

This book provides a social critique of what advertising does to our feelings.

Arthur Asa Berger, *Ads, Fads, and Consumer Culture: Advertising's Impact on American Character and Society,* 3rd ed. (Rowman and Littlefield, 2007)

This book has a number of contemporary examples and covers critical analysis methods, sexuality in advertising, global advertising, and neuromarketing.

Alissa Quart, *Branded: The Buying and Selling of Teenagers* (Basic Books, 2003)

This book reflects on the impact advertising has on today's typical college student.

Students are also encouraged to examine some of the academic journals that deal with issues of advertising in a number of venues, such as *The Journal of Advertising Ethics, Ethics and Society,* and *The Journal of Mass Media Ethics,* and to become familiar with Web sites that call attention to examples of blurring ads and ethical practices.

Internet References . . .

Advertising Age

The Web site of Advertising Age magazine provides access to articles and features about media advertising, such as the history of television advertising.

http://adage.com

Advertising World

This site is maintained by the Advertising Department of the University of Texas and contains links to material on a variety of advertising topics and issues.

http://advertising.utexas.edu/world/index.asp

Entertainment Software Association

Entertainment Software Association (ESA) serves the business and public affairs needs of video game publishers. Its sections on public policy and games in life provide extensive information about the benefits of video games.

www.theesa.com

The U.S. Department of Health and Human Services

This Web site helps women with issues of body image, nutrition, and body image.

www.womenshealth.gov/body-image/

Center for Media and Public Affairs

This site offers information about ongoing debates concerning media fairness and impact, with particular attention to political campaigns and political journalism.

www.cmpa.com

Center for Media and Democracy

The Center for Media and Democracy regularly posts interesting items on the interface between politics and advertising.

www.prwatch.org/

Project Censored

Project Censored often reports on attempts by the ad industry to control information.

www.projectcensored.org/

News and Politics

*A*t *one time, one of the most hotly debated questions about media was whether media content demonstrated a liberal or conservative bias. In recent years, this question has receded, while other, more important issues have risen to the fore. Since the FCC began to revise ownership restrictions for media outlets, and information control has grown throughout the Iraq War, news and politics have begun to be viewed through a slightly different social lens. Issues about news control are now far more complicated than in the days when Walter Lippmann wrote about the ideal of objectivity. While many cities and regions once had many newspapers, now they may have one. Broadcast news dominated the airwaves by powerful networks. Today, a person is as likely to start the day with checking the news on the Internet as they are to pick up a newspaper or watch TV sometime through the day. One of the most popular "news" programs for college-aged students is on Comedy Central. The issues in this section address three important, contemporary topics, and lead us toward discussions of how much, and what type of information we actually use.*

- Does Fake News Mislead the Public?
- Will Evolving Forms of Journalism Be an Improvement?
- Do Social Media Encourage Revolution?

ISSUE 7

Does Fake News Mislead the Public?

YES: Julia R. Fox, Glory Koloen, and Volkan Sahin, from "No Joke: A Comparison of Substance in *The Daily Show with Jon Stewart* and Broadcast Network Television Coverage of the 2004 Presidential Election Campaign," *Journal of Broadcasting and Electronic Media* (June 2007)

NO: Barry A. Hollander, from "Late-Night Learning: Do Entertainment Programs Increase Political Campaign Knowledge for Young Viewers?" *Journal of Broadcasting and Electronic Media* (December 2005)

Learning Outcomes

After reading this issue, you should be able to:

- Discuss the consequences of fake news for political knowledge.
- Evaluate sources of political information.
- Describe the links among news, political knowledge, and engagement.
- Describe the difference between youth and adult knowledge and voting patterns.

ISSUE SUMMARY

YES: This study examined political coverage of the first presidential debate and the political convention on *The Daily Show* and on network nightly newscasts. The study found the network coverage to be more hype than substance, and *The Daily Show* to be more humor than substance. The amount of substantive information between the two newscasts was about the same for both the story and for the entire half-hour program.

NO: Barry Hollander examined learning from comedy and late-night programs. National survey data were used to examine whether exposure to comedy and late-night programs actually informs viewers, focusing on recall and recognition. Some support is found for the prediction that the consumption of such programs is more associated with recognition of information than with actual recall.

T raditionally, journalism has been defined as what appears in newspapers, newsmagazines, and electronic media news programming. In the age of the Internet, simple "medium-based" descriptions of news are no longer accurate. Shifting trends in media usage see young voters turning to comedic sources for information, rather than traditional media. Programs such as *The Daily Show with Jon Stewart* are cited by youth as among the most important sources of political information.

If an enlightened citizenry is one of the foundations of a successful democracy, what are the consequences of this shift for an informed electorate? Fewer than 20 percent of youth read a newspaper daily. Television is still the public's—including youth's—main source of campaign news. Nontraditional and Internet source use is on the rise, but is not the major news source for youth. Within the age group 18–29, 27 percent reported that they got *no* news yesterday.

This generational shift in declining audience is matched with a decline in average political engagement. Younger citizens have lower rates of news and current affairs awareness. In addition to knowing less, this group cares less, votes less, and follows the news less than their elders. Additionally, youth today are less likely to trust political systems, or believe that they can have an influence. Many in the media industries believe that in their adult years individuals will follow the media patterns of their youth, thus the decline in newspapers and traditional television newscasts will certainly continue.

More discouraging is the continued lack of political knowledge within the youth age group. The 2004 Pew Report finds, however, that the most knowledgeable Americans were those who use the Internet (primarily using Web-based versions of traditional media sites), listeners of National Public Radio, and readers of newsmagazines. By comparison, the least knowledgeable Americans got their news from comedy and late-night TV shows, more often viewed by youth. The effects of advocacy journalism on television are being felt in that about 40 percent of the public believe that news is biased in favor of one of the two parties. This is matched by the 40 percent who say there is no bias.

This pattern continues in this decade: Young people still know the least. In a 2007 Pew Study of Public Knowledge of Current Affairs, only 15 percent of 18–29 year olds were among the most informed third of the public. At the other end of the scale, 56 percent of this age group fell into the lowest knowledge group. Across all age levels, 35 percent of the population were in the highest third in knowledge level. These low levels of knowledge correlate with political engagement and, not surprising, news interest. Of those with low knowledge levels, only 53 percent were registered to vote. For the high knowledge level group, the number is 90 percent. Only 16 percent of low knowledge level individuals enjoy keeping up with the news, compared to 69 percent of those at the high level. Yet comedic news is popular with youth: 21 percent of this age group are among the regular audience of the *Daily Show/Colbert Report*. Within the high knowledge group across all ages, 54 percent of the audience of the *Daily Show/Colbert Report* were in the high knowledge group.

In "No Joke," Fox, Koloen, and Sahin compare the substantive information in network newscasts with substantive information in *The Daily Show with Jon Stewart*. Their surprising conclusion is that level of substance is remarkably similar across the shows. Perhaps the shift to comedic news will begin to engage viewers who would not be involved without the humor and skepticism of fake news.

Hollander wonders what we learn from fake news. His question is simple: Does late-night and comedic news exposure actually inform viewers? He distinguishes between recall and recognition memory. Recognition memory is the less demanding measure, asking to recognize some fact or person from a list. Recall asks the respondent to know the answer. Hollander found the consumption of comedic viewers to be more related to recognition than to recall. Journalism functions to maintain the level of knowledge and involvement necessary for a democracy. In this increasingly diverse world of media forms, what is the implication of fake news for journalism and for democracy?

There are two issues entangled in these readings; the first has to do with the worth of fake news in contemporary society. Does it function to invite knowledge and debate within society, or is it mere entertainment? The lines between news and entertainment have long been blurred. Consider, just one example, the frequent insertion of celebrity news into front pages of newspapers and packages on national newscasts. The line between journalists and the public is now blurring even more. Consider news and political bloggers, who have had major influence when they have upon occasion broken news stories before the mainstream media. Do we define journalism by where it appears or by how it functions in society? Part of this first question is a related question of worth: Does fake news function to invite knowledge and debate, or does it promote cynicism? Comedic news has captured the public imagination. The August 2007 *Critical Studies in Mass Communication* journal featured a humorous debate concerning Jon Stewart. Hart and Hartelius accuse Stewart of the sin of "unbridled political cynicism," luring youth into abandoning conventional society and attempts to foster social change, or into shunning involvement in civic and political issues. Continuing with the lighthearted tone, but serious issues, Bennett defends the importance of comedy in an age of cynicism and argues that it breeds instead an independence of perspective.

The second question has to do with the chief audience of the currently popular fake news: youth. Are they disadvantaged as citizens by their reliance on this form of news? Is it somehow less substantive than "real" news? Fox and colleagues think not. Does its presentation style inhibit learning? Hollander fears so. These are among the few works that have seriously studied this phenomenon, so additional research is needed. What are the questions that you think researchers need to ask? Part of what is implied by this concern for the youth audience is the fear that participation in the political life of our democracy will be harmed by nontraditional news sources. Is it information that threatens the political involvement of youth? What other factors influence youth engagement in political and civic issues? And most importantly, what can be done to enhance that engagement and participation?

YES  Julia R. Fox, Glory Koloen, and Volkan Sahin

No Joke

The 2004 elections saw the highest turnout among voters under 30 in more than a decade ("Election Turnout," 2005). As this age group becomes more important in the political process it has also shifted trends in media usage. In particular, young voters are turning to comedic sources for campaign information, rather than more traditional news formats (Pew Research Center, 2004a). What are the implications of this new trend in information seeking, given the presumption that a successful democracy depends on an informed electorate (Williams & Edy, 1999)? Can a humorous political news source possibly be as informative as traditional political news sources? To answer such questions requires multiple studies addressing a wide range of related concerns. Yet, to date there has been little scholarly attention to and no systematic examination of how comedic television messages compare to more traditional television news messages as sources of substantive political information. This study begins to address the questions raised by this new trend by systematically comparing *The Daily Show with Jon Stewart* and broadcast television network newscasts as sources of political campaign information, using content analysis to compare the quality and quantity of 2004 presidential campaign information provided by *The Daily Show with Jon Stewart* and television networks.

Media Dependency Theory

Communication scholars have long considered providing information about the world to be a central function of media (Fox, 2003; Lasswell, 1948; Lippmann, 1921; Price & Roberts, 1987; Wright, 1974). Among the classic writings in this area, Lippmann (1921) noted that the pictures in one's head of the world outside are based on information provided by the press, particularly for the world beyond one's direct experience. Media theorists DeFleur and Ball-Rokeach (1989) define this relationship with media as one of dependency based on goals and resources. According to their media dependency theory, media control information resources that are important for individual goals, such as goals of social understanding (Ball-Rokeach, 1998; DeFleur & Ball-Rokeach, 1989). For issues and events outside of direct experience, people lack information needed to create social meaning, which creates ambiguity (Ball-Rokeach, 1998).

Media can fill those voids with second-hand information that is central to constructions of social reality (Ball-Rokeach, 1998). Such media effects on knowledge and beliefs, as well as behaviors, are more likely when media serve a central information function (Ball-Rokeach, 1998; DeFleur & Ball-Rokeach, 1989). "If, out of habit or necessity, we incorporate the media system as a major vehicle for understanding, then the media system takes on a certain power to influence how we think, feel, and act" (DeFleur & Ball-Rokeach, 1989, p. 316).

For political information, in particular, most people have very little direct contact with politicians and get most of their political information from the media. Media dependency theory suggests, then, that it is critically important to examine the content of mediated political communication as such information may well be used as the basis for political knowledge, attitudes, and behaviors. Such examinations should, of course, include traditional sources of news on which people have relied for decades for political information, such as the broadcast television networks' nightly newscasts. But media dependency theory suggests it is also critical to examine emerging and increasingly important mediated sources of political information, as media dependencies are considered to be a function of expectations about the potential utility of the media content (DeFleur & Ball-Rokeach, 1989). Given the growing number of young voters who say they expect *The Daily Show with Jon Stewart* to fulfill their political information needs, it begs the question as to whether those needs can be satisfied with that show as well as they can be with more traditional television news coverage of political information.

The Daily Show with Jon Stewart as a Source of Campaign Information

More than 20 million under-30 voters cast their ballots in the 2004 presidential election, marking the highest voter turnout for that age group in more than 12 years (Fleischer, 2004; "Under-30," 2004). As voter turnout among this age group increased, news sources of political information for these voters shifted away from the broadcast television networks and toward comedy programs such as *The Daily Show with Jon Stewart*. Specifically, a Pew Research Center (2004a) nationwide survey found the percentage of under-30 respondents (21%) who said they relied regularly upon comedy shows such as *The Daily Show with Jon Stewart* for campaign information was the same as the percentage of under-30 respondents (23%) who said they regularly relied upon the television networks' evening news for campaign information. The percentage of under-30 respondents who said they relied on comedy shows for campaign information is more than double the percentage found in a similar Pew study in 2000 (9%), while the percentage of under-30 voters who regularly relied on broadcast network news declined to almost half of what was found in 2000 (39%) (Pew Research Center, 2004a). Furthermore, television ratings during the Iowa Caucus, New Hampshire primary, and State of the Union address found more male viewers in the 18- to 34-year-old demographic watched *The Daily Show with Jon Stewart* than network news ("Young America's," 2004).

Despite the growing reliance in recent years among young voters on comedy programs for campaign information, there has been precious little systematic examination of this information source, and no published systematic comparison of substantive political coverage in *The Daily Show with Jon Stewart* with traditional television newscasts. In discussing whether or not *The Daily Show with Jon Stewart* should be considered real "news," McKain (2005) describes how the format and formal structural features (e.g. "live" reports) of *The Daily Show with Jon Stewart* mimic those of traditional television newscasts. He also discusses how much of *The Daily Show with Jon Stewart* focuses on skewering broadcast and cable network television news coverage of politics as well as politicians' efforts to spin that coverage. McKain goes so far as to consider whether those who only get their news from *The Daily Show with Jon Stewart* will "get" the jokes without benefit of learning factual information first from traditional news sources. And, he points out that, occasionally, content first presented on *The Daily Show with Jon Stewart*, notably John Edwards announcing his candidacy on the show, is later covered as legitimate news by traditional news outlets. But McKain never makes a direct comparison between the substantive political content presented on *The Daily Show with Jon Stewart* and on more traditional television newscasts.

What would such a comparison find? First, the sources must be considered separately in terms of their substantive political content. Concerning the relative amount of substantive political information presented on *The Daily Show with Jon Stewart*, it seems somewhat obvious that a systematic analysis is likely to find considerably more humorous content than substantive political information on the show. While *The Daily Show with Jon Stewart* was nominated for a Television Critics Association award for "Outstanding Achievement in News and Information" in 2003 and in 2005 and won the award in 2004 ("Comedy Central's," 2003; "The Daily Show's," 2005), Stewart insists that he is a comedian, not a journalist, and that his program is a comedy show, not a newscast (Armour, 2005; Davies, 2005; Gilbert, 2004; "*The Jon Stewart*," 2004). Thus, this study predicts:

H_1: Both the video and audio emphasis in *The Daily Show with Jon Stewart* will be on humor rather than substance.

The question remains, however, as to how this new source of political information will stack up to more traditional sources of television news as far as substantive political information is concerned.

Broadcast Television Network News as a Source of Campaign Information

Broadcast television networks were American's primary source of news and information about presidential elections for much of the second half of the 20th century (Baker & Dessart, 1998; "Despite Uncertain," 2000; Fox, Angelini, & Goble, 2005; Graber, 1993; Pew Research Center, 2002). In 2000, cable television news sources surpassed the broadcast television networks' as the primary source of political campaign information ("Despite Uncertain," 2000). Still, there are a number of compelling reasons to compare coverage of the most recent presidential election presented on the broadcast television networks and on *The Daily Show with Jon Stewart*.

First, the trend found in the Pew (2004a) study findings suggests that broadcast network news is being supplanted by comedy programs as a regular source of campaign information for young adults. Furthermore, the broadcast network newscasts still have millions more viewers than cable and still draw the largest audience for a news program at a particular time (Johnson, 2004; Lazaroff, 2004). Finally, given the passing of Peter Jennings and the retirements of Tom Brokaw and Dan Rather, all within 9 months of the 2004 presidential election, this particular election campaign marks a significant historic moment in broadcast journalism, as it was the last presidential election campaign that the three long-time broadcast television network news anchors covered.

A robust finding from previous studies since the 1970s has been the emphasis on hype rather than on more substantive matters, often described in terms of issue versus image, in the broadcast television networks' coverage of presidential election campaigns (Broh, 1980, 1983; Clancey & Robinson, 1985; Farnsworth & Lichter, 2003; Fox et al., 2005; Graber, 1976, 1980; Hofstetter, 1981; Lichter, Amundson, & Noyes, 1988; Lichter & Lichter, 1996; Patterson, 1977, 1980; Patterson & McClure, 1976). For example, an examination of the final 2 weeks of network coverage of the 1988, 1992, 1996, and 2000 election campaigns found the emphasis to be on horse race and hoopla rather than on campaign issues and candidate qualifications (Fox et al., 2005). While that study specifically examined the final 2 weeks of campaign coverage, other studies examining a longer period, for example from the traditional start of the general campaign after Labor Day, have found a similar emphasis on horse race over more substantive coverage during those years (Farnsworth & Lichter, 2003; Lichter & Lichter, 1996).

Given the lack of substantive coverage found in previous studies, this study is expected to replicate those findings. Specifically:

H_2: The video and audio emphasis in the broadcast network newscasts will be on hype rather than substance.

The bigger question posed here is whether there will be more substance in the broadcast television networks' coverage or in *The Daily Show with Jon Stewart*'s coverage. Given the long-established emphasis on hype rather than substance in television network campaign coverage, it is not at all clear whether a carefully conducted content analysis would find broadcast television network coverage to be more substantive than coverage on *The Daily Show with Jon Stewart*. While Stewart is the first to say that his program is a comedy show and not a news show (Davies, 2005; "The Jon Stewart," 2004), instances such as his telling the hosts of CNN's *Crossfire* that their show was hurting America and telling the host of NPR's *Fresh Air* that, in asking probing questions, he's doing what journalists often don't do clearly show his interest in substantive reporting (Cook, 2004; Davies, 2005; Ryan, 2005). Thus, this study poses the following research question:

> RQ₁: Will there be more substance in the video and audio of the broadcast television networks' coverage than in the video and audio of *The Daily Show with Jon Stewart*'s coverage of the 2004 presidential election?

Method

This study compares the emphasis on hype versus substance in the broadcast television networks' coverage of the first presidential debate and the Democratic and Republican conventions in 2004, the emphasis on humor versus substance in the same debate and convention coverage on *The Daily Show with Jon Stewart*, and the substantive coverage presented on *The Daily Show with Jon Stewart* and in the broadcast television networks' coverage of the first debate and the party conventions.

Debate and Convention Coverage

As noted, other studies have sampled content from the final weeks of a campaign or from the general campaign time frame to examine political news coverage (Farnsworth & Lichter, 2003; Fox et al., 2005; Lichter & Lichter, 1996). However, there is also good reason to specifically examine coverage of debates and conventions. Conventions offer the candidates a chance to present their views on what they consider to be the important issues facing the nation (Scheele, 1984; Sesno, 2001; Trent & Friedenberg, 2004) and are critically important for shoring up political bases and reaching out to independent voters (Dearin, 1997). Political conventions increase voter attention to the campaign, often through news media coverage of the conventions rather than first-hand viewing of the convention proceedings (Jamieson, Johnston, Hagen, Waldman, & Kenski, 2000). As the election draws nearer, the candidates square off in the presidential debates, giving voters an opportunity to compare the candidates and their stands on issues (Just, Crigler, & Wallach, 1990). Although much of the information presented in the debates may have been presented earlier in the campaign, many voters are just beginning to pay attention to campaign messages during late September and October, when the debates are usually held (Jamieson & Adasiewica, 2000). While debates tend to reinforce preexisting candidate preferences, they are particularly important for activating supporters and can sway undecided voters (Kraus, 1979; Lang & Lang, 1961; Lowery & DeFleur, 1983; Middleton, 1962; Ranney, 1979; Salant, 1962; Willis, 1962).

Concept Operationalization

Following a coding scheme developed in previous research (Fox et al., 2005), substantive coverage, as a meta-concept, is categorized by the concepts of campaign issues and candidate qualifications while hype, as a meta-concept, is categorized by the concepts of horse race and hoopla. Indicators of campaign issues are references to or images of issues included in the party platforms such as defense and security, the economy, the environment, education, health care, and crime. Indicators of candidate qualifications are references to or images of the candidates' experience, such as political accomplishments and political positions held. Indicators of horse race are references to or images of the campaign contest, such as who's ahead and behind in the polls, campaign strategies and tactics, and political endorsements. Indicators of hoopla are references to or images of activities and items related to campaign events and their trappings, such as photo opportunities, rallies, flag-waving, hand-shaking, baby kissing, ball throwing, crowds, balloons, and celebrities.

This study also includes categories for humor, a meta-concept categorized by the concepts of joking and laughing. Joking is indicated by funny music, silly and untrue statements, silly voices, tone of voice (sarcastic or mocking or a sudden change in pitch or volume), silly faces (raised eyebrows or a skewed, wide-open or pinched mouth), mocking faces, silly or exaggerated gestures, and obviously altered images. Laughter is indicated by sounds of laughing or chuckling, smiling, and eye crinkling.

Sampling

For the convention coverage, this study used a saturation sample by examining all newscasts from ABC's *World News Tonight with Peter Jennings*, CBS's *Evening News with Dan Rather*, and NBC's *The Nightly News with Tom Brokaw* and all *The Daily Show with Jon Stewart* programs that covered the conventions; specifically, the study examined the broadcast television networks' nightly news programs on July 26–30, August 30 and 31, and September 1–3, and *The Daily Show with Jon Stewart* on July 27–30, August 31, and September 1–3.

Only the first presidential debate is examined in this study as the second debate, a town hall-style debate held on a Friday night, was not covered by ABC's *World News Tonight with Peter Jennings*, CBS's *Evening News with Dan Rather*, and NBC's *The Nightly News with Tom Brokaw* or *The Daily Show with Jon Stewart*, nor was the third debate covered by *The Daily Show with Jon Stewart*.

Coding

Because the audio and video channels in television news stories carry separate and sometimes conflicting messages (Fox et al., 2005), this study examines the coverage in the audio and video channels separately. The coding instrument was modified from one developed in a previous study (Fox et al., 2005) to include the additional categories of joking and laughing. Nominal codings were made for network, date, study coder, and whether the story was about the presidential election. Stories coded were read by the newscast anchors or were packaged by reporters, including the anchor lead-ins to reporters' stories. Story length (in seconds) was recorded for each story in each program in the study sample. In addition, the amount of time (in seconds) in the audio and video messages devoted to horse race, hoopla, campaign issues, candidate qualifications, joking, and laughter was also coded for stories about the presidential election. Coding directions, category definitions, examples, and sample coding sheets were provided to study coders during coder training.

Reliability

When coding interval or ratio-level data, such as the number of seconds of network evening news coverage devoted to a topic, Pearson's correlation coefficient (r) is used to measure the degree to which coders vary together in their observations (Riffe, Lacy, & Fico, 1998). This study uses Pearson correlation coefficients from distances correlations, which measure similarities or dissimilarities between pairs of cases based on particular variables of interest (Fox et al., 2005; Fox & Park, 2006). Here, pairs of coders were compared for similarities in their codings of the study categories—audio horse race, audio hoopla, audio issue, audio qualifications, audio joking, audio laughing, video horse race, video hoopla, video issue, video qualifications, video joking, and video laughing. The Pearson correlation for interval data is parsimonious in that it indicates how similar two coders are on all of these variables by rendering one statistic (Fox et al., 2005; Fox & Park, 2006). But this same statistic also provides a more complete picture of coder reliability compared to other measures as it provides detailed information about where reliability problems might be occurring among the particular study coders, unlike other measures of coder reliability for multiple coders that only render one statistic for the entire group of coders (Fox et al., 2005; Fox & Park, 2006). Study coders each coded a network newscast and one program of *The Daily Show with Jon Stewart* to test coder reliability. Pearson correlation coefficients from the distances correlations indicated that the data coders had both high intercoder reliability (Pearson correlation coefficients $r = .988$ or higher) and intracoder reliability (Pearson correlation coefficients $r = .975$ or higher).

Results

An analysis of variance was run prior to analyzing the data, using network as the independent variable, to examine whether the three broadcast television networks varied significantly in their coverage of the coding categories. No significant differences were found. In addition, separate analyses for each political convention found similar emphases on hype versus substance for the broadcast networks and similar emphases on humor versus substance for *The Daily Show with Jon Stewart* for both the Democratic and the Republican conventions.

Not surprisingly, the average amounts of video [60.27] and audio [114.73] humor were significantly more than the average amounts of video [2.16] and audio [19.78] substance in *The Daily Show with Jon Stewart* stories about the presidential election.

Also as predicted, the average amounts of video [58.18] and audio [80.69] hype were significantly more than the average amounts of video [2.2] and audio [26.13] substance in the broadcast network news stories about the presidential election.

Interestingly, the average amounts of video and audio substance in the broadcast network news stories were not significantly different than the average amounts of visual and audio substance in *The Daily Show with Jon Stewart* stories about the presidential election (see Table 1).

It should be noted that the broadcast network news stories about the presidential election were significantly shorter, on average, than were *The Daily Show with Jon Stewart* stories about the presidential election. Thus, the argument could be made that while the amount of substance per story was not significantly different, the proportion of each story devoted to substance was greater in the network news stories than in stories from *The Daily Show with Jon Stewart*. On the other hand, the proportion of stories per half hour program devoted to the election campaign was greater in *The Daily Show with Jon Stewart* than in the broadcast network newscasts. Thus, the analysis was run again using the half-hour program, rather than the story, as the unit of analysis. The results showed that there was still no significant difference in the average amounts of video and audio substance per program on *The Daily Show with Jon Stewart* and on the broadcast network newscasts (see Table 2).

Table 1

Substance in the Network News and *The Daily Show with Jon Stewart* Stories

RQ1: Audio/Video Substance	Network News		The Daily Show		Significance Test		
	M	SD	M	SD	t	d	p (two-tailed)
Video substance	2.29	5.37	2.16	8.95	−0.11	165	p = .91
Audio substance	26.13	33.38	19.78	36.05	1.00	165	p = .32

Table 2

Substance in the Network News and *The Daily Show with Jon Stewart* Programs

RQ1: Audio/Video Substance	Network News		The Daily Show		Significance Test		
	M	SD	M	SD	t	d	p (two-tailed)
Story length	135.40	60.20	233.16	80.00	−8.07	165	p < .011
Video substance	9.03	9.33	8.89	17.13	−0.3	40	p = .97
Audio substance	102.94	75.59	81.33	92.63	.73	40	p = .47

Discussion

At first blush, the increasing reliance among young voters on comedic sources of political information appears to turn the long-held assumption of rational citizens making informed, thoughtful decisions (Noelle-Neumann, 1995; Schudson, 1995) on its ear. Not surprisingly here, in keeping with Stewart's insistence that he is a comedian not a journalist, this study found considerably more humor than substance in *The Daily Show with Jon Stewart*'s political coverage. Yet, this study also found Stewart's program to be just as substantive as the broadcast networks' campaign coverage, regardless of whether the story or the program was used as the unit of analysis. As we've known for years that the broadcast networks place substantial emphasis on insubstantial information in their political coverage, this finding is perhaps not altogether surprising, either.

Although the two sources were found here to be equally substantive, are they equally informative? There is debate among scholars as to how well soft news shows, in which *The Daily Show with Jon Stewart* is categorized by some (Baumgartner & Morris, 2006), can inform their viewers. Baum (2002, 2003) concludes from survey research that soft news may help inform an otherwise inattentive public, although Hollander's (1995) survey data found viewing late-night programs was unrelated to general knowledge about the campaign. However, Hollander's study did not specifically examine viewing of *The Daily Show with Jon Stewart*. To the contrary, the University of Pennsylvania's National Annenberg Election survey found younger viewers of *The Daily Show with Jon Stewart* answered more political questions correctly than respondents who did not watch that show ("Stewart's 'stoned slackers,'" 2004).

Experimental research may well substantiate this correlational survey data suggestion that viewers may actually process and remember substantive information presented on *The Daily Show with Jon Stewart* better than when it is presented on more serious sources of political information. When viewers see positive messages they are appetitively activated (in an approach mode toward the message) and tend to encode more information than when they are aversively activated while viewing a negative message (Fox, Park, & Lang, 2006; Lang, 2006a, 2006b; Lang, Sparks, Bradley, Lee, & Wang, 2004). Previous studies have found that political coverage is often negative. For example, media coverage of presidential debates tends to include a greater proportion of attacks and a smaller proportion of acclaims compared to the actual candidate utterances during the debates (Benoit & Currie, 2001; Reber & Benoit, 2001). Thus, traditional television news campaign stories may activate the aversive motivational system. While such coverage is clearly different than, say, gory and graphic war coverage, which would clearly activate the aversive system, studies have found physiological indications of aversive system activation for socially as well as biologically threatening information (Blanchette, 2006; Lethbridge, Simmons, & Allen, 2002; McRae, Taitano, Kaszniak, & Lane), and in some cases the contemporary social threats elicited stronger responses than their biological counterparts (Blanchette, 2006). In contrast, although *The Daily Show with Jon Stewart* may also be negative in tone, the appetitive system is likely to be activated by the humor on *The Daily Show with Jon Stewart* and by the audience's laughter, which may elicit emotional contagion (McDonald & Fredin, 2001). Additionally, the audience laughter may elicit automatic attentional responses called orienting responses that bring additional processing resources to the viewing task (Lang, 2000).

For that matter, onset of visual information on screen also elicits orienting responses (Lang, 2000). Yet, in one of the limitations of this study, only the total time during which visuals were present on screen was coded here and not the frequency of visual onsets.

Clearly, there is much more to be examined in considering the phenomenon that *The Daily Show with Jon Stewart* has become, particularly experimental research to examine differences in the ways in which viewers process and remember political information presented on that show compared to more traditional, serious television newscasts. Also, other content analyses might examine differences in tone between *The Daily Show with Jon Stewart* and more traditional news sources, for example examining whether one source is more negative or more biased toward a particular political party. Other experiments might examine the impact of that emphasis on viewer attitudes, perhaps similar to Baumgartner and Morris's (2006) examination of effects on candidate evaluations and voter efficacy, but using a broader efficacy scale than used by those authors. Studies could also examine whether younger voters may be particularly susceptible to media dependency effects from *The Daily Show with Jon Stewart*. As Sears (1986) points out, this age group, particularly at the lower end of the age range, tends to have less "crystallized" social and political attitudes than older adults (p. 521). Previous studies have found that voters who are less partisan tend to be more influenced by media than those who are more set in their views (Chaffee, 2001; Chaffee & Choe, 1980; Lazarsfeld, Berelson, & Gaudet, 1944; Mendelsohn & O'Keefe, 1975). Thus, these younger voters, with more fluid social and political attitudes, may be even more susceptible to media dependency effects than their older counterparts. Indeed, a recent analysis (Baumgartner & Morris, 2006) of Pew Center (2004b) data found viewing *The Daily Show with Jon Stewart*, which regularly skewers traditional news media coverage (McKain, 2005), was significantly related to respondents 18–25 saying they were less likely to trust what news organizations say, but the same was not true for older viewers of the show.

In the meantime, the data reported here offer the first systematic comparison of substantive information presented in campaign coverage on *The Daily Show with Jon Stewart* and more conventional television news sources of political information. The results provide valuable information on the substantive quality of this increasingly important source of campaign information for young voters. The findings should allay at least some of the concerns about the growing reliance on this nontraditional source of political information, as it is just as substantive as the source that Americans have relied upon for decades for political news and information. However, while this is true in a comparative sense, in an absolute sense neither of the sources examined here was particularly substantive, which should give pause to broadcast news executives in particular, and more generally to all politicians, citizens, and scholars concerned with the important informative function that mass media, particularly television news sources, serve in this democracy.

References

Armour, T. (2005, April 24). It's a dirty job . . . *Chicago Tribune*, sec. 7, p. 18.

Baker, W., & Dessart, G. (1998). *Down the tube: An inside account of the failure of American television*. New York: Basic Books.

Ball-Rokeach, S. (1998). A theory of media power and a theory of media use: Different stories, questions, and ways of thinking. *Mass Communication and Society*, 1(1/2), 5–40.

Baum, M. (2002). Sex, lies, and war: How soft news brings foreign policy to the inattentive public. *American Political Science Review*, 96(1), 91–109.

Baum, M. (2003). Soft news and political knowledge: Evidence of absence or absence of evidence? *Political Communication*, 20, 173–190.

Baumgartner, J., & Morris, J. (2006). "The Daily Show" effect: Candidate evaluations, efficacy, and American youth. *American Politics Research*, 34(3), 341–367.

Benoit, W. L., & Currie, H. (2001). Inaccuracies in media coverage of the 1996 and 2000 presidential debates. *Argumentation and Advocacy*, 38(1), 28–39.

Blanchette, I. (2006). Snakes, spiders, guns, and syringes: How specific are evolutionary constraints on the detection of threatening stimuli? *The Quarterly Journal of Experimental Psychology*, 59(8), 1394–1414.

Broh, C. A. (1980). Horse-race journalism: Reporting the polls in the 1976 presidential election. *Public Opinion Quarterly*, 44, 515–549.

Broh, C. A. (1983). Presidential preference polls and network news. In W. C. Adams (Ed.), *Television coverage of the 1980 presidential campaign* (pp. 29–48). Norwood: Ablex Publishing Corporation.

Chaffee, S. (2001). Studying the new communication of politics. *Political Communication*, 18, 237–244.

Chaffee, S., & Cho, S. (1980). Time of decision and media use during the Ford-Carter campaign. *Public Opinion Quarterly*, 44, 53–69.

Clancey, M., & Robinson, M. J. (1985). General election coverage: Part I. In M. Robinson & A. Ranney (Eds.), *The mass media in campaign 84: Articles from Public Opinion magazine* (pp. 27–33). Washington, DC: American Enterprise Institute for Public Policy Research.

Comedy Central's "The Daily Show with Jon Stewart" honored with four TCA awards nominations. (2003, June 5). . . .

Cook, J. (2004, November 24). CBS' Rather to sign off as news anchor. *Chicago Tribune*, sec. 1, pp. 1, 14.

"The Daily Show's" Jon Stewart wins prestigious TCA award. (2005, July 25). . . .

Davies, D. (Host). (2005, July 22). *Fresh Air* [Radio broadcast]. Philadelphia, PA: WHYY.

Dearin, R. D. (1997). The American dream as depicted in Robert J. Dole's 1996 presidential nomination acceptance speech. *Presidential Studies Quarterly*, 27(1), 698–711.

DeFleur, M., & Ball-Rokeach, S. (1989). *Theories of mass communication* (5th ed.). White Plains, NY: Longman, Inc.

Despite uncertain outcome campaign 2000 highly rated. (2000). Washington, DC. Retrieved July 30, 2001, from Election turnout in 2004 was highest since 1968. (2005, January 16). *Hoosier Times*, p. A6.

Farnsworth, S. J., & Lichter, S. R. (2003). *The nightly news nightmare: Network television's coverage of U.S. presidential elections, 1988–2000*. Lanham, MD: Rowman & Littlefield Publishers, Inc.

Fleischer, M. (2004, November 3). *Youth turnout up sharply in 2004* [Press release]. Washington, DC: The Center for Information & Research on Civic Learning & Engagement.

Fox, J. R. (2003). The alarm function of mass media: A critical study of "The plot against America," a special edition of NBC Nightly News with Tom Brokaw. In N. Chitty, R. Rush, & M. Semati (Eds.), *Studies in terrorism: Media scholarship and the enigma of terror* (pp. 55–71). Penang, Malaysia: Southbound (in association with the *Journal of International Communication*).

Fox, J. R., Angelini, J. R., & Goble, C. (2005). Hype versus substance in network television coverage of presidential election campaigns. *Journalism and Mass Communication Quarterly*, *82*(1), 97–109.

Fox, J. R., & Park, B. (2006). The "I" of embedded reporting: An analysis of CNN coverage of the "Shock and Awe" campaign. *Journal of Broadcasting & Electronic Media*, *50*, 36–51.

Fox, J. R., Park, B., & Lang, A. (2006, June). *Complicated emotional messages produce liberal bias: Effects of valence and complexity on sensitivity and criterion.* Top paper presented to the Information Systems Division at the International Communication Association annual conference, Dresden, Germany.

Gilbert, M. (2004, December 30). Pop culture swung wildly left, right in election year. *Chicago Tribune*, sec. 2, p. 2.

Graber, D. A. (1976). Press and TV as opinion resources in presidential campaigns. *Public Opinion Quarterly*, *40*, 285–303.

Graber, D. A. (1980). *Mass media and American politics*. Washington, DC: Congressional Quarterly Press.

Graber, D. A. (1993). *Mass media and American politics* (4th ed.). Washington, DC: Congressional Quarterly Press.

Hofstetter, C. R. (1981). Content analysis. In D. D. Nimmo & K. R. Sanders (Eds.), *Handbook of political communication* (pp. 529–560). Beverly Hills, CA: Sage Publications.

Hollander, B. (1995). The new news and the 1992 presidential campaign: Perceived vs. actual political knowledge. *Journalism and Mass Communication Quarterly*, *72*(4), 786–798.

Jamieson, K. H., & Adasiewicz, C. (2000). What can voters learn from election debates? In S. Coleman (Ed.), *Televised election debates: International perspectives* (pp. 25–42). New York: St. Martin's Press, Inc.

Jamieson, K. H., Johnston, R., Hagen, M. G., Waldman, P., & Kenski, K. (2000). *The public learned about Bush and Gore from conventions; half ready to make an informed choice.* Philadelphia: Annenberg Pubic Policy Center.

Johnson, S. (2004, November 28). The future of network news: Follow the money. *Chicago Tribune*, sec. 7, pp. 1, 8–9.

The Jon Stewart and undecided voter connection. (2004, September 20). New York: Fox News Network. . . .

Just, M., Crigler, A., & Wallach, L. (1990). Thirty seconds or thirty minutes: What viewers learn from spot advertisements and candidate debates. *Journal of Communication, 40*(3), 120–133.

Kraus, S. (Ed.). (1979). *The great debates: Carter v. Ford, 1976.* Bloomington: Indiana University Press.

Lang, A. (2000). The limited capacity model of mediated message processing. *Journal of Communication, 50*(1), 46–70.

Lang, A. (2006a). Motivated cognition (LC4MP): The influence of appetitive and aversive activation on the processing of video games. In P. Messarsis & L. Humphries (Eds.), *Digital media: Transformation in human communication* (pp. 237–254). New York: Peter Lang Publishing.

Lang, A. (2006b). Using the limited capacity model of motivated mediated message processing to design effective cancer communication messages. *Journal of Communication, 56*(Suppl.), S57–S81.

Lang, A., Sparks, J. V., Bradley, S. D., Lee, S., & Wang, Z. (2004). Processing arousing information: Psychophysiological predictors of motivated attention. *Psychophysiology, 41*(Suppl. 1), S61.

Lang, K., & Lang, G. E. (1961). Ordeal by debate: Viewer reactions. *Public Opinion Quarterly, 25,* 277–288.

Lasswell, H. (1948). The structure and function of communication in society. In L. Bryson (Ed.), *The communication of ideas* (pp. 37–51). New York: Harper and Row.

Lazaroff, L. (2004, November 24). Audience decline an old story. *Chicago Tribune,* sec. 3, pp. 1, 8.

Lazarsfeld, P., Berelson, B., & Gaudet, H. (1944). *The People's Choice.* New York: Columbia University Press.

Lethbridge, R., Simmons, J., & Allen, N. (2002). All things unpleasant are not equal: Startle reflex modification while processing social and physical threat. *Psychophysiology, 39*(Suppl. 1), S51.

Lichter, S. R., Amundson, D., & Noyes, R. (1988). *The video campaign: Network coverage of the 1988 primaries.* Washington, DC: American Enterprise Institute and the Center for Media and Public Affairs.

Lichter, S. R., & Lichter, L. S. (1996). Campaign '96 final: How TV news covered the general election. *Media Monitor.* Washington, DC: Center for Media and Public Affairs.

Lippmann, W. (1921). *Public opinion.* New York: Macmillan Company.

Lowery, S. A., & DeFleur, M. L. (1983). *Milestones in mass communication research.* New York: Longman.

McDonald, D., & Fredin, E. (2001, May). *Primitive emotional contagion in coviewing.* Paper presented to the Information Systems Division at the International Communication Association 51st annual conference, Washington, DC.

McKain, A. (2005). Not necessarily not the news: Gatekeeping, remediation, and *The Daily Show. The Journal of American Culture, 28*(4), 415–430.

McRae, K., Taitano, E., Kaszniak, A., & Lane, R. (2004). Differential skin conductance response to biologically and non-biologically relevant IAPS stimuli at brief exposure durations before a backward mask. *Psychophysiology*, *41*(Suppl. 1), S60.

Mendelsohn, H., & O'Keefe, G. (1975). *The people choose a president: Influences on voter decision making.* New York: Praeger Publishers.

Middleton, R. (1962). National TV debates and presidential voting decisions. *Public Opinion Quarterly*, *26*, 426–429.

Noelle-Neumann, E. (1995). Public opinion and rationality. In T. Glasser & C. Salmon (Eds.), *Public opinion and the communication of consent* (pp. 33–54). New York: The Guilford Press.

Patterson, T. E. (1977). The 1976 horserace. *The Wilson Quarterly*, *1*, 73–79.

Patterson, T. E. (1980). *The mass media election: How Americans choose their president.* New York: Praeger Publishers.

Patterson, T. E., & McClure, R. D. (1976). *The unseeing eye: The myth of television power in national politics.* New York: Paragon Books.

Pew Research Center for the People & the Press. (2002, June 9). *Public's news habits little changed by September 11.* Washington, DC. Retrieved August 15, 2002, from http://people-press.org

Pew Research Center for the People & the Press. (2004a, January 11). *Cable and Internet loom large in fragmented political universe: Perceptions of partisan bias seen as growing.* Washington, DC.

Pew Research Center for the People & the Press. (2004b, June 8). *Online news audience larger, more diverse.* Washington, DC.

Price, V., & Roberts, D. (1987). Public opinion processes. In C. Berger & S. Chaffee (Eds.), *Handbook of communication science* (pp. 781–816). Newbury Park, CA: Sage.

Ranney, A. (Ed.). (1979). *The past and future of presidential debates.* Washington, DC: American Enterprise Institute for Public Policy Research.

Reber, B. H., & Benoit, W. L. (2001). Presidential debate stories accentuate the negative. *Newspaper Research Journal*, *22*(3), 30–43.

Rifle, D., Lacy, S., & Fico, F. (1998). *Analyzing media messages: Using quantitative content analysis in research.* Mahwah, NJ: Lawrence Erlbaum Associates, Inc.

Ryan, M. (2005, April 8). Good decision: Putting "Indecision" on DVD. *Chicago Tribune*, sec. 2, p. 2.

Salant, R. S., (1962). The television debates: A revolution that deserves a future. *Public Opinion Quarterly*, *26*, 335–350.

Scheele, H. Z. (1984). Ronald Reagan's 1980 Acceptance Address: A focus on American values. *Western Journal of Speech Communication*, *48*(1), 51–61.

Schudson, M. (1995). *The power of news.* Cambridge, MA: Harvard University Press.

Sears, D. (1986). College sophomores in the laboratory: Influences of a narrow data base on social psychology's view of human nature. *Journal of Personality and Social Psychology*, *51*(3), 515–530.

Sesno, F. (2001). Let's cover the conventions. *The Harvard International Journal of Press/Politics*, *6*(1), 11–15.

Stewart's "stoned slackers"? Not quite. (2004, September 28). Atlanta, GA: CNN. com. . . .

Trent, J. S., & Friedenberg, R. V. (2004). *Political campaign communication: Principles and practices* (5th ed.). Lanham, MD: Rowman & Littlefield.

Under-30 voters top 20 million. (2004, November 6). *The Herald-Times*, p. A5.

Williams, B., & Edy, J. (1999). Basic beliefs, democratic theory, and public opinion. In C. Glynn, S. Herbst, G. O'Keefe, & R. Shapiro (Eds.), *Public Opinion* (pp. 212–245). Boulder, CO: Westview Press.

Willis, E. F. (1962). Little TV debates in Michigan. *Quarterly Journal of Speech, 48,* 15–23.

Wright, C. (1974). The nature and functions of mass communication. In J. Civikly (Ed.), *Messages: A reader on human communication* (pp. 241–250). New York: Random House. (Reprinted from *Mass communication: A sociological perspective,* pp. 11–23, by C. Wright, Ed., 1959, New York: Random House).

Young America's news source: Jon Stewart. (2004, March 2). CNN.com. . . .

Barry A. Hollander  NO

Late-Night Learning

The fragmenting mass media environment has created a host of new ways people say they learn about public affairs. In the early 1990s, researchers explored the role of the "new news" in U.S. politics, particularly the influence of talk radio (Hollander, 1994, 1995). An emerging body of scholarly work has expanded this analysis to entertainment-based television and how it affects political perceptions and knowledge. The scope ranges widely to include television talk shows (Prior, 2003), dramas such as *The West Wing* (Holbert, Pillion, et al., 2003; Parry-Giles & Parry-Giles, 2002; Rollins & O'Connor, 2003), situation comedies (Holbert, Shah, & Kwak, 2003), police dramas (Holbert, Shah, & Kwak, 2004), and the political content of late-night comedy shows (Moy, Xenos, & Hess, 2004; Niven, Lichter, & Amundson, 2003; Parkin, Bos, & van Doom, 2003).

Among the concerns is whether entertainment programs actually inform viewers, specifically younger people who may get their news from late-night television hosts such as Jay Leno or comedy programs like *The Daily Show*. Anecdotal evidence and surveys suggest that for many young people, such programs and their hosts are perceived as vital sources of political information and news (Pew Research Center, 2000, 2002, 2004). Not everyone is convinced, especially Stewart, the host of *The Daily Show*. "I still think that's a fallacy that they get most of their news from us," Stewart told television critics (McFarland, 2004, ¶ 14).

Not all knowledge is the same. Whether viewers of entertainment-based programs learn about public affairs is reminiscent of earlier concerns about the informative power of television news as compared to print sources, most often newspapers. Shoemaker, Schooler, and Danielson (1989) argued that medium differences and their subsequent effects were best addressed through understanding the differences between recall versus recognition of political information. This position is echoed by those who examined the differential effects of intentional and incidental exposure to information (Eagle & Leiter, 1964; Stapel, 1998). In brief, what viewers glean from such programs may be a function of many factors: the cognitive effort expended, political interest and sophistication, and exactly what kind of knowledge is tapped in surveys or questionnaires. This study presents two tests of knowledge—recall and recognition—and argues that entertainment-based programs are better suited for the latter in terms of understanding what they contribute to a viewer's public affairs knowledge, particularly for younger viewers.

Political Knowledge

An enlightened citizenry remains one of the foundations of a successful and thriving democracy, and yet the U.S. public is relatively uninformed about their political world (Bennett, 1996). Despite advances in education and an exploding number of available news sources, scholars have discovered no corresponding increase in political knowledge (Neuman, 1986; Smith, 1989). As Delli Carpini and Keeter (1992) noted: "To say that much of the public is uninformed about much of the substance of politics and public policy is to say nothing new" (p. 19).

Measures of newspaper use are often associated with political knowledge (Becker & Dunwoody, 1982; Chaffee & Tims, 1982; Chaffee, Zhao, & Leshner, 1994; Pettey, 1988; but see also Weaver & Drew, 1995). Exposure to or reliance on television news has not fared as well (Becker & Whitney, 1980; Patterson & McClure, 1976), although a few studies have uncovered a positive relationship (e.g., Zhao & Chaffee, 1995). To make sense of these findings, some have suggested that how people orient toward a medium (McLeod & McDonald, 1985), attend to a medium (Chaffee & Schleuder, 1986), or involve themselves with a medium (Shoemaker et al., 1989) can mask the existence of positive effects on knowledge. These approaches are similar to that of Salomon's (1983) position that people assess the amount of cognitive effort necessary for a particular medium and expend only that amount, with television perceived as requiring the least amount of effort and therefore leading to reduced learning as compared to print, which is perceived to require greater mental effort. The result is a self-fulfilling prophecy, with print information generating superior learning as compared to television or video presentations.

Taken together, these studies suggest that measures of recall alone may not be sensitive enough to uncover the effects of televised entertainment-based programming. Intention to learn or attention to a message is often associated with superior recall, whereas incidental exposure to a message leads to greater recognition of information (Beals, Mazis, Salop, & Staelin, 1981; Eagle & Leiter, 1964; Stapel, 1998). When involvement is high, measures of recall perform best, but in situations in which only marginal interest exists, recognition is often the best measurement strategy (Singh & Rothschild, 1983). Thus, television is ill suited for measures of recall as compared to print. Some argue the differences lie in left-brain versus right-brain processing, in which print learning is best tapped by asking recall questions and television learning is best tapped by recognition questions (Krugman, 1977, but see du Plessis, 1994, for an alternate view).

Entertainment Media and Politics

This discussion is particularly apt when considering the emergence of entertainment-based media as a form of political communication. Indeed, interpersonal conversations now rely on the fictional television content in addition to news as people make sense of their social and political world (Delli Carpini & Williams, 1996). Popular late-night and comedy programs have taken an increasingly political bent, with the number of political jokes on late-night TV steadily rising from 1989 to 2000 (Parkin et al., 2003). Thus, the audience is exposed to campaign politics and public affairs as part of the entertainment whole, but the quality of the information remains in doubt. Late-night humor's focus on the presidency and presidential candidates, for example, rarely includes issue content and instead highlights the miscues of political actors (Niven et al., 2003). The audience of such entertainment-oriented talk shows and comedy programs is often less educated and interested in politics than the mainstream news audience (Davis & Owen, 1998; Hamilton, 2003), suggesting viewers less capable of making sense of the political content. Indeed, in an examination of talk radio, Hollander (1995) found that among less educated listeners, exposure to such programs led to a sense of feeling informed but was unrelated to actual campaign knowledge. Among listeners of greater education, talk radio exposure was related to both the feeling of being informed and campaign information holding, suggesting that greater cognitive ability and motivation brought about by education increases the ability to glean useful information from such programs.

Most studies find no relationship between entertainment-based or "soft" news and political knowledge (Chaffee et al., 1994; Hollander, 1995; McLeod et al., 1996; Pfau, Cho, & Chong, 2001; Prior, 2003), and an analysis by Parkin et al. (2003) reports a negative relationship. This is not to say watching entertainment programs is unrelated to how people make sense of the political world. Such programs can influence perceptions of political actors or how people process political information (Moy et al., 2004; Pfau et al., 2001).

The question of how much is actually learned from entertainment television remains open to debate, and some argue that passive learning or awareness of issues does occur from casual television viewing (see Baum, 2003, for a discussion). As Shoemaker et al. (1989) noted in their examination of differences among newspaper-reliant and television-news-reliant respondents, the kind of knowledge one measures can help explain many of the confusing and contradictory findings from previous studies. In addition, the gratifications sought from such viewing can also play a role (Becker & Whitney, 1980), and thus, we need to consider more than mere exposure to a medium in order to understand how it may influence the ways in which people process public affairs information. Therefore, the following hypothesis was posited:

> H_1: Viewing comedy and late-night programs for political information will be associated with recognition of campaign knowledge but not with recall of campaign knowledge.

A number of other factors can also influence processing strategies and information processing, such as political sophistication, cognitive ability, and motivation. The self-reported reliance of younger viewers on entertainment-based fare has drawn both popular and academic attention, making age a normative factor of interest and one often associated with political sophistication and motivation. Shoemaker et al. (1989) found age to be a significant factor in their recall and recognition study in terms of reliance on either newspapers or television news. Younger respondents recalled more election facts only if they relied on newspapers for their campaign information, suggesting that their peers who relied on television news were either unable or unmotivated to process information from that medium. In a similar vein, Young (2004) found people with greater political knowledge to be largely unaffected by late-night programming, but those with less knowledge were more volatile in their candidate evaluations depending on how much they watched such programming. Baum (2005) also found that politically unengaged voters who watch entertainment TV were more influenced by such heuristics in their perceptions of candidates. Given that age and political knowledge are often negatively correlated (Delli Carpini & Keeter, 1996) and that younger persons might be expected to rely on television-based fare for information, this suggests that younger respondents may be less successful at tests of recall as compared to recognition. Therefore, the following hypotheses were posited:

> H_2: Younger viewers of entertainment programs will be more likely than older viewers to identify such programs as a method of learning about political campaigns.

> H_3: Watching such programs for campaign information will be associated with recognition of campaign events for younger viewers but not with recall of campaign events.

Method

Data were drawn from the January 2004 Political Communications Study conducted by the Pew Research Center for the People and the Press. This national telephone survey of 3,188 adults includes a battery of questions tapping the use of various media sources, from print to television, and a small set of items asking for recall and recognition of events in the campaign for the Democratic Party nomination. In addition, the availability of a large number of demographic and political variables allows for stringent multivariate controls in subsequent analyses.

Entertainment Media Measures

Rather than focus on mere exposure to a medium or category of programs, the analysis here examines those who say they use various programs specifically for the purpose of keeping up with the election campaign. Survey respondents were asked a battery of possible sources of such information and whether they use them to "learn something about the presidential campaign or the candidates."[1] Responses could range from 1 (*never*) to 4 (*regularly*), creating a 4-point scale for each category of programming or specific program. The 15 possible sources include 2 of most interest here: late-night TV shows such as *Letterman* and *Leno* and comedy shows such as *Saturday Night Live* and *The Daily Show*. In addition, respondents answered questions about religious radio shows, talk radio, the Internet, local TV news, national network broadcast news, cable news networks, C-SPAN, TV magazine shows, NPR, public broadcasting news, morning TV news shows, political talk shows such as CNN's *Crossfire* and CNBC's *Hardball*, and Sunday morning network talk shows.

Political Knowledge

The survey provides a small set of questions that tap both recall and recognition of events tied to the Democratic Party as candidates vied for its nomination to face incumbent President George W. Bush. Recall is measured by two questions: one asking if a respondent can correctly identify which Democratic presidential candidate served as an Army general (Wesley Clark) and which served as majority leader in the House of Representatives (Richard Gephardt). Correct responses were coded as 1, and all other responses were coded as 0, with the responses summed to create an index that ranged from 0 (*none of the questions answered correctly*) to 2 (*both items answered correctly*). There is a strong relationship between answering these two questions correctly ($\chi^2 = 921.3$, $p < .001$, Kendall's τ_b ordinal-by-ordinal correlation $= .54$, $p < .001$, Cronbach's $\alpha = .70$). Recognition is measured by asking respondents if they had heard of Al Gore's endorsement of Howard Dean and of Dean's comment about wanting to win the votes of "guys with Confederate flags in their pickup trucks." Respondents were presented a 3-point scale ranging from 1 (*never heard of it*) to 3 (*heard a lot*). These responses were summed into a index with a range from 0 (*never heard of either incident*) to 6 (*heard a lot about both incidents*). The two items are highly correlated ($r = .46$, $p < .001$, Cronbach's $\alpha = .63$).

Analytic Strategy

The first step is to establish who uses the various media to learn about political campaigns through bivariate analysis in tandem with demographic and political variables, specifically whether younger respondents are more likely to identify late-night and comedy programs as sources of information. The true test of these relationships will follow with multivariate analysis in which the "usual suspects" of political knowledge research are used as either statistical controls or as interaction terms to address the three hypotheses. These controls are age, education, gender, income, race, campaign interest, newspaper exposure, political participation, strength of ideology, and strength of partisanship.[2] Newspaper exposure was included because among all media variables, it is the one that in the literature consistently predicts political knowledge. Interaction terms with age are also included to test the third hypothesis.

Results

Patterns of Media Use

Respondents who said they used late-night and comedy television programs to learn about the political campaign also tended to use other media for the same information.[3] Age was significantly associated with these two kinds of programming, with the younger the respondent, the more likely he or she was to name late-night and comedy programs as an information source, supporting the hypothesized relationships.[4] The audience of these two types of programming—at least those who identify it as an important source of campaign news—tended to be younger rather than older, minority, more male than female, leaning toward the Democratic Party, politically liberal rather than conservative, and somewhat more interested in political campaigns. Indeed, few significant differences exist between the audience of these two kinds of programming, although age has a greater association with comedy viewing ($r = -.32$, $p < .01$) than with late-night television viewing ($r = -.19$, $p < .01$).[5]

Overall, most respondents did not score well on the test of recall, with 62% unable to answer either of the two questions in the survey. The index created from these two items had a mean of 0.6 ($SD = 0.8$), whereas the recognition index had a mean of 3.6 ($SD = 1.3$). . . . Recall knowledge was negatively correlated with watching late-night programs ($r = -.09$, ns) and comedy programs ($r = -.05$, $p < .01$), whereas recognition was unrelated to either media variable ($r = .02$, ns, and $r = -.00$, ns, respectively). The lack of a relationship with recognition is at odds with other studies, which suggest that such a measure might be the best method for tapping the kinds of knowledge gleaned from such programs. It is also important to note that using the other media for campaign news was often positively associated with both recall and recognition. Given the high correlation between late-night and comedy viewing and the correlation patterns with the key dependent variables among the various media, these two sources appear to have more in common with each other than with other communication channels.

Multivariate Analyses

A more stringent test is provided by . . . regression, which statistically controls for the effects of demographic and political factors. . . . The predictive power demonstrated by the demographic factors [of age, education, income, sex, and race] is particularly revealing, with all five achieving statistical significance. The political factors perform less well, although campaign interest and reading newspapers do contribute significantly to the model. The final step [enters] the two entertainment-based media. . . . Despite the large number of statistical controls, watching late-night programming to learn about the news was significantly associated with recall and recognition, but in opposite directions as predicted by Hypothesis 1. Watching late-night programs was negatively associated with recall ($\beta = -.06$, $p < .01$) and positively associated with recognition ($\beta = .05$, $p < .01$). The results for comedy television use do not support the hypothesis, with use of these programs for campaign information being unrelated to both recall ($\beta = -.03$, ns) and recognition ($\beta = .01$, ns).

Hypothesis 2 predicted that age would be significantly associated with program viewing. By regressing the demographic and political factors listed previously on use of both programs, age was the most powerful predictor, far outstripping the predictive power of other variables.[6] This hypothesis was supported.

To answer Hypothesis 3 on whether age and viewing act together to explain campaign knowledge, interaction terms were created. The interaction of age and watching late-night programs for campaign news was negatively related to recall ($\beta = -.04$, $p < .05$) but not significantly associated with recognition ($\beta = -.02$, ns). . . . That is, for young people at the lowest and highest levels of viewing late-night programs, the recall of campaign information is relatively low as compared to more moderate viewing of such programs. Older respondents demonstrate more of a linear relationship. This suggests a function of diminishing returns for younger viewers in how much they actually learn from late-night programs. The interaction term of age with comedy television viewing created a similar result on recall ($\beta = -.05$, $p < .01$) but also achieved statistical significance on recognition as well ($\beta = -.04$, $p < .05$). Although comedy viewing alone was not associated with either knowledge measure, when combined with age the results suggest that young people do receive a modest benefit from viewing comedy programs in terms of both recall and recognition.

Summary

As predicted in the hypothesis, younger viewers identified comedy and late-night television programs as a source of political campaign news. In addition, there was some support for the prediction that the consumption of such programming, particularly late-night television shows, was more associated with recognition than recall. Little support was found, however, for the hypothesized interaction between age and media use in predicting recognition but not recall. For example, watching comedy programs for news improved both recognition and recall for younger viewers, but age made no difference in the relationship between watching late-night programs and recognition of political information. However, age did interact with late-night viewing and recall but not in the expected direction, with younger respondents contradicting the general tendency of a negative relationship between viewing such programs and recall of campaign information.

Conclusion

This study began with a basic question: Do young people learn about a political campaign from such entertainment fare as late-night and comedy television programs? That a younger audience is drawn to such content is without doubt, and in surveys and anecdotal accounts, they often identify *The Daily Show* and similar programs as the source of their political information. The research here supports the idea that younger people seek out entertainment-based programs to keep up with a political campaign and that watching such programs is more likely to be associated with recognition of campaign information than it is with recall of actual information. This is an important difference. Previous research has identified two key methods of measuring political knowledge—recall and recognition. Successful recall of factual information is often associated with use of the print media, particularly newspapers, and scholars suggest that lower motivation and differences in how information is processed makes tests of recognition the preferred method of measuring the effects of television news—and by extension such entertainment-based programming as comedy and late-night shows. In addition, some have found that age can play an important role in the ability to answer public affairs questions.

Overall, younger viewers do appear to get more out of such programs as compared to older viewers, although in some cases it is a matter of diminishing returns. Beyond moderate levels of viewing late-night programs, the improvement in recall disappears while the improvement in recognition increases. Or to put it another way, late-night television viewing increases what young people think they know about a political campaign but provides at best modest improvements to actual recall of events associated with the campaign.

Does political knowledge truly matter? As Rousseau (1762/1968) wrote: "The very right to vote imposes on me the duty to instruct myself in public affairs, however little influence my voice may have in them" (p. 49). Democratic theory rests on the assumption of an informed electorate, and there is some fear that viewers face a diet of empty calories and may "fill up" on programming that does little to actually improve their knowledge about public affairs and political campaigns, a finding reminiscent of Hollander's (1995) results concerning education and listening to talk radio and the effects on actual versus perceived knowledge.

Some 20 years ago, Postman (1985) warned that a reliance on perpetual entertainment and trivia will harm public conversation, placing the nation and its culture at risk. A demand that all content be entertaining, even the most serious questions of politics and public affairs, appears a trend that has captured the attention of the youngest in society. As the political content of comedy and late-night television programs continues to rise, as does an audience turned off by mainstream news sources, then the significance of this exposure increases to the point where, for many, they become the lone source of news. Such a possibility seems to stun host Jon Stewart, who says the possibility either "says something terrible about news organizations, or something terrible about the comedy we're doing, or terrible about teenagers" (McFarland, 2004, ¶ 9). There is some good news here, that young people are capable of gleaning at least modest amounts of campaign information from such content, but how competent it leaves them to participate in a meaningful manner remains an open question.

Notes

1. The items were randomized to control for the influence of question order. For some items, a split-method was used, meaning half of the respondents were randomly assigned to receive one of two program questions. The split variables are religious radio shows such as *Focus on The Family*, talk radio shows, local TV news about your viewing area, TV news magazine shows such as *60 Minutes, 20/20*, and *Dateline*, and morning television shows such as *The Today Show* and *Good Morning America*. In these cases, half of the 3,188 respondents received these items, and half did not.

2. The strength of partisanship and ideology measures are the typical folded scales in which extremes on party identification and political ideology are

scored as high, and scores in the middle of both measures are scored as low. These measures then set aside the direction of a respondent's ideological or partisan leanings and instead focus on how strongly they feel about either political factor.

3. Indeed there is some suggestion here of a response bias, given the positive correlations found between late-night and comedy viewing and all of the other media save one, a hardly surprising nonsignificant relationship between watching comedy programs and listening to religious radio programming. The most powerful correlation in the analysis, however, is between both late-night and comedy TV for information ($r = .50, p < .001$), suggesting a significant overlap in the viewing of these two genres to learn about campaign information.

4. However, age also is associated with using other channels for campaign information. Younger users are more likely to also report getting information from the Internet, C-SPAN, talk radio, NPR, and cable news channels such as CNN. Older respondents favor TV news magazines, religious radio, public broadcasting, Sunday morning political talk shows, local television news, and national television news broadcasts.

5. Minor differences can be found, although most are of little substantive difference. Newspaper exposure, for example, is negatively correlated with late-night viewing ($r = -.06, p < .01$) but is unrelated to watching comedy shows ($r = -.03, ns$). In addition, education is weakly but positively associated with comedy viewing ($r = .07, p < .01$) but not with late-night viewing ($r = .01, ns$). Overall, a weak trend in correlations suggests that late-night viewing, as compared to comedy viewing, is somewhat more tied to less use of regular news and less education. However, no differences can be seen in partisan or ideological strength, ties to a specific party or ideology, or in campaign interest, making any suggestion of audience differences here more speculative than likely.

6. No table provided. The top predictors of late-night television viewing were age ($\beta = -.20, p < .01$), income ($\beta = -.07, p < .01$), and campaign interest ($\beta = .07, p < .01$). The top predictors of comedy show viewing were age ($\beta = -.31, p < .01$), campaign interest ($\beta = .09, p < .01$), and race ($\beta = -.08, p < .01$). The only difference other than the relative predictive power of age between the two variables is the role of newspaper reading ($\beta = -.05, p < .01$, for late-night television, and $\beta = -.00, ns$, for comedy shows).

References

Baum, M. A. (2003). Soft news and political knowledge: Evidence of absence or absence of evidence? *Political Communication, 20*, 173–190.

Baum, M. A. (2005). Talking the vote: Why presidential candidates hit the talk show circuit. *American Journal of Political Science, 49*, 213–234.

Beals, H., Mazis, M. B., Salop, S. C., & Staelin, S. (1981). Consumer search and public policy. *Journal of Consumer Research, 8*, 11–22.

Becker, L. B., & Dunwoody, S. (1982). Media use, public affairs knowledge and voting in a local election. *Journalism Quarterly, 59*, 212–218.

Becker, L. B., & Whitney, D. C. (1980). Effects of media dependencies: Audience assessment of government. *Communication Research, 7*, 95–120.

Bennett, S. E. (1996). "Know-nothings" revisited again. *Political Behavior*, 18, 219–233.

Chaffee, S. H., & Schleuder, J. (1986). Measurement and effects of attention to media news. *Human Communication Research*, 13, 76–107.

Chaffee, S. H., & Tims, A. R. (1982). News media use in adolescence: Implications for political cognitions. In M. Burgoon (Ed.), *Communication yearbook 6* (pp. 736–758). Beverly Hills, CA: Sage.

Chaffee, S. H., Zhao, X., & Leshner, G. (1994). Political knowledge and the campaign media of 1992. *Communication Research*, 21, 305–324.

Davis, R., & Owen, D. (1998). *New media and American politics*. New York: Oxford University Press.

Delli Carpini, M. X., & Keeter, S. (1992). The public's knowledge of politics. In J. D. Kennamer (Ed.), *Public opinion, the press, and public policy* (pp. 19–40). Westport, CT: Praeger.

Delli Carpini, M. X., & Keeter, S. (1996). *What Americans know about politics and why it matters*. New Haven, CT: Yale University Press.

Delli Carpini, M. X., & Williams, B. A. (1996). Constructing public opinion: The uses of fictional and nonfictional television in conversations about the environment. In A. N. Crigler (Ed.), *The psychology of political communication* (pp. 149–175). Ann Arbor: University of Michigan Press.

du Plessis, E. (1994). Recognition versus recall. *Journal of Advertising Research*, 34, 75–91.

Eagle, M., & Leiter, E. (1964). Recall and recognition in intentional and incidental learning. *Journal of Experimental Psychology*, 68, 58–63.

Hamilton, J. T. (2003). *All the news that's fit to sell: How the market transforms information into news*. Princeton, NJ: Princeton University Press.

Holbert, R. L., Pillion, O., Tschida, D. A., Armfield, G. G., Kinder, K., Cherry, K., et al. (2003). The *West Wing* as endorsement of the American presidency: Expanding the domain of priming in political communication. *Journal of Communication*, 53, 427–443.

Holbert, R. L., Shah, D. V., & Kwak, N. (2003). Political implications of prime-time drama and sitcom use: Genres of representation and opinions concerning women's rights. *Journal of Communication*, 53, 45–60.

Holbert, R. L., Shah, D. V., & Kwak, N. (2004). Fear, authority, and justice: The influence of TV news, police reality, and crime drama viewing on endorsements of capital punishment and gun ownership. *Journalism and Mass Communication Quarterly*, 81, 343–363.

Hollander, B. A. (1994). Patterns in the exposure and influence of the Old News and the New News. *Mass Comm Review*, 21, 144–155.

Hollander, B. A. (1995). The new news and the 1992 presidential campaign: Perceived versus actual campaign knowledge. *Journalism and Mass Communication Quarterly*, 72, 786–798.

Krugman, H. E. (1977). Memory without recall, exposure without perception. *Journal of Advertising Research*, 17, 7–12.

McFarland, M. (2004). Young people turning comedy shows into serious news source. *Seattle Post-Intelligencer*. . . .

McLeod, J. M., Guo, Z., Daily, K., Steele, C. A., Horowitz, E., & Chen, H. (1996). The impact of traditional and nontraditional media forms in the 1992 presidential election. *Journalism and Mass Communication Quarterly, 73*, 401–416.

McLeod, J. M., & McDonald, D. G. (1985). Beyond simple exposure: Media orientations and their impact on political processes. *Communication Research, 12*, 3–33.

Moy, P., Xenos, M. A., & Hess, V. K. (2004, May). *Priming effects of late-night comedy.* Paper presented at the annual meeting of the International Communication Association, New Orleans, LA.

Neuman, W. R. (1986). *The paradox of mass politics: Knowledge and opinion in the American electorate.* Cambridge, MA: Harvard University Press.

Niven, D., Lichter, S. R., & Amundson, D. (2003). The political content of late night comedy. *Press/Politics, 8*, 118–133.

Parkin, M., Bos, A., & van Doom, B. (2003, November). *Laughing, learning and liking: The effects of entertainment-based media on American politics.* Paper presented at the annual meeting of the Midwest Political Science Association, Chicago.

Parry-Giles, T., & Parry-Giles, S. J. (2002). The *West Wing's* prime time presidentality: Mimesis and catharsis in a postmodern romance. *Quarterly Journal of Speech, 88*, 209–227.

Patterson, T. E., & McClure, R. (1976). *The unseeing eye: The myth of television power in national elections.* New York: Putman's.

Pettey, G. R. (1988). The interaction of the individual's social environment, attention and interest, and public affairs media use on political knowledge holding. *Communication Research, 15*, 265–281.

Pew Research Center for the People and the Press. (2000, February 5). *The tough job of communicating with voters.* . . .

Pew Research Center for the People and the Press. (2002, June 9). *Public's news habits little changed since September 11.* . . .

Pew Research Center for the People and the Press. (2004, January 11). *Cable and Internet loom large in fragmented political news universe.* . . .

Pfau, M., Cho, J., & Chong, K. (2001). Communication forms in U.S. presidential campaigns: Influences on candidate perceptions and the democratic process. *Press/Politics, 6*, 88–105.

Postman, N. (1985). *Amusing ourselves to death: Public discourse in the age of show business.* New York: Viking.

Prior, M. (2003). Any good news in soft news? The impact of soft news preference on political knowledge. *Political Communication, 20*, 149–171.

Rollins, P. C., & O'Connor, J. E. (2003). *The West Wing: The American presidency as television drama.* Syracuse, NY: Syracuse University Press.

Rousseau, J.-J. (1968). *The social contract* (M. Cranston, Trans.). Harmondworth, England: Penguin. (Original work published 1762)

Salomon, G. (1983). Television watching and mental effort: A social psychological view. In J. Bryant & D. R. Anderson (Eds.), *Children's understanding of television: Research on attention and comprehension* (pp. 181–198). New York: Academic.

Shoemaker, P. J., Schooler, C., & Danielson, W. A. (1989). Involvement with the media: Recall versus recognition of election information. *Communication Research, 16*, 78–103.

Singh, S. N., & Rothschild, M. L. (1983). Recognition as a measure of learning from television commercials. *Journal of Marketing Research, 20*, 235–248.

Smith, E. R. A. N. (1989). *The unchanging American voter*. Berkeley: University of California Press.

Stapel, J. (1998). Recall and recognition: A very close relationship. *Journal of Advertising Research, 38*, 41–45.

Weaver, D., & Drew, D. (1995). Voter learning in the 1992 presidential election: Did the "nontraditional" media and debates matter? *Journalism and Mass Communication Quarterly, 72*, 7–17.

Young, D. G. (2004). Late-night comedy in election 2000: Its influence on candidate trait ratings and the moderating effects of political knowledge and partisanship. *Journal of Broadcasting & Electronic Media, 48*, 1–22.

Zhao, X., & Chaffee, S. H. (1995). Campaign advertisements versus television news as sources of political issue information. *Public Opinion Quarterly, 59*, 41–65.

EXPLORING THE ISSUE

Does Fake News Mislead the Public?

Critical Thinking and Reflection

1. Considering these articles, what are the important differences between fake news and network news? What consequences will these differences promote?
2. Is fake news better than no news?
3. How is news knowledge related to news consumption? Can you be an informed citizen without relying on news?
4. Does fake news promote cynicism or appropriate skepticism?
5. Why are youth and adult knowledge and voting patterns so different?

Is There Common Ground?

In this case the common ground is easy to identify. If the overarching goal of this issue is to ponder the links among news viewing, political knowledge, and civic and political involvement, one answer comes from our observations of the 2008 election of President Obama. Throughout this issue a causal chain of events has been implied: become involved with the news, from that exposure develop political awareness and knowledge, based on that political awareness and knowledge, become an active voter and perhaps even become involved in civic and political processes. The 2008 election galvanized the country and reminded us of an early finding of mass communication research: the importance of interpersonal contacts.

The 2008 election got people talking and excited. The issues were very real, the historical nature of the election exciting, bringing in many who had previously been indifferent and increasing minority participation. In this case, engagement and participation did not develop in the nice causal chain outlined above. Now the question becomes, "Will this engagement continue, or was it only a fluke of circumstance?"

Additional Resources

Robert Love, "Before Jon Stewart," *Columbia Journalism Review* (March/April 2007)

Love outlines the history of fake news, ranging from Hearst to the "yellow press" to video news releases. He reveals a long and undistinguished history of journalistic fakes.

John Pavlik, "Fake News," *Television Quarterly* (2005)

Pavlik details his experience as an interviewee for *The Daily Show*. His careful retelling of his experience, from the point of view of an established department head in a major mass communication program, is both humorous and troubling.

Jeffrey P. Jones, *Entertaining Politics: Satiric Television and Political Engagement* (2009)

Jeffrey Jones examines fake news as they function to call traditional media into question. The book dismisses persistent claims that these programs have cynical effects and create misinformed young citizens, demonstrating instead how such programming provides for an informed, active, and meaningful citizenship.

Amarnath Amarasingam, *The Stewart/Colbert Effect: Essays on the Real Impacts of Fake News* (2011)

The 10 essays in this collection explore the issues engendered by the popularity of entertainment news, including the role of satire in politics, the declining level of trust in traditional sources of media, the shows' cathartic or informational function, and the ways in which these shows influence public opinion.

ISSUE 8

Will Evolving Forms of Journalism Be an Improvement?

YES: The Economist, from "The People Formerly Known as the Audience," *The Economist* (vol. 399:8741, pp. 9–12, July 7, 2011)

NO: Alex Jones, from "The Iron Core," in *Losing the News* (Oxford University Press, 2009)

Learning Outcomes
After reading this issue, you should be able to:
• Define consumer generated content.
• Define the iron core.
• Contrast the iron core to opinion journalism.
• Evaluate the dangers and opportunities of the traditional system and the evolving forms of journalism.

ISSUE SUMMARY

YES: In a special report *The Economist* studies "The People Formerly Known as the Audience" to argue that social media allow a wider range of people to take part in gathering, filtering, and distributing the news. A torrent of information is being posted on the Internet, creating a role for people—not limited to journalists—to evaluate, verify, and create meaning.

NO: Alex Jones describes the iron core of journalism as fact-based accountability journalism, an expensive, intensive search for information that holds those with power accountable. Opinion journalism, quasi-news programs, and even entertainment media rely on the iron core for their substance. Whether journalism that produces the iron core will continue to function as is needed is his concern.

Has the time come to discard the journalistic models of the past? In this digital age, where new platforms for communication emerge routinely, what do the new models offer? Before you read further, take a moment to write one way in which you think journalism needs to improve. What change would you like to see? A major change emerging in the digital age has been the rise of participatory journalism. Participatory journalism can take two forms: civic journalism and independent digital voices. Civic journalism refers to the journalistic practice of engaging communities in dialogue. Many media outlets have tried to strengthen their ties to the community by encouraging comment and reporting about important civic concerns. This can happen in a variety of ways, including inviting comment, convening citizen panels, changing journalistic practices to listen and reflect more thoroughly on citizen viewpoints, and surveying the community to identify community needs. Often these discussions take place on the media outlet's Web site. A concept that you may have heard used is "hyper local." A hyper local focus reports intensely on events and issues within a well-defined community and is intended primarily for consumption by residents of that community. It almost always relies on user-generated content as well as professionally developed reporting. Many believe that "localism" will save local newspapers, radio, and television stations because it will distinguish them from readily available national voices.

The second form of participatory journalism refers to the explosion of voices that have developed as independent news reporting and commentary. "User-generated content" is a broad term for all the ways in which individuals have expanded opportunity to produce and distribute their ideas and products across the Internet. There are blogs, digital newsletters, Web sites, YouTube videos, and more, where individuals report and comment on the news.

In 2011, *The Economist* published a special section on the future of news. One article focused on the ways in which social media are creating as well as contributing to the national and international news stream. Their point is straightforward: News is no longer in the hands of journalists. It is now as they describe it "an ecosystem" wherein journalists, sources, readers, and viewers exchange information. Rosen describes it as a shift in the tools of production to the audience. After an initial period of hostility, news organizations are now using this changed ecosystem as an adjunct to traditional media. Traditional media face a series of challenges in using this information: How do you verify accounts? How do you protect sources? When do you run with information that you can't verify in the new 24/7 news cycle? But all of these are issues of traditional media; they are mostly not issues for the bloggers, tweeters, photographers, videographers, and Facebook posters. Within the realm of social media, content providers are developing their own methods of curating, coordinating, and developing socially constructed meaning for what is observed. Will consumer-generated content be an adjunct to more traditional media, or will it replace traditional journalism entirely?

That is certainly what Alex Jones fears. He fears the loss of the iron core of journalism, the accountability reporting that holds power to account. Much is absent from the iron core. Opinion pieces, talk shows, arts and entertainment news, sports, and even entertainment news programs such as *20/20* are outside the core. Some of these, he argues, are derived from the core. Without what he terms "accountability news," he is concerned with what will remain. The core, he notes, is enveloped by a thick blanket of talk and opinion. This conversation takes place all across our country, but what will it be based on if the iron core is not in place? Who, for example, will even try to fact-check the information permeating the talk/opinion envelope? Jones acknowledges that the crisis is financial. Economic concerns and the Internet have placed the iron core in jeopardy. If social responsibility is replaced by financial necessity, the loss will be grave. With these evolutions, he asserts, high-end journalism is dying in America. His point is straightforward. Journalism is a profession. It requires full-time commitment and consistent attention. It cannot become the province of the occasional commentator.

For another perspective on whether emerging forms of journalism will be an improvement, consider the views of Eran Ben-Porath in his article "Internal Fragmentation of the News: Television News in Dialogical Format and Its Consequences for Journalism," *Journalism Studies* (2007). He argues that the primary change in journalism in this era has been the shift from traditional practices to dialogic formats in which conversationally based news has become predominant. When dialogue, rather than reporting, is the format, the authority of the journalist is lessened, conversationalists are often not journalists but commentators or partisan spokespersons, and the audience changes from receivers of information to witnesses of conversation. In addition to diminished authority of the reporter, Ben-Porath argues for diminished authority and accountability for the news organization; the organization did not make the "claims"; their guests did. Thus, the organization's accountability for accuracy is diminished. He also asserts that question-asking, rather than fact-checking, become the norm. These changes are taking place most visibly in television news, but are also playing out extensively on the Internet. Does this mean that the evolving forms of journalistic practice will continue this drift to conversation rather than reporting? As a colleague said, "News is expensive; opinion is cheap."

Concerns such as these should lead us back to fundamental questions about media and society. Freedom of the press is granted in the First Amendment. What does that freedom mean for the operation of the press? Questions of this sort are studied within normative theories of mass communication. Normative theory asks about ideal ways to structure and operate news systems. A group called the Hutchins Commission on Freedom of the Press released a report in 1947 that introduced the social responsibility theory of the press. A few of the principles in that report were that media (1) had certain obligations to society, (2) which obligations were to be met by setting high professional standards of informativeness, truth, accuracy, objectivity, and balance, and that (3) journalists should be accountable to society as well as to their employers. This general perspective is sometimes communicated by the brief phrase, "with rights come obligations." How does the current media system fare in fulfilling these goals? How well do the evolving forms of journalism fulfill these same goals?

An international group prepared a statement "In Defense of Journalism as a Public Trust" (search Poynter.org under that title for the full announcement). The group concluded that market pressures are undermining journalism to the detriment of the public interest. They conclude with the strong statement, "It is this fundamental role of the press to inform and empower citizens that is being endangered." John Hockenberry is disillusioned about the ability of professional journalism to survive in the current corporate environment. Based on his experience at *Dateline NBC,* he explores the timidity of those in charge of newsrooms. He found that fear of corporate owners, of audience response, and of technology cripples authentic journalism. He describes a process of deciding which stories would air that was influenced by corporate ownership and timid management. With the focus clearly on audience size, Hockenberry argues that television news has "lost its most basic journalistic instincts in its search for the audience-driven sweet spot, the 'emotional center' of the American people." His pessimistic conclusion is that television news has lost its center in its search for numbers. Technology is freeing communication, and that may be good news for the news (*Technology Review,* 2008).

John Carroll provides a clear statement of the business and professional issues that make these changes in journalism such an important debate. In a speech at the University of Kentucky titled "The Future (We Hope) of Journalism," he asks three crucial questions: Who, in the digital future, will do the reporting? What principles, if any, will guide the journalism of the digital age? Will we have journalistic institutions that are strong enough, and independent enough, to serve as a counterweight to big government and big corporations? You can find this speech at www.poynter.org.

As you read and debate these selections, return to the one suggestion you made about how journalism needs to improve. What kinds of changes could make your suggestion happen? Would citizen journalism help? Or would your suggestion require more traditional journalistic practice? Participatory journalism offers the hope of broader community engagement in civic issues. But are there downsides to this focus? Does journalism lose some of its autonomy it it allows citizens to lead in reporting decisions? Does citizen journalism run the risk of involving citizens, but having their input minimized by the news outlets? As we consider the comments of David Simon, we need to consider the willingness of the American public to pay for high-quality journalism. As an abstract concept, we would probably agree that we want quality, but how many of us are willing to pay for the subscription fees that newspapers now charge? How many of us are willing to pay for our news at all in this age of free access to information on the Internet? These and many other questions are all part of trying to envision a future for journalism in the digital age.

YES

The Economist

The People Formerly Known as the Audience

Social-media technologies allow a far wider range of people to take part in gathering, filtering and distributing news. The announcement that Barack Obama would shortly appear on television came late in the evening on May 1st. "POTUS to address the nation tonight at 10.30 pm eastern time," tweeted Dan Pfeiffer, communications director at the White House. This caused an explosion of speculation on Twitter. Had Muammar Qaddafi been killed in an air strike? Had Osama bin Laden been tracked down at last? At first these two theories had roughly equal support, measured by the volume of tweets. But then Keith Urbahn, chief of staff for Donald Rumsfeld, a former defence secretary, had a call from a well-connected television news producer who wanted to interview Mr Rumsfeld about the killing of bin Laden. Mr Urbahn tweeted: "So I'm told by a reputable person they have killed Osama bin Laden. Hot damn."

His message quickly rippled across Twitter. Television news channels began to report the story, which was confirmed by Mr Obama an hour later. It subsequently turned out that Sohaib Athar, a computer consultant living in Abbottabad, the Pakistani village where bin Laden had been hiding, had unwittingly described the operation as it happened in a series of tweets ("A huge window-shaking bang here in Abbottabad . . . I hope it's not the start of something nasty").

The next day a picture that purported to show bin Laden's bloodied face began to circulate online, but on Twitter it was swiftly exposed as a fake. A week later a statement on an obscure website attributed to bin Laden's son Omar, calling his father's killing "criminal" and his burial at sea demeaning, was reported around the world after a link to it was tweeted by Leah Farrall, a counter-terrorism analyst. All this shows how social media are changing journalism, says Mark Jones, global communities editor at Reuters, a news agency: "Every aspect of that story was on Twitter."

Surveys in Britain and America suggest that 7–9% of the population use Twitter, compared with almost 50% for Facebook. But Twitter users are the "influencers," says Nic Newman, former head of future media at the BBC and now a visiting fellow at the Reuters Institute at Oxford University. "The audience isn't on Twitter, but the news is on Twitter," says Mr Jones.

Thanks to the rise of social media, news is no longer gathered exclusively by reporters and turned into a story but emerges from an ecosystem in which journalists, sources, readers and viewers exchange information. The change began around 1999, when blogging tools first became widely available, says Jay Rosen, professor of journalism at New York University. The result was "the shift of the tools of production to the people formerly known as the audience," he says. This was followed by a further shift: the rise of "horizontal media" that made it quick and easy for anyone to share links (via Facebook or Twitter, for example) with large numbers of people without the involvement of a traditional media organisation. In other words, people can collectively act as a broadcast network.

At first many news organisations were openly hostile towards these new tools. In America the high point of the antagonism between bloggers and the mainstream media was in late 2004, when "60 Minutes," an evening news show on CBS, alleged on the basis of leaked memos that George Bush junior had used family connections to win favourable treatment in the Air National Guard in the 1970s. Bloggers immediately questioned the authenticity of the memos. A former CBS News executive derided blogging as "a guy sitting in his living room in his pyjamas writing what he thinks." But the bloggers were right. CBS retracted the story and Dan Rather, one of the most respected names in American news, resigned as the show's anchor in early 2005.

But in the past few years mainstream media organisations have changed their attitude. The success of the Huffington Post, which launched in May 2005 with a combination of original reporting by members of staff, blog posts from volunteers (including many celebrity friends of Arianna Huffington's, the site's co-founder) and links to news stories on other sites, showed the appeal of what Ms Huffington calls a "hybrid" approach that melds old and new, professional and amateur. Newspapers and news channels have since launched blogs of their own, hired many bloggers and allowed readers to leave comments, as on blogs. They also invite pictures, video and other contributions from readers and seek out material published on the internet, thus incorporating non-journalists into the news system.

Journalists are becoming more inclined to see blogs, Facebook, Twitter and other forms of social media as a valuable adjunct to traditional media (and sometimes a corrective to them). "We see these things as being highly complementary to what we do," says Martin Nisenholtz of the *New York Times*. Many journalists who were dismissive about social media have changed their tune in the past few months as their value became apparent in the coverage of the Arab uprisings and the Japanese earthquake, says Liz Heron, social-media editor at the *New York Times*.

The View from the Street

When a young Tunisian, Mohammed Bouazizi, set himself on fire on December 17th to protest against the police confiscating his fruitstall and the lack of jobs for young people, his action prompted demonstrations by other youths in the town of Sidi Bouzid. A video of one protest, led by Mr Bouazizi's mother, was posted on Facebook, where it was seen by the new-media team at Al Jazeera; a satellite news broadcaster founded in 1996 and based in Qatar that has become the Arab world's most influential media outlet. Al Jazeera showed the video on air, and by the time Bouazizi died of his burns on January 4th protests had broken out across Tunisia and spread across the Arab world.

Marc Lynch, an expert on Middle Eastern media at George Washington University, says social media and satellite television worked together to draw attention to the Arab spring. Social media spread images of protesters in Tunisia that might otherwise have been suppressed by the regime, he wrote on his blog at Foreign Policy. "But it was the airing of these videos on Al Jazeera . . . which brought those images to the mass Arab public and even to many Tunisians who might otherwise not have realised what was happening."

The staff in Al Jazeera's Arabic and English newsrooms had, as it happened, undergone intense social-media training only the month before. "It was just in time," says Moeed Ahmad, the network's head of new media. Although Al Jazeera had used material from the internet in its coverage before, in Tunisia there was no other choice, because it had no reporters on the ground. With its journalists freshly trained in the use of such material, theory was quickly put into practice.

The training was the culmination of a two-year initiative to make better use of social media throughout Al Jazeera, prompted by the realisation during the three-week Gaza war of 2008–09 that the channel's audience was swiftly moving online. This meant convincing journalists that social media are not a threat, but "the biggest assets you can have." Instead of flying a reporter somewhere to cover a story, Al Jazeera can draw upon networks of trusted volunteers whose credibility has been established. It also has a website, called Sharek, where photos and videos can be submitted for use (once verified) in Al Jazeera's television and online reports.

Other news organisations are working along similar lines. Sharek, launched in 2008, seems to have been inspired by CNN's iReport website. Over 750,000 people have volunteered as iReporters, and reports have been submitted from every country on earth. CNN's coverage of the Japanese earthquake in March, which drew heavily on iReport material, won it its best ratings in more than five years. "Because it happened so suddenly and in such a remote area, having the extra iReport material was enormously helpful," says Mark Whitaker, managing editor of CNN. "I just see it growing." But it is always vetted before being used on air, he adds.

Verifying material to ensure it is suitable for broadcasting can be an elaborate process, says Mohamed Yehia of BBC Arabic. Journalists examine photographs and video footage for recognisable landmarks, street signs, vehicles or weapons to determine whether images really come from a particular city or region. Sound can help. Shadows can indicate the time of day. Comparing weather reports with date stamps can reveal whether a video or photograph really was taken on a particular date. Even when verified, such material will not be used if it identifies people and puts them in danger, Mr Yehia adds.

Checking snippets of information posted on Twitter is more difficult. Tweets can be a useful way to gauge the public mood about an issue and are now often incorporated into news coverage as digital "vox pops." Many journalists use Twitter to solicit leads, find sources or ask for information. But

Twitter is a public forum where anyone can say anything. Neal Mann, a producer who works for Sky News, a British satellite-news channel controlled by News Corporation, says he thinks it is a journalist's duty to provide reliable information, on Twitter as elsewhere. He works with a network of trusted contacts around the world whose tweets he passes on to his followers. By contrast, Andy Carvin, a social-media strategist at NPR who has become known for this monitoring of Twitter during the Arab spring, does not attempt to check the accuracy of every tweet before publishing it. Instead, he asks his followers to help assess the trustworthiness of individual tweets.

Either way, there is clearly a role for people--including journalists, but not limited to them—to select, filter and analyse the torrent of information being posted on the internet. "There still is an editorial function that needs to happen—there still needs to be someone who really makes sense of it all," says Jack Dorsey, co-founder of Twitter. This process is known in social-media jargon as "curation," and a growing number of tools is available to do the job. Storify, for example, is a website that lets users arrange items of social media (including tweets, Facebook posts, videos from YouTube and photos from Flickr) into chronological narratives. The resulting narrative can then be embedded into pages on other sites. Keepstream and Storyful work in a similar way. All this raises the question whether some stories may be better covered by constantly updated streams of tweets than by traditional articles. By providing more raw material than ever from which to distil the news, in short, social media have both done away with editors and shown up the need for them. News organisations are already abandoning attempts to be first to break news, focusing instead on being the best at verifying and curating it, says Mr Newman. But like other aspects of journalism, this role is now open to anyone.

As well as getting involved (if they choose) in newsgathering, verification and curation of news, readers and viewers have also become part of the news-distribution system as they share and recommend items of interest via e-mail and social networks. "If searching for news was the most important development of the past decade, sharing news may be among the most important of the next," noted a recent study of online news consumption in America by the Pew Research Centre's Project for Excellence in Journalism. Typically around 20–30% of visitors to the websites of big news organisations come from Google's search engine or its news site, Google News.

The proportion of visitors referred from Facebook is smaller, but growing quickly as social-sharing features become more commonplace and easier to use. With a single click of a Facebook "Like" button, for example, you can recommend a story, video or slideshow to your entire network of friends. Some news sites present visitors with a list of stories recommended by their friends because they reckon an endorsement from someone you know carries extra weight. "This year you'll see more and more news sites where referrals from social networks exceed those from search engines," says Joshua Benton of the Nieman Journalism Lab. "Facebook is beginning to join Google as one of the most influential players in driving news audiences," observes the Pew study, as social sharing steers readers to the stories that are most popular among their social circle.

Letting your network of friends guide you to stuff you might find interesting makes a lot of sense, says Nick Denton, founder of Gawker Media, a network of popular blogs. Friends are a good proxy for one's tastes, he says, and social recommendation is far more efficient than maintaining lists of keywords relating to topics of interest. Better still, "you get the serendipity that people said was going to be lost with personalised news." At the same time, says Bret Taylor, chief technology officer at Facebook, social recommendations are "recreating the watercooler" by increasing the odds that, in a fragmented media landscape, friends and family members will have seen the same things.

Flipboard, an app that runs on the iPad, goes a stage further. It can compile an entire personalised magazine, with flippable pages, in which the articles are items recommended by the user's contacts on Facebook and Twitter. Other news apps and websites, including News.me, Zite and Trove, do similar things. John-Paul Schmetz, a veteran of the German media industry and the co-founder of Cliqz, another social-recommendation start-up, says such services are needed because the explosion of content online in the past decade means "you spend a lot of time filtering, and you don't spend much time reading."

Rather than relying solely on human editors or mindless algorithms to find the best content, he says, it makes sense to use a hybrid approach, analysing contacts and behaviour on social networks to find items of interest. Mr Denton, however, is worried that the shift towards social filtering of news is making news organisations too dependent on Facebook. "It's eating their lunch," he says. Facebook's Mr Taylor insists that there is no conflict because his firm does not produce content but merely provides "valuable distribution" for it.

The Feeling Is Mutual

Clearly readers and viewers are getting steadily more involved in gathering, filtering and distributing news. The Guardian's Alan Rusbridger calls this process the "mutualisation" of news. "If you are open to contributions from others, you generally end up with richer, better, more diverse and expert content than if you try to do it alone," he says. Involving thousands of readers through "crowdsourcing" also lets news outlets do things that would otherwise be impractical, such as searching through troves of documents looking for interesting material.

Rather than thinking of themselves as setting the agenda and managing the conversation, news organisations need to recognise that journalism is now just part of a conversation that is going on anyway, argues Jeff Jarvis, a media guru at the City University of New York. The role of journalists in this new world is to add value to the conversation by providing reporting, context, analysis, verification and debunking, and by making available tools and platforms that allow people to participate. All this requires journalists to admit that they do not have a monopoly on wisdom. "Ten years ago that was a terribly threatening idea, and it still is to some people," says Mr Rusbridger. "But in the real world the aggregate of what people know is going to be, in most cases, more than we know inside the building."

A Pew Research Centre survey published in March 2010 found that 37% of American internet users, or 29% of the population, had "contributed to the creation of news, commented about it or disseminated it via postings on social-media sites like Facebook or Twitter". The figure is probably much higher today, because the Pew survey predates the introduction in April 2010 of the Facebook "Like" button, which makes sharing a news story (or anything else) as simple as clicking a mouse. Only a small proportion of these people provide content as well as commenting and sharing. But, as Mr Rosen points out, even if just 1% of the audience is now involved in the news system, that's millions of new people. "It isn't true that everyone is a journalist," he says. "But a lot more people are involved."

The Iron Core

Imagine a sphere of pitted iron, grey and imperfect like a large cannonball. Think of this dense, heavy ball as the total mass of each day's serious reported news, the iron core of information that is at the center of a functioning democracy. This iron core is big and unwieldy, reflecting each day's combined output of all the professional journalism done by news organizations—newspapers, radio and television news, news services such as the Associated Press and Reuters, and a few magazines. Some of its content is now created by new media, nonprofits, and even, occasionally, the supermarket tabloids, but the overwhelming majority still comes from the traditional news media.

This iron core does not include Paris Hilton's latest escapade or an account of the Yankees game or the U.S. Open. It has no comics or crossword puzzle. No ads. It has no stories of puppies or weekend getaways or recipes for cooking great chili. Nor does it include advice on buying real estate, investing in an IRA, movie reviews, or diet tips. There is nothing wrong with any of these things. Indeed, pleasant and diverting stories are far more appealing to most people than the contents of the core, which some find grim, boring, or riddled with bias.

It has no editorials and does not include the opinions of columnists or op-ed writers or political bloggers. These things are *derived* from the core. They are made possible because there *is* a core. Their point of departure is almost always information gleaned from the reporting that gives the core its weight, and they serve to spread awareness of the information that is in the core, to analyze it and interpret it and challenge it. Opinion writers pick and choose among what the core provides to find facts that will further an argument or advance a policy agenda. But they are outside the core, because they almost always offer commentary and personal observation, not original reporting.

Inside the core is news from abroad, from coverage of the war in Iraq to articles describing the effort to save national parks in Mozambique. There is news of politics, from the White House to the mayor's office. There is an account of a public hearing on a proposal to build new ball fields and an explanation of a regional zoning concept that might affect property values. There is policy news about Medicare reform and science news about global warming. There is news of business, both innovation and scandal, and even sporting news of such things as the abuse of steroids. An account of the battle within

From *Losing the News: The Future of the News That Feeds Democracy* by Alex S. Jones (Oxford University Press, 2009), pp. 1–6, 7–8, 12–19, 20–22, 25, 27. Copyright © 2009 by Oxford University Press, Ltd. Reprinted by permission.

the local school board about dress codes is there, along with the debate in the state legislature over whether intelligent design should be taught as science. The iron sphere is given extra weight by investigative reports ranging from revelations that prisoners at the county jail are being used to paint the sheriffs house to the disclosure that the government is tapping phones without warrants as part of the war on terror.

What goes into this cannonball is the daily aggregation of what is sometimes called "accountability news," because it is the form of news whose purpose is to hold government and those with power accountable. This is fact-based news, sometimes called the "news of verification" as opposed to the "news of assertion" that is mostly on display these days in prime time on cable news channels and in blogs.

Traditional journalists have long believed that this form of fact-based accountability news is the essential food supply of democracy and that without enough of this healthy nourishment, democracy will weaken, sicken, or even fail.

For more than a century, this core of reported news has been the starting place for a raucous national conversation about who we are as a people and a country. Just as the Earth is surrounded by a blanket of atmosphere, so too is this core enveloped by a thick layer of talk and opinion. The conversation—which seems more like an endless family squabble—takes place on editorial pages and in letters to the editor, in opinion columns and on Sunday morning talk shows, on *The O'Reilly Factor* and the radio programs of Rush Limbaugh and Don Imus, in blogs on the Internet and press releases, over dining-room tables, beside water coolers and in barrooms, in political cartoons and on *The Daily Show with Jon Stewart*.

. . .The core also feeds the entertainment industry, which has its own powerful voice in the national conversation. The quasi-news programs on television, such as *Today* and *20/20*, look to the core for ideas and inspiration. Some pure entertainment programs, such as *The West Wing*, come directly from the core, and even the silliest of sitcoms and nastiest of hip-hop lyrics are often linked to it in some murky way. No matter where the conversation about public affairs takes place, it is almost always an outgrowth of that daily iron cannonball.

The biggest worry of those concerned about news is that this iron core is in jeopardy, largely because of the troubles plaguing the newspaper business. It is the nation's newspapers that provide the vast majority of iron core news. My own estimate is that 85 percent of professionally reported accountability news comes from newspapers, but I have heard guesses from credible sources that go as high as 95 percent. While people may *think* they get their news from television or the Web, when it comes to this kind of news, it is almost always newspapers that have done the actual reporting. Everything else is usually just a delivery system, and while resources for television news have plunged and news on commercial radio has all but disappeared, the real impact on iron core news has been from the economic ravaging of newspapers.

Until now, the iron core of news has been somewhat sheltered by an economic model that was able to provide extra resources beyond what readers—and advertisers—would financially support. This kind of news is expensive to produce, especially investigative reporting. And there are indications that a lot of people aren't really interested. In the media economy of the future, cold metrics will largely determine what is spent on news. The size and quality of the iron core will be a direct reflection of what the audience for it will economically support. Demand will rule, and that may well mean that, as a nation, we will be losing a lot of news. There will be a bounty of talk—the news of assertion—but serious news, reported by professional journalists, is running scared.

Inside the core, there is a hierarchy of news, each type important in its own way. The first tier could be thought of as bearing witness. This is no small service to democracy, and is the meat and potatoes of accountability news in that it lets citizens know the fundamentals of what is happening in their world and in the corridors of power. Much of the headline news, both of the White House and around the world, is the act of journalists bearing witness to events. Firsthand coverage of disasters such as Hurricane Katrina and of wars in Afghanistan and Iraq are examples of this kind of bearing-witness journalism at its most challenging. Similarly, the reporter who tells you what happened at the mayor's press conference or at the school board meeting is bearing witness. Being a reliable surrogate for the public—the nation's eyes and ears—is most of what goes into the core, and it is also the most straightforward form of journalism. The burden for the reporter is to tell it straight and get as much of the truth as is possible.

But bearing witness is frequently not enough—indeed, not nearly enough for important issues. It opens the door to the second tier of core journalism, which can be thought of as "following up." Good journalists rarely stop with bearing witness. That is the point of departure for the second step of finding out what more is to be known and answering the all-important question "why?"—seeking reasons that often are not apparent at the moment of bearing witness. This is the journalism that requires being able to stay with a story rather than simply visit it and then move on to the next thing. It means listening to the mayor's press conference and then finding out what was behind the decision or policy that was announced. It is staying with the war rather than parachuting in, doing a quick report, and leaving on the next plane. It is sometimes simply being able to confirm what seemed to be the truth at the moment of bearing witness, but may have been a selective representation. It requires time to follow up, and it demands—and in turn creates—expertise and sophistication about what is being reported.

Next up the hierarchy of core news is what might be called "explanatory journalism," which takes even more time and expertise. This is the product of boring deeply into a subject, speaking to sources, unearthing data, gathering facts, and mastering complexity. It is the kind of reporting that compares the confusing options for older Americans as they try to choose between prescription plans and that examines—without prejudice—the evidence for and against the reality of global warming and presents the result in a form that is illuminatingly fair-minded. It could be thought of as following up on steroids, and if following up takes effort and dogged curiosity, explanatory journalism takes deeper knowledge and expertise, and even more time.

Finally, at the top of the reporting chain, is investigative reporting. This is the toughest kind of journalism because it not only takes time and great expertise, it must be done in the face of efforts to keep information secret. Inherent in the concept of investigative reporting is that it is news that someone with power does not want the public to know. Often, it starts with a reporter simply bearing witness. In perhaps the most celebrated example, in 1972 Bob Woodward was a low-level metro reporter at the *Washington Post,* on the job for only nine months, when five men broke into the Democratic National Headquarters in the Watergate complex and got caught wearing rubber surgical gloves and carrying fancy bugging equipment and $2,300 in cash. Both Woodward and another metro reporter, Carl Bernstein, worked on the first-day page-one story, along with eight other *Post* reporters, and they didn't even get a byline. But they then attacked the story like wolverines, and the *Post* won a Pulitzer Prize for Public Service for its coverage of the Watergate scandal. As Alicia Shepard points out in her article "The Myth of Watergate, Woodward and Bernstein," the story released a deluge of reportorial energy as the nation's best news organizations competed for scoops. The *Los Angeles Times* was first to get one of the burglars on the record in a hard-hitting interview. In his book *Richard Nixon, Watergate and the Press,* Louis Liebovich said that within six months of the break-in, the *Post* had produced 201 staff-written stories, but the *New York Times* had published 99 and the *Los Angeles Times* 45. Important investigative work was also done by the *Washington Star, Time, Newsweek,* and CBS. The aggregate of their work was the fruit of thousands of man-hours by talented reporters, and it took every bit of that commitment by news organizations to finally force the truth to emerge. . . .

The problem is financial. Building the relationships and trust that generate high-stakes investigative reporting requires a news organization's patient support. A skilled investigative reporter can cost a news organization more than $250,000 a year in salary and expenses for only a handful of stories. Single projects can sometimes take months or even years. A few years ago, the *Los Angeles Times* allowed three reporters to work for three years, one of them virtually full-time, on a story that resulted in exposing a glaring bit of unexpected evil. The series, which was entitled "Guardians for Profit," told of how predatory opportunists manipulated the system to get themselves legally appointed guardians of elderly people without the victims' knowledge or wish. These vulnerable seniors had no close family, but did have assets, and their new "guardians"—with the law behind them—were able to take over their lives and plunder at will. The multipart series rocked Los Angeles and prompted a severe tightening in laws involving appointed guardianships. But the series cost hundreds of thousands of dollars in salaries and expenses.

This kind of reporting also often means incurring legal risks and igniting the wrath of powerful interests, which is one reason there is so little of it on the Web. The economic muscle of a major news organization, with lawyers and libel insurance, is all but essential. While it does not make up the greatest quantity of core reporting, it is the weightiest reporting of all when it comes to accountability. In the changing news economy, each form of core news is in jeopardy of shrinking in proportion to how expensive it is to produce, which will mean that investigative, explanatory, and follow-up news stand to get hit hardest. But even bearing-witness news—especially if it incurs significant expense, such as foreign reporting—is facing a bleak prospect. The hollowed-out iron core of the future may well be mostly a compendium of the simplest, cheapest kind of bearing-witness news, generated by a corps of general assignment reporters whose job is to fill a quota of publishable copy rather than to cover a beat with depth. News staffs are shrinking, and the most experienced and highly paid reporters and editors are usually the target. As they leave the journalistic ranks, the iron core steadily hollows out. . . .

Until recently, iron core reporting in all of its forms has been artificially protected and subsidized because of an American bargain in which public service was harnessed to voracious capitalism as news spawned a business. In the 18th century, newspapers tended to be subsidized political organs or promotional vehicles for businesses whose real profit came from commercial printing. The *business* of news was a product of technological advances in the 19th century that were as revolutionary in their time as digital technology has been in ours. . . .

When new technology made it practical to manufacture newspapers quickly and cheaply, a new economic model was born, based on selling advertising, which in turn required attracting the largest possible audience.

The devil's bargain was struck as newspapers sought to marry commerce with the social responsibility of preserving a free press, which had been singled out for protection by the First Amendment as a mission close to sacred. They elected to fulfill that mission not by printing narrow political broadsides but by publishing *news,* which was the foundation of a modern free press and also had a far broader potential audience, a decided virtue. Newspaper owners, who were now businessmen, were interested in attracting an audience so they cut the price per copy. . . . These new mass audience newspapers used news to draw a crowd. The money to pay for gathering that news was to come from advertising. The self-interest of creating high profits was accompanied by the understanding that a significant part of those profits would be used for the public purpose of providing news.

However, the bargain was neither that simple nor that pure. While serious—if still partisan—news on politics and public affairs was one of the things that owners put into the columns of their papers, it was hardly the only thing—and perhaps was never the principal appeal of the burgeoning newspaper business. Scandal, crime, and gossipy social and celebrity news were staples of most newspapers, especially in the penny press. Newspaper "crusades" for various social reforms had the added—often, primary—appeal of whipping up circulation. For instance, William Randolph Hearst's campaign to drag America into a war with Spain over Cuba was, at least in part, a gimmick to boost sales.

Soon pictures and cartoons, poetry and book serials, and sports, and all kinds of other things were poured into a newspaper's pages—anything that would lure readers into buying a paper. . . . For advertisers, the content was only important in that it brought readers whose eyes passed over their solicitations to buy pots, pans, and patent medicines. The iron core style of news may have been the ostensible heart of newspapers, but the reality was that both advertising and lighter, racier content outpaced serious news from the start.

To the best of my knowledge, no one has ever tried to measure just how much of what has appeared in newspapers over the decades could be considered iron core news. My best guess is that the amount of serious reporting on important topics would average around 15 percent. . . . This was true from the period in the 1800s when commercial newspapers were born, and it has remained consistent for 150 years. The total amount of this kind of news grew with the size of newspapers, but the percentage seems to have remained virtually constant. About half the space in a typical newspaper is devoted to advertising. If roughly 15 percent is core news, the other 35 percent is taken up with crowd-pleasing soft news, features, comics, gimmicks, editorials, entertainments, amusements, and such. Even in the elite newspapers, the percentages don't vary much. The *New York Times, Washington Post,* and *Los Angeles Times* all devote reams of space to sports, entertainment, and other non-core news. . . .

It would be like unscrambling an egg to try to put a precise number on how many people have bought newspapers for their serious news, as opposed to the smorgasbord of entertaining fare to be found there. But it seems reasonable to think that if there had been clamor for more serious news by newspaper readers, they would have been accommodated. That there was no such clamor for a century and a half suggests that publishers got the percentage about right, for a mass audience with an interest—but a limited interest—in such news.

But it was the prospect of doing serious news that drew most of the best reporters and editors to journalism. Reporting accountability news carried the most prestige. It was the most expensive to produce, took the most time, often got the biggest play, and required the greatest expertise. Much of the other content was provided by syndicates and services or reporters lower in the pecking order. But serious news required employing an experienced news staff that expected raises and vacations, health insurance and pensions, and took themselves increasingly seriously as professionals.

It is this kind of news that is recognized in prizes and awards, which in turn validate the newspaper's inevitable claim to be fulfilling not just a commercial but a societal role. It was this kind of news that was thought important enough to be protected by the First Amendment—though what the amendment actually protected was free expression rather than high-quality news. Even so, in the 20th century, the public service of publishing iron core news was what gave newspaper owners a mantle of honor and respectability that went nicely with their growing profits.

No matter the real reason for subscribing to a newspaper, those who bought one got the news too. It came with the package. The result was a virtuous circle of profitability and public service. The greatest news expense was for serious journalism, which was not necessarily the part of the paper that prompted the most sales, but which was in the public interest. A cascade of amusing and titillating material swelled the paper's audience, which in turn brought in the bountiful ad revenues that were used to pay for the serious news that by itself would likely not have attracted an audience of sufficient size. From the 1980s until recently, the paper almost certainly made handsome profits, the public was served with both news and entertainment, and few in the newsroom spent much time thinking about the fact that their salaries were paid by people who had limited or even no interest in the journalistic work they did. Newspaper readers who didn't really want that kind of news had to buy it anyway because it came with the paper. They presumably would glance at the iron core news, or even read it carefully upon occasion, but they didn't seek it out. For this group of indeterminate size, the serious news was essentially a bonus that came with the sport section or the ads—which, in themselves, were a major attraction.

The readers who cared intensely about serious news were able to get a report far richer than what could have been supported had it depended on their readership alone. As the 20th century progressed, both radio and television adopted the same essential formula, though the time in their broadcasting day devoted to iron core news was even less than the 15 percent in newspapers. The essential point from a business perspective was that serious news almost certainly got a disproportionate share of the revenue from advertising, based on raw popularity of content. And the public benefited.

Digital technology—and especially the Internet—is rapidly blowing that long-standing economic model to smithereens. Traditional news was already in trouble, but the digital revolution has hit the news business with crushing force. And as the old mass communication model is rapidly being replaced by one of increasingly narrow specialized audiences, the department store is becoming a mall of boutiques. Serious news, which had been the sheltered child, is increasingly being cast into a cruel world to sink or swim on its own. It has gone from being protected—a bit like dairy farmers—to something more like a pure market environment. And while some view the market as the best arbiter of what lives and dies, allowing unfettered market forces to rule is increasingly seen as having a high social price. Wal-Mart, for instance, is resisted in communities where people fear their local merchants will be swept away. To its opponents, the benefits of a megastore are not worth the small businesses that would be lost, and with them a sense of community.

I grew up in the 1950s, and the plight of newspapers reminds me of the situation faced by local hardware stores when the big chain stores began to appear. On Main Street in my hometown, there were three hardware stores in the same block. They were sleepy places where everything seemed to go in slow motion, but each had its own group of loyal customers of long standing among the county's farmers. . . . They competed with each other, but there was enough business to sustain them. Then the world changed on them, and they did what any businessman would do. The big outfits charged less, so they tried to find new ways to make a buck and at the same time cut their expenses. Employees were let go. Extending credit became a luxury they could ill afford. They trimmed their inventory to the bone and stocked only the most popular items that they felt sure they could sell. But in doing so they lost their character and the personal connection with their customers. And, of course, they all went out of business. . . .

There is no evil here. The farmers embraced the lower prices they got from the big stores. They were sorry to see the old stores pass, but it seemed inevitable. The old hardware merchants did what they could to save their businesses, and their decisions to cut costs and try to lure the farmers in new ways seemed to make sense. But the market prevailed and they were swept away. I'm not sure the traditional news industry is like these hardware stores, but it is having much the same reaction to the disruptive change that is threatening its livelihood. News organizations are trying, rationally, to save their business, but that is not the same thing as saving the news. Indeed, they increasingly view their news operations—especially the part of the budget that goes for iron core news—as an expense that doesn't contribute as much as it costs. In the media world now evolving, the resources of a news operation will be whatever its audience can generate and the focus of a newsroom will likely be whatever the market prefers. In a world of virtually infinite choices, just where this new equilibrium will be struck for iron core news is uncertain at best.

While many Americans sense that something calamitous is happening with news, the air of crisis is most acute not among the public but in the nation's newsrooms. Of the problems that constitute the news crisis, the one next in importance to the eroding core of accountability news is the crisis of leadership and morale inside the world of journalism. Even at the elite news organizations, reporters and editors and news executives as a group are discouraged, ... because many of them have begun to doubt their calling. Editors who once brought galvanizing energy and a zestful moral outrage to the news and sought to inspire their newsrooms are now obliged to spend most of their time managing budgets and devising new ways to get by with less. Reporters are watching news jobs disappear all over the country as corporations that own news organizations cut costs. With jobs increasingly scarce, journalists cling to positions that are less and less focused on what made most of them yearn to be in news in the first place. Instead of a job that they regarded as valuable and exciting and serving a larger public purpose, many have come to feel they are on a treadmill of mediocrity, asked only to provide a quota of "content" that will fill the news columns at the lowest cost. And any executive running a news organization who resists the home office on budget targets is apt to have a short tenure. . . .

In 2006, the newspaper industry went into a collective panic about the decline in newspaper circulation and ad revenues, which was especially acute in lucrative classified advertising. The reason classified advertising is so highly profitable is that, despite the relatively low cost of each ad, the cumulative revenue from a page of classified advertising comes to more than the income from a full-page ad elsewhere in the paper. Newspaper advertising is sold on the basis of a price per column inch, and inch for inch, a page of classified advertising brings in far more cash than a single ad that covers a page and thereby merits a discounted column-inch price.

Craigslist.com, the free classified Web site, and other searchable Internet sites have played havoc with newspaper classified ads. For instance, craigslist has made itself an alternative to the sorts of ads that have traditionally appeared in the back pages of newspapers. On craigslist, you can create a listing to sell unused exercise equipment or find a rental apartment, and it costs nothing. It is simple to use, searchable, and allows you to [post] photographs of what you want to sell. Similar online sites for selling cars and finding jobs have proven devastatingly effective compared to the old way. For newspapers, for which classified advertising has been a crucial financial artery, the rise of such sites has been devastating, and the erosion is growing worse. While newspapers are creating online capabilities of their own for classifieds, it's hard to compete pricewise with free.

As the audience declines and advertisers experiment with new media, newspaper advertising and circulation revenues are under enormous pressure and are declining at many papers. To make things worse, the costs of labor and newsprint—a newspaper's two highest expenses—have spiraled up. Contractual agreements are making increased salaries unavoidable, and the cost of newsprint has increased dramatically in the past few years. Profit levels of over 20 percent had become commonplace at newspapers, and the squeeze between declining revenues and unavoidable cost increases has sent newspapers into a tailspin. In many cases, the newspaper companies have huge debt obligations from buying other papers in more optimistic times, only to see the revenues dwindle that are needed to pay interest and principal. The reaction at many newspapers has been to cut news staffs—including people who create the type of news that much of the audience considers boring and is expensive, requiring the best, most experienced reporters, who also command the highest salaries. Increasingly, this kind of news is viewed more as a luxury than an essential, and even a turnoff to readers who prefer to know what's up with Hollywood.

As a result, the iron core is in trouble.

A case can be made that the core will not only survive, but grow more weighty through new forms of news media, such as Web-based citizen journalism and journalistic bloggers. Traditional media are trying to find news ways to report news that will appeal to a younger, Web-savvy audience, and creating new publications and Web sites in response to reader tastes. Perhaps that is what will happen. But so far, we appear to be losing this important kind of news far faster than we are replacing it.

Even worse, the sense of social responsibility that has long existed at traditional news organizations is in retreat. This has been true for some time, but a gradual slackening in commitment to news as a social responsibility has become a headlong rout because of the panicky scramble to shore up profit margins. News and business have always been linked in the United States, and traditional news organizations have been commercial enterprises that had profit as a priority. But there was also the parallel priority of social stewardship.

This stewardship was at best uneven, especially in times of financial crunch. It would, of course, be ridiculous to idealize journalism. There was no Golden Age in which the typical publisher was a self-sacrificing paragon, eager to demonstrate his rectitude by trading profits for high ideals. There were a few of those, but they were always the exceptions. Nor was there an Arcadia when news was not sometimes compromised by laziness, human error, greed, and bias. Journalism is a human endeavor, with all the attendant weaknesses.

But it would be just as wrong to suggest that nothing has shifted in the values of the news business, and that the overwhelming power of market thinking has not had a corrosive impact on those values. . . .

The unhappy truth is that newspapers that sought to retain readers by investing in their newsrooms have not been able to show that this strategy pays off with a surge in circulation. The argument that quality will keep readers is not one that can easily be demonstrated. It appears that newspaper readership is a habit and one that is predictably generational. The members of the World War II generation were devout newspaper readers, the Baby Boomers significantly less so, and many of today's young people think of newspapers and all traditional news as anachronisms.

Part of the news crisis is finding a solution that will pay the significant costs of generating the accountability news that is essential to our democracy and still allow an acceptable profit. This is a riddle that has yet to be solved, and so the iron cannonball of accountability news continues to grow lighter and shrink. But if within the traditional media a commitment to a social stewardship becomes mere window dressing and an empty boast, the loss will be terrible indeed. . . .

Indeed, the reason that losing the news—the accountability news—is so important is that a dearth of reliable information will force us to chart our national path with pseudo news and opinion that may be more appealing but will be far less reliable. The news in that pitted, old iron sphere was far from perfect, but it was—and is—essential.

EXPLORING THE ISSUE

Will Evolving Forms of Journalism Be an Improvement?

Critical Thinking and Reflection

1. How can the benefits of content generated from around the world be best integrated into traditional media systems? Is that the inevitable outcome? Is it the best outcome?
2. Will evolving forms of journalism and economic pressure defeat the iron core? Can current markets support quality journalism?
3. Should Internet "journalists" receive First Amendment protection? What journalistic standards should guide the digital age?

Is There Common Ground?

We can envision a continuum with traditional journalism on one end and consumer-generated content on the other. Yet both articles seem to suggest that a hybrid model may be the way into the future. Certainly, that is what we are seeing today as newspapers, television, even magazines integrate consumer-generated information into their content. I am not sure, however, that such a hybrid would satisfy those on opposite ends of the spectrum.

From one side, traditional journalism is still the voice of authority using consumer-generated content at its discretion. These voices from everywhere are providing information without context or verification, perhaps spreading misinformation or exacerbating problems. From the other side of the spectrum, traditional journalism is slow to react, misses important information because of its journalistic practices, and treats the consumer-generated content with disdain. Currently, there exists détente between the two positions. It is hard to predict whether it will hold.

Additional Resources

Howard Kurtz, *Reality Show: Inside the Last Great Television News War* (2007)

Kurtz gives an insider look at news production and judgment at the three legacy networks.

Leonard Downie and Robert Kaiser, *The News about the News: American Journalism in Peril* (2003)

See this volume for a look at how the state of newspaper journalism has changed in the Internet age, from *Washington Post* editors Downie and Kaiser.

Dan Gillmor, *We the Media: Grassroots Journalism by the People, for the People* (2006)

To read more extensively about the hope that online journalism will fundamentally change journalism in a positive manner, see Gillmor (2006).

ISSUE 9

Do Social Media Encourage Revolution?

YES: Clay Shirky, from "The Political Power of Social Media," *Foreign Affairs* (vol. 90, p. 1, January/February 2011)

NO: Malcolm Gladwell, from "Small Change: Why the Revolution Will Not Be Tweeted," *The New Yorker* (vol. 86, p. 30, October 2010)

Learning Outcomes

After reading this issue, you should be able to:

- Define the instrumental versus the environmental view and explain the conservative dilemma.
- Discuss how the power of weak ties limits social media influence.
- Analyze the connections among political systems, economic conditions, and communications in revolutions.

ISSUE SUMMARY

YES: Clay Shirky considers the ways social media have been used to organize protest and promote social change. He writes about short- and long-term consequences of social media use, but notes that the most important impact of social media use is in the promotion of a civil society and lasting change. Social media, he argues, can create shared awareness, which makes it harder for repressive regimes to maintain the status quo.

NO: Malcolm Gladwell argues that social media is unlikely to make a difference. Social change requires powerful and interpersonal ties. It is interpersonal connections that will motivate social activism, he asserts. Social media may be effective in the short term, but cannot generate the levels of commitment necessary to effect social change.

An iconic photograph shows a solitary protestor standing in front of tanks entering Tiananmen Square in 1989. The medium that had supported students involved in these series of protests was the fax machine. As world media heard about the demonstrations, they converged on Beijing and watched as the events of that June day unfolded. Pictures and newspaper articles about the use of fire hoses and police dogs on anti-segregation marchers in 1963 Birmingham, Alabama were considered powerful in the creation of anti-segregationist sentiment throughout the United States. Media as powerful witness to confrontation is an important function of the press. Clay Shirky and Malcolm Gladwell force us to think about whether there are more interactive ways that media may encourage social revolution in today's digital age.

The Arab Spring refers to a wave of revolutionary demonstrations and protests occurring in the Arab World since they began in December of 2010 with the self-immolation of an impoverished street vendor in protest of the confiscation of the produce he sold and the mistreatment he routinely endured from civil authorities. This sparked violent protests that swept the country, as people demonstrated against corruption, the absence of political freedom, and poor living conditions. By the end of January, the president of Tunisia had resigned. Tunisia was the first in a series of anti-government protests that swept the Arab world. The consequences will be felt for many years, and much of the world anxiously awaits the outcomes of these regime changes in terms of international relations. Revolutions occurred in Tunisia and Egypt; a civil war in Libya; civil uprisings in Syria, Bahrain, and Yemen; and sustained protests that forced governmental changes in many other Arab countries.

Social media have been a feature of these protests and were used to raise awareness, coordinate action, and organize strategy. One Egyptian protestor tweeted, "We use Facebook to schedule the protests, Twitter to coordinate, and YouTube to tell the world." Egyptians were so successful in using mobile media to organize demonstrations that the Egyptian government shut down much of the country's Internet system in a brief and unsuccessful attempt to quell public protest. The articles in this issue cite many examples of how social media has been used in political confrontations. Andrew Sullivan famously wrote, "The revolution will be tweeted." Clay Shirky and Malcolm Gladwell debate that premise.

Clay Shirky offers an in-depth analysis of the political impact of social media. He writes about the ways in which social media have been used to organize protest, but sees the most important impact of social media in promoting civil society and long-term social reform. He argues that the ability of social media to create "shared awareness" is a powerful function of social media, and catapults the regimes in power into a "conservative dilemma" of limited options to preserve the status quo. He offers his insights into the ways in which the United States can adopt policies on Internet access that can help, rather than hinder, social change. He urges that the United States abandon its instrumental view of social media for an environmental view that promotes principles, rather than trying to create change.

Malcolm Gladwell argues that social media is unlikely to make a difference. Social media, he argues, is effective for low-involvement activities. The power of social media in the extensive social networks of many friends is both its strength and weakness. The weak ties of individuals to their Internet and social media communities do not produce the level of interpersonal connection that will motivate courageous social activism. He uses examples from the civil rights era to demonstrate the need for strong and personal connection to a cause in order to create the levels of commitment and involvement needed to effect social change.

Philip Howard in "The Arab Spring's Cascading Effects" (*Miller-McCune*, February 23, 2011) urges us not to underestimate the risks that protestors took by overemphasizing the role of technology. The dichotomy between face to face as strong ties and text messages as weak ones is false. Images of friends being beaten, he argues, is what drew people into the streets. Increasingly, those appeals come digitally. Then the digital storytelling spread across North Africa and the Middle East, and the inspiring stories of success began to prompt a belief that social change could occur in other countries as well. From this he draws a hopeful conclusion: A network of citizens now has political power because of social media. The Arab Spring has brought down dictators. Can it now bring democracy to the region?

The recent work of Evgeny Morozov is attracting attention for his darker predictions about the use of Internet and social media in revolution. In his book, *The Net Delusion: The Dark Side of Internet Freedom* (Public Affairs, 2011), high hopes that the Internet would usher in an age of democracy in previously closed societies are, he argues, beginning to fade. Technology was supposed to empower the people, who would inevitably rebel. He decries cyber-utopian visions of the power of the Internet to promote democracy that refuse to acknowledge its downside. Instead, he argues, it has become a tool of authoritarian governments who use it as a propaganda tool, to suppress free speech and for surveillance. Governments under challenge, in his observations of former Soviet regimes, began to experiment with censorship and soon became adept at social media, paying bloggers to extol the government and search out information on the opposition. In contrast to cyber-utopian perspectives, Morozov warns that the idea of Internet freedom might have dire implications for the future of democracy. He argues that the Internet in general, and social media in particular, have become an arena of threat for those opposing repressive regimes. To salvage the Internet's promise, Morozov urges the West to drop our net delusions and be informed by a realistic assessment of costs and benefits, as well as a commitment to long-term social change.

Hindman offers another insight into the relationship of online media and democracy. In his book, *The Myth of Digital Democracy* (Princeton University Press, 2009), Hindman argues that the perception of the Internet as fostering democratic and grassroots direct political speech is a myth. He explores what he deems the myth that the Internet has given political "voice" to the previously voiceless and facilitated debate and deliberation. The Internet may allow millions to speak, but who is being heard? Instead, he argues that Internet political speech is dominated by search engines that return the most popular sites, which favor media and political elites. Although there may be millions of sites, only a relative few have substantial audiences and these parallel the dominant media: legacy newspaper, magazine, and television sites; major browsers; and a very few influential Internet-only sites or blogs. In short, the grassroots may have spoken, but who is listening?

Ironically, at least one author argues that an important precursor to the Tunisian revolution was another social media event: WikiLeaks documented the greed and corruption of the Tunisian president and his family. The leaked documents were dispatches from U.S. diplomats who described lavish homes, sumptuous banquets, and even a large tiger that lived in the compound. Soon a "TuniLeaks" site was created in Tunisia to share these documents and their contents were reported on Al Jazeera. It was humiliating to the Tunisian people to have this information published to the world. Humiliating, in particular, because much of these excesses were already known, but nothing had been done about them. Not a month later, the produce vendor set himself on fire and the protests began. Similar dispatches caused outrage in Egypt, Libya, Bahrain, and Yemen. Were these a catalyst for revolution? See J. Bachrach, "WikiHistory: Did the Leaks Inspire the Arab Spring?" in the July/August 2011 issue of *World Affairs Journal*.

The lessons of history do not always apply to the future. Malcolm Gladwell illuminates some seminal actions during the early Civil Rights movements that he argues required strong interpersonal ties to be successful. But as noted in the introduction, pictures and newspaper articles created anti-segregationist sentiment in the United States. In China, the world watched Tiananmen Square, and ironically, the world knew to watch because of the messages sent out of the country by fax. Is it so hard to think that social media may play an important role in the revolutions of the future?

What seems clear is that these opposing positions probably both contain truth. Social media can coordinate, incite, and motivate revolution. Revolution cannot occur without a strong social undercurrent that opposes those in power. These commitments were probably forged in discussions and debates in homes, offices, shops, and streets. Social media may be able to create that sense of "share awareness" that begins to tie people together in a common cause. But it probably takes a commitment to change to keep moving forward in light of significant opposition. What lights the match? What fans the flame? And, what fuels the fire long term? It may never be possible to unravel the unique factors that combine to make a revolution.

YES

Clay Shirky

The Political Power of Social Media

Technology; the Public Sphere, and Political Change

On January 17, 2001, during the impeachment trial of Philippine President Joseph Estrada, loyalists in the Philippine Congress voted to set aside key evidence against him. Less than two hours after the decision was announced, thousands of Filipinos, angry that their corrupt president might be let off the hook, converged on Epifanio de los Santos Avenue, a major crossroads in Manila. The protest was arranged, in part, by forwarded text messages reading, "Go 2 EDSA. Wear blk." The crowd quickly swelled, and in the next few days, over a million people arrived, choking traffic in downtown Manila.

The public's ability to coordinate such a massive and rapid response— close to seven million text messages were sent that week—so alarmed the country's legislators that they reversed course and allowed the evidence to be presented. Estrada's fate was sealed; by January 20, he was gone. The event marked the first time that social media had helped force out a national leader. Estrada himself blamed "the text-messaging generation" for his downfall.

Since the rise of the Internet in the early 1990s, the world's networked population has grown from the low millions to the low billions. Over the same period, social media have become a fact of life for civil society worldwide, involving many actors—regular citizens, activists, nongovernmental organizations, telecommunications firms, software providers, governments. This raises an obvious question for the U.S. government: How does the ubiquity of social media affect U.S. interests, and how should U.S. policy respond to it?

As the communications landscape gets denser, more complex, and more participatory, the networked population is gaining greater access to information, more opportunities to engage in public speech, and an enhanced ability to undertake collective action. In the political arena, as the protests in Manila demonstrated, these increased freedoms can help loosely coordinated publics demand change.

The Philippine strategy has been adopted many times since. In some cases, the protesters ultimately succeeded, as in Spain in 2004, when demonstrations organized by text messaging led to the quick ouster of Spanish Prime

From *Foreign Affairs*, January/February 2011, pp. 28–41. Copyright © 2011 by Council on Foreign Relations, Inc. Reprinted by permission of Foreign Affairs. www.ForeignAffairs.com

Minister José María Aznar, who had inaccurately blamed the Madrid transit bombings on Basque separatists. The Communist Party lost power in Moldova in 2009 when massive protests coordinated in part by text message, Facebook, and Twitter broke out after an obviously fraudulent election. Around the world, the Catholic Church has faced lawsuits over its harboring of child rapists, a process that started when The Boston Globes 2002 expose of sexual abuse in the church went viral online in a matter of hours.

There are, however, many examples of the activists failing, as in Belarus in March 2006, when street protests (arranged in part by e-mail) against President Aleksandr Lukashenko's alleged vote rigging swelled, then faltered, leaving Lukashenko more determined than ever to control social media. During the June 2009 uprising of the Green Movement in Iran, activists used every possible technological coordinating tool to protest the miscount of votes for Mir Hossein Mousavi but were ultimately brought to heel by a violent crackdown. The Red Shirt uprising in Thailand in 2010 followed a similar but quicker path: protesters savvy with social media occupied downtown Bangkok until the Thai government dispersed the protesters, killing dozens.

The use of social media tools—text messaging, e-mail, photo sharing, social networking, and the like—does not have a single preordained outcome. Therefore, attempts to outline their effects on political action are too often reduced to dueling anecdotes. If you regard the failure of the Belarusian protests to oust Lukashenko as paradigmatic, you will regard the Moldovan experience as an outlier, and vice versa. Empirical work on the subject is also hard to come by, in part because these tools are so new and in part because relevant examples are so rare. The safest characterization of recent quantitative attempts to answer the question, Do digital tools enhance democracy? . . . is that these tools probably do not hurt in the short run and might help in the long run—and that they have the most dramatic effects in states where a public sphere already constrains the actions of the government.

Despite this mixed record, social media have become coordinating tools for nearly all of the world's political movements, just as most of the world's authoritarian governments (and, alarmingly, an increasing number of democratic ones) are trying to limit access to it. In response, the U.S. State Department has committed itself to "Internet freedom" as a specific policy aim. Arguing for the right of people to use the Internet freely is an appropriate policy for the United States, both because it aligns with the strategic goal of strengthening civil society worldwide and because it resonates with American beliefs about freedom of expression. But attempts to yoke the idea of Internet freedom to short-term goals—particularly ones that are country-specific or are intended to help particular dissident groups or encourage regime change—are likely to be ineffective on average. And when they fail, the consequences can be serious.

. . . The U.S. government should maintain Internet freedom as a goal to be pursued in a principled and regime-neutral fashion, not as a tool for effecting immediate policy aims country by country. It should likewise assume that progress will be incremental and, unsurprisingly, slowest in the most authoritarian regimes.

The Perils of Internet Freedom

In January 2010, U.S. Secretary of State Hillary Clinton outlined how the United States would promote Internet freedom abroad. She emphasized several kinds of freedom, including the freedom to access information (such as the ability to use Wikipedia and Google inside Iran), the freedom of ordinary citizens to produce their own public media (such as the rights of Burmese activists to blog), and the freedom of citizens to converse with one another (such as the Chinese public's capacity to use instant messaging without interference).

Most notably, Clinton announced funding for the development of tools designed to reopen access to the Internet in countries that restrict it. This "instrumental" approach to Internet freedom concentrates on preventing states from censoring outside Web sites, such as Google, YouTube, or that of *The New York Times*. It focuses only secondarily on public speech by citizens and least of all on private or social uses of digital media. According to this vision, Washington can and should deliver rapid, directed responses to censorship by authoritarian regimes.

The instrumental view is politically appealing, action-oriented, and almost certainly wrong. It overestimates the value of broadcast media while underestimating the value of media that allow citizens to communicate privately among themselves. It overestimates the value of access to information, particularly information hosted in the West, while underestimating the value of tools for local coordination. And it overestimates the importance of computers while underestimating the importance of simpler tools, such as cell phones. . . .

New media conducive to fostering participation can indeed increase the freedoms Clinton outlined, just as the printing press, the postal service, the telegraph, and the telephone did before. One complaint about the idea of new media as a political force is that most people simply use these tools for commerce, social life, or self-distraction, but this is common to all forms of media. Far more people in the 1500s were reading erotic novels than Martin Luther's "Ninety-five Theses," and far more people before the American Revolution were reading *Poor Richard's Almanack* than the work of the Committees of Correspondence. But those political works still had an enormous political effect.

. . . Today's dissident movements will use any means possible to frame their views and coordinate their actions; it would be impossible to describe the Moldovan Communist Party's loss of Parliament after the 2009 elections without discussing the use of cell phones and online tools by its opponents to mobilize. Authoritarian governments stifle communication among their citizens because they fear, correctly, that a better-coordinated populace would constrain their ability to act without oversight.

Despite this basic truth—that communicative freedom is good for political freedom—the instrumental mode of Internet statecraft is still problematic. It is difficult for outsiders to understand the local conditions of dissent. External support runs the risk of tainting even peaceful opposition as being directed by foreign elements. Dissidents can be exposed by the unintended effects of novel tools. A government's demands for Internet freedom abroad can vary from country to country, depending on the importance of the relationship, leading to cynicism about its motives.

The more promising way to think about social media is as long-term tools that can strengthen civil society and the public sphere. In contrast to the instrumental view of Internet freedom, this can be called the "environmental" view. According to this conception, positive changes in the life of a country, including pro-democratic regime change, follow, rather than precede, the development of a strong public sphere. This is not to say that popular movements will not successfully use these tools to discipline or even oust their governments, but rather that U.S. attempts to direct such uses are likely to do more harm than good. Considered in this light, Internet freedom is a long game, to be conceived of and supported not as a separate agenda but merely as an important input to the more fundamental political freedoms.

The Theater of Collapse

Any discussion of political action in repressive regimes must take into account the astonishing fall of communism in 1989 in eastern Europe and the subsequent collapse of the Soviet Union in 1991. Throughout the Cold War, the United States invested in a variety of communications tools, including broadcasting the Voice of America radio station, hosting an American pavilion in Moscow (home of the famous Nixon-Khrushchev "kitchen debate"), and smuggling Xerox machines behind the Iron Curtain to aid the underground press, or samizdat. Yet despite this emphasis on communications, the end of the Cold War was triggered not by a defiant uprising of Voice of America listeners but by economic change. As the price of oil fell while that of wheat spiked, the Soviet model of selling expensive oil to buy cheap wheat stopped working. As a result, the Kremlin was forced to secure loans from the West, loans that would have been put at risk had the government intervened militarily in the affairs of non-Russian states. In 1989, one could argue, the ability of citizens to communicate, considered against the background of macroeconomic forces, was largely irrelevant.

But why, then, did the states behind the Iron Curtain not just let their people starve? After all, the old saying that every country is three meals away from revolution turned out to be sadly incorrect in the twentieth century; it is possible for leaders to survive even when millions die. Stalin did it in the 1930s, Mao did it in the 1960s, and Kim Jong II has done it more than once in the last two decades. But the difference between those cases and the 1989 revolutions was that the leaders of East Germany, Czechoslovakia, and the rest faced civil societies strong enough to resist. The weekly demonstrations in East Germany, the Charter 77 civic movement in Czechoslovakia, and the Solidarity movement in Poland all provided visible governments in waiting.

The ability of these groups to create and disseminate literature and political documents, even with simple photocopiers, provided a visible alternative to the communist regimes. For large groups of citizens in these countries, the political and, even more important, economic bankruptcy of the government was no longer an open secret but a public fact. This made it difficult and then impossible for the regimes to order their troops to take on such large groups.

Thus, it was a shift in the balance of power between the state and civil society that led to the largely peaceful collapse of communist control. The state's ability to use violence had been weakened, and the civil society that would have borne the brunt of its violence had grown stronger. When civil society triumphed, many of the people who had articulated opposition to the communist regimes—such as Tadeusz Mazowiecki in Poland and Vaclav Havel in Czechoslovakia—became the new political leaders of those countries. Communications tools during the Cold War did not cause governments to collapse, but they helped the people take power from the state when it was weak.

The idea that media, from the Voice of America to samizdat, play a supporting role in social change by strengthening the public sphere echoes the historical role of the printing press. As the German philosopher Jürgen Habermas argued in his 1962 book, The Structural Transformation of the Public Sphere, the printing press helped democratize Europe by providing space for discussion and agreement among politically engaged citizens, often before the state had fully democratized. . . .

Political freedom has to be accompanied by a civil society literate enough and densely connected enough to discuss the issues presented to the public. In a famous study of political opinion after the 1948 U.S. presidential election, the sociologists Elihu Katz and Paul Lazarsfeld discovered that mass media alone do not change people's minds; instead, there is a two-step process. Opinions are first transmitted by the media, and then they get echoed by friends, family members, and colleagues. It is in this second, social step that political opinions are formed. This is the step in which the Internet in general, and social media in particular, can make a difference. As with the printing press, the Internet spreads not just media consumption but media production as well—it allows people to privately and publicly articulate and debate a welter of conflicting views.

A slowly developing public sphere, where public opinion relies on both media and conversation, is the core of the environmental view of Internet freedom. As opposed to the self-aggrandizing view that the West holds the source code for democracy—and if it were only made accessible, the remaining autocratic states would crumble—the environmental view assumes that little political change happens without the dissemination and adoption of ideas and opinions in the public sphere. Access to information is far less important, politically, than access to conversation. Moreover, a public sphere is more likely to emerge in a society as a result of people's dissatisfaction with matters of economics or day-to-day governance than from their embrace of abstract political ideals.

To take a contemporary example, the Chinese government today is in more danger of being forced to adopt democratic norms by middle-class members of the ethnic Han majority demanding less corrupt local governments than it is by Uighurs or Tibetans demanding autonomy. Similarly, the One Million Signatures Campaign, an Iranian women's rights movement that focuses on the repeal of laws inimical to women, has been more successful in liberalizing the behavior of the Iranian government than the more confrontational Green Movement.

For optimistic observers of public demonstrations, this is weak tea, but both the empirical and the theoretical work suggest that protests, when effective, are the end of a long process, rather than a replacement for it. Any real commitment by the United States to improving political freedom worldwide should concentrate on that process—which can only occur when there is a strong public sphere.

The Conservative Dilemma

Disciplined and coordinated groups, whether businesses or governments, have always had an advantage over undisciplined ones: they have an easier time engaging in collective action because they have an orderly way of directing the action of their members. Social media can compensate for the disadvantages of undisciplined groups by reducing the costs of coordination. . . . As a result, larger, looser groups can now take on some kinds of coordinated action, such as protest movements and public media campaigns, that were previously reserved for formal organizations. For political movements, one of the main forms of coordination is what the military calls "shared awareness," the ability of each member of a group to not only understand the situation at hand but also understand that everyone else does, too. Social media increase shared awareness by propagating messages through social networks. The anti-Aznar protests in Spain gained momentum so quickly precisely because the millions of people spreading the message were not part of a hierarchical organization.

The Chinese anticorruption protests that broke out in the aftermath of the devastating May 2008 earthquake in Sichuan are another example of such ad hoc synchronization. The protesters were parents, particularly mothers, who had lost their only children in the collapse of shoddily built schools, the result of collusion between construction firms and the local government. . . . When the schools collapsed, citizens began sharing documentation of the damage and of their protests through social media tools. The consequences of government corruption were made broadly visible, and it went from being an open secret to a public truth.

The Chinese government originally allowed reporting on the post-earthquake protests, but . . . began arresting protesters and threatening journalists when it became clear that the protesters were demanding real local reform and not merely state reparations. . . . Beijing was afraid of the possible effects if this awareness became shared: it would have to either enact reforms or respond in a way that would alarm more citizens. After all, the prevalence of camera phones has made it harder to carry out a widespread but undocumented crackdown.

This condition of shared awareness—which is increasingly evident in all modern states—creates what is commonly called "the dictator's dilemma" but that might more accurately be described by the phrase coined by the media theorist Briggs: "the conservative dilemma," so named because it applies not only to autocrats but also to democratic governments and to religious and business leaders. The dilemma is created by new media that increase public access to speech or assembly; with the spread of such media, whether photo-copiers or Web browsers, a state accustomed to having a monopoly on public speech finds itself called to account for anomalies between its view of events and the public's. The two responses to the conservative dilemma are censor-ship and propaganda. But neither of these is as effective a source of control as the enforced silence of the citizens. The state will censor critics or produce propaganda as it needs to, but both of those actions have higher costs than simply not having any critics to silence or reply to in the first place. But if a government were to shut down Internet access or ban cell phones, it would risk radicalizing otherwise pro-regime citizens or harming the economy. . . .

Popular culture also heightens the conservative dilemma by providing cover for more political uses of social media. Tools specifically designed for dissident use are politically easy for the state to shut down, whereas tools in broad use become much harder to censor without risking politicizing the larger group of otherwise apolitical actors. Ethan Zuckerman of Harvard's Berkman Center for Internet and Society calls this "the cute cat theory of digital activ-ism." Specific tools designed to defeat state censorship (such as proxy servers) can be shut down with little political penalty, but broader tools that the larger population uses to, say, share pictures of cute cats are harder to shut down.

For these reasons, it makes more sense to invest in social media as gen-eral, rather than specifically political, tools to promote self-governance. The norm of free speech is inherently political and far from universally shared. To the degree that the United States makes free speech a first-order goal, it should expect that goal to work relatively well in democratic countries that are allies, less well in undemocratic countries that are allies, and least of all in undemocratic countries that are not allies. But nearly every country in the world desires economic growth. Since governments jeopardize that growth when they ban technologies that can be used for both political and economic coordination, the United States should rely on countries' economic incentives to allow widespread media use. In other words, the U.S. government should work for conditions that increase the conservative dilemma, appealing to states' self-interest rather than the contentious virtue of freedom, as a way to create or strengthen countries' public spheres.

Social Media Skepticism

There are, broadly speaking, two arguments against the idea that social media will make a difference in national politics. The first is that the tools are them-selves ineffective, and the second is that they produce as much harm to democratization as good, because repressive governments are becoming better at using these tools to suppress dissent.

The critique of ineffectiveness, most recently offered by Malcolm Glad-well in The New Yorker, concentrates on examples of what has been termed "slacktivism," whereby casual participants seek social change through low-cost activities, such as joining Facebook's "Save Darfur" group, that are long on bumper-sticker sentiment and short on any useful action. The critique is correct but not central to the question of social media's power; the fact that barely committed actors cannot click their way to a better world does not mean that committed actors cannot use social media effectively. Recent protest movements . . . have used social media not as a replacement for real-world action but as a way to coordinate it. As a result, all of those protests exposed participants to the threat of violence, and in some cases its actual use. In fact, the adoption of these tools (especially cell phones) as a way to coordinate and document real-world action is so ubiquitous that it will probably be a part of all future political movements.

This obviously does not mean that every political movement that uses these tools will succeed, because the state has not lost the power to react. This points to the second, and much more serious, critique of social media as tools for political improvement—namely, that the state is gaining increasingly sophisticated means of monitoring, interdicting, or co-opting these tools. The use of social media, the scholars Rebecca MacKinnon of the New America Foundation and Evgeny Morozov of the Open Society Institute have argued, is just as likely to strengthen authoritarian regimes as it is to weaken them. The Chinese government has spent considerable effort perfecting several systems for controlling political threats from social media. The least important of these is its censorship and surveillance program. Increasingly, the government recognizes that threats to its legitimacy are coming from inside the state and that blocking the Web site of *The New York Times* does little to prevent grieving mothers from airing their complaints about corruption.

The Chinese system has evolved from a relatively simple filter of incoming Internet traffic in the mid-1990s to a sophisticated operation that not only limits outside information but also uses arguments about nationalism and public morals to encourage operators of Chinese Web services to censor their users and users to censor themselves. Because its goal is to prevent information from having politically synchronizing effects, the state does not need to censor the Internet comprehensively; rather, it just needs to minimize access to information.

Authoritarian states are increasingly shutting down their communications grids to deny dissidents the ability to coordinate in real time and broadcast documentation of an event. This strategy also activates the conservative dilemma, creating a short-term risk of alerting the population at large to political conflict. When the government of Bahrain banned Google Earth after an annotated map of the royal family's annexation of public land began circulating, the effect was to alert far more Bahrainis to the offending map than knew about it originally. So widely did the news spread that the government relented and reopened access after four days.

Such shutdowns become more problematic for governments if they are long-lived. When antigovernment protesters occupied Bangkok in the summer of 2010, their physical presence disrupted Bangkok's shopping district, but the state's reaction, cutting off significant parts of the Thai telecommunications infrastructure, affected people far from the capital. The approach creates an additional dilemma for the state—there can be no modern economy without working phones—and so its ability to shut down communications over large areas or long periods is constrained.

In the most extreme cases, the use of social media tools is a matter of life and death, as with the proposed death sentence for the blogger Hossein Derakhshan in Iran (since commuted to 19 and a half years in prison) or the suspicious hanging death of Oleg Bebenin, the founder of the Belarusian opposition Web site Charter 97. Indeed, the best practical reason to think that social media can help bring political change is that both dissidents and governments think they can. All over the world, activists believe in the utility of these tools and take steps to use them accordingly. And the governments they contend with think social media tools are powerful, too, and are willing to harass, arrest, exile, or kill users in response. One way the United States can heighten the conservative dilemma without running afoul of as many political complications is to demand the release of citizens imprisoned for using media in these ways. Anything that constrains the worst threats of violence by the state against citizens using these tools also increases the conservative dilemma.

Looking at the Long Run

To the degree that the United States pursues Internet freedom as a tool of statecraft, it should de-emphasize anti-censorship tools, particularly those aimed at specific regimes, and increase its support for local public speech and assembly more generally. Access to information is not unimportant, of course, but it is not the primary way social media constrain autocratic rulers or benefit citizens of a democracy. Direct, U.S. government–sponsored support for specific tools or campaigns targeted at specific regimes risk creating backlash that a more patient and global application of principles will not.

This entails reordering the State Department's Internet freedom goals. Securing the freedom of personal and social communication among a state's population should be the highest priority, closely followed by securing individual citizens' ability to speak in public. This reordering would reflect the reality that it is a strong civil society—one in which citizens have freedom of assembly—rather than access to Google or YouTube, that does the most to force governments to serve their citizens.

As a practical example of this, the United States should be at least . . . worried about . . . South Korea's requirement that citizens register with their real names for certain Internet services, . . . an attempt to reduce their ability to surprise the state with the kind of coordinated action that took place during the 2008 protest in Seoul. If the United States does not complain as directly about this policy as it does about Chinese censorship, it risks compromising its ability to argue for Internet freedom as a global ideal.

More difficult, but also essential, will be for the U.S. government to articulate a policy of engagement with the private companies and organizations that host the networked public sphere. Services based in the United States, such as Facebook, Twitter, Wikipedia, and YouTube, and those based overseas, such as QQ (a Chinese instant-messaging service), WikiLeaks (a repository of leaked documents whose servers are in Sweden), Tuenti (a Spanish social network), and Naver (a Korean one), are among the sites used most for political speech, conversation, and coordination. And the world's wireless carriers transmit text messages, photos, and videos from cell phones through those sites. How much can these entities be expected to support freedom of speech and assembly for their users? . . . it is unlikely that without some legal framework, as exists for real-world speech and action, moral suasion will be enough to convince commercial actors to support freedom of speech and assembly.

It would be nice to have a flexible set of short-term digital tactics that could be used against different regimes at different times. But the requirements of real-world statecraft mean that what is desirable may not be likely. Activists in both repressive and democratic regimes will use the Internet and related tools to try to effect change in their countries, but Washington's ability to shape or target these changes is limited. Instead, Washington should adopt a more general approach, promoting freedom of speech, freedom of the press, and freedom of assembly everywhere. And it should understand that progress will be slow. Only by switching from an instrumental to an environmental view of the effects of social media on the public sphere will the United States be able to take advantage of the long-term benefits these tools promise—even though that may mean accepting short-term disappointment.

Malcolm Gladwell  **NO**

Small Change: Why the Revolution Will Not Be Tweeted

Social media can't provide what social change has always required.

At four-thirty in the afternoon on Monday, February 1, 1960, four college students sat down at the lunch counter at the Woolworth's in downtown Greensboro, North Carolina. They were freshmen at North Carolina A. & T., a black college a mile or so away.

"I'd like a cup of coffee, please," one of the four, Ezell Blair, said to the waitress.

"We don't serve Negroes here," she replied.

The Woolworth's lunch counter was a long L-shaped bar that could seat sixty-six people, with a standup snack bar at one end. The seats were for whites. The snack bar was for blacks. Another employee, a black woman who worked at the steam table, approached the students and tried to warn them away. "You're acting stupid, ignorant!" she said. They didn't move. Around five-thirty, the front doors to the store were locked. The four still didn't move. Finally, they left by a side door. Outside, a small crowd had gathered, including a photographer from the Greensboro *Record*. "I'll be back tomorrow with A. & T. College," one of the students said.

By next morning, the protest had grown to twenty-seven men and four women, most from the same dormitory as the original four. The men were dressed in suits and ties. The students had brought their schoolwork, and studied as they sat at the counter. On Wednesday, students from Greensboro's "Negro" secondary school, Dudley High, joined in, and the number of protesters swelled to eighty. By Thursday, the protesters numbered three hundred, including three white women, from the Greensboro campus of the University of North Carolina. By Saturday, the sit-in had reached six hundred. People spilled out onto the street. White teenagers waved Confederate flags. Someone threw a firecracker. At noon, the A. & T. football team arrived. "Here comes the wrecking crew," one of the white students shouted.

By the following Monday, sit-ins had spread to Winston-Salem, twenty-five miles away, and Durham, fifty miles away. The day after that, students at Fayetteville State Teachers College and at Johnson C. Smith College, in Charlotte, joined in, followed on Wednesday by students at St. Augustine's College and Shaw University, in Raleigh. On Thursday and Friday, the protest crossed state lines, surfacing in Hampton and Portsmouth, Virginia, in Rock Hill, South Carolina, and in Chattanooga, Tennessee. By the end of the month, there were sit-ins throughout the South, as far west as Texas. "I asked every student I met what the first day of the sitdowns had been like on his campus," the political theorist Michael Walzer wrote in *Dissent*. "The answer was always the same: 'It was like a fever. Everyone wanted to go.'" Some seventy thousand students eventually took part. Thousands were arrested and untold thousands more radicalized. These events in the early sixties became a civil-rights war that engulfed the South for the rest of the decade—and it happened without e-mail, texting, Facebook, or Twitter.

The world, we are told, is in the midst of a revolution. The new tools of social media have reinvented social activism. With Facebook and Twitter and the like, the traditional relationship between political authority and popular will has been upended, making it easier for the powerless to collaborate, coordinate, and give voice to their concerns. When ten thousand protesters took to the streets in Moldova in the spring of 2009 to protest against their country's Communist government, the action was dubbed the Twitter Revolution, because of the means by which the demonstrators had been brought together. A few months after that, when student protests rocked Tehran, the State Department took the unusual step of asking Twitter to suspend scheduled maintenance of its Web site, because the Administration didn't want such a critical organizing tool out of service at the height of the demonstrations. "Without Twitter the people of Iran would not have felt empowered and confident to stand up for freedom and democracy," Mark Pfeifle, a former national-security adviser, later wrote, calling for Twitter to be nominated for the Nobel Peace Prize. Where activists were once defined by their causes, they are now defined by their tools. Facebook warriors go online to push for change. "You are the best hope for us all," James K. Glassman, a former senior State Department official, told a crowd of cyber activists at a recent conference sponsored by Facebook, A. T. & T., Howcast, MTV, and Google. Sites like Facebook, Glassman said, "give the U.S. a significant competitive advantage over terrorists. Some time ago, I said that Al Qaeda was 'eating our lunch on the Internet.' That is no longer the case. Al Qaeda is stuck in Web 1.0. The Internet is now about interactivity and conversation."

These are strong, and puzzling, claims. Why does it matter who is eating whose lunch on the Internet? Are people who log on to their Facebook page really the best hope for us all? As for Moldova's so-called Twitter Revolution, Evgeny Morozov, a scholar at Stanford who has been the most persistent of digital evangelism's critics, points out that Twitter had scant internal significance in Moldova, a country where very few Twitter accounts exist. Nor does it seem to have been a revolution, not least because the protests—as Anne Applebaum suggested in the *Washington Post*—may well have been a bit of stagecraft cooked up by the government. (In a country paranoid about Romanian revanchism, the protesters flew a Romanian flag over the Parliament building.) In the Iranian case, meanwhile, the people tweeting about the demonstrations were almost all in the West. "It is time to get Twitter's role in the events in Iran right," Golnaz Esfandiari wrote, this past summer, in *Foreign*

Policy. "Simply put: There was no Twitter Revolution inside Iran." The cadre of prominent bloggers, like Andrew Sullivan, who championed the role of social media in Iran, Esfandiari continued, misunderstood the situation. "Western journalists who couldn't reach—or didn't bother reaching?—people on the ground in Iran simply scrolled through the English-language tweets post with tag #iranelection," she wrote. "Through it all, no one seemed to wonder why people trying to coordinate protests in Iran would be writing in any language other than Farsi."

Some of this grandiosity is to be expected. Innovators tend to be solipsists. They often want to cram every stray fact and experience into their new model. As the historian Robert Darnton has written, "The marvels of communication technology in the present have produced a false consciousness about the past—even a sense that communication has no history, or had nothing of importance to consider before the days of television and the Internet." But there is something else at work here, in the outsized enthusiasm for social media. Fifty years after one of the most extraordinary episodes of social upheaval in American history, we seem to have forgotten what activism is.

Greensboro in the early nineteen-sixties was the kind of place where racial insubordination was routinely met with violence. The four students who first sat down at the lunch counter were terrified. "I suppose if anyone had come up behind me and yelled 'Boo,' I think I would have fallen off my seat," one of them said later. On the first day, the store manager notified the police chief, who immediately sent two officers to the store. On the third day, a gang of white toughs showed up at the lunch counter and stood ostentatiously behind the protesters, ominously muttering epithets such as "burr-head nigger." A local Ku Klux Klan leader made an appearance. On Saturday, as tensions grew, someone called in a bomb threat, and the entire store had to be evacuated.

The dangers were even clearer in the Mississippi Freedom Summer Project of 1964, another of the sentinel campaigns of the civil-rights movement. The Student Nonviolent Coordinating Committee recruited hundreds of Northern, largely white unpaid volunteers to run Freedom Schools, register black voters, and raise civil-rights awareness in the Deep South. "No one should go *anywhere* alone, but certainly not in an automobile and certainly not at night," they were instructed. Within days of arriving in Mississippi, three volunteers—Michael Schwerner, James Chaney, and Andrew Goodman— were kidnapped and killed, and, during the rest of the summer, thirty-seven black churches were set on fire and dozens of safe houses were bombed; volunteers were beaten, shot at, arrested, and trailed by pickup trucks full of armed men. A quarter of those in the program dropped out. Activism that challenges the status quo—that attacks deeply rooted problems—is not for the faint of heart.

What makes people capable of this kind of activism? The Stanford sociologist Doug McAdam compared the Freedom Summer dropouts with the participants who stayed, and discovered that the key difference wasn't, as might be expected, ideological fervor. "*All* of the applicants—participants and withdrawals alike—emerge as highly committed, articulate supporters of the goals and values of the summer program," he concluded. What mattered more was an applicant's degree of personal connection to the civil-rights movement. All the volunteers were required to provide a list of personal contacts—the people they wanted kept apprised of their activities—and participants were far more likely than dropouts to have close friends who were also going to Mississippi. High-risk activism, McAdam concluded, is a "strong-tie" phenomenon.

This pattern shows up again and again. One study of the Red Brigades, the Italian terrorist group of the nineteen-seventies, found that seventy per cent of recruits had at least one good friend already in the organization. The same is true of the men who joined the mujahideen in Afghanistan. Even revolutionary actions that look spontaneous, like the demonstrations in East Germany that led to the fall of the Berlin Wall, are, at core, strong-tie phenomena. The opposition movement in East Germany consisted of several hundred groups, each with roughly a dozen members. Each group was in limited contact with the others: at the time, only thirteen per cent of East Germans even had a phone. All they knew was that on Monday nights, outside St. Nicholas Church in downtown Leipzig, people gathered to voice their anger at the state. And the primary determinant of who showed up was "critical friends"—the more friends you had who were critical of the regime the more likely you were to join the protest.

So one crucial fact about the four freshmen at the Greensboro lunch counter—David Richmond, Franklin McCain, Ezell Blair, and Joseph McNeil—was their relationship with one another. McNeil was a roommate of Blair's in A. & T.'s Scott Hall dormitory. Richmond roomed with McCain one floor up, and Blair, Richmond, and McCain had all gone to Dudley High School. The four would smuggle beer into the dorm and talk late into the night in Blair and McNeil's room. They would all have remembered the murder of Emmett Till in 1955, the Montgomery bus boycott that same year, and the showdown in Little Rock in 1957. It was McNeil who brought up the idea of a sit-in at Woolworth's. They'd discussed it for nearly a month. Then McNeil came into the dorm room and asked the others if they were ready. There was a pause, and McCain said, in a way that works only with people who talk late into the night with one another, "Are you guys chicken or not?" Ezell Blair worked up the courage the next day to ask for a cup of coffee because he was flanked by his roommate and two good friends from high school.

The kind of activism associated with social media isn't like this at all. The platforms of social media are built around weak ties. Twitter is a way of following (or being followed by) people you may never have met. Facebook is a tool for efficiently managing your acquaintances, for keeping up with the people you would not otherwise be able to stay in touch with. That's why you can have a thousand "friends" on Facebook, as you never could in real life.

This is in many ways a wonderful thing. There is strength in weak ties, as the sociologist Mark Granovetter has observed. Our acquaintances—not our friends—are our greatest source of new ideas and information. The Internet lets us exploit the power of these kinds of distant connections with marvellous efficiency. It's terrific at the diffusion of innovation, interdisciplinary collaboration, seamlessly matching up buyers and sellers, and the logistical functions of the dating world. But weak ties seldom lead to high-risk activism.

In a new book called "The Dragonfly Effect: Quick, Effective, and Powerful Ways to Use Social Media to Drive Social Change," the business consultant Andy Smith and the Stanford Business School professor Jennifer Aaker tell the story of Sameer Bhatia, a young Silicon Valley entrepreneur who came down with acute myelogenous leukemia. It's a perfect illustration of social media's strengths. Bhatia needed a bone-marrow transplant, but he could not find a match among his relatives and friends. The odds were best with a donor of his ethnicity, and there were few South Asians in the national bone-marrow database. So Bhatia's business partner sent out an e-mail explaining Bhatia's plight to more than four hundred of their acquaintances, who forwarded the e-mail to their personal contacts; Facebook pages and YouTube videos were devoted to the Help Sameer campaign. Eventually, nearly twenty-five thousand new people were registered in the bone-marrow database, and Bhatia found a match.

But how did the campaign get so many people to sign up? By not asking too much of them. That's the only way you can get someone you don't really know to do something on your behalf. You can get thousands of people to sign up for a donor registry, because doing so is pretty easy. You have to send in a cheek swab and—in the highly unlikely event that your bone marrow is a good match for someone in need—spend a few hours at the hospital. Donating bone marrow isn't a trivial matter. But it doesn't involve financial or personal risk; it doesn't mean spending a summer being chased by armed men in pickup trucks. It doesn't require that you confront socially entrenched norms and practices. In fact, it's the kind of commitment that will bring only social acknowledgment and praise.

The evangelists of social media don't understand this distinction; they seem to believe that a Facebook friend is the same as a real friend and that signing up for a donor registry in Silicon Valley today is activism in the same sense as sitting at a segregated lunch counter in Greensboro in 1960. "Social networks are particularly effective at increasing motivation," Aaker and Smith write. But that's not true. Social networks are effective at increasing *participation*—by lessening the level of motivation that participation requires. The Facebook page of the Save Darfur Coalition has 1,282,339 members, who have donated an average of nine cents apiece. The next biggest Darfur charity on Facebook has 22,073 members, who have donated an average of thirty-five cents. Help Save Darfur has 2,797 members, who have given, on average, fifteen cents. A spokesperson for the Save Darfur Coalition told *Newsweek*, "We wouldn't necessarily gauge someone's value to the advocacy movement based on what they've given. This is a powerful mechanism to engage this critical population. They inform their community, attend events, volunteer. It's not something you can measure by looking at a ledger." In other words, Facebook activism succeeds not by motivating people to make a real sacrifice but by motivating them to do the things that people do when they are not motivated enough to make a real sacrifice. We are a long way from the lunch counters of Greensboro.

The students who joined the sit-ins across the South during the winter of 1960 described the movement as a "fever." But the civil-rights movement was more like a military campaign than like a contagion. In the late nineteen-fifties, there had been sixteen sit-ins in various cities throughout the South, fifteen of which were formally organized by civil-rights organizations like the N.A.A.C.P. and CORE. Possible locations for activism were scouted. Plans were drawn up. Movement activists held training sessions and retreats for would-be protesters. The Greensboro Four were a product of this groundwork: all were members of the N.A.A.C.P. Youth Council. They had close ties with the head of the local N.A.A.C.P. chapter. They had been briefed on the earlier wave of sit-ins in Durham, and had been part of a series of movement meetings in activist churches. When the sit-in movement spread from Greensboro throughout the South, it did not spread indiscriminately. It spread to those cities which had preexisting "movement centers"—a core of dedicated and trained activists ready to turn the "fever" into action.

The civil-rights movement was high-risk activism. It was also, crucially, strategic activism: a challenge to the establishment mounted with precision and discipline. The N.A.A.C.P. was a centralized organization, run from New York according to highly formalized operating procedures. At the Southern Christian Leadership Conference, Martin Luther King, Jr., was the unquestioned authority. At the center of the movement was the black church, which had, as Aldon D. Morris points out in his superb 1984 study, "The Origins of the Civil Rights Movement," a carefully demarcated division of labor, with various standing committees and disciplined groups. "Each group was task-oriented and coordinated its activities through authority structures," Morris writes. "Individuals were held accountable for their assigned duties, and important conflicts were resolved by the minister, who usually exercised ultimate authority over the congregation."

This is the second crucial distinction between traditional activism and its online variant: social media are not about this kind of hierarchical organization. Facebook and the like are tools for building *networks*, which are the opposite, in structure and character, of hierarchies. Unlike hierarchies, with their rules and procedures, networks aren't controlled by a single central authority. Decisions are made through consensus, and the ties that bind people to the group are loose.

This structure makes networks enormously resilient and adaptable in low-risk situations. Wikipedia is a perfect example. It doesn't have an editor, sitting in New York, who directs and corrects each entry. The effort of putting together each entry is self-organized. If every entry in Wikipedia were to be erased tomorrow, the content would swiftly be restored, because that's what happens when a network of thousands spontaneously devote their time to a task.

There are many things, though, that networks don't do well. Car companies sensibly use a network to organize their hundreds of suppliers, but not to design their cars. No one believes that the articulation of a coherent design philosophy is best handled by a sprawling, leaderless organizational system. Because networks don't have a centralized leadership structure and clear lines of authority, they have real difficulty reaching consensus and setting goals. They can't think strategically; they are chronically prone to conflict and error.

How do you make difficult choices about tactics or strategy or philosophical direction when everyone has an equal say?

The Palestine Liberation Organization originated as a network, and the international-relations scholars Mette Eilstrup-Sangiovanni and Calvert Jones argue in a recent essay in *International Security* that this is why it ran into such trouble as it grew: "Structural features typical of networks—the absence of central authority, the unchecked autonomy of rival groups, and the inability to arbitrate quarrels through formal mechanisms—made the P.L.O. excessively vulnerable to outside manipulation and internal strife."

In Germany in the nineteen-seventies, they go on, "the far more unified and successful left-wing terrorists tended to organize hierarchically, with professional management and clear divisions of labor. They were concentrated geographically in universities, where they could establish central leadership, trust, and camaraderie through regular, face-to-face meetings." They seldom betrayed their comrades in arms during police interrogations. Their counterparts on the right were organized as decentralized networks, and had no such discipline. These groups were regularly infiltrated, and members, once arrested, easily gave up their comrades. Similarly, Al Qaeda was most dangerous when it was a unified hierarchy. Now that it has dissipated into a network, it has proved far less effective.

The drawbacks of networks scarcely matter if the network isn't interested in systemic change—if it just wants to frighten or humiliate or make a splash—or if it doesn't need to think strategically. But if you're taking on a powerful and organized establishment you have to be a hierarchy. The Montgomery bus boycott required the participation of tens of thousands of people who depended on public transit to get to and from work each day. It lasted a *year*. In order to persuade those people to stay true to the cause, the boycott's organizers tasked each local black church with maintaining morale, and put together a free alternative private carpool service, with forty-eight dispatchers and forty-two pickup stations. Even the White Citizens Council, King later said, conceded that the carpool system moved with "military precision." By the time King came to Birmingham, for the climactic showdown with Police Commissioner Eugene (Bull) Connor, he had a budget of a million dollars, and a hundred full-time staff members on the ground, divided into operational units. The operation itself was divided into steadily escalating phases, mapped out in advance. Support was maintained through consecutive mass meetings rotating from church to church around the city.

Boycotts and sit-ins and nonviolent confrontations—which were the weapons of choice for the civil-rights movement—are high-risk strategies. They leave little room for conflict and error. The moment even one protester deviates from the script and responds to provocation, the moral legitimacy of the entire protest is compromised. Enthusiasts for social media would no doubt have us believe that King's task in Birmingham would have been made infinitely easier had he been able to communicate with his followers through Facebook, and contented himself with tweets from a Birmingham jail. But networks are messy: think of the ceaseless pattern of correction and revision, amendment and debate, that characterizes Wikipedia. If Martin Luther

King, Jr., had tried to do a wiki-boycott in Montgomery, he would have been steamrollered by the white power structure. And of what use would a digital communication tool be in a town where ninety-eight per cent of the black community could be reached every Sunday morning at church? The things that King needed in Birmingham—discipline and strategy—were things that online social media cannot provide.

The bible of the social-media movement is Clay Shirky's "Here Comes Everybody." Shirky, who teaches at New York University, sets out to demonstrate the organizing power of the Internet, and he begins with the story of Evan, who worked on Wall Street, and his friend Ivanna, after she left her smart phone, an expensive Sidekick, on the back seat of a New York City taxicab. The telephone company transferred the data on Ivanna's lost phone to a new phone, whereupon she and Evan discovered that the Sidekick was now in the hands of a teen-ager from Queens, who was using it to take photographs of herself and her friends.

When Evan e-mailed the teen-ager, Sasha, asking for the phone back, she replied that his "white ass" didn't deserve to have it back. Miffed, he set up a Web page with her picture and a description of what had happened. He forwarded the link to his friends, and they forwarded it to their friends. Someone found the MySpace page of Sasha's boyfriend, and a link to it found its way onto the site. Someone found her address online and took a video of her home while driving by; Evan posted the video on the site. The story was picked up by the news filter Digg. Evan was now up to ten e-mails a minute. He created a bulletin board for his readers to share their stories, but it crashed under the weight of responses. Evan and Ivanna went to the police, but the police filed the report under "lost," rather than "stolen," which essentially closed the case. "By this point millions of readers were watching," Shirky writes, "and dozens of mainstream news outlets had covered the story." Bowing to the pressure, the N.Y.P.D. reclassified the item as "stolen." Sasha was arrested, and Evan got his friend's Sidekick back.

Shirky's argument is that this is the kind of thing that could never have happened in the pre-Internet age—and he's right. Evan could never have tracked down Sasha. The story of the Sidekick would never have been publicized. An army of people could never have been assembled to wage this fight. The police wouldn't have bowed to the pressure of a lone person who had misplaced something as trivial as a cell phone. The story, to Shirky, illustrates "the ease and speed with which a group can be mobilized for the right kind of cause" in the Internet age.

Shirky considers this model of activism an upgrade. But it is simply a form of organizing which favors the weak-tie connections that give us access to information over the strong-tie connections that help us persevere in the face of danger. It shifts our energies from organizations that promote strategic and disciplined activity and toward those which promote resilience and adaptability. It makes it easier for activists to express themselves, and harder for that expression to have any impact. The instruments of social media are well suited to making the existing social order more efficient. They are not a natural enemy of the status quo. If you are of the opinion that all the world needs is a little buffing around the edges, this should not trouble you. But if you think that there are still lunch counters out there that need integrating it ought to give you pause.

Shirky ends the story of the lost Sidekick by asking, portentously, "What happens next?"—no doubt imagining future waves of digital protesters. But he has already answered the question. What happens next is more of the same. A networked, weak-tie world is good at things like helping Wall Streeters get phones back from teen-age girls. *Viva la revolución.*

EXPLORING THE ISSUE

Do Social Media Encourage Revolution?

Critical Thinking and Reflection

1. Are social media a source of shared awareness or simply a useful tool in social change?
2. If a repressive regime fears shared awareness of social problems, will responses to social protests become increasingly violent? What might or might not influence that reaction to the conservative dilemma?
3. Is social media constrained by the power of weak ties? What limits would that put on its utility?
4. Does the use of social media put protests at risk?
5. What communication policies should the United States pursue to advance civil society and moderate abuses of power? Should they be more instrumental or environmental?

Is There Common Ground?

An avalanche of magazine articles and academic publications are surely being written at this moment to more clearly evaluate the impact of social media on the Arab Spring. What the verdict of history will be is unclear. There is common ground between our two authors. Both acknowledge the ability of social media to accomplish important short term goals such as bringing people together at a certain time and place for a protest. Both agree that personal contact is essential. Neither believes that social media functions alone in generating revolution. Shirky discusses the political and economic conditions under which the Arab Spring took place. Gladwell paints a picture of the courage required by those who undertook civil disobedience in the face of segregationist laws and traditions that exacted a high price from those who overstepped their bounds.

Fundamentally, our authors disagree on the long-term political power of social media. Gladwell would agree that it can be a useful tool. Shirky would argue that a more important function of social media is its ability to bring people together, to promote discussion and debate, and to create a shared awareness of the issues that they face.

Additional Resources

Mahjoob Zweiri and Emma Murphy, *The New Arab Media: Technology, Image and Perception* (Ithaca Press, 2011)

This volume examines the growth of new media in the Middle East. Topics include: Al-Jazeera, Internet development, satellite TV, and the use of media for diplomacy and reflecting developments within the Arab world.

Robin Wright, *Rock the Casbah: Rage and Rebellion Across the Islamic World* (Simon & Schuster, 2011)

The author explores the emerging struggle that she sees with the Muslim world to defy extremism. She argues that within the Arab world many are struggling to rescue the faith, reform political systems, and achieve basic human rights.

This story is still being written. Explore through your college and university library databases the articles that are being written about the causes and consequences of the Arab Spring.

Internet References . . .

American Civil Liberties Union

This official site of the ACLU provides a general introduction of issues involving individual rights.

www.aclu.org

Fairness and Accuracy in Reporting (FAIR)

FAIR is a national media watch group that offers criticism of media bias and censorship. FAIR advocates for greater diversity in the press and scrutinizes media practices that marginalize public interest, minority, and dissenting viewpoints.

www.fair.org

The Federal Communications Commission (FCC)

This official site of the FCC provides comprehensive information about the rules and guidelines, official inquiries, and other operations of this complex agency.

www.fcc.gov

Freedom Forum

Freedom Forum is a nonpartisan international foundation dedicated to free press and free speech, and in helping media and the public understand one another. The Web site includes extensive resources and excellent discussion of issues of free speech and press, as well as religion, technology, and international issues. The Press Watch area is intriguing.

www.freedomforum.org

CQ Researcher

Type "Broadcast Indecency" into the search engine for access to a full report on issues of broadcast indecency including extensive background material, a historical recap, an analysis of current issues, and additional resources.

http://library.cqpress.com/cqresearcher/

Peabody Archives, University of Georgia

Since 1941, the University of Georgia Grady College has been home to the Peabody Awards, which recognize the best of broadcast programming. This archive of winners features news, entertainment, educational, children's, and documentary programming.

www.libs.uga.edu/media/index.html

Television News Archive, Vanderbilt University

Since 1968, the Television News Archive has systematically recorded, abstracted, and indexed national television newscasts. This database is the guide to the Vanderbilt University collection of network television news programs.

http://tvnews.vanderbilt.edu

Law and Policy

*F*or the media, the First Amendment entails both rights and responsibilities. How to ensure that these responsibilities will be met is the subject of much of communications law and legislative action. What are the valid limits of the rights of free press? How should society respond when First Amendment rights are in conflict with other individual rights? What changes will the new technology force upon our operation of these rights? The issues in this section deal with who should be responsible for media content and with the rights of groups who find that content inappropriate. We also examine a context in which we question the meaning of "copyright" and whether the laws pertaining to intellectual property rights are still relevant in today's media-saturated world.

- Is Hate Speech in the Media Directly Affecting Our Culture?

- Does Online Communication Compromise the Rights of an Individual When Information Is "Anonymous?"

- Do Copyright Laws Protect Ownership of Intellectual Property?

ISSUE 10

Is Hate Speech in the Media Directly Affecting Our Culture?

YES: **Henry A. Giroux**, from "Living in a Culture of Cruelty: Democracy as Spectacle," *Truthout* (September 2, 2009)

NO: **Georgie Ann Weatherby and Brian Scoggins**, from "A Content Analysis of Persuasion Techniques Used on White Supremacist Websites," *Journal of Hate Studies* (vol. 4, 2005–2006)

Learning Outcomes

After reading this issue, you should be able to:

- Understand the range of issues that comprise questionable content in media, and understand how different media forms change the relationship between senders and receivers of messages.

- Apply not only your own individual interpretation of these scholars' essays, but also should question the context for each; for example, is the world becoming a "meaner" place?

- Know what role media plays in socialization. You should be able to evaluate these ideas and consider their broader implications.

- Evaluate the basis for the claims of these authors and consider any flaws in logic or perspective.

- Explain how these viewpoints can inform readers of broader, yet related issues.

- Discuss one of the most cherished freedoms in American life; the right to free speech.

ISSUE SUMMARY

YES: In this essay, Henry Giroux questions how and why our culture has become so mean spirited. By addressing media content in news and popular fare, he analyzes how the politics of a "pedagogy of hate" has become an exercise in power that ultimately has created a "culture of cruelty." As part of this imposed philosophy, citizens have begun to question and undermine our government's responsibility to protect their interests.

NO: Georgie Ann Weatherby and Brian Scoggins examine the content of the Web pages of four extremist groups on the Internet and discuss the persuasive techniques each uses. They find that the sites draw from traditional tactics that "soft-pedal" positions that emphasize recruiting, while downplaying the messages of hate.

T he term "hate speech" often means different things to different people. The First Amendment to the Constitution ensures freedom of speech, but, in general, hate speech is exempted from the First Amendment. What actually constitutes hate speech is where the difficulties begin. In most cases, hate speech demonstrates some level of contempt for other people, but the term is meant to convey the deliberate bias toward and discrimination against persons that could be incited because of the form of hate speech. This definition becomes murkier when we think of the political ideology behind criticizing others, or the levels to which persuasive tactics may hide the actual intention of hate.

In these selections, the authors do not quarrel with the intentions of hate speech, but rather with the way disguised forms of hate speech exist in different forms of media. Henry Giroux is highly critical of popular media that mask the politics of hate in the process of understanding the production of cultural meaning. By examining specific media texts, he identifies how information and entertainment media normalize a culture of cruelty by disguising meanness and power in entertaining ways, thereby creating cultural products that value the beating of homeless people, contempt for noncommercial public spheres, and scorn for those who are disenfranchised.

Arguing from the perspective of the indirect, or limited, effects of media, Georgie Ann Weatherby and Brian Scoggins investigate how four white supremacist Web sites present information that may appear benign but mask the ideologies of the groups they represent. They investigate the persuasive tactics of The National Alliance, which is part of the neo-Nazi movement; the Imperial Klans of America, which is connected to the Ku Klux Klan; the Aryan Nations, which is a part of the Christian Identity movement; and a less well-known site called Stormfront. By presenting their ideas to the mainstream society, these groups attempt to gain compliance from persons who may be recruited to the extremist group's side.

In the United States, our history of hate speech legislation often is targeted toward groups that exhibit bigotry or contempt for racial, ethnic, religious, or gender groups. In particular, we have had a long history of extremist groups of all kinds, hoping to use the media to defend their positions and recruit new members. When the ideas or methods of a group are viewed as possibly contemptuous, the case usually reaches the courts. In 1989, the Ku Klux Klan approached a cable television company in Kansas City, Missouri, for the purpose of showing a program on the local community access station. The city council decided to withdraw the public access channel completely (*Missouri Knights of the Ku Klux Klan v. Kansas City*, 723 F. Supp. 1347, 1989). The Klan sued the city based on their denial of First Amendment right to free speech and won. The city had to reinstitute the public access channel, and the Klan was able to run their program.

This type of right to free speech exists in most forms of media in the United States, but the issue has become even more extreme in the case of the Internet, where there is so much freedom to post information. In both mainstream media (as Giroux writes) and on the Internet where extremist Web sites exist (as Weatherby and Scoggins write), we can see how hate speech is sanctioned, practiced, and, in some cases, endorsed by the public. Is hate speech infiltrating our society? We think that these selections pose this important question as well as many others.

Social mores and values change over time, and there is no doubt that many people do not critically examine their own biases and behaviors, but media help us examine these issues through a wider lens. Since the Civil Rights Movement in the United States, broader awareness has been given to issues of diversity, difference, and equality. We might want to question whether our own insecurities contribute to a meaner world, when we expect to see a broader range of images and symbols in the media that hopefully, suggest a multicultural, more accepting set of images, visual messages, and content. At the same time, the migration from "mass" media to more personal forms suggests that consumers can easily seek out content that more clearly aligns with their own biases and perceptions. In this case, then, the Internet in particular, can be both a democratizing medium, as well as a storehouse of messages designed to pander to individual preconceived notions. As the selections in this issue demonstrate, we may be experiencing a cumulative effect of people privileging their own biases, rather than thinking more broadly about appropriate socialization and social inclusion.

Hate speech is almost always evaluated based upon the context in which it is presented. The Supreme Court has adjudicated many cases in which the debate around messages has revolved around the meaning of "free speech" and "hate speech." As articulated in the First Amendment, is "free speech" extended to everyone, or just to those who have the responsibility of informing the public of the surveillance of the environment and of the impact of social movements? Are bloggers given the same rights as journalists, and do regular citizens have the right to "free speech" in both public and private communications?

Hate speech has always been an important topic on campuses where speech codes often exist to protect people. Timothy C. Schiell's *Campus Hate Speech on Trial* (University of Kansas, 2009) is an in-depth analysis of a number of important situations in which controversial positions on hate speech have become prevalent on campuses.

Hate speech is closely aligned with the idea of the "Fighting-Words Doctrine," first articulated in *Chaplinsky v. New Hampshire* (315 U.S. 568 (1942)). In this case, Chaplinsky was convicted of violating a New Hampshire statute that had been designed to prohibit inflammatory words—words that could be insightful or offensive or insulting language aimed at a public official. When the Supreme Court heard the case, they agreed that public officials, and anyone, for that matter, should not be subjected to language that could upset the peace of the community. In particular, the "fighting words" included those that had no social value, but that were possibly lewd, obscene, profane, or libelous, as well as those that upset the social interest in moral discourse.

As you review the YES and NO selections in this issue, we ask you to consider whether hate speech or a "culture of meanness" is infiltrating our society? We think that these selections pose this important question as well as many others.

YES

Henry A. Giroux

Living in a Culture of Cruelty: Democracy as Spectacle

Under the Bush administration, a seeping, sometimes galloping, authoritarianism began to reach into every vestige of the culture, giving free rein to those anti-democratic forces in which religious, market, military and political fundamentalism thrived, casting an ominous shadow over the fate of United States democracy. During the Bush-Cheney regime, power became an instrument of retribution and punishment was connected to and fueled by a repressive state. A bullying rhetoric of war, a ruthless consolidation of economic forces, and an all-embracing free-market apparatus and media driven pedagogy of fear supported and sustained a distinct culture of cruelty and inequality in the United States. In pointing to a culture of cruelty, I am not employing a form of left moralism that collapses matters of power and politics into the discourse of character. On the contrary, I think the notion of a culture of cruelty is useful in thinking through the convergence of everyday life and politics, of considering material relations of power—the disciplining of the body as an object of control—on the one hand, and the production of cultural meaning, especially the co-optation of popular culture to sanction official violence, on the other. The culture of cruelty is important for thinking through how life and death now converge in ways that fundamentally transform how we understand and imagine politics in the current historical moment—a moment when the most vital of safety nets, health care reform, is being undermined by right-wing ideologues. What is it about a culture of cruelty that provides the conditions for many Americans to believe that government is the enemy of health care reform and health care reform should be turned over to corporate and market-driven interests, further depriving millions of an essential right?

Increasingly, many individuals and groups now find themselves living in a society that measures the worth of human life in terms of cost-benefit analyses. The central issue of life and politics is no longer about working to get ahead, but struggling simply to survive. And many groups, who are considered marginal because they are poor, unemployed, people of color, elderly or young, have not just been excluded from "the American dream," but have become utterly redundant and disposable, waste products of a society that no longer considers them of any value. How else to explain the zealousness in which social safety nets have been dismantled, the transition from welfare to workfare (offering little job training programs and no child care), and recent acrimony over health care reform's public option? What accounts for the passage of laws that criminalize the behavior of the 1.2 million homeless in the United States, often defining sleeping, sitting, soliciting, lying down or loitering in public places as a criminal offence rather than a behavior in need of compassionate good will and public assistance? Or, for that matter, the expulsions, suspensions, segregation, class discrimination and racism in the public schools as well as the more severe beatings, broken bones and damaged lives endured by young people in the juvenile justice system? Within these politics, largely fueled by market fundamentalism—one that substitutes the power of the social state with the power of the corporate state and only values wealth, money and consumers—there is a ruthless and hidden dimension of cruelty, one in which the powers of life and death are increasingly determined by punishing apparatuses, such as the criminal justice system for poor people of color and/or market forces that increasingly decide who may live and who may die.

The growing dominance of a right-wing media forged in a pedagogy of hate has become a crucial element providing numerous platforms for a culture of cruelty and is fundamental to how we understand the role of education in a range of sites outside of traditional forms of schooling. This educational apparatus and mode of public pedagogy is central to analyzing not just how power is exercised, rewarded and contested in a growing culture of cruelty, but also how particular identities, desires and needs are mobilized in support of an overt racism, hostility towards immigrants and utter disdain, coupled with the threat of mob violence toward any political figure supportive of the social contract and the welfare state. Citizens are increasingly constructed through a language of contempt for all noncommercial public spheres and a chilling indifference to the plight of others that is increasingly expressed in vicious tirades against big government and health care reform. There is a growing element of scorn on the part of the American public for those human beings caught in the web of misfortune, human suffering, dependency and deprivation. As Barbara Ehrenreich observes, "The pattern is to curtail financing for services that might help the poor while ramping up law enforcement: starve school and public transportation budgets, then make truancy illegal. Shut down public housing, then make it a crime to be homeless. Be sure to harass street vendors when there are few other opportunities for employment. The experience of the poor, and especially poor minorities, comes to resemble that of a rat in a cage scrambling to avoid erratically administered electric shocks."

A right-wing spin machine, influenced by haters like Rush Limbaugh, Glenn Beck, Michael Savage and Ann Coulter, endlessly spews out a toxic rhetoric in which: all Muslims are defined as jihadists; the homeless are not victims of misfortune but lazy; blacks are not terrorized by a racist criminal justice system, but the main architects of a culture of criminality; the epidemic of obesity has nothing to do with corporations, big agriculture and advertisers selling junk food, but rather the result of "big" government giving people food stamps; the public sphere is largely for white people, which is being threatened by immigrants and people of color, and so it goes. Glenn Beck, the alleged voice of the common man, appearing on the "Fox & Friends" morning show, calls President Obama a "racist" and then accuses him of "having a deep-seated hatred for white people or the white culture." Nationally syndicated radio host Rush Limbaugh unapologetically states that James Early Ray, the confessed killer of Martin Luther King Jr., should be given a posthumous Medal of Honor, while his counterpart in right-wing hate, talk radio host Michael Savage, states on his show, "You know, when I see a woman walking around with a burqa, I see a Nazi. That's what I see—how do you like that?—a hateful Nazi who would like to cut your throat and kill your children." He also claims that Obama is "surrounded by terrorists" and is "raping America." This is a variation of a crude theme established by Ann Coulter, who refers to Bill Clinton as a "very good rapist." Even worse, Obama is a "neo-Marxist fascist dictator in the making," who plans to "force children into a paramilitary domestic army." And this is just a small sampling of the kind of hate talk that permeates right-wing media. This could be dismissed as loony right-wing political theater if it were not for the low levels of civic literacy displayed by so many Americans who choose to believe and invest in this type of hate talk. On the contrary, while it may be idiocy, it reveals a powerful set of political, economic and educational forces at work in miseducating the American public while at the same time extending the culture of cruelty. One central task of any viable form of politics is to analyze the culture of cruelty and its overt and covert dimensions of violence, often parading as entertainment.

Underlying the culture of cruelty that reached its apogee during the Bush administration was the legalization of state violence, such that human suffering was now sanctioned by the law, which no longer served as a summons to justice. But if a legal culture emerged that made violence and human suffering socially acceptable, popular culture rendered such violence pleasurable by commodifying, aestheticizing and spectacularizing it. Rather than being unspoken and unseen, violence in American life had become both visible in its pervasiveness and normalized as a central feature of dominant and popular culture. Americans had grown accustomed to luxuriating in a warm bath of cinematic blood, as young people and adults alike were seduced with commercial and military video games such as "Grand Theft Auto" and "America's Army," the television series "24" and its ongoing Bacchanalian fête of torture, the crude violence on display in World Wrestling Entertainment and Ultimate Fighting Championship, and an endless series of vigilante films such as "The Brave One" and "Death Sentence," in which the rule of law is suspended by the viscerally satisfying images of men and women seeking revenge as laudable killing machines—a nod to the permanent state of emergency and war in the United States. Symptomatically, there is the mindless glorification and aestheticization of brutal violence in the most celebrated Hollywood films, including many of Quentin Tarantino's films, especially the recent "Death Proof," "Kill Bill" 1 & 2, and "Inglorious Bastards." With the release of Tarantino's 2009 bloody war film, in fact, the press reported that Dianne Kruger, the co-star of "Inglorious Bastards," claimed that she "loved being tortured by Brad Pitt [though] she was frustrated she didn't get an opportunity to get frisky with her co-star, but admits being beaten by Pitt was a satisfying experience."

This is more than the aestheticization of violence, it is the normalization and glorification of torture itself.

If Hollywood has made gratuitous violence the main staple of its endless parade of blockbuster films, television has tapped into the culture of cruelty in a way that was unimaginable before the attack on the US on September 11. Prime-time television before the attacks had "fewer than four acts of torture" per year, but "now there are more than a hundred." Moreover, the people who torture are no longer the villains, but the heroes of prime-time television. The most celebrated is, of course, Jack Bauer, the tragic-ethical hero of the wildly popular Fox TV thriller "24." Not only is torture the main thread of the plot, often presented "with gusto and no moral compunction," but Bauer is portrayed as a patriot, rather than a depraved monster, who tortures in order to protect American lives and national security. Torture, in this scenario, takes society's ultimate betrayal of human dignity and legitimates the pain and fear it produces as normal, all the while making a "moral sadist" a television celebrity. The show has over 15 million viewers, and its glamorization of torture has proven so successful that it appears to have not only numbed the public's reaction to the horrors of torture, but it is so overwhelmingly influential among the US military that the Pentagon sent Brig. Gen. Patrick Finnegan to California to meet with the producers of the show. "He told them that promoting illegal behavior in the series . . . was having a damaging effect on young troops." The pornographic glorification of gratuitous, sadistic violence is also on full display in the popular HBO television series "Dexter," which portrays a serial killer as a sympathetic, even lovable, character. Visual spectacles steeped in degradation and violence permeate the culture and can be found in various reality TV shows, professional wrestling and the infamous Jerry Springer Show. These programs all trade in fantasy, glamorized violence and escapism. And they share similar values. As Chris Hedges points out in his analysis of professional wrestling, they all mirror the worst dimensions of an unchecked and unregulated market society in which "winning is all that matters. Morality is irrelevant. . . . It is all about personal pain, vendettas, hedonism and fantasies of revenge, while inflicting pain on others. It is the cult of victimhood."

The celebration of hyper-violence, moral sadism and torture travels easily from fiction to real life with the emergence in the past few years of a proliferation of "bum fight" videos on the Internet, "shot by young men and boys who are seen beating the homeless or who pay transients a few dollars to fight each other." The culture of cruelty mimics cinematic violence as the agents of abuse both indulge in actual forms of violence and then further celebrate the barbarity by posting it on the web, mimicking the desire for fame and recognition, while voyeuristically consuming their own violent cultural productions. The National Coalition for the Homeless claims that "On YouTube in July 2009, people have posted 85,900 videos with 'bum' in the title [and] 5,690 videos can be found with the title 'bum fight,' representing . . . an increase of 1,460 videos since April 2008." Rather than problematize violence, popular culture increasingly normalizes it, often in ways that border on criminal intent. For instance, a recent issue of Maxim, a popular men's magazine, included "a blurb titled 'Hunt the Homeless' [focusing on] a coming 'hobo convention' in Iowa and says 'Kill one for fun. We're

87 percent sure it's legal.' " In this context, violence is not simply being transformed into an utterly distasteful form of adolescent entertainment or spectacularized to attract readers and boost profits, it becomes a powerful pedagogical force in the culture of cruelty by both aligning itself and becoming complicit with the very real surge of violence against the homeless, often committed by young men and teenage boys looking for a thrill. Spurred on by the ever reassuring presence of violence and dehumanization in the wider culture, these young "thrill offenders" now search out the homeless and "punch, kick, shoot or set afire people living on the streets, frequently killing them, simply for the sport of it, their victims all but invisible to society." All of these elements of popular culture speak stylishly and sadistically to new ways in which to maximize the pleasure of violence, giving it its hip (if fascist) edginess.

Needless to say, neither violent video games and television series nor Hollywood films and the Internet (or for that matter popular culture) cause in any direct sense real world violence and suffering, but they do not leave the real world behind either. That is too simplistic. What they do achieve is the execution of a well-funded and highly seductive public pedagogical enterprise that sexualizes and stylizes representations of violence, investing them with an intense pleasure quotient. I don't believe it is an exaggeration to claim that the violence of screen culture entertains and cleanses young people of the burden of ethical considerations when they, for instance, play video games that enabled them to "casually kill the simulated human beings whose world they control." Hollywood films such as the "Saw" series offer up a form of torture porn in which the spectacle of the violence enhances not merely its attraction, but offers young viewers a space where questions of ethics and responsibility are gleefully suspended, enabling them to evade their complicity in a culture of cruelty. No warnings appear on the labels of these violent videos and films, suggesting that the line between catharsis and desensitization may become blurred, making it more difficult for them to raise questions about what it means "to live in a society that produces, markets, and supports such products." But these hyper-violent cultural products also form part of a corrupt pedagogical assemblage that makes it all the more difficult to recognize the hard realities of power and material violence at work through militarism, a winner-take-all economy marked by punishing inequalities and a national security state that exhibits an utter disregard for human suffering. Even the suffering of children, we must note, as when government officials reduce the lives of babies and young children lost in Iraq and Afghanistan to collateral damage. Tragically, the crime here is much more than symbolic.

The ideology of hardness and cruelty runs through American culture like an electric current, sapping the strength of social relations and individual character, moral compassion and collective action, offering up crimes against humanity that become fodder for video games and spectacularized media infotainment, and constructing a culture of cruelty that promotes a "symbiosis of suffering and spectacle." As Chris Hedges argues,

> Sadism is as much a part of popular culture as it is of corporate culture. It
> dominates pornography, runs . . . through reality television and trash-talk
> programs and is at the core of the compliant, corporate collective.

Corporatism is about crushing the capacity for moral choice. And it has its logical fruition in Abu Ghraib, the wars in Iraq and Afghanistan, and our lack of compassion for the homeless, our poor, the mentally ill, the unemployed and the sick.

Bailouts are not going to address the ways in which individual desires, values and identities are endlessly produced in the service of a culture of cruelty and inequality. Power is not merely material; it is also symbolic and is distributed through a society in ways we have never seen before. No longer is education about schooling. It now functions through the educational force of the larger culture in the media, Internet, electronic media and through a wide range of technologies and sites endlessly working to undo democratic values, compassion and any viable notion of justice and its accompanying social relations. What this suggests is a redefinition of both literacy and education. We need, as a society, to educate students and others to be literate in multiple ways, to reclaim the high ground of civic courage, and to be able to name, engage and transform those forms of public pedagogy that produce hate and cruelty as part of the discourse of common sense. Otherwise, democracy will lose the supportive institutions, social relations and culture that make it not only possible but even thinkable.

Georgie Ann Weatherby
and Brian Scoggins

A Content Analysis of Persuasion Techniques Used on White Supremacist Websites

The Internet has made it possible for people to access just about any information they could possibly want. Conversely, it has given organizations a vehicle through which they can get their message out to a large audience. Hate groups have found the Internet particularly appealing, because they are able to get their uncensored message out to an unlimited number of people. This is an issue that is not likely to go away. The Supreme Court has declared that the Internet is like a public square, and it is therefore unconstitutional for the government to censor websites (*Reno et al. v. American Civil Liberties Union et al.* 1997). Research into how hate groups use the Internet is necessary for several reasons. First, the Internet has the potential to reach more people than any other medium. Connected to that, there is no way to censor who views what, so it is unknown whom these groups are trying to target for membership. It is also important to learn what kinds of views these groups hold and what, if any, actions they are encouraging individuals to take. In addition, ongoing research is needed because both the Internet and the groups themselves are constantly changing.

The research dealing with hate websites is sparse. The few studies that have been conducted have been content analyses of dozens of different hate sites. The findings indicate a wide variation in the types of sites, but the samples are so broad that no real patterns have emerged.

This study will focus on the content and the use of persuasive techniques of four major white supremacist websites. Three of them are major groups connected to larger movements: the National Alliance connected to the Neo-Nazi movement, the Imperial Klans of America connected to the Ku Klux Klan, and the Aryan Nations connected to the Christian Identity movement. In addition, the study will be examining a large site named Stormfront that is not affiliated with any group.

This study will catalogue what parts of the site hate groups use for attracting people, how their extremist views are disguised, what types of age, gender, and educational demographics they are appealing to, and what kinds of attempts they make to recruit potential members. Its primary focus is to

From *Journal of Hate Studies*, vol. 4, no. 1, 2005–2006, pp. 9–13, 17–18, 20–23. Copyright ©
2006 by Gonzaga University Institute for Action Against Hate. Reprinted by permission.

examine the efforts that are made on the site to indoctrinate visitors into white supremacist beliefs. Since the views expressed on the sites are extremist, it is hypothesized that the compliance techniques of foot-in-the-door technique (when something small is requested first to make compliance more likely for a larger request) and low-ball technique (when only part of what a request entails is made known) will be used. This study will examine the extent to which these techniques are present on the sites.

Literature Review

The theories in which this study is grounded are compliance techniques that, if present on the website, would serve to make the site more appealing to potential members of mainstream society. Foot-in-the-door technique is a theory of social psychology that holds that a person will be more likely to accede to a request if he or she previously has agreed to a smaller, related request. Generally, gaining compliance with a request is the purpose of foot-in-the-door technique. It is not a new idea to use this technique to change people's perspectives. It is believed to be one of the basic tactics used in Korean brainwashing. Furthermore, it is one of the techniques that Nazi propaganda minister Joseph Goebbles used in his attempts to spread the racism that was vital to Hitler's rise to power.

Low-ball technique is a technique wherein compliance is gained by not telling the person the whole story. This method is often intertwined with foot-in-the-door technique. This is in fact how most propaganda works. The person or organization trying to persuade tells only part of the story. Low-ball technique includes the site's explanations and a defense of the viewpoints expressed on it. In telling only one side, the websites are more likely to sound reasonable and appealing to others. When people do not know both sides or the whole story, they are much more likely to comply, and compliance will change their self-perception.

Freedman and Fraser did pioneering work with foot-in-the-door technique. Their study included two experiments in which they compared the likelihood of people's complying with a large request if they were first asked to comply with a smaller request and if they were not. They found that only 22% of people who were asked only the large request agreed to it, whereas 53% of the people who agreed to the initial small request agreed to the large request. When the researchers controlled for the variable of familiarity with the experimenter, they found it to be insignificant, which indicates that people do not comply because they feel as if they know the person making the request. When they looked at the factor of merely agreeing to the request and not actually following through, they found that it was only slightly less of an indication of compliance. This means that just the act of agreeing to the request is a significant part of the effect.

This study was very significant in that it uncovered some of the basic principles concerning how and why foot-in-the-door technique works. The basic idea was that once someone has agreed to any action, no matter how small, he tends to feel more involved than he did before, which leads to a change in self-perception and attitude. This is very relevant to the present study, because this is the kind of self-perception change that is hypothesized to take place when the foot-in-the-door technique is used on websites.

Bem found that cognitive dissonance is a necessary element when changing one's self-perception, if the changed perception conflicts with the person's original beliefs. Cognitive dissonance occurs when a person holds two views that are in conflict with one another. The way a person deals with this dissonance will vary, but regardless of that, it causes a person anxiety, and therefore he or she will want to resolve it. When trying to appeal to potential members, these groups will structure their websites to make them appear more likeable and less extreme; this would be an example of low-ball technique. A change in self-perception comes about more easily if a person does not have set beliefs about something. In this case, cognitive dissonance may not occur and a change in beliefs could come as soon as some propaganda gets its foot in the door.

The people that are most likely to be susceptible to this technique are those with low self-esteem or values that, while mainstream, remain closer to those of extremists. Bramel found that when something is in conflict with a person's self-perception, it causes more arousal and subsequently is viewed as bad. However, the opposite is true as well: the more closely an idea matches a person's self-perception, the more likely it is to be viewed as not as bad. Thus hate groups seeking to recruit people from the mainstream are likely to have greater success if they are welcoming, and downplay or disguise their actual beliefs, as McDonald has already observed. This is why foot-in-the-door and low-ball techniques are expected to be prevalent.

There are three other major compliance techniques as well: door-in-the-face, pique, and that's-not-all techniques. Door-in-the-face technique is demonstrated when someone initially is asked to perform a large request, and then is asked to perform a smaller one. Pique technique refers to arousing someone's interest with something unusual. In that's-not-all technique, a rather large request is made, followed by the offering of incentives for following the request. These techniques are not considered in this study, for the reason that they would not be effective in changing people's beliefs. This is so because in this situation, extremists are striving to make their viewpoint look appealing to those in the mainstream. These other techniques, if used, would further polarize the group from the mainstream, making its members seem more extreme or outlandish, which would not cause people to sympathize or associate with them; consequently, they would not change anyone's self-perception.

The Internet has become an excellent medium for recruitment. However, recruitment was not the main goal of these groups at first. Even today, there are many other ways in which white supremacist sites use the Internet. The history of white supremacist groups on the Internet began in 1983 when George Dietz put up a computer bulletin board system named Liberty Bell. The West Virginian Neo-Nazi used it to post various white supremacist information such as holocaust denial, racist, and anti-Semitic material.

A year later, the Aryan Nations and White Aryan Resistance set up bulletin boards of their own in an attempt to help connect right-wing extremists from all over. Included in the content of the postings on the Aryan Nations site were listings of various Jewish headquarters, with messages attached encouraging surfers to take action against them.

The White Aryan Resistance was even more focused on inciting violence; however, their activities caught up with them when they were held liable for the death of an Ethiopian immigrant at the hands of two skinheads for the amount of $12.5 million. Already by 1985, hate groups online were being monitored by watchdog groups such as the Anti-Defamation League.

By the early 1990s, bulletin boards were being replaced by discussion boards. These allowed more people the opportunity to contribute their own extremist views. By this time, the Internet was also being used by hate groups to encourage their strategy of leaderless resistance. The goal was to have people take matters into their own hands, operating in underground cells unaffiliated with any particular group. William Pierce's 1978 novel, the *Turner Diaries,* is a model of this tactic. In the book, the main character starts a race war by bombing the FBI building (this was the model Timothy McVeigh used in his attack on the Federal Building in Oklahoma City). Other groups have promoted RAHOWA (or racial holy war) on their sites and generally encouraged leaderless resistance.

The Internet offers groups the opportunity to reach unprecedented numbers of people with these ideas. It further allows groups to implicitly encourage leaderless resistance, glorifying real-life terrorists such as Robert Mathews, Gordon Kahl, and David Tate. It allows lone wolves the ability to keep up on events, stay informed about the group, and get ideas while protecting the group from liability.

Now that the Internet is more widely used and accessible, groups use it for many of the same purposes, but have expanded its role to include more intricate methods of recruiting. Groups are able to appeal to a wide range of age groups and people with different ideologies by allowing them easy access to what interests them.

There are hundreds of racist websites, all of which have different objectives and means by which they attempt to arrive at those objectives. . . . Grant and Chiang . . . looked at 157 racist websites. They found that recruitment appeared to be a main objective for many sites that were making attempts to reach more impressionable surfers. These attempts occasionally included kids' pages, but much more commonly were links to multimedia, merchandise, racist music, and video games.

The Internet allows hate groups to control their image in terms of how they wish to appear to the public. Groups are able to appear much more respectable, and nearly all are choosing to take this route. Among the sites included in this analysis, overt support of violence (even by violent groups) was seen infrequently, and claims that groups were unbiased, not racist, and not hate groups were made fairly often. Indeed, a great many sites were lacking in overt bigotry, especially on the home page.

An ostensibly non-offensive and objective site is one of the things that is effective in preparing to use foot-in-the-door and low-ball technique. The first step is to make the site friendlier and apparently closer to people's mainstream views. Doing so will make the ideas presented more likely to be considered, as they are perceived as being closer to people's self-perception. . . .

The National Alliance is the largest Neo-Nazi group in the U.S., despite the death of its leader and founder, William Pierce, in 2002. The West Virginia-based group was founded in the 1970s and since then has grown a great deal, thanks to Pierce. Erich Gliebe took over as the head of the NA after Pierce's death. The group uses several mediums in addition to the Internet, including radio, flyers, video games, magazines, and newsletters. . . . One of the main focuses of the National Alliance is recruiting: "To attract new followers, NA leaders and members have used billboards, hung organizational banners in prominent locations, rented booths at gun shows, posted their propaganda materials on public property and distributed NA literature in suburban neighborhoods and on college campuses." In addition, the National Alliance owns Resistance Records, a label for white power music meant to attract younger people. It also publishes Pierce's books, the *Turner Diaries* and another book called *Hunter,* which details a race war. These measures have influenced a number of terrorist acts and hate crimes. All of these efforts toward recruitment are intended to get NA members' foot in the door so that they can attract a greater number of people. The National Alliance takes a much less direct approach when it comes to letting people know they are out there. Thus we surmise that the group is more concerned with recruitment and indoctrination than they are with spreading a hateful message.

The Aryan Nations was chosen for this study because, while it has ties to Neo-Nazis, it is one of the largest and most visible representations of the Christian Identity movement. The Christian Identity Church is based on the presupposition that Aryans are God's chosen people and Jews are the offspring of Satan. The Aryan Nations was established in the mid-1970s by Richard Butler, and since then it has grown under his leadership. At the time of Butler's death in 2004, the group was bankrupt as a result of a Southern Poverty Law Center lawsuit against it; currently the group is run by August Kreis, who has led it into disarray. The mediums for recruitment used by this group are Internet websites, posters, videos, chat rooms, conferences, and online bulletin boards. Its members can also be linked to numerous hate crimes and terrorist acts that have occurred since the 1970s.

The Ku Klux Klan is a group that is fragmented into many various factions. In general, its members all share the same beliefs and ideologies. Their basic goal since the group's genesis in 1866 has been to lash out at minority groups who they feel are responsible for any change in lifestyle or hardship they experience. Today their focus appears (at least to the outside observer) to be inward, on such things as taking pride in their heritage. They have also made an effort to clean up their image in order to mainstream the organization. This study will examine the Imperial Klans of America, chosen because they are the largest single group within the KKK. The mediums they use to reach people are leaflets, mass mailings, the Internet, and rallies. All of these rely on compliance techniques; however, this study is concerned only with those used on the Internet. Most of these techniques would not be effective in changing a person's self-perception, and therefore are not effective methods of recruitment. They are used simply to let the public know that the Klan is out there.

Stormfront.org is the largest white supremacist site on the Internet. Don Black is the founder and operator of the website. It has numerous links to sites all across the world. It can most accurately be described as a forum, but what makes Stormfront unique is that it is very inclusive of all other white supremacist sites. It was chosen for the very fact that it is by far the largest white supremacist site on the Internet. . . .

The findings of this study were for the most part what was expected. The sites appear to be used largely as recruiting tools. There were many examples of foot-in-the-door technique and low-ball technique. Stormfront had the most instances of the techniques with 154; next was the National Alliance with 76; then came the Imperial Klans of America with 72; and last was the Aryan Nations with 40 instances. When contrasted with examples of overtly racist or offensive parts of the site, it was found that the overwhelming majority of the content for three of the sites paints their parent group in a positive light. Stormfront had only 2 examples of overtly racist or offensive material, the Imperial Klans of America 3, and the National Alliance 0. What was unexpected was the open virulence of the Aryan Nations, who had 20 overtly racist and offensive portions on their site. The quantity of racist and offensive portions of the site is important to note because even a few instances of a site's overtly stating its message have a strong impact on the viewer. Such directness serves to negate many of the efforts of the sites to appear mainstream and reasonable.

There are many differences and similarities that were found between the sites. The National Alliance separated itself from the other sites by its complete lack of overtly offensive areas on its website. That is not to say that there is nothing offensive about the message of the site; however, to a person with little or no knowledge of white supremacism looking at the site, it might not immediately appear offensive and racist. The site lacked any racial epithets; instead, it explained why the group holds its beliefs and cites evidence to support those beliefs. The absence of overt hostility makes it impossible to place the site in a ratio. It appears to be appealing most to a better-educated, middle-class demographic. Evidence for this assertion can be gleaned from a section in which the group profiles those involved in the National Alliance. In the profile section two middle-class housewives explain why they wanted to join. The National Alliance owns a rather extensive publishing company, Vanguard books. There are 600 books available through the site, many of which appear to be unaffiliated with the white supremacy movement. Both of these are examples of foot-in-the-door technique, but the member profile is also an example of subculture theory being used. It is interesting that two women are profiled. The choice of female profiles shows whom the group is trying to target: people who would not normally be associated with an extremist group. Another telling fact was that there was no link to the group's music label, Resistance Records. The absence of the link has changed since December of 2003. The missing link is further evidence that the group is targeting exclusively an older, more educated generation. The same is true of their radio show, which appeals to people who would have the time and desire to listen to such things during the day. It is clear from this study that the National Alliance is the group in the study that is most heavily focused on trying to appear mainstream.

The Imperial Klans of America and Stormfront have very similar approaches when it comes to attracting people. As was stated earlier, the overtly racist and offensive parts of the site have a huge impact. So even though there is a large discrepancy between the ratios, it does not appear that great when visiting the sites. Stormfront has a ratio of 77:1, the IKA a ratio of 24:1. Stormfront covers all of the demographics. It has discussion forums for teens and for women, as well as an entire kids' site.

Among the more notable parts of the site is the section for the scholarship essay competition. An essay is a small request, yet the power to change someone's self-perception through getting him to agree to write one is a huge step in indoctrinating young minds. Using this same principle, the kids' page attached to the site suggests that any students having to do a report on Martin Luther King would do well to use the resource of martinlutherking .org. This is a site that appears legitimate, but makes Martin Luther King out to be a villain and hate-monger. It is also noteworthy that the kids' page has a large collection of writings explaining the history of the white race. Stormfront makes great use of low-ball technique. The site goes to extreme lengths to explain the group's views and the problems caused by minorities. This low-ball technique accounts for 111 of the 154 instances of efforts to recruit used on this site.

Stormfront has a variety of areas that are dedicated to all age groups and genders. Furthermore, there are discussion forums for all sorts of different interests. There are forums for health and fitness, homemaking, business, poetry, theology, and personal ads, just to name a few. It is a very inclusive site with respect to white supremacists.

It was somewhat surprising that a site unaffiliated with any particular groups would have so much of its content tailored to prospective members. This suggests that Don Black, the site's creator, is more concerned with changing people's beliefs than with having them take any sort of action, such as joining a particular group or committing a certain act. This orientation is similar to that of the IKA.

The Imperial Klans of America have made a distinct effort to separate themselves from their menacing past. This was evident from the disclaimer on the site, which stated that the group does not condone any acts of violence whatsoever. This claim is ironic because historically the Klans are the oldest and most violent group. The reason for the disclaimer is to protect the group from legal liability if a person was to commit a hate crime based on the information on their site. The disclaimer also serves a secondary purpose: to give the impression that the IKA is nonviolent. Like Stormfront, they have a broad discussion forum, though it is somewhat smaller. They have a selection of specific forums to choose from, such as homemaking, Bible studies, education and home schooling, and unrevised history, to name a few. These categories are evidence that they are trying to appeal to women as well. This site had no specific section for young kids, but promoted Nordic Fest, a White Power music festival that would appeal to teens in general.

In keeping with tradition, their primary enemies were blacks. They have a very long section entitled "Black Hate Crimes Against Whites," in which they explain how the crime statistics people see are skewed toward favoring blacks. The different points made here accounted for 19 different examples of the efforts to recruit. Nothing was overtly racist; rather, it was made to look well-researched and scholarly. As one example, on the part entitled "Martin Luther King, The Truth," which tells about the torture of whites in South Africa at the hands of blacks, there is a toll-free hotline at the bottom of the page. Its mere presence made the group appear to be a reputable organization.

While much of the site was professionally done and much of the work appeared scholarly, there were some blatantly racist and offensive images. There were pictures up from a recent cross "lighting" the group had held. There were also advertisements for Nordic Fest, the annual White Power music festival sponsored by the IKA. By far the most offensive material on the site was the printable flyers. These flyers could not possibly be intended for anything other than shock value and for threatening minorities. It is clearly this group's goal to have people distribute the flyers in order to harass the groups depicted in them. Often they depicted minorities in a dehumanizing fashion, as ready to prey on whites.

The Aryan Nations was the black sheep of the sites studied, with a ratio of 2:1. Half of their 40 instances of foot-in-the-door or low-ball technique were different writings explaining the national socialist movement. The rest were simple things like links to contact them and the implication of a nonprofit .org URL. There were very few efforts to appeal to a broader range of people. It should be noted that several of the links that would likely have led to parts of the site that could have been coded as attempts to recruit did not work. The faulty links are most likely a result of the internal disarray that plagues the group. Consequently they are probably not devoting much time or effort to the upkeep of the website. . . .

EXPLORING THE ISSUE

Is Hate Speech in the Media Directly Affecting Our Culture?

Critical Thinking and Reflection

1. Hate speech and creating a hostile environment for someone can be forms of defamation. Recent legislation (such as the Meagan Meir Cyberbullying Prevention Act) has made it a criminal act to use online communication media for the purposes of creating a hostile environment for someone (see Issue 17). Is online "meanness" different from creating a culture of hostility or addressing someone face-to-face?
2. If you look at the people around you, the information you get from media, and the way people in the media talk to each other—do you see evidence of meanness? What are the long-term prospects for living in a society that allows certain mean-spirited words and confrontations without challenge? Is this the type of world you would like to inhabit?
3. How do children learn through socialization? Can children be expected to understand the difference between hostility, hate, and fear? Can adults?

    In considering the perspectives of the authors, do you agree with Giroux that our culture is becoming a meaner place? Are you concerned about the availability of the Internet to groups who have a specific agenda that may, possibly, violate someone else's civil rights?
4. Do today's contemporary media forms challenge the meaning and intent of the First Amendment? Should there be situations in which some groups in society should be protected from the views of others in "public" forums?

Is There Common Ground?

We spend a good deal of time posing questions about the role of the media in the *Taking Sides* book; how regulations and policies change over time, and how we, as individuals make sense of the world around us. In the YES and NO selections, we look to society as the place in which a number of attitudes, biases, and learned behaviors are contested.

Surely, if you examined Supreme Court transcripts about the sanctity of the First Amendment and its application to evolving forms of media, you would see a variety of viewpoints from the Supreme Court Justices. Some take the First Amendment as "absolute," while others consider the contemporary environment and context in which to judge how broadly the First Amendment may apply in specific situations. Hate Speech may not be covered by the First Amendment, but the range of hostile behaviors, terms, and epithets can easily fall into the "gray" areas between the absolutist and contextual interpretations. The number and range of specific contexts for this discussion are very large.

Additional Resources

In a 2008 public symposium in New York City, organized by New Criterion and the Foundation for Defense of Democracies, the issue of hate speech and Islam/U.S. relationships in media was addressed in *Free Speech in an Age of Jihad: Libel Tourism, "Hate Speech" and Political Freedom.*

Janis L. Judson and Donna M. Bertazzoni, *Law, Media, and Culture, the Landscape of Hate* (Peter Lang, 2002).

This book is a collection of problems of hate speech and media images in popular culture.

The American Civil Liberties Union (ACLU) has a Web site specifically dedicated to issues and problems of hate speech on campus:

www.aclu.org/free-speech/hate-speech-campus

The Huffington Post recorded an interesting article about Facebook's use of hate speech, and its targets—women (written on 10/4/11):

www.huffingtonpost.com/2011/10/04/facebook-hate-speech-women_n_993800.html

Cultivation theory is an accepted idea in media studies, that suggests that people who watch mean, violent, or caustic media performances may interpret the rest of the world to be more mean. The Web site below briefly describes the mean world syndrome—an idea and phrase coined by George Gerbner:

http://meanworldsyndrome.com/

ISSUE 11

Does Online Communication Compromise the Rights of an Individual When Information Is "Anonymous?"

YES: Neil Swidey, from "Inside the Mind of the Anonymous Online Poster," *Boston.com* (June 20, 2010)

NO: Ian Lloyd, from "Privacy, Anonymity and the Internet," *Electronic Journal of Comparative Law* (vol. 13, no. 1, March 2009)

Learning Outcomes

After reading this issue, you should be able to:

- Apply some basic concepts regarding private technology in public places to consider whether "anonymity" or "privacy" is possible.
- Many of the technologies we use today—the Internet and cell phones, in particular—give us the illusion that we can have private communications in public places. Is this really possible?
- Understand how technologies always leave "trails" or "breadcrumbs" that can lead a knowledgeable person (or hacker) to expose their media use.
- Evaluate your own behavior, particularly in public places, and hopefully, apply some common sense rules and guidelines to your media use.
- Analyze a situation in which technology leads us to think one thing (providing an illusion of anonymity or privacy) while creating a situation in which anonymity or privacy can be easily violated. Should new laws be created to solve these problems?

YES: Neil Swidey addresses the issue of anonymous online posters who register their opinions on the *Boston Globe* Web site, www .Boston.com. He discusses how some abusive and vitriolic postings sometimes have to be eliminated by site moderators, and how important it is to some people to have access to posting their opinions online. Unlike traditional newspapers, where comments to the editor contain a reader's name and address, the anonymous poster sometimes becomes so offensive that the nature and value of online commentary are called into question.

NO: In examining the legal relationship between privacy and anonymity, Ian Lloyd provides both a legal approach toward protecting privacy and anonymity, and provides examples of how everyday behavior challenges our expectations of anonymity and privacy when data collections violate a person's reasonable expectation of privacy. He writes that although the legal approach toward more online communication attempts to protect personal rights, good intentions often backfire, and life in the digital age comes with some possible breaches of trust.

Ever since the Internet became available for public use, the element of *trust* that had been a part of the concept undergirding the use of the Internet and the World Wide Web has been tested by individuals, companies interested in data mining, and those who see the distribution form as a means of reaching targeted consumers. The early developers had not taken into consideration the fact that the Internet might be used for spam, identity theft, cyberbullying, hacking, or other harmful purposes, and both the Internet and the Web evolved with little regulation, bearing little similarity to other forms of media for which we had preexisting principles, guidelines, regulations, and laws.

The unique characteristics of the Internet and the Web allow users to present themselves anonymously, through the use of pseudonyms, avatars, or other means of disguising their real names and identities. For the most part, these online identities bear little or no resemblance to actual users' real-life identities. Most of the time, the "alternate identities" pose no problem and are harmless, but sometimes the rules and practices of people engaging in online communication clash or violate principles, guidelines, or practices that had been adopted to protect earlier forms of communication through media forms that provided greater transparency and required great responsibility and accountability on behalf of the users.

The First Amendment to the Constitution of the United States guarantees freedom of speech and freedom of the press, but these rights assume a level of responsibility on the part of those who exercise these freedoms. Traditional newspapers often invited comments from readers, and would often feature many of them on the op-ed page, or in a section titled "Letters to the Editor." Now, however, as Neil Swidey informs us, editors of online publications sometimes have to moderate the flow and number of comments posted by readers, and sometimes cut off anonymous posters who may use inflammatory language, or post for purposes of exercising their own views that may push the First Amendment to its limits in terms of civility.

British professor Ian Lloyd discusses how tenuous notions of privacy and anonymity are, and takes the perspective that the legal dimension of anonymity has been explored far less than the legal definition of privacy. Using a number of examples, he shows how attempts to protect anonymity and privacy are often taken by law enforcement, civil organizations, and businesses, although these efforts are sometimes thwarted by the multiple layers of information that actually provide a data mine that makes it easier, rather than harder, to identify someone. He discusses policies that put a statute of limitations on the amount of time organizations (like Google, for example) can keep records of use before they are "anonymized" but concludes that contemporary use of anonymous information online is just as vulnerable to misuse as earlier forms of data collection in other media and for other purposes.

Life in the digital age brings many new possibilities and challenges, but it also raises questions about older policies and practices that do not transfer easily to online communication. As you read these two selections, you may want to consider the number of ways in which low-cost, immediate, international distribution systems of information call earlier practices and policies into question.

Undoubtedly, the lines often blur between privacy and anonymity; and there are good reasons to be concerned about whether online communication leads one to violate the rights of others, as well as the problem of exposing one's self to practices that inadvertently violate their own rights. There are a number of misconceptions about how the law can protect a person in online communication, and how "absolute" privacy and anonymity can possibly exist in an information age.

As Lloyd writes, lifestyles that use technology to a great degree often have the effect of making one feel anonymous, but at the same time the promise of controlling our identities is often taken away from us without our knowledge. The positive and negative effects of relying more on online communication for personal reasons as well as for effective business purposes is in itself, complicated. Young people, particularly pre-teens and teenagers live more of their lives online than older adults, and the thought that online communication is a private activity is no justification for posting personal information that may actually harm someone.

There is great agreement that privacy and anonymity should be protected, but little agreement on how it can be accomplished. Many students have found that friends have posted unflattering (or embarrassing) pictures of them online without their knowledge. Many employers do a search of online information that exists about potential employees, and often, the unflattering or embarrassing pictures can prevent someone from getting a job—if the employer interprets those pictures to exercise a lapse of good taste or good conduct. Similarly, information posted anonymously with the intent to cause harm or embarrass someone can be traced through computer records, and the author can be charged with defamation of character if the information actually causes someone harm.

The most effective way of controlling privacy, anonymity, and a person's basic human rights comes from efforts to exercise control over personal information. The Electronic Frontier Forum (EFF.org) has several web pages dedicated to explaining that anonymity is a right, conferred by the U.S. Constitution, and it criticizes many organizations for challenging or violating that right. On January 30, 2011, EFF criticized *Facebook's* new policy on selling personal information of *Facebook* users to advertisers, and claimed that it violates the trust of its users. If the positions of the two authors in this issue are right, we can expect to see many more challenges to notions of privacy and anonymity online in the future.

An important feature of this issue is that often, people who assume anonymity, leave "trails" of information that actually identifies them, in some form or another. We often don't consider the technological structures of newer media (like the Internet and cell phones), nor do we realize that the idea of using technology in public places actually records our use, including the time, and often, our identifying information. Think for a moment of a situation in which someone was using a public computer terminal in a library; he or she types in his or her password, perhaps a credit card number, and a good amount of information about what sites he visits. If the person forgets to clear the cache of the computer, this information is easily accessible to the next user, who can research the recent history of the computer's use.

Similarly, whenever we purchase things online, or access certain sites, we allow our computers and cell phones to store information in "cookies" on the hard drives. Anyone who then uses these technologies has a wealth of information about the original user, including passwords, address books, and all sorts of personal data.

As you can see, the issues go far beyond overhearing someone on a cell phone in a public place, discussing intimate details with a friend, or having a conversation that might be more appropriately held behind closed doors. And, there is always the possibility of someone forwarding electronic messages to others, as we have seen recently in the scandals surrounding political figures using cell phones for sexting, or in the British *News of the World* cell phone hacking scandals—both situations in which the perpetrators thought they could hide behind their online anonymity, only to be disgraced and humiliated once the information so easily came to light.

Perhaps our current laws and expectations with regard to private information may need to be evaluated and reconsidered, but until there is a systematic examination of public policy, the only way we can protect our own identities and our privacy is to become more knowledgeable consumers and users of media, in our own lives.

YES

Neil Swidey

Inside the Mind of the
Anonymous Online Poster

On Monday, May 17, [2010] at 2 p.m., a breaking news article headlined "Obama's aunt given OK to stay in United States" hits the home page of Boston.com. In a matter of seconds, the first anonymous online comment appears. A reader with the handle of Peregrinite writes, "of course she can . . . can someone appeal."

Certain topics never fail to generate a flood of impassioned reactions online: immigration, President Obama, federal taxes, "birthers," and race. This story about Obama's Kenyan aunt, who had been exposed as an illegal immigrant living in public housing in Boston and who was now seeking asylum, manages to pull strands from all five of those contentious subjects.

In the next few minutes, several equally innocuous posts follow, including a rare comment in favor of the judge's decision. Then the name-calling begins. At 2:03 p.m., a commenter with the pseudonym of Craptulous calls the aunt, Zeituni Onyango, a "foreign free-loader." Seconds later comes the lament from Redzone 300: "Just another reason to hate are [sic] corrupt government."

News websites from across the country struggle to maintain civility in their online comments forums. But given their anonymous nature and anything-goes ethos, these forums can sometimes feel as ungovernable as the tribal lands of Pakistan.

At Boston.com, the website of *The Boston Globe*, a team of moderators—or "mods"—monitor the comments. Actually, with just one or two mods on per shift, and an average of more than 6,000 comments posted every day, on every corner of the site, the mods could never hope to monitor all the simultaneous chatter. Instead, they focus on evaluating the "abuse reports" that commenters file against one another. For Steve Morgan, a veteran editor who coordinates the monitoring, the color of trouble is red. The crimson message at the top of his computer screen keeps a running total of the abuse reports that are awaiting action. Some complaints don't ultimately turn up abuse—coarse language, ad hominem attacks, and the like—but rather just a political stance that the person doing the complaining doesn't care for. So a mod needs to evaluate each complaint and decide either to remove the comment or let it stand.

Over the next two hours, the comments about Obama's aunt keep flying, the abuse reports continue to climb, and the mods scramble to remove the many posts—both conservative and liberal—that they determine have crossed the line. Some comments are enlightening, on both sides of the issue. (Madriver1 offers statistics showing that, of nearly 40,000 asylum requests filed last year, more than one-quarter were granted.) Some are unintentionally funny. (GLOBEREADER83 chastises another commenter for having written "good grammar" instead of "proper grammar," but in both cases misspells it as *grammer*.) And many are not just mean, but make-you-want-to-shower nasty. There are references to Muslim bombers, Somalian pirates, "teabaggers and xenophobes," America becoming "a 3rd world socialist hellhole," and crude comparisons between Aunt Zeituni and James Brown, and between the first family and farm animals.

At 3:41 p.m., when the commentary has degenerated into all-out combat, hummlarry writes, "Obama is Kenyan and he is illegal and president. We have been invaded by non-Americans and the liberals are to blame. I hope that one of the liberals feels the pain by being broken into by a needy illegal and then maybe they will get it. Deport them all."

Not long after that, Boston.com staffers take the drastic and relatively rare step of turning off the comments function on that particular article. (For certain types of stories, such as those involving personal tragedies, the comments section is turned off from the start.) Poof—hundreds of comments about Obama's aunt disappear.

Too many abuse reports had been pouring in; by day's end, the total number would be 1,330—twice the daily average for the previous month. More than that, the commentary had reached its tipping point. The pros of hosting a robust, freewheeling conversation had become outweighed by the cons of all the venom and nastiness, by people who are allowed to name-call without any obligation to reveal their own names.

The raging commentary on Obama's aunt is a microcosm of the thorny problem many websites are grappling with right now over what to do with anonymous comments. At many of these sites, executives have begun to ask themselves: How did we get into this thicket, and is there a sensible way out? But a more basic question needs to be answered first: Who are these people who spend so much of their days posting anonymous comments, and what is motivating them?

Newspapers find themselves in a strange position. People wanting to have a letter to the editor printed in the paper have long been required to provide their name, address, and a daytime phone number. Yet on the websites owned by these same newspapers, all it usually takes to be handed a perpetual soapbox is an active e-mail address.

After years of letting anonymity rule online, many media heavyweights, from *The Washington Post* to *The Huffington Post,* have begun to modify their policies. The goal is to take the playground back from anonymous bullies and give greater weight to those willing to offer, in addition to strong views, their real names.

Others, like *The (Cleveland) Plain Dealer*, are probably wishing they'd taken that step earlier. In March, the paper outed a local judge for allegedly posting comments on Cleveland.com under the handle lawmiss that included critical commentary on cases and individuals appearing before her in court. The judge denied authorship and is now suing the paper and its affiliated companies for $50 million. Her denials might seem a smidge south of persuasive, and *The Plain Dealer* may well have been journalistically suspect had it not gone public with the information once it discovered it. But the judge has a valid point about her expectations of anonymity.

In another suit, a Louisiana public official sued 11 anonymous posters last month for comments on *The Times-Picayune* website that he said were malicious and untruthful. (He didn't sue the website—under federal law, sites are generally not legally responsible for defamatory postings by readers—but rather asked that it disclose the commenters' names. He later dropped the suit.) No matter who you believe in each of these cases, it's a haunted house that anonymity built.

Anonymous commentary is a push and pull between privacy and trust, and the implications extend beyond news sites to include Web reviews for everything from books to technology to hotel rooms. Online postings can sway political opinion and heavily influence whether products or businesses thrive or fail. They can make or break reputations and livelihoods. On one side, anonymous comments give users the freedom to be completely candid in a public forum. On the other, that freedom can be abused and manipulated to spread lies or mask hidden agendas. With all that in the balance, the thinking goes, shouldn't we know who's saying these things?

Clearly, anonymity is under attack. Even the Chinese government has had enough, announcing last month it would begin a push to end unnamed online comments. And, really, there's not much that officials in Beijing don't already know about who's saying what within their borders.

Still, the nameless nature of the Web is so embedded in the culture that it will be hard to change the rules now. And as newspaper websites struggle to maintain their central role hosting the community conversation and work to increase the time users spend on their sites, scrapping anonymity isn't such a clear-cut call.

I've always loved finding the hidden gems in online comments—the surprising slice of data that makes me question one of my political assumptions, the pithy one-liner that makes me laugh out loud. But those gems seem increasingly rare amid all the yelling and hollow rage and predictable talking points.

If we hope to clean up the online conversation, we need a better understanding of the select group of people doing most of the talking. Studies have shown that participation rates in online social communities tend to follow something called the "90-9-1" rule. About 90 percent of the people are "lurkers," that is, watching but not actively contributing; 9 percent are infrequent contributors; and 1 percent are, to borrow a term from the fast-food industry, the heavy users.

McDonald's and Burger King have teams of researchers who do nothing but try to understand the patterns, desires, and quirks of their heavy users, their best customers. However, yet another unfortunate byproduct of anonymity is that news sites know precious little about their most active commenters.

Stanley Talabach is a man of routine. He wakes up at 5 every morning and by 6 has made his way down to the dark kitchen of his North Attleborough town house. He consumes a breakfast consisting of a cocktail of Mountain Dew and orange juice, a multivitamin, 25 milligrams of diuretic (for mild hypertension), an adult dose of baby aspirin, folic acid, and a banana.

He then logs on to the desktop computer that functions as the centerpiece of his kitchen table, and goes to three different sites—Boston.com, BostonHerald.com, and MSN.com—to check his horoscope. That the three seldom agree on how a Pisces like him will fare that day has done little to dampen his enthusiasm for the astral arts. If the Boston.com horoscope offers five stars, it puts an extra spring in his step.

Talabach knows housekeeping is not one of his strengths, but as a twice-divorced, semi-retired 66-year-old credit analyst who lives alone, he doesn't feel the need to impress anyone. He assures me the walls and the blinds on the kitchen slider were once white, but I see no evidence of their ever having been anything other than a brownish yellow. "That's thanks to these," he says, holding up a pack of Berkley unfiltered cigarettes. Next to his computer he keeps a blue ashtray that is more like a small urn.

After the horoscopes, Talabach turns to the articles posted on Boston.com and makes his daily transformation, from Stanley to Xenophonic.

Let's clear this up right now: It's not Xeno*phobic*, but Xeno*phonic*, a common mistake, especially by those reading his comments on immigration, one of his favorite topics. Although he is an unenrolled voter, he is a proud conservative, and there are few issues that get him more worked up than illegal immigration. A couple come close: unions, affirmative action, and anything having to do with Ted Kennedy.

"I don't care where you came from to come here ILLEGALLY, GO BACK!" he wrote last month in a comment attached to an article about Governor Deval Patrick blasting Arizona's new immigration law. "Did we all see where some wise guy students in California took down the American flag, hoisted the MEXICAN flag and put the American flag beneath it . . . UPSIDE DOWN? Ahnold should have sent in the National Guard to remove the Mexican Flag and rehoist the American flag."

Although some liberal commenters accuse him of being xenophobic, Talabach says he has no quarrel with outsiders. His father emigrated from Albania, a detail of his biography he often invokes in his posts on immigration, as he did in the closing to his comment about the Mexican flag: "FYI son of an immigrant that came here LEGALLY."

His political views have been shaped unmistakably by his life experience. Knowing that his father followed the rules to come to the States, worked hard every day of his life, and served eight years in the US Army, Talabach is offended when he perceives new immigrants looking for shortcuts. Recalling that he himself made $1.90 an hour at his first job, but he got to take home 85 percent of his pay, Talabach is on guard against any sniff of wasteful spending by a federal and state government that combine to "relieve me of 26, 27, 28 percent of my pay." Feeling he was passed over for promotions during the 1970s and '80s in favor of female and minority candidates he saw as less qualified, he loathes "first" articles, like those touting the first Hispanic Supreme Court justice. "Why do we need to keep score?" he'll thunder.

He posts most of his comments in the morning, before heading to work in Mansfield. Ever since he decided to semi-retire about three years ago, his schedule has been 8:30 a.m. to 12:30 p.m., though he usually shows up at work at 7:10 a.m., taking the extra time to read the paper. He's been at his current job for 11 years and says that for at least nine of them, he never missed a single day of work.

Other than the occasional conversation with his boss, almost all of his political discussions take place in the form of online comments.

When he gets home, he'll look to see how other commenters have responded to his earlier posts. There's a "Recommend" button on the comments page on Boston.com, where people can give their thumbs up to posted comments. This is the metric by which Talabach judges his daily performance. He recalls the time his comment on a column titled "My Lazy American Students" drew hundreds of "Recommends." Leaning back in his chair, with his left arm resting on his thick belly and his right arm jingling change in his pocket, he smiles. "There were more than 600 comments, and at least half of them agreed with me!"

I ask him if he has any hobbies. He points to a large wall hanging behind him. "I made this rug," he says, before adding, "I made those two clocks," and pointing to a pair nearby. "They came in a kit." I ask him if he has a workshop in the house. He shakes his head. "No, I made all of these things when I was living at my old house in Foxborough." Then it dawns on me. He told me earlier that he'd been living in his current place for more than a decade. So much for current hobbies.

He has no wife, no children, and a job requiring just 20 hours a week. He doesn't follow sports, doesn't hang out at bars or go on many trips beyond the occasional visit to play the slots at Twin River, and isn't involved in any organizations to speak of. But he is extremely active in his community. It just happens to be one that only exists online.

Despite his strong views, he is generally a responsible member of that community. Every once in a while he'll find one of his comments on Boston .com has been removed because he went too far. . . . Occasionally, he'll commit the common commenter sin of weighing in on an article without having read it, and be called on it when his objection turns out to have been covered in the fifth paragraph.

But, overall, he plays by the rules, works hard at this commenter job of his, and, in a way, serves his community. After reading his posts and spending time with him, I believe him when he tells me that, even though he's anonymous online, he would never write anything that he wouldn't say "*mano a mano.*" That, incidentally, strikes me as a pretty good standard for separating the stand-up commenters from the cowardly name-callers.

One more thing about this anonymous heavy user named Xenophonic. He's never been all that anonymous. The full name his parents gave him at his christening is the same one his father was given back in Albania: Xenophon Stanley Talabach.

I reached out to dozens of Boston.com heavy users like Xenophonic. Actually, to protect the privacy of users, I wasn't handed their e-mail addresses. Instead, I gave a list of the commenters with whom I wanted to speak to Boston .com's director of user engagement, Teresa Hanafin, who then e-mailed the commenters directly, telling them they could contact me if they wanted to be interviewed. (I chose to focus on Boston.com users for obvious reasons: It's got the biggest regional reach and it's where I could hope to get the most complete picture of online users.) My list included a wide range of posters: conservatives and liberals, people who comment on articles and people who spend their time on the themed message boards, the reasonable types and the all-caps troublemakers. I made it clear that I wouldn't reveal anyone's identity without their permission.

Those willing to talk included people on the left and the right, males and females, people passionate about sports and people passionate about politics and people passionate about passion (the Love Letters crowd). Somewhat surprisingly, many had no problem with my using their real names in the article, though a few offered some understandable reasons why they didn't want to be identified.

But here are the people I didn't hear back from: the screamers, troublemakers, and trolls (Internet slang for people behind inflammatory posts). Not a single one. The loudest, most aggressive voices grew mum when asked to explain themselves, to engage in an actual discussion. The trolls appear to prize their anonymity more than anyone else.

Michael Sol Pollens is not a troll, but he is a heavy user. He explains that he spent three decades as a private detective, focusing mostly on fraud investigations, before suffering a nervous breakdown. He turned in his detective's license and began writing detective fiction. He quickly discovered that posting comments online could be a therapeutic way to kick off his early-morning writing schedule. "I get up at 4, fire up a little incense, fire up some rock music, and go at it," says the 51-year-old.

Pollens posts on Boston.com, NYTimes.com, and elsewhere under the same pen name he uses for his fiction, KurtLarsen. When he worked as a PI, Pollens was careful not to have his photo taken, but he's more relaxed about identity these days. (He recently got his detective's license back.) When I interviewed him in the lilac study of the Malden home he shares with his wife, he had no hesitation about also being videotaped. Curiously, his only request was that he be allowed to wear his shades. He includes a link to his website, KurtLarsen.net, in his posts, and that website includes a reference to his real name.

Pollens, who peppers his sentences with a sometimes exhausting series of literary references, comments most frequently on stories about post-9/11 civil rights infringements and the Arab-Israeli conflict. (He is Jewish but is a tough critic of the Israeli government's treatment of Palestinians.) At his most productive, he posts up to four comments a day. He is every bit as liberal as Xenophonic is conservative, but the appeal for his participation is similar, and he is equally focused on his "Recommends" standing. "I do enjoy the community nature of this," he says.

That community can morph in fascinating ways. In the comments section on articles about Arab-Israeli relations, Pollens found a poster named Shamu who was preaching from the same pulpit. "I like what you say," Pollens wrote Shamu at one point, inviting Shamu to contact him offline. Shamu did. They've since become friends and have had dinner together several times.

Shamu, it turns out, is a therapist from the North Shore. Out of sensitivity to his clients, he tries to keep his political views private and asked me not to include his real name. He says that months of reading KurtLarsen posts had given him such insight into Pollens that by the time they met, there were few surprises. "I am amazed by how well you can know somebody through the Internet," Shamu says. "When you actually meet, you're just adding a face and body inflections."

Then again, sometimes those impressions formed online can turn out to be off base. Yoshimi25 is one of the most faithful contributors to On the Front Burner, a Red Sox discussion board on Boston.com. On game nights, she'll spend five hours or more on the board—posting comments before, during, and after the game.

Yoshimi25 hasn't lived in the Boston area for nearly two decades. Still, her heart beats for Boston. I met her and her 18-year-old daughter when they returned to the area from Ohio for a recent vacation. Both were wearing Red Sox championship T-shirts.

When I ask Yoshimi25 her age, she says, "Forty-three—exactly two months younger than Tim Wakefield." A divorced freelance artist who uses finger quotes when referring to her "social life," Yoshimi25 says, "I don't have many close friends in Ohio." Her friends on Boston.com fill that void. She feels she's gotten to know quite a bit about her fellow heavy users. "I know Lloyd-Dobler has two kids, and they must be young, because he talks about putting them to bed at 8 o'clock," she says. "I know jesseyeric is in a local band."

Once when a troll attacked Yoshimi25, hurling ugly anti-Asian slurs at her, her friends on the boards rose to her defense. Most people assume Yoshimi25 is Asian. In fact, she is a blue-eyed Irish-American named Kelly. Her Eastern-sounding handle comes from her days practicing martial arts. Yoshimi25 says that because the Front Burner message board is such an intimate group, the regulars on it tend to behave well, even though they're anonymous. "Although I can say anything I want without consequences," she says, "you should behave as though there are consequences."

That gets to the heart of the problem. The comments sections on many general-interest news sites lack both the carrot and the stick for encouraging responsible behavior. The carrot is the cohesion of a group you don't want to disappoint, like Yoshimi25's Front Burner community. The stick is the shame associated with having your real name publicly attached to embarrassing behavior. Without these two levers, the social contract breaks down.

Steve Yelvington knows this terrain as well as anyone. In the mid-1980s, he began hosting dial-up bulletin boards as a hobby. Most of the people on them used pseudonyms, but because it was a coherent group, the social contract remained strong. In 1994, he was the founding editor of the Star Tribune Online in Minneapolis (now Startribune.com), which Minnesota's largest newspaper began as a pre-Web platform that required participants to provide not only their real names but also a credit card number. Yet with the arrival of the Web and the proliferation of online forums, anonymity began to take hold, fueled, in particular, by the way the early dominant service provider, America Online, gave each account the option for multiple screen names.

"As the conversational spaces get larger," Yelvington says, "the bonds that tie people together get weaker."

The 57-year-old Yelvington is now a new-media strategist working with Morris Publishing Group, whose holdings include 13 daily papers from Florida to Alaska. His goal is to clean up the playground of online comments while preserving some measure of anonymity, so that, say, a closeted gay student would still feel comfortable posting a comment about the climate at his high school. To strike this balance, Yelvington is pushing Morris sites to insist on collecting (but not publishing) real names and street addresses for everyone who comments, yet allow users to continue to post under pseudonyms. "That gives us a reasonably powerful tool for detecting troublemakers," he says. "Most of the troublemakers tend to lie about their name and address, but they lie poorly."

Still, that approach would have done nothing to prevent the mess that the *The Plain Dealer* found itself in with the judge and lawmiss's comments. To avoid minefields like that, Howard Owens, a former digital executive at Gatehouse Media, insists on real names for anyone posting on TheBatavian.com, the news site he publishes in Batavia, New York.

Under Yelvington's plan, Owens says, readers wouldn't know if the JIMY23 posting a comment blasting the mayor is really the guy planning to challenge him in the next election. And if the managers of the news site figure that out, it puts them in an awful bind.

Owens insists that a no-anonymity rule is not just good journalism but good business as well. "My competitor allows anonymous comments," he says. "We don't. We get 10 times what they get. My users are more willing to engage in conversation, because they know who they are arguing with." Almost all the heavy users I spoke with said they would continue to comment even if they had to provide their real name.

While news organizations debate scrapping anonymity, the ground may be shifting beneath them. With all of our identifying information getting sliced, diced, and sold, by everyone from credit card companies to Facebook, is there really such a thing as the anonymous Web anymore? Consider this demonstration from the late '90s by Carnegie Mellon University computer science professor Latanya Sweency. She took three commonly available data points: sex (male), ZIP code (02138), and date of birth (July 31, 1945). Those seemingly anonymous attributes could have described lots of people, right? Actually, no. She proved they could belong to just one person: former governor William Weld. She tells me that 87 percent of Americans can now be identified with just these three data points.

Maybe the best approach to getting people to behave better online is just reminding them how easy it is to figure out who they really are.

Ian Lloyd  **NO**

Privacy, Anonymity and the Internet

Scott McNealy, chairman of SUN, one of the leading Internet companies, famously commented of the online world and its likely development. 'You have zero privacy already. Get over it.' . . .

How can a person have zero privacy and yet operate in an environment where no one knows who or what he, she or it is? Trying to reconcile seemingly incompatible expectations is nothing new for the law and it is suggested that both views have elements of validity. In this particular context, the approaches highlight, it is submitted, a crucial distinction between notions of privacy and of anonymity. The legal dimension of the latter concept has hitherto been relatively little explored yet, it is suggested, may furnish a sturdier basis for the protection of individual rights and freedoms for the majority of the population than what is sometimes stigmatised as, perhaps correctly, more elitist concept of privacy.

The relationship between privacy and anonymity is complex perhaps akin to that between conjoined siblings. Both share common, and frequently vital, organs but also have capacity for independent action. . . .

Although the concept of privacy is extremely broad in its scope, what might be regarded as the classical aspect of the right is the wish to prevent others knowing both who we are and what we are doing. For the vast majority of the population, unless we are enjoying or enduring a Warholian fifteen minutes of fame, our actions, at least when linked to our identity are of little concern to anyone other than close family and friends. . . .

For many, typically but by no means exclusively, of a younger age, online life is becoming an integral component of their personal life. Social networking sites have acquired massive penetration. It is a rare media event today that does not seek to access and make use of information presented on social networking sites with references to postings on such sites. It is also relatively common for employers or potential employers to conduct searches seeking information about individual's social networking activities. Accounts (and photographs) of alcohol fuelled nights out may sit uneasily alongside a carefully crafted CV and soberly dressed interview candidate. Given that the decision to participate in a social networking site is entirely optional and the dissemination options and possibilities made as clear as is ever the case on the Internet, it is difficult to argue that such activities constitute any form of infringement of privacy except perhaps on the basis that individuals may well be unaware of the fact that their spontaneous actions may leave permanent trails in cyberspace. Perhaps rather than talking in terms of privacy, the message should be that by making information available in such a public forum and linking it to a name, individuals are giving up their anonymity. The Information Commissioner's office has produced guidance aimed specifically at young persons concerning the risks associated with such on-line activities. Much the same could be said of a wide range of on-line activities. Millions of people have signed up for store loyalty cards either unaware or uncaring that they are giving away information identifying them and their purchases. Perhaps most potentially intrusive is the Nectar card which links across a range of suppliers both on the High Street and in the field of on-line retailing where more than 200 outlets, including such well known names as Amazon and E-Bay, participate in the scheme. Although it is claimed that only limited data is collated centrally such coverage means that virtually every purchase an individual makes could be linked by a single identifying number.

Every action on line leaves traces, often more extensive than is likely to be the case in the real world. A visit to an on-line bookstore, for example might be analogised to entering a high street store only to have an employee watching and recording every book picked up and examined. The use of cookies allows continuing linkage between a site and a particular computer. Surveillance devices in the workplace allow employers to monitor the activities and efficiency of individuals. At a potentially extreme level, the United States Patent Office has published an application from Microsoft for a system which will monitor an employee's heart rate, body temperature, blood pressure and movement. It is claimed that the system will automatically detect signs of stress or illness. At a rather simpler but perhaps more threatening level, evidence is mounting regarding the scale of surveillance currently conducted by employers regarding the on-line activities of employees. . . .

Indeed the term to 'Google' has become a widely accepted verb. There has been ongoing debate between Google and European data protection authorities concerning the length of time for which data relating to searches is retained in a format which permits identification of at least the computer from which the request originated. Until 2007, such data was retained for 2 years before being anonymised. Following discussions it has recently been announced that data will be rendered anonymous after nine months, a period which is still longer than the 6 months sought by the European Union's Article 29 Working Party on Data Protection. Extensive records will also be maintained by Internet Service Providers (a term which may well include employers).

Considerable publicity has recently been given to proposals to introduce a new system for targeting on line adverts to users dependent upon their browsing history. Some of the United Kingdom's major ISPs, including BT and Virgin have signed up to a system known as Webwise developed by a company called Phorm although none have yet implemented the system. In part concerns relate to Phorm's previous business activities which may be described as operating on the boundary of acceptable conduct in relation to the use of spyware software—a practice which involves the use of cookies to monitor the operations carried out on a computer. If the scheme is what the developers claim, it might be seen as a rare case of a poacher turning gamekeeper.

Effectively the system notes the URLs of the web sites visited by a user and then searches the sites compiling a list of key words. This can then be linked to the user in order to build up a profile which could be used to target marketing. An advertiser specialising in offering travel services might, for example, want to target marketing at web users who have previously visited sites selling airline or train tickets.

At first sight the proposal seems a horrifying intrusion on privacy and indeed many commentators are of this opinion. Perhaps not surprisingly the developers of the system take a different view with their web site proclaiming that Webwise revolutionises online advertising by setting a new, higher standard on privacy and anonymity. Designed with both user privacy and targeting effectiveness as equal priorities, the result is a technology that, for the first time, ISPs, their Internet user customers, and all participants in the online advertising ecosystem can trust.

Key to the system is the claim that it allocates a random number to each individual and that this is the only form of data which it keeps on the individual. A user will have a contract with an ISP for provision of Internet access. The ISP in turn enters into a contract with Webwise. The first time the user accesses the Internet after the Webwise contract is implemented a randomly generated number will be allocated and linked to a cookie placed on the user's computer.

The Webwise hardware and software acts as a filter between the ISP's equipment and web sites. When the user types a URL in his or her browser the Webwise system categorises the relevant web site, in a manner not too dissimilar to that used by traditional search engines, albeit perhaps more limited in scope. A visit to, for example, an airline booking site might be referenced against 'airline' 'ticketing' 'reservations' or similar terms. Over time, the system will build up a more and more detailed profile of the browsing habits of the user and this could be made available to advertisers so that the messages which appear on the user's screen are tailored to the browsing habits identified. A user who regularly visits web sites connected with travel might receive adverts relating to offers on flights or hotel accommodation. A further feature claimed for the system is that it will maintain a list of sites associated with fraudulent activity and cause a warning to be displayed if a user attempts to navigate to such a site.

It is stressed in publicity that users can opt out from the system either on a permanent or a temporary basis. A number of ISPs have indicated that they will offer the system on an 'opt in' basis. It does not appear clear, however, how the opt-out system will work at a technical level and in particular whether their traffic will still be routed through the Webwise system.

Some support for the system has come from sources normally closely associated with unconditional support for individual privacy. The basis for the approval appears to lie in an acceptance that safeguards are such that there is a high degree of assurance that anonymity will be preserved. . . .

As in so many cases concerned with Internet based activities, the key issue is one of trust. A Privacy Examination report was commissioned by the developers of Webwise from the well established consultancy firm Ernst and Young. This expressed the view that the system complied with the developer's claims regarding privacy protection but with the rider that:

> Because of inherent limitations in control, error or fraud may occur and not be detected. Furthermore, the projection of any conclusions, based on our findings, to future periods is subject to the risk that the validity of such conclusions may be altered because of changes made to the Service or controls, or a deterioration in the degree of effectiveness of the controls.

With continuing increases in processing power, it is becoming more and more difficult to be assured of anonymity. In 2006 AOL placed on the Internet data relating to search requests made by millions of its subscribers. The assumption was that as no names or other identifiers such as the IP address of the computer [were] used to conduct a search, the individuals concerned would remain anonymous. Instead each user was allocated a randomly generated number. Although no names were published, in at least some cases it proved possible to identify individuals following analysis of their search history. One case concerned a user allocated the identifying number 4417749. As was reported:

> No.4417749 conducted hundreds of searches over a three-month period on topics ranging from "numb fingers" to "60 single men" to "dog that urinates on everything."
> Search by search, click by click, the identity of AOL user No.4417749 became easier to discern. There are queries for several people with the last name Arnold, for "landscapers in Lilburn," Georgia, and for "homes sold in shadow lake subdivision gwinnett county georgia."
> It did not take much investigating to follow that data trail to Thelma Arnold, a 62-year-old widow who lives in Lilburn, frequently researches her friends' medical ailments and loves her three dogs. "Those are my searches," she said, after a reporter read part of the list to her over the phone.

The case may well be an isolated one, but there is no doubt that the issue of preserving anonymity is assuming increasing importance in the context of activities such as national censuses. The possibility to compare data across a diverse range of sources undoubtedly challenges, at least in a small number of cases, the anonymity previously promised by law in the conduct of censuses. . . .

At a positive level, electronic communications allow individuals to communicate in a way that can minimise the impact of any disability from which they may suffer. In a very real sense the Internet may promote goals of social inclusion. Actions may, of course be motivated by more malign considerations with the classic example being that of paedophiles who present a fictitious personality in the attempt to persuade children to agree to face to face meetings. Such tactics and techniques are not novel. In the mid 1990's a much publicised case concerned a 32 year old man passing himself off as a 17 year old in order to attend school and obtain sufficient exam passes to be offered a place at medical school. This may have been a somewhat extreme case and there is no doubt that the Internet allows greater flexibility for users to choose the personality that they want to present to others. Instances have been reported of males presenting themselves (apparently very convincingly) as females in Internet fora. In a real sense there is privacy in electronic communications because we have great control over the image we present. Anonymity is a different matter. If an individual accesses the Internet from an Internet café in order to browse web sites, and pays cash for the privilege, there is the prospect of a good degree of anonymity. In almost every other situation our Internet usage will leave trails which can be traced to a particular computer and, at least by inference, from there to a particular individual. Such a prospect has come as a less than welcome surprise to a considerable number of Internet users who have acted in the belief that they enjoyed anonymity or at least pseudonimity in the sense that their postings would have appeared under a chosen pseudonym rather than a real name. . . .

From Knowledge to Information, from Privacy to Anonymity

Especially as we move from village or close family communities to the more anonymous and impersonal lifestyles associated with much of modern life, traditional notions of privacy are perhaps of limited relevance to most persons. It is often a cause for concern that modern life confers too much privacy, to the extent that the weak vulnerable can suffer in isolation. The right to be left alone is surely of limited interest to the frail invalid who has little or no human contact for months at a time. Shopping in a hypermarket—even more shopping on line—involves minimal genuine human contact. In the Middle Ages the philosopher Francis Bacon referred to the fact that 'knowledge is power.' Today it is commonplace to assert that 'information is power' and to recite the mantra that we live in an 'information society.' The change in semantics is reflective of a massive change in society. Knowledge is essentially a human commodity with all the flaws and failings associated with imperfect beings. In the twentieth century a popular BBC comedy show, 'Open All Hours' featured Ronnie Barker as a small shop keeper in a stereotypical northern England close knit community. A running theme in the show concerned his efforts, invariably successful, to use his intimate knowledge of his regular customers to persuade them to purchase the goods he wished to sell rather than those which they had originally intended to buy. Today, of course, loyalty card data and analysis of transaction records allow stores to target marketing based on customer's known buying habits. The effect may be the same but there will be little or no human knowledge of the particular individuals. Beyond use of data for marketing purposes, examples have also been reported of the use of data in connection with criminal investigations. In one case a magistrate was convicted of theft when he found and kept a Rolex watch in a supermarket. Critical evidence for the prosecution came from his loyalty card records which placed him in the supermarket at the same time as the watch was lost by its rightful owner. Illustrating the durability of such records, the facts only came to light more than 2 years after the event. The then Home Secretary David Blunkett sparked off considerable debate several years ago when in making a defence of the government's proposals to introduce ID cards he suggested that individuals had more to fear from supermarket loyalty cards. . . .

We can all be identified in myriad ways and in some respects that serves to at least limit the extent to which our anonymity might be compromised. Widespread use of a single identifier poses obvious dangers in terms of the ability to link data from a disparate range of sources.

It is important not to lose sight of the benefits which information technology generally and the Internet in particular has brought. Massive amounts of information are made available to everyone which previously would have been the preserve of a select few. Search technology, epitomised by the new verb 'to Google' has become an established feature of many person's business and personal lives. . . .

It is virtually impossible to participate in modern society and demand complete anonymity any more than we can seek absolute privacy. What does need to be considered more carefully is the nature and extent of the consequences that may follow from a substantial diminution to our right and ability to conduct our affairs under conditions of anonymity. Silly, thoughtless and unkind actions are as much a part of the human condition as more admired qualities. If people cannot commit small sins, they may more easily be tempted to attempt more serious offences. We perhaps interfere with genetics at our peril.

Technology has a major part to play in law enforcement but it should not operate in isolation and a major concern about current United Kingdom policy is that policy changes are being introduced in an ad hoc and barely considered manner. A prime example, perhaps, is the DNA database maintained by police authorities. Already the largest of its kind in the world, it operates without any specific statutory authority or parliamentary oversight. Its existence marks a significant change in the nature of much policing activity. From seeking to identify an individual criminal the question today is often whose DNA profile matches material obtained at the scene of a crime?

But what is the solution? All the evidence is to the effect that the young and members of certain ethnic minorities are disproportionately represented on the database. Should we seek to include everyone? Just as privacy is sometimes considered to be an elitist concept favouring the rich and powerful and providing little benefit to the average person, so anonymity could be seen as excluding vulnerable minorities. Calls have been made from some eminent people, including senior judges, for everyone's details to be included in the database. It is tempting to draw an analogy with fingerprint technology in the 19th century but the reality is that storage and processing capabilities at that time would have made a system of universal fingerprinting difficult if not completely impossible. Today at the technical level, universal DNA profiling is a simple task. If the political decision were to be taken, universal coverage would be a relatively simply technical matter. . . .

Many questions and, unfortunately, few answers. No laws can guard against every accident or every eventuality. Many of the best documented instances of information misuse predate the computer age. Prior to the Second World War the Dutch government maintained elaborate systems of population registers. Designed to assist efficient administration, details were held including name, address and religious affiliation. Not intrinsically objectionable until the Second World War erupted, Holland was occupied and the Nazis obtained a list of the name and address of every Jew in Holland. Whilst the motives of those who seek personal data today may be benign and even laudable, data can have a very long life and a change in circumstances may result in data supplied for one purpose being put to another. Especially at the stage of collecting data, the human being behind the data may well be a matter of little or no interest but if anonymity is lost the consequences may be profound.

EXPLORING THE ISSUE

Does Online Communication Compromise the Rights of an Individual When Information Is "Anonymous?"

Critical Thinking and Reflection

1. Using the definitions that Ian Lloyd provides in NO selection, do you think that anonymity and privacy are two different things, or, in which cases, might they be related?
2. Are you aware of the protocols that different technologies impose over keeping a record of interactions over them? Is privacy becoming less "important" in a society in which we use so many technologies in public places?
3. If you examine your behavior and behavior of your friends using technologies in public places, do you ever feel that you are violating a sense of privacy? Has anyone ever said something to you that made you feel uncomfortable, when you realize that others may hear personal information about you, or loved ones?
4. Who should be responsible for safeguarding the privacy of others?

Is There Common Ground?

Traditionally, we have invoked the Fourth Amendment to the Constitution as interpreting our right to personal privacy in our own homes, but how does that hold up when we use technologies to communicate in public settings? So many uses of our technologies allow a certain level of remaining anonymous—but as Swidey clearly indicates, this type of anonymity may not really be possible.

Recently, some social networks (like Google+) have required that all users take out accounts in their own, legal names, rather than with pseudonyms or aliases. The real reason for this is that the information we share on social networks is often sold to third parties (like advertisers), so constructing an accurate portrayal of users is important to the networks—but are you willing to give up information about your consumer habits, the people with whom you communicate, and your online behaviors to these businesses? The selections in this issue are just the "tip of the iceberg" when it comes to clarifying personal information, our desire to be anonymous, in some cases, and our use of contemporary technologies in today's social world.

Additional Resources

National Public Radio, "Gotcha! Why Online Anonymity May Be Fading," www.npr.org/templates/story/story.php?storyId=112450627 (National Public Radio, 2009).

Since the production of the above story in 2009, more examples of the question of anonymity and Internet use have emerged.

On February 14, 2011, the U.S. Senate announced that Senator Al Franken was named to chair a new subcommittee on privacy, technology, and the law, for Congress:

http://franken.senate.gov/?p=press_release&id=1315

The American Civil Liberties Union (ACLU) recently reported on the first 25 years of privacy in an online world:

www.aclu.org/blog/technology-and-liberty/online-privacy-law-
turns-quarter-century-old-today

The Australian *Sydney Morning Journal* recently wrote about social networks demanding that users not hide behind pseudonyms or anonymous postings:

www.smh.com.au/technology/technology-news/death-of-anonymity-online-
has-et-users-fuming-20110905-1jtda.html

Business Week discusses the problem of an anonymous blogger called Gay Girl in Damascus who was writing a blog, but was later found out to be a 40-year-old woman in Scotland. This type of anonymous "outing" is described in:

www.businessweek.com/technology/content/jun2011/tc20110620_
748404.htm

ISSUE 12

Do Copyright Laws Protect Ownership of Intellectual Property?

YES: Siva Vaidhyanathan, from "Copyright Jungle," *Columbia Journalism Review* (September/October 2006)

NO: Stephanie C. Ardito, from "MySpace and YouTube Meet the Copyright Cops," *Searcher* (May 2007)

Learning Outcomes

After reading this issue, you should be able to:

- Understand what current copyright restrictions protect.
- Discuss whether authors of original material should retain the right to make a profit off of their intellectual endeavors. If not, what type of material would we lose?
- Consider the range of issues that are encompassed by copyright legislation, like who should be responsible for policing copyright and ownership restrictions. Were these laws created to protect the financial interests of artists and creators, or are copyright restrictions more of a moral issue?
- Evaluate contemporary technology and its ability to obfuscate copyright laws and policies.

ISSUE SUMMARY

YES: In this selection, Siva Vaidhyanathan discusses how applications of copyright to music, film, publishing, and software companies all result in a complex system of trying to protect original ownership of intellectual property. The author gives several examples, including Google's efforts to digitize entire libraries, but reminds us that copyright also gives owners the right to say no.

NO: Stephanie Ardito examines how social networking sites have created problems for protecting copyright, because laws and enforcement of copyright law are so difficult. She believes big media companies and social networking sites will ultimately give up trying to enforce copyright, because it is too expensive and time consuming.

Copyright, or the legal protection of ownership of original materials in a tangible, fixed medium, has a long history. U.S. copyright law was established in 1790, and was based on the British Licensing Act of 1662, created not long after the invention of the printing press and the distribution of printed materials to the masses. In 1886, the Berne Convention resulted in copyright principles for most nations of the globe, and established principles for fair and equitable treatment for original authors of artifacts resulting from scientific and creative endeavors.

Once digital technology began to make it easy and cheap to duplicate media content with virtually no signal degradation, the foundation of the old copyright law began to crumble. Now, when it is possible for someone to record, edit, and rearrange material into a new form, like that often posted on MySpace or YouTube, it becomes increasingly difficult to police the ownership of the original material.

The authors of these selections provide a number of examples to show how copyright law is being challenged in a number of ways. Siva Vaidhyanathan focuses on the adaptation of traditional print media to electronic form, and discusses how copyright, file sharing, plagiarism, and fair use have all become muddled in the world of digital forms of media. Stephanie Ardito focuses more on social networking sites on which anyone can post creative works of their own—often using material from other sources. She discusses how various companies have attempted to create service agreements that place the responsibility for copyright clearance on the person posting information, not the company distributing the message. She further explains how the legal agreements are complicated, difficult to enforce, and probably doomed to extinction. She also discusses digital rights management and attempts to protect copyright, which have not served their purpose as well as one might hope.

The positions taken for this issue raise many more questions as well. If it does become increasingly difficult to protect one's creative products, will there be a chilling effect on innovation, or will different structures of payment or control of the product have to be considered? Who does copyright violation actually hurt? Can the definition of fair use be extended to a greater number of media forms, or uses of content?

At this time in history, newer technologies, like digital forms, are challenging older laws and practices that had been created to protect earlier forms of media. How might industries change in the future, if the economic base of copyright is eroded? What other laws, regulations, and practices could also be challenged by the growth of user-friendly, low-cost digital technologies? The answers to these questions are put into perspective by Professor Vaidhyanathan, who reminds us that "the copyright system will help determine the richness and strength of democracy in the twenty-first century."

One of the most difficult aspects about copyright is that depending on how the law is enforced, the result can be a form of censorship. The challenge, then, is to find the balance of protecting original work that truly belongs to an author who justifiably can claim credit for the work it took to produce something, versus creating an atmosphere that either does not recompense an author, or shifts all work into public domain.

As courts have tried to sort out problems with traditional copyright legislation and newer technologies, several attempts have been made to narrow the focus of the application of the law. The court case that resulted in a consumer's right to record film and television programs off of the television came from *Universal City Studios, Inc. v. Sony Corp. of America, 659 F.2d 963* (9th Cir. 1981), but stipulated that the copy was to be for personal use only. The current Copyright Act allows consumers to duplicate CDs and computer software for backup purposes, and to modify them as necessary, but all of these court cases favored the consumer with clear stipulation that duplicated material cannot and should not be sold to anyone else.

Problems with copyright become much more difficult when people post things on the Internet, digitally manipulate images, or link to other Web sites. Does the content copied from one form take on a new identity as "creative, original work" when an artist (or home consumer) manipulates images and puts them into a new form—such as taking still pictures and animating them, then posting them on the Web? How might a wiki, like Wikipedia, inadvertently violate copyright? It may come as no surprise that copyright law is one of the fastest growing topics and areas of specializations in law schools around the country.

In addition to the way a home consumer might harmlessly use someone else's copyrighted work, organizations that deal with fairness legal issues are concerned about their involvement in abuses of copyright, and their liability. James G. Neal writes in "Copyright Is Dead . . . Long Live Copyright," *American Libraries* (December 2002, pp. 48–51) of the problems public institutions have with trying to police the Internet and duplication technologies in their organizations. Heather Green's article, "Whose Video Is It, Anyway? YouTube's Runaway Success Has Opened a Pandora's Box of Copyright Issues," *BusinessWeek* (August 7, 2006, p. 38), explains how businesses should be aware of copyright violations. Rob Pegorano, the technology writer for the *Washington Post*, has written a series of articles on copyright infringements, including "Time to Face the Music on File Sharing" (February 15, 2007, p. D1).

As you consider the many sides of the debate on copyright and digital technology, it might be useful to think of how different persons might respond to the issues. For example, how might a screenwriter think about file sharing of his or her film, downloaded from the Internet? How would the author of a book feel about electronic distribution of the book he or she wrote, if no royalties, or lesser royalties were paid for the copies of the work? How do those people who work in the important—yet often less visible fields—such as CD package design, feel about digital duplication? And of course, what would the position of an independent retailer be on the elimination of copyrighted works for sale? How would you feel if a paper you wrote over a long period of time was posted to the Internet and other people used your work without attributing credit to you?

Several authors have written about the problems in today's schools, because students make assumptions about material and do not credit the authors. For example, in a survey conducted among high school students, the majority of students thought that what was on the Internet was in the public domain, and therefore, did not need to be cited. In another study, students complained that when they cut and pasted information from the Internet, it was sometimes difficult to change the fonts and typeface to make the research paper look good. Often, students assume that since Wikipedia is collaboratively written, that attribution of source is not necessary when using Wikipedia as a source of information. In each of these cases, the assumptions are incorrect, and students should be aware that copyright does require attribution of ideas and quoted material; therefore, if you use information from the Internet, Wikipedia, or any number of blogs, news sources, or any other information from the Internet, you are expected to cite the attribution for the ideas that you are using.

YES

Siva Vaidhyanathan

Copyright Jungle

Last May [2005], Kevin Kelly, *Wired* magazine's "senior maverick," published in *The New York Times Magazine* his predictive account of flux within the book-publishing world. Kelly outlined what he claimed will happen (not might or could—*will*) to the practices of writing and reading under a new regime fostered by Google's plan to scan millions of books and offer searchable texts to Internet users.

"So what happens when all the books in the world become a single liquid fabric of interconnected words and ideas?" Kelly wrote. "First, works on the margins of popularity will find a small audience larger than the near-zero audience they usually have now. . . . Second, the universal library will deepen our grasp of history, as every original document in the course of civilization is scanned and cross-linked. Third, the universal library of all books will cultivate a new sense of authority. . . ."

Kelly saw the linkage of text to text, book to book, as the answer to the information gaps that have made the progress of knowledge such a hard climb. "If you can truly incorporate all texts—past and present, multilingual—on a particular subject," Kelly wrote, "then you can have a clearer sense of what we as a civilization, a species, do know and don't know. The white spaces of our collective ignorance are highlighted, while the golden peaks of our knowledge are drawn with completeness. This degree of authority is only rarely achieved in scholarship today, but it will become routine."

Such heady predictions of technological revolution have become so common, so accepted in our techno-fundamentalist culture, that even when John Updike criticized Kelly's vision in an essay published a month later in *The New York Times Book Review*, he did not so much doubt Kelly's vision of a universal digital library as lament it.

As it turns out, the move toward universal knowledge is not so easy. Google's project, if it survives court challenges, would probably have modest effects on writing, reading, and publishing. For one thing, Kelly's predictions depend on a part of the system he slights in his article: the copyright system. Copyright is not Kelly's friend. He mentions it as a nuisance on the edge of his dream. To acknowledge that a lawyer-built system might trump an engineer-built system would have run counter to Kelly's sermon.

Much of the press coverage of the Google project has missed some key facts: most libraries that are allowing Google to scan books are, so far, providing

From *Columbia Journalism Review*, September/October 2006, pp. 42–48. Copyright © 2006 by Columbia Journalism Review. Reprinted by permission.

only books published before 1923 and thus already in the public domain, essentially missing most of the relevant and important books that scholars and researchers—not to mention casual readers—might want. Meanwhile, the current American copyright system will probably kill Google's plan to scan the collections of the University of Michigan and the University of California system—the only libraries willing to offer Google works currently covered by copyright. In his article, Kelly breezed past the fact that the copyrighted works will be presented in a useless format—"snippets" that allow readers only glimpses into how a term is used in the text. Google users will not be able to read, copy, or print copyrighted works via Google. Google accepted that arrangement to limit its copyright liability. But the more "copyright friendly" the Google system is, the less user-friendly, and useful, it is. And even so it still may not fly in court.

Google is exploiting the instability of the copyright system in a digital age. The company's struggle with publishers over its legal ability to pursue its project is the most interesting and perhaps most transformative conflict in the copyright wars. But there are many other battles—and many other significant stories—out in the copyright jungle. Yet reporters seem lost.

Copyright in recent years has certainly become too strong for its own good. It protects more content and outlaws more acts than ever before. It stifles individual creativity and hampers the discovery and sharing of culture and knowledge. To convey all this to readers, journalists need to understand the principles, paradoxes, licenses, and limits of the increasingly troubled copyright system. Copyright is not just an interesting story. As the most pervasive regulation of speech and culture, the copyright system will help determine the richness and strength of democracy in the twenty-first century.

The Copyright Wars

It's not that the press has ignored copyright. Recent fights have generated a remarkable amount of press. Since Napster broke into the news in 2000, journalists have been scrambling to keep up with the fast-moving and complicated stories of content protection, distribution, and revision that make up the wide array of copyright conflicts.

During this time of rapid change it's been all too easy for reporters to fall into the trap of false dichotomies: hackers versus movie studios; kids versus music companies; librarians versus publishers. The peer-to-peer and music-file-sharing story, for instance, has consistently been covered as a business story with the tone of the sports page: winners and losers, scores and stats. In fact, peer-to-peer file sharing was more about technological innovation and the ways we use music in our lives than any sort of threat to the commercial music industry. As it stands today, after dozens of court cases and congressional hearings, peer-to-peer file-sharing remains strong. So does the music industry. The sky did not fall, our expectations did.

The most recent headline-grabbing copyright battle involved *The Da Vinci Code*. Did Dan Brown recycle elements of a 1982 nonfiction book for his bestselling novel? The authors of the earlier book sued Brown's publisher,

Random House U.K., in a London court in the spring of 2006 in an effort to prove that Brown lifted protected elements of their book, what they called "the architecture" of a speculative conspiracy theory about the life of Jesus. In the coverage of the trial, some reporters—even in publications like *The New York Times*, *The Washington Post*, and *The San Diego Union-Tribune*—used the word "plagiarism" as if it were a legal concept or cause of action. It isn't. Copyright infringement and plagiarism are different acts with some potential overlap. One may infringe upon a copyright without plagiarizing and one may plagiarize—use ideas without attribution—without breaking the law. Plagiarism is an ethical concept. Copyright is a legal one.

Perhaps most troubling, though, was the way in which the *Da Vinci Code* story was so often covered without a clear statement of the operative principle of copyright: one cannot protect facts and ideas, only specific expressions of ideas. Dan Brown and Random House U.K. prevailed in the London court because the judge clearly saw that the earlier authors were trying to protect ideas. Most people don't understand that important distinction. So it's no surprise that most reporters don't either.

Reporters often fail to see the big picture in copyright stories: that what is at stake is the long-term health of our culture. If the copyright system fails, huge industries could crumble. If it gets too strong, it could strangle future creativity and research. It is complex, and complexity can be a hard thing to render in journalistic prose.

The work situation of most reporters may also impede a thorough understanding of how copyright affects us all. Reporters labor for content companies, after all, and tend to view their role in the copyright system as one-dimensional. They are creators who get paid by copyright holders. So it's understandable for journalists to express a certain amount of anxiety about the ways digital technologies have allowed expensive content to flow around the world cheaply.

Yet reporters can't gather the raw material for their craft without a rich library of information in accessible form. When I was a reporter in the 1980s and 1990s, I could not write a good story without scouring the library and newspaper archives for other stories that added context. And like every reporter, I was constantly aware that my work was just one element in a cacophony of texts seeking readers and contributing to the aggregate understanding of our world. I was as much a copyright user as I was a copyright producer. Now that I write books, I am even more aware of my role as a taker and a giver. It takes a library, after all, to write a book.

The Right to Say No

We are constantly reminded that copyright law, as the Supreme Court once declared, is an "engine of free expression." But more often these days, it's instead an engine of corporate censorship.

Copyright is the right to say no. Copyright holders get to tell the rest of us that we can't build on, revise, copy, or distribute their work. That's a fair bargain most of the time. Copyright provides the incentive to bring work to market. It's impossible to imagine anyone anteing up $300 million for *Spider-Man 3* if we did not have a reasonable belief that copyright laws would limit its distribution to mostly legitimate and moneymaking channels.

Yet copyright has the potential of locking up knowledge, insight, information, and wisdom from the rest of the world. So it is also fundamentally a *conditional* restriction on speech and print. Copyright and the First Amendment are in constant and necessary tension. The law has for most of American history limited copyright—allowing it to fill its role as an incentive-maker for new creators yet curbing its censorious powers. For most of its 300-year history, the system has served us well, protecting the integrity of creative work while allowing the next generation of creators to build on the cultural foundations around them. These rights have helped fill our libraries with books, our walls with art, and our lives with song.

But something has gone terribly wrong. In recent years, large multinational media companies have captured the global copyright system and twisted it toward their own short-term interests. The people who are supposed to benefit most from a system that makes ideas available—readers, students, and citizens—have been excluded. No one in Congress wants to hear from college students or librarians.

More than ever, the law restricts what individuals can do with elements of their own culture. Generally the exercise of copyright protection is so extreme these days that even the most innocent use of images or song lyrics in scholarly work can generate a legal threat. Last year one of the brightest students in my department got an article accepted in the leading journal in the field. It was about advertising in the 1930s. The journal's lawyers and editors refused to let her use images from the ads in question without permission, even though it is impossible to find out who owns the ads or if they were ever covered by copyright in the first place. The chilling effect trumped any claim of scholarly "fair use" or even common sense.

What Has Changed

For most of the history of copyright in Europe and the United States, copying was hard and expensive, and the law punished those who made whole copies of others' material for profit. The principle was simple: legitimate publishers would make no money after investing so much in authors, editors, and printing presses if the same products were available on the street. The price in such a hypercompetitive market would drop to close to zero. So copyright created artificial scarcity.

But we live in an age of abundance. Millions of people have in their homes and offices powerful copying machines and communication devices: their personal computers. It's almost impossible to keep digital materials scarce once they are released to the public.

The industries that live by copyright—music, film, publishing, and software companies—continue to try. They encrypt video discs and compact discs so that consumers can't play them on computers or make personal copies. They monitor and sue consumers who allow others to share digital materials over the Internet. But none of these tactics seem to be working. In fact, they have been counterproductive. The bullying attitude has alienated consumers. That does not mean that copyright has failed or that it has no future. It just has a more complicated and nuanced existence.

Here is the fundamental paradox: media companies keep expanding across the globe. They produce more software, books, music, video games, and films every year. They charge more for those products every year. And those industries repeatedly tell us that they are in crisis. If we do not radically alter our laws, technologies, and habits, the media companies argue, the industries that copyright protects will wither and die.

Yet they are not dying. Strangely, the global copyright industries are still rich and powerful. Many of them are adapting, changing their containers and their content, but they keep growing, expanding across the globe. Revenues in the music business did drop steadily from 2000 to 2003—some years by up to 6.8 percent. Millions of people in Europe and North America use their high-speed Internet connections to download music files free. From Moscow to Mexico City to Manila, film and video piracy is rampant. For much of the world, teeming pirate bazaars serve as the chief (often only) source of those products. Yet the music industry has recovered from its early-decade lull rather well. Revenues for the major commercial labels in 2004 were 3.3 percent above 2003. Unit sales were up 4.4 percent. Revenues in 2004 were higher than in 1997 and comparable to those of 1998—then considered very healthy years for the recording industry. This while illegal downloading continued all over the world.

Yet despite their ability to thrive in a new global/digital environment, the companies push for ever more restrictive laws—laws that fail to recognize the realities of the global flows of people, culture, and technology.

Recent changes to copyright in North America, Europe, and Australia threaten to chill creativity at the ground level—among noncorporate, individual, and communal artists. As a result, the risk and price of reusing elements of copyrighted culture are higher than ever before. If you wanted to make a scholarly documentary film about the history of country music, for example, you might end up with one that slights the contribution of Hank Williams and Elvis Presley because their estates would deny you permission to use the archival material. Other archives and estates would charge you prohibitive fees. We are losing much of the history of the twentieth century because the copyright industries are more litigious than ever.

Yet copyright, like culture itself, is not zero-sum. In its first weekend of theatrical release, *Star Wars Episode III: Revenge of the Sith* made a record $158.5 million at the box office. At the same time, thousands of people downloaded high-quality pirated digital copies from the Internet. Just days after the blockbuster release of the movie, attorneys for 20th Century Fox sent thousands of "cease-and-desist" letters to those sharing copies of the film over the Internet. The practice continued unabated.

How could a film make so much money when it was competing against its free version? The key to understanding that seeming paradox—less control, more revenue—is to realize that every download does not equal a lost sale. As the Stanford law professor Lawrence Lessig has argued, during the time when music downloads were 2.6 times those of legitimate music sales, revenues dropped less than 7 percent. If every download replaced a sale, there would be no commercial music industry left. The relationship between the free version and the legitimate version is rather complex, like the relationship between a public library and a book publisher. Sometimes free stuff sells stuff.

Checks and Unbalances

Here's a primer for reporters who find themselves lost in the copyright jungle: American copyright law offers four basic democratic safeguards to the censorious power of copyright, a sort of bargain with the people. Each of these safeguards is currently at risk:

1. First and foremost, copyrights eventually expire, thus placing works into the public domain for all to buy cheaply and use freely. That is the most important part of the copyright bargain: We the people grant copyright as a temporary monopoly over the reproduction and distribution of specific works, and eventually we get the material back for the sake of our common heritage and collective knowledge. The works of Melville and Twain once benefited their authors exclusively. Now they belong to all of us. But as Congress continues to extend the term of copyright protection for works created decades ago (as it did in 1998 by adding twenty years to all active copyrights) it robs the people of their legacy.

2. Second, copyright restricts what consumers can do with the text of a book, but not the book itself; it governs the content, not the container. Thus people may sell and buy used books, and libraries may lend books freely, without permission from publishers. In the digital realm, however, copyright holders may install digital-rights-management schemes that limit the transportation of both the container and the content. So libraries may not lend out major portions of their materials if they are in digital form. As more works are digitized, libraries are shifting to the lighter, space-saving formats. As a result, libraries of the future could be less useful to citizens.

3. Third, as we have seen, copyright governs specific expressions, but not the facts or ideas upon which the expressions are based. Copyright does not protect ideas. But that is one of the most widely misunderstood aspects of copyright. And even that basic principle is under attack in the new digital environment. In 1997, the National Basketball Association tried to get pager and Internet companies to refrain from distributing game scores without permission. And more recently, Major League Baseball has tried, but so far has failed, to license the use of player statistics to limit "free riding" firms that make money facilitating fantasy baseball leagues. Every Congressional session, database companies try to create a new form of intellectual property that protects facts and data, thus evading the basic democratic right that lets facts flow freely.

4. Fourth, and not least, the copyright system has built into it an exception to the power of copyright: fair use. This significant loophole, too, is widely misunderstood, and deserves further discussion.

Generally, one may copy portions of another's copyrighted work (and sometimes the entire work) for private, noncommercial uses, for education, criticism, journalism, or parody. Fair use operates as a defense against an accusation of infringement and grants confidence to users that they most likely will not be sued for using works in a reasonable way.

On paper, fair use seems pretty healthy. In recent years, for example, courts have definitively stated that making a parody of a copyrighted work is considered "transformative" and thus fair. Another example: a major ruling in 2002 enabled image search engines such as Google to thrive and expand beyond simple Web text searching into images and video because "thumbnails" of digital photographs are considered to be fair uses. Thumbnails, the court ruled, do not replace the original in the marketplace.

But two factors have put fair use beyond the reach of many users, especially artists and authors. First and foremost, fair use does not help you if your publisher or distributor does not believe in it. Many publishers demand that every quote—no matter how short or for what purpose—be cleared with specific permission, which is extremely cumbersome and often costly.

And fair use is somewhat confusing. There is widespread misunderstanding about it. In public forums I have heard claims such as "you can take 20 percent" of a work before the use becomes unfair, or, "there is a forty-word rule" for long quotes of text. Neither rule exists. Fair use is intentionally vague. It is meant for judges to apply, case by case. Meanwhile, copyright holders are more aggressive than ever and publishers and distributors are more concerned about suits. So in the real world, fair use is less fair and less useful.

The Biggest Copy Machine

Fair use is designed for small ball. It's supposed to create some breathing room for individual critics or creators to do what they do. Under current law it's not appropriate for large-scale endeavors—like the Google library project. Fair use may be too rickety a structure to support both free speech and the vast dreams of Google.

Reporters need to understand the company's copyright ambitions. Google announced in December 2004 that it would begin scanning in millions of copyrighted books from the University of Michigan library, and in August 2006 the University of California system signed on. Predictably, some prominent publishers and authors have filed suit against the search-engine company.

The company's plan was to include those works in its "Google Book Search" service. Books from the library would supplement both the copyrighted books that Google has contracted to offer via its "partner" program with publishers and the uncopyrighted works scanned from other libraries, including libraries of Harvard, Oxford, and New York City. While it would offer readers full-text access to older works out of copyright, it would provide only "snippets" of the copyrighted works that it scans without the authors' permission from Michigan and California.

Google says that because users will only experience "snippets" of copyrighted text, their use of such material should be considered a fair use. That argument will be tested in court. But whether those snippets constitute fair use is just one part of the issue. To generate the "snippets," Google is scanning the entire works and storing them on its servers. The plaintiffs argue that the initial scanning of the books itself—done to create the snippets from a vast database—constitutes copyright infringement, the very core of copyright. Courts will have to weigh whether the public is better served by a strict and clear conception of copyright law—that only the copyright holder has the right to give permission for any copy, regardless of the ultimate use or effect on the market—or a more flexible and pragmatic one in which the user experience matters more.

One of the least understood concepts of Google's business is that it copies everything. When we post our words and images on the Web, we are implicitly licensing Google, Yahoo, and other search engines to make copies of our content to store in their huge farms of servers. Without such "cache" copies, search engines could not read and link to Web pages. In the Web world, massive copying is just business as usual.

But through the library project, Google is imposing the norms of the Web on authors and publishers who have not willingly digitized their works and thus have not licensed search engines to make cache copies. Publishers, at first, worried that the Google project would threaten book sales, but it soon became clear that project offers no risk to publishers' core markets and projects. If anything, it could serve as a marketing boon. Now publishers are most offended by the prospect of a wealthy upstart corporation's "free-riding" on their content to offer a commercial and potentially lucrative service without any regard for compensation or quality control. The publishers, in short, would like a piece of the revenue, and some say about the manner of display and search results.

Copyright has rarely been used as leverage to govern ancillary markets for goods that enhance the value or utility of the copyrighted works. Publishers have never, for instance, sued the makers of library catalogs, eyeglasses, or bookcases. But these are extreme times.

The mood of U.S. courts in recent years, especially the Supreme Court, has been to side with the copyright holder in this time of great technological flux. Google is an upstart facing off against some of the most powerful media companies in the world, including Viacom, News Corporation, and Disney—all of which have publishing wings. Courts will probably see this case as the existential showdown over the nature and future of copyright and rule to defend the status quo. Journalists should follow the case closely. The footnotes of any court decision could shape the future of journalism, publishing, libraries, and democracy.

Out of the Jungle

Google aside, in recent years—thanks to the ferocious mania to protect everything and the astounding political power of media companies—the basic, democratic checks and balances that ensured that copyright would not operate as an instrument of private censorship have been seriously eroded. The most endangered principle is fair use: the right to use others' copyrighted works in a reasonable way to promote important public functions such as criticism or education. And if fair use is in danger then good journalism is also threatened. Every journalist relies on fair use every day. So journalists have a self-interest in the copyright story.

And so does our society. Copyright was designed, as the Constitution declares, to "promote the progress" of knowledge and creativity. In the last thirty years we have seen this brilliant system corrupted and captured by the very industries that the old laws fostered. Yet the complexity and nuanced nature of copyright battles make it hard for nonexperts to grasp what's at stake.

So it's up to journalists to push deeper into stories in which copyright plays a part. Then the real challenge begins: explaining this messy system in clear language to a curious but confused audience.

Stephanie C. Ardito  **NO**

MySpace and YouTube Meet the Copyright Cops

Since the dawn of the Internet, many of us have marveled at the ground-breaking novelty of Internet sites that seem to appear from nowhere, gain rapid popularity, and become staples on everyone's set of bookmarks. The founders of these sites do not usually come from traditional content providers, so the phenomenon of Web-based services such as Yahoo!, Amazon, Travelocity, MapQuest, and Google continue to amaze us.

And just when we think there can't possibly be any more innovation, along come social networking and video-sharing sites such as MySpace and YouTube and their hundreds of imitators.

As these companies take off and continue to soar, inevitably, it seems, the copyright infringement lawsuits begin, often initiated by the traditional media powerhouses which feel threatened by the upstarts' popularity. The truly groundbreaking Internet companies manage to survive. Negotiations and settlements are worked out, conglomerates with bottomless financial pockets come to the rescue, or deep-rooted media companies finally accept the need to change their business paradigms or lose their considerable customer base.

The latest round of battles is occurring within the music and movie industries. The background and conflicts are no different than what we've seen before. Ten years ago, the scientific, technical, and medical (STM) publishers resisted placing full-text articles on the Internet. These publishers worried about losing expensive annual subscriptions if individual articles were easily accessible for purchase, as well as about how to collect royalties on multiple copies of articles circulating on the Web. Although struggling with customer demand for replication of Web services inspired by Internet technology, publishers finally figured out how to make their content widely and instantly available. Now publishers struggle with open access and end users (both authors and readers) going directly to the Web. The music and movie industries are bound to do the same.

The New Reality

A former employee of mine will graduate from music school this year. His dream is to earn a living as a jazz drummer. Recently, he created a MySpace page, listing upcoming band engagements, announcing his availability as a

private instructor, and providing videos and audio clips of his live performances. There are no copyright notices on the page, but Matt shared his opinion
that the original purpose of MySpace was to make budding artists known. If
his videos and music show up somewhere else on the Internet or if users download the clips, Matt doesn't care. Copyright won't become an issue for him
until he's famous. His major concern now is to get his name known.

As for school policies and educational efforts informing kids about copyright, teachers at my nephews' and niece's high schools and colleges do not
discuss the ramifications of downloading content from the Internet. English
and computer science teachers who require electronic copies of papers talk to
their students about plagiarism and warn students that their compositions are
being run against the Turnitin . . . to verify originality.

However, colleges and universities may soon intensify instructional efforts
to enlighten students about copyright, including possible litigation initiated
around the illegal downloading and storing of videos and music. On Feb. 28,
2007, the Recording Industry Association of America (RIAA) announced another
round of lawsuits against college students for copyright infringements. . . .

Regarding my own personal experience with the social networking sites,
I will admit that I'm a frequent user of YouTube. A while back, I saw a VH1 documentary on Meat Loaf, in which the television show played clips from Meat
Loaf's *Bat Out of Hell* video. Being a fan, after the program ended, I immediately went to YouTube and looked for the full videos of a couple of songs from
the album—"You Took the Words Right Out of My Mouth" and "Paradise by
the Dashboard Light" (a particular favorite of mine). I was tempted to download the videos to my computer so I could view them whenever the mood
struck, but my niece told me that the videos remain on YouTube "forever," so
I wouldn't have a problem finding them whenever I wanted. Since I still worry
that someday the copyright police will knock on my door, take my computer,
and lock me up in copyright jail, I listened to my niece's advice and did not
download the videos.

However, my niece's assertion that videos stay on YouTube into infinity
isn't true. I'm also a celebrity news junkie. Earlier this year, I was intrigued
about the scuttlebutt surrounding the Justin Timberlake/Scarlett Johannsson
video, "What Goes Around . . . Comes Around." I had seen clips of a steamy
swimming pool scene from the video and immediately went to YouTube
to find it. And there it was. In fact, there were several uploads of the video
from a number of the site's users. I watched the entire video to see what
the fuss was about and told my neighbor about it. Of course she asked me
for the URL, but when I went back to look for the video on YouTube, it had
vanished. Since Sony, the legal distributor, allows "sharing" of the video
directly from its Musicbox Web site, I emailed the URL to my neighbor. . . .
I suspect that Sony must have warned YouTube to take the illegal copies off
its site.

So, what prompts my nephews, niece, colleagues, and me to go to
MySpace and YouTube to view grainy, unprofessional, uploaded videos and
audios recorded on camera phones and camcorders versus searching the
music label or movie studio Web sites for the originals? The answer lies in the

ease and convenience of MySpace and YouTube. Without much fuss and no required registration, you can quickly identify videos of interest, see which ones are the most popular with others (both sites rank videos by the number of hits received, similar to Amazon's "Top Sellers"), click on the videos you want to watch, and, within a matter of seconds, have them appear on your screen. In comparison, the traditional media companies often require users to download special software to view videos and click through several pages of terms and conditions before gaining access. Even when that access is finally granted, you may sit for several minutes waiting for the videos to download to your screen. Since consumers want instant gratification, the established players need to learn some lessons from MySpace and YouTube. So, let's review the genesis and appeal of these two Web sites.

YouTube

Founded in February 2005, YouTube is typical of many startup Internet companies. It originated in a garage, followed quickly by significant funding from a venture capital company, in this case, Sequoia Capital. At first, users shared personal videos, but as the Web site's popularity grew rapidly, YouTube contracted with traditional content providers (television and movie studios and record labels) to load commercial clips. In less than a year, the video and user statistics were staggering. The company claims that 65,000 videos are uploaded daily, with consumers watching more than 100 million videos a day. Twenty million unique users, mainly in the 18–49 age range, view the Web site monthly.

In October 2006, Google, also initially funded by Sequoia Capital, bought YouTube for $1.65 billion. YouTube has struggled to find advertising revenue, so it should benefit from Google's ownership and experience in generating revenue. Although YouTube faced some copyright legal challenges from the music industry prior to Google's purchase, lawsuits seemed to have multiplied since the takeover. Some industry analysts speculate this litigiousness stems from the arrival of Google's deep financial pockets. For now, Google doesn't seem deterred by the legal wrangling.

YouTube's Boilerplate

Let's take a look at YouTube's copyright notices. Within the Terms of Use document . . . section 4 deals with Intellectual Property Rights. The section's statements are typical of the notices we see on the Web sites of publishers, database producers, and other content providers:

> The content on the YouTube Website, except all User Submissions (as defined below), including without limitation, the text, software, scripts, graphics, photos, sounds, music, videos, interactive features and the like ("Content") and the trademarks, service marks and logos contained therein ("Marks"), are owned by or licensed to YouTube, subject to copyright and other intellectual property rights under United States and foreign laws and international conventions. Content on the Website is provided to you AS IS for your information and personal use only

and may not be used, copied, reproduced, distributed, transmitted, broadcast, displayed, sold, licensed, or otherwise exploited for any other purposes whatsoever without the prior written consent of the respective owners. YouTube reserves all rights not expressly granted in and to the Website and the Content. You agree to not engage in the use, copying, or distribution of any of the Content other than expressly permitted herein, including any use, copying, or distribution of User Submissions of third parties obtained through the Website for any commercial pur- poses. If you download or print a copy of the Content for personal use, you must retain all copyright and other proprietary notices contained therein. You agree not to circumvent, disable or otherwise interfere with security related features of the YouTube Website or features that prevent or restrict use or copying of any Content or enforce limitations on use of the YouTube Website or the Content therein.

As with traditional content providers who negotiate author contracts, those who upload original videos "grant YouTube a worldwide, non-exclusive, royalty-free, sublicenseable and transferable license to use, reproduce, distrib- ute, prepare derivative works of, display, and perform the User Submissions in connection with the YouTube Website and YouTube's (and its successor's) busi- ness, including without limitation for promoting and redistributing part or all of the YouTube Website (and derivative works thereof) in any media formats and through any media channels."

But YouTube goes one step further than traditional publishers and data- base producers by granting "each user of the YouTube Website a non-exclusive license to access your User Submissions through the Website, and to use, reproduce, distribute, prepare derivative works of, display and perform such User Submissions as permitted through the functionality of the Website and under these Terms of Service." In other words, as I interpret this clause, those who upload videos they have created own the rights to their works. In the publishing world of newspapers, journals, and books, authors generally turn over their rights to the publishers, who then own the authors' works into perpetuity.

By clicking on the Terms of Use, YouTube's registered users also agree they will not submit any copyrighted material, with YouTube reserving the right to remove content if it detects infringement. YouTube cites the Digital Millennium Copyright Act (DMCA) of 1998 as the company's guideline for dealing with potential copyright violations, requiring written communication if copyright holders find their intellectual property has been illegally uploaded to the YouTube Web site. . . . DMCA seems to protect YouTube and Google from lawsuits if the infringing works are removed when copyright holders notify them, but actual litigation that would give us precedent has yet to be established.

In a separate document, "Copyright Tips,". . . . YouTube admits: "The most common reason we take down videos for copyright infringement is that they are direct copies of copyrighted content and the owners of the copyrighted con- tent have alerted us that their content is being used without their permission." YouTube mentions "fair use," providing links to four Web sites that outline the factors considered to establish fair use status: U.S. Copyright Office; . . . Stanford University Libraries and Academic Information Resources; . . . Copyright Web site LLC; . . . and the Chilling Effects Clearinghouse. . . .

MySpace

MySpace . . . was founded in 2003 as a social networking Web site. In 2005, Rupert Murdoch's News Corporation acquired MySpace as part of a $580 million acquisition, with the "lifestyle portal" now a unit of Fox Interactive Media Inc. Users must be at least 14 to join MySpace (one must be 13 to access YouTube), but I'm not sure how this is enforced on either site.

The MySpace Terms of Use Agreement is similar to YouTube's and applies to users who are Visitors (those who browse the Web site) or Members (those who register). . . . Under the section titled Proprietary Rights in Content on MySpace.com, when members display, publish, or post any content on the Web site, MySpace acknowledges that ownership rights belong to members, but members grant MySpace "a limited license to use, modify, publicly perform, publicly display, reproduce, and distribute such Content solely on and through the MySpace Services." The license is "non-exclusive . . . fully-paid and royalty-free (meaning that MySpace.com is not required to pay you for the use on the MySpace Services of the Content that you post), sublicenseable (so that MySpace.com is able to use its affiliates and subcontractors such as Internet content delivery networks to provide the MySpace Services), and worldwide (because the Internet and the MySpace Services are global in reach)." Members must "warrant" that the posted content "does not violate the privacy rights, publicity rights, copyrights, contract rights or any other rights of any person" and agree "to pay for all royalties, fees, and any other monies owing any person by reason of any Content posted . . . through the MySpace Services."

The Agreement includes a "partial" list of 27 prohibitive content activities. Illicit activities include promoting an "illegal or unauthorized copy of another person's copyrighted work, such as providing pirated computer programs or links to them, providing information to circumvent manufacture-installed copy-protect devices, or providing pirated music or links to pirated music files." Advertising and paid commercial activity is also prohibited. As with YouTube, MySpace includes several paragraphs on liabilities and disclaimers.

The Agreement is dated Oct. 25, 2006, coinciding with MySpace's announcement that the company had implemented a filtering system to identify copyrighted materials posted by its users. The audio fingerprinting technology came from Gracenote . . . , a California-based company specializing in the organization of digital music. Music files uploaded by MySpace users are run against Gracenote's MusicID software and Global Media Database to detect copyright infringements.

In February 2007, MySpace announced the implementation of a second program to block videos containing copyrighted content posted by its users. In this case, digital fingerprinting technology licensed from Audible Magic . . . is used to screen and block videos.

YouTube seems to lag behind MySpace in applying filtering technology. The company hoped to introduce a new mechanism to filter out unauthorized videos by the end of 2006. On Feb. 22, 2007, the *Mercury News* reported that Google had signed a deal with Audible Magic to provide its filtering technology on the YouTube Web site. However, YouTube and Audible Magic had not directly issued an "official" statement about such a deal as of that date, nor would either company comment.

Storms of Litigation

On Oct. 11, 2006, *The Wall Street Journal* interviewed two copyright experts about the Google purchase of YouTube: John Palfrey, a Harvard University law professor and director of the Berkman Center for Internet & Society . . . , and Stan Liebowitz, an economics professor at the University of Texas at Dallas and director of the Center for the Analysis of Property Rights and Innovation. . . . Mr. Palfrey said, "Google is no stranger to copyright risk. Much to their credit, Google has not let a lack of precision in the copyright context stop them from taking on major projects. The YouTube deal is no exception. As with Google News and the Libraries Project, the YouTube technology and service is going to make some people—competitors and people elsewhere in the value chain alike—somewhat unhappy."

Mr. Liebowitz agreed with Palfrey: "Google is no stranger to these issues. Its attempt (the library project) to copy all the books in existence without getting copyright permission in advance has led to a lawsuit against it by copyright owners. Perhaps there are economies of scale in fighting such lawsuits. I also agree that YouTube is no Napster. Nevertheless, whether there will be copyright litigation depends on several issues. Although the purpose of YouTube might be to encourage home-grown creative endeavors, some portion of YouTube files have been pure copyrighted files with no home-grown component, although it appears that YouTube has taken them down when requested."

Palfrey expressed his opinion that if users agree to YouTube's Terms of Service agreement—"not to post anything that violates anyone else's copyright," and YouTube removes copyrighted works immediately that come to the company's attention—then YouTube and Google should be protected by the DMCA if lawsuits are filed. If the companies ignore or don't respond to claims of infringement, he considered litigation inevitable.

In fairness to YouTube, the company has quickly responded when notified about copyrighted materials, not only from media conglomerates, but also from individual directors and writers. For example, in July 2006, journalist Robert Tur sued YouTube for posting a video he had shot of a white truck driver named Reginald Denny being dragged out of his truck and beaten during the Los Angeles riots in 1992. When YouTube learned of the lawsuit, the video was immediately removed. Shortly before Google's purchase of YouTube, the Japanese Society for Rights of Authors, Composers and Publishers notified the company of nearly 30,000 illegal clips floating around the YouTube Web site. Again, when alerted, YouTube removed the offending clips.

Preceding the sale of YouTube to Google, a flurry of announcements appeared regarding potential content deals with Sony, Bertelsmann, Universal Music, and CBS. While the CBS talks ultimately broke down, YouTube brokered a deal with the British Broadcasting Company to load selective BBC news and entertainment content on the company Web site. Analysts forecast that Google's significant financial resources would prompt an immediate upsurge in copyright litigation after the company's takeover of YouTube. In fact, as this issue of *Searcher* went to press, lawsuits were being announced on a daily basis, so many, that it was difficult for me to keep up. For example, on Jan. 18, 2007, competitor News Corp. subpoenaed YouTube for the identity of users who uploaded full episodes of Fox's TV show *24* before the episodes debuted. Apparently, YouTube gave in to Fox's pressure and identified the users.

In addition, Viacom Inc.—which owns MTV, Nickelodeon, Comedy Central, and Paramount, not to mention, the immortal *I Love Lucy* and *Perry Mason* TV series—ordered YouTube to remove more than 100,000 video clips. Viacom had been in discussions with YouTube to keep the videos on the Web site. Some critics speculated that Viacom may have demanded the removal of the videos to force YouTube into a quicker royalty arrangement, rather than let negotiations drag on indefinitely. Since Comedy Central's *The Daily Show with Jon Stewart* is among the most heavily viewed videos on the YouTube Web site, industry analysts thought Viacom's strategy would compel YouTube to immediately agree on terms favorable to Viacom. As of this writing, YouTube and Google had not budged.

Shortly after the breakdown in talks, on March 13, 2007, Viacom filed a lawsuit against Google and YouTube, seeking more than $1 billion in damages for "160,000 unauthorized clips of Viacom's programming . . . viewed more than 1.5 billion times" on the YouTube Web site. Some critics commented that Viacom not only wants control over its media programs, but doesn't like its materials displayed along side the work of amateurs on YouTube, mainly because the unprofessional videos turn off advertisers. However, the real truth may lie in the threat Viacom is experiencing over YouTube's popularity and the significant Google resources supporting the Web site. Interestingly, in the month prior to the lawsuit announcement, Viacom signed a licensing deal with Joost . . . , a company whose technology will be used to load videos from Viacom's television networks onto the Internet. One has to wonder if Viacom entered into the Joost deal knowing that the lawsuit against Google and YouTube would follow. The Viacom lawsuit will be the one to watch, as the company will argue that YouTube had direct knowledge of the illegal videos and profited from the postings (i.e., most likely citing Section 512 from the DMCA safe harbor clause).

In an ironic twist, on March 22, 2007, the Electronic Frontier Foundation (EFF) sued Viacom on behalf of MoveOn.org and Brave New Films. In August 2006, the two companies had created and uploaded a video, *Stop the Falsiness,* to YouTube. The video parodied *The Colbert Report,* another popular Comedy Central program owned by Viacom, and included clips from the show as well as original interviews. EFF argues that Viacom unlawfully asked YouTube to remove the video parody, which EFF claims was protected by free speech and fair use. Google and YouTube are not named in the lawsuit.

Another conglomerate, Vivendi (and its subsidiary, Universal Music Group), has received frequent press coverage for its aggressive tactics in filing copyright infringement lawsuits against social networking and video Web sites. The company continues to pressure MySpace and YouTube to pay royalties, either by forcing users to "pay-per-play" or by sharing ad revenues. These tactics are being blasted by critics, who write that customers are alienated when media companies fail to adopt to new technology.

As an aside, in early February 2007, a privately held video-sharing company called Veoh Networks, Inc. was formed by media giants Time Warner and Michael Eisner (former Disney Chairman and CEO) and various investment firms. In a bit of irony, considering the corporate backgrounds of the founders, Veoh found itself facing copyright infringement lawsuits less than a week after its video Web site debuted.

Watching and Waiting

Some media giants are choosing to stay out of the copyright fray but continue to cautiously watch legal developments at their competitors. For example, late in 2006, Warner Music chose not to sue YouTube for uploading songs and videos, but rather, negotiated a deal to share revenue from ads placed next to Warner material. Warner's strategy differed sharply from the approach employed against Napster nearly 6 years ago. In that case, a class action suit from a number of music companies shut down Napster.

Commenting on the Viacom lawsuit against YouTube, Paul Cappuccio, Time Warner's general counsel, expressed his opinion that "companies should reach a compromise . . . We are still of the opinion that we can negotiate a business solution with YouTube that will efficiently identify and filter out unauthorized copyrighted works while also allowing us to license copyright works to them for a share of revenue."

Some conglomerates decide to sit back because they have found themselves between a rock and a hard place. Illegal videos and music give them exposure and may help to generate sales. Sound familiar? Years ago, information professionals pleaded with traditional publishers to allow access to individual articles and to consider alternative forms of electronic advertising to generate revenue, foreseeing that money (and profits) could be made without paying for annual subscriptions. Back then, we called the publishers dinosaurs. Now, the media conglomerates are being labeled with the same term.

Personally, I think the media giants will eventually calm down and learn to work with social networking and video Web sites. Otherwise, these outlets risk losing their substantial customer base, not to mention access to revolutionary marketing strategies and technologies that only upstart Internet companies can seem to initiate. For example, YouTube is piloting some innovative advertising programs that may allay the fears of the conglomerates, while at the same time, rewarding them with revenue. One program, called "participatory video ads," is being embraced by companies such as General Motors,

Adidas, and Coca-Cola. These firms have purchased YouTube video space to spotlight their brands. As with personal videos placed on the Web site, users can rate and comment on the commercially made videos.

In a separate marketing development, on Feb. 22, 2007, Fox Interactive Media (owner of MySpace) announced that it had acquired Strategic Data Corporation. Like DoubleClick . . . Strategic Data is a digital advertising company. Fox hopes to use Strategic Data's systems to persuade more users to click on ads placed on the MySpace Web site.

Until the media giants simmer down, however, MySpace and YouTube will face legal battles over copyrighted music and movie clips for some time to come. The confrontations will be fierce, but Google and News Corp. have significant financial resources and large legal staffs to handle the lawsuits. In fact, after its takeover of YouTube, Google set aside more than $200 million (funded through stock held in escrow) to cover future litigation costs.

As we went to press, News Corp. and NBC Universal announced plans to launch a legally pure, video distribution network some view as a potential competitor to YouTube. Scheduled to launch this summer, the new service will stock an online video site with masses of TV shows and videos, plus clips that users will be allowed to modify and share. Partners in the project already include the usual Google competitors—AOL, MSN, and Yahoo!. Television library content will be advertiser-supported and free to users. Some outlets will support mashups and online communities. Downloading movies will require user payments.

Digital Rights Management and the Steve Jobs Controversy

Like the digital object identifier (DOI) technology developed by publishers to tag and track electronic copyrighted works, media companies have created features in digital rights management (DRM) technology to make it difficult for users to copy or transfer audio and video files. Generally, technologies to thwart file sharing have failed, with media companies relying on their own personnel to scan the Internet for unauthorized copies. Even after threatening the offending parties, content providers continue to struggle in tracking down the same illegal copies likely to appear elsewhere on the Web.

On Feb. 6, 2007, Apple's Steve Jobs posted an essay on his company's Web site . . . entitled "Thoughts on Music." Jobs proposed that digital rights management (DRM) software preventing music reproduction and piracy be eliminated, so that songs could be played on any device. Apple licenses music rights from the "big four" music companies: Universal, Sony BMG, Warner, and EMI. According to Jobs, these companies "control the distribution of over 70% of the world's music." When Apple started its iTunes service, the company "was able to negotiate landmark usage rights at the time, which include allowing users to play their DRM protected music on up to 5 computers and on an unlimited number of iPods. Obtaining such rights from the music companies was unprecedented at the time, and even today is unmatched by most other digital music services. However, a key provision of our agreements with the music companies is that if our DRM system is compromised and their music becomes playable on unauthorized devices, we have only a small number of weeks to fix the problem or they can withdraw their entire music catalog from our iTunes store. . . . So far we have met our commitments to the music companies to protect their music, and we have given users the most liberal usage rights available in the industry for legally downloaded music."

The controversy with Jobs' posting comes with his proposal to completely abolish blocking DRM protections. He wrote: "Imagine a world where every online store sells DRM-free music encoded in open licensable formats. In such a world, any player can play music purchased from any store, and any store can sell music which is playable on all players." Jobs justifies such an open source solution because he believes that DRM systems have never worked to prevent music piracy. He claims that music CDs are completely unprotected, so that "all the music distributed on CDs can be easily uploaded to the Internet, then (illegally) downloaded and played on any computer or player. In 2006, under 2 billion DRM-protected songs were sold worldwide by online stores, while over 20 billion songs were sold completely DRM-free and unprotected on CDs by the music companies themselves. The music companies sell the vast majority of their music DRM-free, and show no signs of changing this behavior, since the overwhelming majority of their revenues depend on selling CDs which must play in CD players that support no DRM system. . . . Convincing [the big four] to license their music to Apple and others DRM-free will create a truly interoperable music marketplace."

Many music industry analysts agree with Jobs—that nothing will prevent piracy. Those who buy iPods are not purchasing many DRM-protected recordings. Rather, consumers purchase music on CDs and download individual tracks into the format of their choice on the iPods. Jobs justified his position on DRMs by providing statistics on what the iTunes store sells: "Today's most popular iPod holds 1000 songs, and research tells us that the average iPod is nearly full. This means that only 22 out of 1000 songs, or under 3% of the music on the average iPod, is purchased from the iTunes store and protected with a DRM. The remaining 97% of the music is unprotected and playable on any player that can play the open formats. It's hard to believe that just 3% of the music on the average iPod is enough to lock users into buying only iPods in the future. And since 97% of the music on the average iPod was not purchased from the iTunes store, iPod users are clearly not locked into the iTunes store to acquire their music."

On the flip side, those opposed to Jobs' proposal to eliminate DRM protections point out the pressure Jobs faces from European fair trade laws that will soon mandate making iTunes music available to non-Apple devices. If an unrestricted MP3 format is adopted across the music industry, any digital device could download music from any source. Looking to the future, Jobs may envision expanding the iTunes concept to movies, TV programs, electronic books, and other media. With DRM blocking eliminated, content from a wide range of formats could be downloaded to any digital device.

On Feb. 15, 2007, Rob Pegoraro, a reporter with *The Washington Post*, succinctly summarized all the fuss whirling in the entertainment industry:

The [DRM] technology can still serve a role in online music or movie rental services, which have drawn far fewer customers than stores like iTunes, but for purchases it does too little to justify its costs. In practice, it only stops copying by the unmotivated, the over-scheduled or the inexperienced—the people most likely to buy a song or movie online as long as they can do so quickly, easily and cheaply. In the music industry, a growing number of outlets beyond the big-name companies, from tiny indie-rock operations to the Philadelphia Orchestra and the Smithsonian Institution's Folkways label, have realized the futility of copy-restriction software and now sell digital downloads in open, unrestricted formats. At this point, this all amounts to little more than expensive psychotherapy for Hollywood executives. It's the height of arrogance for them to keep sending us the bill.

My thoughts exactly! . . .

EXPLORING THE ISSUE

Do Copyright Laws Protect Ownership of Intellectual Property?

Critical Thinking and Reflection

1. Is there any difference in the way copyright protects the rights of an original author in different forms of media, such as film, television, print, the Internet, or in the area of digitally produced media?
2. If copyright were not upheld, what jobs would disappear? Who could afford to be a professional writer, filmmaker, musician, or other performance artist?
3. Our current legal system can be expensive and cumbersome, but it is the best recourse for the creator of original material to protect their financial interests in his or her work. Can you suggest other alternatives for how individuals can protect their ownership rights?
4. You may want to examine other approaches toward a more contemporary idea about protecting one's intellectual property. Are there other ways of controlling information, such as through encryption methods, "copyleft" (see below) or licensing agreements?

Is There Common Ground?

Undoubtedly, today's digital technologies duplicate information easily, and make it possible to copy material that has the same quality as an original. We use so many of these technologies in the privacy of our own homes, and think of the technologies as tools that mediate information and its use that it is easy to have a lax viewpoint about protecting the ownership of original property. Some organizations take the position that copyright actually prevents creativity, and have offered alternatives to the traditional laws. For example, "copyleft" is an idea that licenses some type of digital data (like video games and other creative activities) and allows users to manipulate original information for free. There are often restrictions on how far copyleft will go, but it does suggest that there is a range of content for which the original author expects users to change and/or manipulate digital data.

One area that is hotly debated is the way electronic publishers of printed material license rights to the original owners of printed information. In today's markets, authors of printed books often agree to a different payment scheme or accountability for their materials once a publisher distributes their work in electronic form. While not everyone is convinced that these new payment schemes will work flawlessly, copyright and the protection of intellectual property will probably remain a hotly contested legal battlefield for some time to come.

Additional Resources

Copyright infringement is a big problem. The following Web site provides clarification on what types of infringement occurs:

**www.clickandcopyright.com/copyright-resources/
copyright-infringement.aspx**

Understanding the Digital Millennium Copyright Act helps clarify what law and policy is most applicable to digital information:

**www.ehow.com/about_6560612_digital-millennium-copyright-act
.html?ref=Track2&utm_source=ask**

EDUCAUSE is a group that attempts to clarify important matters for colleges and students. Their clarifications on copyright are printed at:

www.educause.edu/Resources/Browse/DMCA/31236

Wired magazine has written about the problems of applying old privacy law in the era of cloud computing:

www.wired.com/threatlevel/2011/10/ecpa-turns-twenty-five/

Internet References . . .

The Electronic Freedom Forum

The Electronic Freedom Forum's site provides a number of examples of hate speech and examples of the use of electronic media, and has a specific set of examples on the principle of "fighting words."

**www.freedomforum.org/packages/first/fightingwords/
casesummaries.htm**

The ACLU

The American Civil Liberties Union (ACLU) maintains a Web site devoted to the issues in this section.

www.aclu.org/technology-and-liberty

www.aclu.org/technology-and-libertyT

The Electronic Frontier Foundation

The Electronic Frontier Foundation also maintains an up-to-date Web site on their positions on anonymity, technology, and privacy.

www.eff.org/issues/privacy

The GNU Project

The GNU Project is one of the leaders of the "copyleft" approach to licensing software. A more in-depth analysis of what this group identifies as copyleft can be found on its Web site.

www.gnu.org/copyleft/

The U.S. Copyright Office

Taking out a legal copyright is actually easy and not very expensive. Information can be found at the U.S. Printing Office's Web site.

www.copyright.gov/

Institute of Electrical and Electronics Engineers (IEEE)

The IEEE's position on the Digital Millennium Copyright Act can be found at the below-mentioned link.

www.ieeeusa.org/policy/positions/DigitalCopyright1109.pdf

Media Business

*I*t is important to remember that media industries are businesses and that they must be profitable in order to thrive. Changes in ownership rules have resulted in a new group of media companies and corporations. Newspapers may be the first major industry to fail. Most have retooled and have focused on smaller, targeted audiences. In this section we discuss what has changed in traditional media outlets, and how new special-interest groups and new technologies are changing the type of media that is available to the public. Are changes to traditional industries inevitable? Are there evolving models of business for the digital age? What aspects of law, regulation, and business practices have come together to change the nature of the media "playing field?" How likely are new services to survive? Is the era of mass media now over?

- Did Consolidation of the Music Industry Hurt Music Distribution?
- Should Newspapers Shut Down Their Presses?
- Do New Business Models Result in Greater Consumer Choice of Products and Ideas?

ISSUE 13

Did Consolidation of the Music Industry Hurt Music Distribution?

YES: **Greg Kot**, from *Ripped: How the Wired Generation Revolutionized Music* (Simon & Schuster, 2009)

NO: **Panos Panay**, from "Rethinking Music: The Future of Making Money as a Performing Musician," in *Rethinking Music: A Briefing Book*, http://cyber.law.harvard.edu/sites/cyber.law.harvard.edu/files/Rethinking_ Music_Briefing_Book_April-25-2011.pdf

---

Learning Outcomes

After reading this issue, you should be able to:

- Understand how rapidly the music industry has changed in recent years, and the controversies that have resulted from these changes.
- Understand that each form of media relies on an industry that is self-perpetuating, and in search of making a profit.
- Apply the ideas from these authors to examine how the music industry has changed, and consider whether other media industries could undergo similar changes.
- Evaluate the many issues related to the way media industries (in this case, the music industry, which encompasses recorded music, radio, performance venues, and the distribution of music) contribute to the economy, and the relationship between commercial production and profit.

ISSUE SUMMARY

YES: Greg Kot explains the business model that dominated the recording industry throughout the 1990s and into the 2000s. In this excerpt, he identifies how rapidly the old business model crumbled and how record executives feared the evolving technological

changes that foretold of an economic model that would revolutionize the corporate music structure.

NO: Panos Panay examines specific changes to the live music scene,
and the growth of niche markets that contributed to the evolution of several new models for the music business. Despite a poor
economy in 2010, fans are becoming more active and involved in
the production of a successful band and/or record. Along with a
new model of entrepreneurship, Panay offers insights to how the
recording industry is evolving.

N ot long ago, the Recording Industry Association of America (RIAA) sued
young people for downloading unauthorized recorded music. For years, the
RIAA campaigned against downloading music for free, claiming that it undermined the financial structure of the music industry. In 1998, Shawn Fanning, a
19-year-old student, developed a free Internet-based, peer-to-peer (P2P) service
that allowed people to share music files through Mp3 technology. By 2001,
Fanning had been taken to court by the RIAA, and the original Napster was
closed, but Fanning sold the logo and the name to Roxio, a company that
legally sold music through the Internet, and since that time, the recording
industry has been in flux, and new business models have emerged to promote
musicians and music.

In this issue, Greg Kot chronicles the power the recording industry had
through consolidation, prior to the shift to digitally downloaded music. Kot, a
Chicago Tribune rock music writer, effectively portrays the power that was held
by corporations at the end of the 1990s. A typical business model in those days
might find a record label executive's interest in a particular musician or group,
and the label would finance the marketing of the artist(s). When the artist
then made money, the label recouped their investments. This system gave rise
to the power of hit music, and if a performer or group became particularly successful, you might expect a number of copy-cats to follow, hoping to cash in
on the public's interest in a new sound, a style, or a genre of music.

After the controversy over free downloads, many questioned whether the
independent musical artist could survive in the newly reframed music industry. Panos Panay, an entrepreneur who invests money in new musical performers, and develops their careers through helping them become independent
business people, writes that those who have accepted the new business model
have had the opportunity to try to control their own success, brand, and creative personae.

At first, some recording artists took extreme positions on this issue.
Metallica was one of the first groups to oppose free downloads, but soon realized that by giving away some music for free, they actually cultivated a broader
following. The Canadian group, *Bare Naked Ladies* (BNL) was among the first
to establish their own record label, and control all aspects of recording,
concert venues, and the sale of derivative product. The band, *They Might Be*

Giants found that writing and performing for television shows (they wrote the theme song for *Malcolm in the Middle,* which ran from 2000–2006, among others) was one such alternative way of making money while cultivating an audience and performing regularly. Now, the music industry is alive and well, but it seldom looks like it did a mere 15 years ago.

We specifically included these selections in this edition of *Taking Sides* because we wanted to show that business models in the media industries are not fixed. They are always undergoing change, and as a result, the opportunities, jobs, and careers in those industries are changing dramatically. For students who hope to work in the media industries, it is important to watch how other industries undergo change, especially in terms of shifting from mass market models to more niche audience models, like the music industry.

This issue also ties together concepts introduced in Issue 12 dealing with copyright and how digital technology challenges laws that were developed with an interest in older business models, with the proliferation of smaller market product, discussed in Anderson's selection in Issue 15.

The media industries are, after all, businesses, and won't thrive for long if they don't make a profit. The history of media content and the economic imperative for the media industries' choices of what to present to the public is one of the most telling tales of the relationship between consumer interest and product availability.

YES

Greg Kot

Ripped: How the Wired Generation Revolutionized Music

Chaos and Transformation

Peter Jenner is a man who knows his "freak-outs"—sixties terminology for an intense, drug-induced emotional experience. He was Pink Floyd's first manager, after all, and he has remained one of the industry's most forward-looking thinkers for forty years. So when he spoke to a room full of music executives in the fall of 2006 at the Future of Music Policy Summit in Montreal, his assessment of their business resonated.

"We are in the midst of a technological freak-out," he said. "The business is broken. . . . Digital technology is fundamentally changing our business in a way that no development of the last two hundred years equals, except the onset of electricity."

Jenner described a worst-case scenario for people who had made a lucrative living as middlemen in the twentieth-century music business, the conduits between musicmakers and consumers. The Internet was making them obsolete.

"We're trying to force a nineteenth- and twentieth-century business model into twenty-first-century technology," he said. "I'm not surprised we're in chaos."

Peer-to-peer file sharing had turned consumers into distributors. CD burners had turned them into manufacturers. This shift in responsibilities left the industry with only one role: as "policeman . . . hostile to consumers . . . [and] stopping progress."

In a report prepared that same year, *Beyond the Soundbytes,* Jenner expanded on his disdain for this shortsighted response: "The flagrant spread of 'Internet piracy' in developed countries is a reflection of the failure of the industry as a whole to develop an appropriate copyright response to the distribution and remuneration options made possible by the new technologies."

He mocked the industry's response to the new challenges posed by Internet distribution and peer-to-peer file sharing: hand-wringing, followed by litigation, in which "the endless predictions of victory reminds one of the Vietnam War."

We were back in the sixties again, when Rock 'n' Roll Inc. was still in its infancy. Now four decades later, it was looking like a relic.

"When five percent of the artists are making ninety-five percent of the money, the system is broken," Daniel Levitin, a McGill University music professor, proclaimed.

Through the breach rushed a new generation of bands and fans empowered by personal computers and broadband Internet connections. Willy-nilly they forged a new world of music distribution that seized control from once all-powerful music and radio conglomerates.

In less than a decade, a new Internet-savvy music hierarchy had been created. Commercial radio, MTV, retail stores, and record companies lost their exclusive tastemaker status, while consumers morphed into de facto music programmers who shared information and music via message boards, Web pages, e-zines, and MP3 blogs.

In the process, more people than ever were creating and consuming music. Without a physical product to sell, costs sunk for recording and distributing music. At the same time, opportunities to be heard increased. In this world, the fringe players could more easily find and build a dedicated audience, and a musical ecosystem encompassing thousands of microcultures began to emerge.

"We're moving into an era of massive niche markets rather than a mass market," Jenner said. This was bad news for people awaiting the next Beatles or the new U2—a band that could unite the masses in a whirlwind of hits and hype. For everybody else, this was an opportunity for more music to flourish in more places than ever.

In this broader, more diversified world, bands such as Montreal's Arcade Fire, Seattle's Death Cab for Cutie, and Omaha's Bright Eyes rose to prominence. They were viral success stories, selling out shows around the world before they were selling albums in the kind of numbers that would make the majors take notice of them.

It was enough to make Death Cab for Cutie's Chris Walla proselytize like a digital evangelist: "This is the golden age of the Internet. The laptop kids have clued in everybody else to what's going on: radio, television, the record industry—they're all following the Internet's lead. Because those kids know their laptop can make their cultural existence more fulfilling than any media corporation."

Who knew a laptop could be so empowering? The music industry sure didn't. But the Internet turned fans into gatekeepers. It also gave bands an independence they never had: the ability to communicate directly with their fans in ways their predecessors never could have imagined.

Consider that when the nineties roared to a close with CDs generating millions in profit, the industry consisted of six multinational record labels, and a single corporation (SFX, soon to be bought out by Clear Channel) that dominated the concert and commercial radio businesses. The primary decisions about what kind of music most of America would hear and how consumers would access that music (through radio, retail, and touring) were essentially being made by a few dozen key executives at a handful of companies.

But that power structure, the by-product of a century's worth of empire building, started to crumble the instant the first music file was ripped onto a computer hard drive and shared online. Metallica and the major labels took the rogue file-swapping service Napster to court in 2000 and held back the Internet tide for a few months. But as independent producer Steve Albini said, "It's like trying to hold back the ocean, like trying to keep the sun from rising every morning. It's a whole new era, except the music industry doesn't know it yet." It would find out soon enough.

In the fall of 2000, Radiohead's *Kid A* was a Napster-fueled hit on the Internet long before it arrived in record stores. The esoteric album barely registered on commercial radio; but it was in heavy rotation on the Net months before its release. The result was a number one album, an extraordinary confluence of underground taste and mass popularity.

The industry responded not with vigorous new ideas, but with strong-arm tactics and threats. It served fans not with digital innovation but with lawsuits—more than twenty thousand in a span of four years, in an attempt to intimidate consumers away from file sharing.

Seven years after *Kid A*, Radiohead released *In Rainbows* through its website, without the aid of a record label.

The cost to fans? "It's up to you," Radiohead told them.

In contrast to the major labels, the band embraced one of the fundamental principles of good business: the customer is always right. It was a moment of clarity, a moment in which the future finally overtook the past. . . .

Consolidated to Death

In February 1999, Sheryl Crow found herself in the strange position of having won a Grammy Award for an album put out by a record label that no longer existed.

In the weeks before the Grammys, A&M—the record label that had signed her, nurtured her career, and overseen her rise from Los Angeles studio singer to international rock star over the previous decade—was gutted and folded into the Interscope label as part of the newly formed Universal Music Group. The demise of A&M was the result of a $10.4 billion purchase of the PolyGram music companies by Seagram.

As the rest of the industry celebrated itself at the Grammys, Crow saw trouble ahead. In her acceptance speech, the singer delivered something of a eulogy for her old label. She was the only artist at the nationally televised ceremony to publicly acknowledge the huge toll exacted by the wave of consolidation that had washed over her profession.

Up until a few months before, she had been working for one of the smaller major-label companies, headed by veteran music executive Al Cafaro; now Cafaro and A&M were gone and she found herself under contract to the world's largest record company, headed by Edgar Bronfman Jr. The immediate costs of the merger were easy to quantify: besides Cafaro, more than twenty-five hundred employees lost their jobs and 250 bands lost their deals with labels such as A&M, Geffen, Mercury, Island, and Motown.

But in the long term, the effects of consolidation would be even more profound, and usher in a decade when the twentieth-century music industry would suddenly find itself fighting for its life, undone by its single-minded pursuit of profit at the expense of the cornerstone principle that had allowed it to thrive for decades: artist development, as nurtured by savvy executives who not only knew their business but knew their music.

Now Cafaro, a music lifer, was out, and Bronfman, a longtime liquor magnate, was in. He'd soon head the biggest music corporation in the world. Bronfman was heir to the Seagram fortune and was running the family business in the nineties when he sought to diversify the company's holdings by branching out into music. As with the other moneymen taking power in the consolidation-heavy nineties, music was not central to his vision but rather a piece in a larger portfolio of products,

Cafaro was one of Crow's champions; he had signed her to her first record deal in 1991 and had allowed her to rerecord her debut album because she was dissatisfied with the initial results. Cafaro's faith was rewarded with a hit: *Tuesday Night Music Club* established Crow as an artist to be reckoned with in 1993. It went on to sell more than 4 million copies and her career flourished; her 1999 Grammy was her sixth.

Yet she wasn't in a particularly celebratory mood in the days after the '99 ceremony.

"It's a frightening time as far as the music industry being an artist-nurturing industry," she said. "Now everything is so numbers-oriented and new artists get one shot, maybe two, to get a hit, and that's it. They sign two-album deals now. I was signed to seven albums and I was given a chance to get on the road and hone my craft. You want artists who have a strong point of view, who have the potential to grow into something wonderful, like Jackson Browne and Joni Mitchell, who found themselves by touring and continuing to write, and their album sales slowly grew. But now artists aren't getting that opportunity because there's pressure to have instant hits."

Consolidation was the era's trendiest business strategy. It caught on because it enabled companies to claim bigger market share, streamline operations by cutting overlapping positions and payroll, and explore new revenue streams. By the late nineties, Wall Street was rife with merger news, and deals that further centralized power in the record, radio, and concert industries were brokered. Power was concentrated in fewer hands than ever: the PolyGram-Universal merger left five multinational conglomerates to run the $14.6 billion-a-year record industry. Ten conglomerates accounted for 62 percent of the gross revenue in the $10.2 billion commercial-radio business, and one company—SFX Entertainment—dominated the $1.5 billion concert-touring industry.

One side effect of this strategy profoundly affected consumers: the price for music spiked. Compact disc prices approached a record $19, even though the manufacturing cost had actually declined since the discs came into the marketplace in the early eighties. Tickets for major shows skyrocketed. Indirectly, an even steeper price was being paid: concerts were being transformed into marketing opportunities for a vast network of products.

Enter New York-based SFX, which bought more than a hundred major concert venues nationwide and then began acquiring tours by major artists underwritten by national advertisers. In 1999, SFX had a hand in producing 60 percent of the two hundred biggest revenue-generating shows; the concert industry had its biggest year ever, with $1.5 billion in sales. The reason? Ticket prices had increased a whopping $10 a ticket, a 30 percent increase over 1998, to an average of $44.

With consolidation came pressure to produce profit. The multinationals were effectively run by their shareholders, who wanted a steady flow of quarterly returns to justify their investment. But in an industry supposedly devoted to creating a highly volatile and unpredictable product—music—this was hardly a sound strategy. How to reconcile the whims of creativity with the need for producing profit on a prescribed schedule?

"That's a big problem because Wall Street is looking for stability—quarter-over-quarter growth—in an industry that is dependent on artists," whose creativity can't be doled out in quarterly spurts, said Michael Nathanson, a New York investment counselor.

His words—delivered in 1999 at the South by Southwest music conference in Austin, Texas—brought silent "Amens" from a roomful of music executives, many of whom must've felt like they were attending their own wake. Each of their jobs was in jeopardy as longtime record labels were folded inside Godzilla-sized multinational corporations.

"Every day the corporation became more and more powerful inside of the company and suddenly it was our total focus, rather than the consumers, or the artists," said Howie Klein, a longtime old-guard executive who ran Reprise Records until he was deemed expendable in 2000. "And at a certain point, it wasn't even the shareholders we were serving, but the Wall Street analysts. We were there for the short-term needs of Wall Street, which is antithetical to the needs of a company that is supposedly founded on music. The industry was built on signing artists with a strong vision, and trusting that vision to do good work over a long period of time. Your job as a record company man was to help them realize that. [Former Warner executive] Lenny Waronker once told me, 'If it's a real artist, you can never go wrong.'"

Klein's view of the industry he once knew is highly romanticized. There were always plenty of bloodsuckers in it for a quick buck. But Klein had his priorities straight. In the eighties, he had started a fine independent label, 415 Records, in his San Francisco bedroom. When he was able to finally pay himself $100 a week, it was a big deal. "I'd never seen a three-figure salary before," he says now with a laugh. Later he was mentored by some of the best minds in the business, including Sire's Seymour Stein and Warner Bros.' Mo Ostin, and he'd help nurture the careers of artists and bands such as Romeo Void, Lou Reed, and Depeche Mode.

To a large extent, those artists built a career by being different. It was their idiosyncrasies that made them interesting and gave them staying power. But the industry of the late nineties didn't want idiosyncrasy. The long-range, career-building view was out. Instant pay-back was in. In the late nineties the acts dominating the charts were marketing triumphs more than creative ones: Britney Spears, 'N Sync, the Backstreet Boys, Ricky Martin, and Will Smith. They were the kind of telegenic, cross-format acts that could be sold quickly through a variety of mediums.

"There is so much pressure on the people at the label to generate profits that the music isn't allowed to breathe and artists aren't allowed to develop," said Moby, who had just signed a deal with an independent label, V2 Records, and released what would be his biggest record, *Play*.

"It makes bad creative sense, and it makes bad business sense. Under the circumstances of the music business right now, Bruce Springsteen and Fleetwood Mac would have been dropped long before they had a hit because their first few records didn't do that well. Prince's first few records were not huge sellers. So the major labels in the pursuit of quarterly profits are shooting themselves in the foot by putting out lowest-common-denominator music that works on the radio but doesn't generate any loyalty. There's no room for idiosyncratic artists. You have to fit the mold, and radio defines that mold. Right now, if you're not a teen pop star, an R&B artist, a hip-hop artist, a generic alternative rock band, or a female singer-songwriter, you might as well not even think about making records."

That mold was set largely by two monoliths: MTV and commercial radio. To get the word out about its latest music, record companies had to do business with both. And both were becoming increasingly narrow outlets for only the most heavily budgeted music. Though MTV launched in 1981 by playing music videos round the clock, it was now much like any other cable television station. Nonmusic programming dominated its schedule, and videos were confined to a select few superstars. Commercial radio was still the kingmaker as far as hits were concerned, and in the consolidation era it was all about centralized decision making. The playlists at commercial stations across the country became increasingly difficult to tell apart.

The trend was accelerated by the 1996 Telecommunications Act, the first major overhaul of U.S. telecommunications law since 1934. It eliminated most media ownership laws. Section 202 of the act, in particular, would prove to have a major impact on music; it required the Federal Communications Commission to eliminate "any provisions limiting the number of AM or FM broadcast stations which may be owned or controlled by one entity nationally."

That decree quickly led to the rapid near monopolization of the radio industry by a handful of corporations, most notably Clear Channel Communications. In 2000, the San Antonio, Texas-based radio conglomerate further expanded its interests by acquiring SFX. It was a move hailed by the company as a triumph of synergy that would enable Clear Channel stations to promote concerts in Clear Channel concert venues. By 2002, the company owned more than twelve hundred radio stations, covering 247 of the nation's top 250 markets, and controlled the biggest concert venues nationwide.

"I think that putting stations in the hands of people who are committed to public service and who are top broadcasters is good for the public," said Randy Michaels, the CEO of Clear Channel from 1999 to 2002. "When we were in the mom-and-pop era, half the radio stations were owned by people who were as interested in playing what they liked as opposed to really serving the public. When you have professional management, who is focused on serving the listener, then of necessity we are obsessed with what the public wants, and we work every day to give them what they want."

But the numbers told a different story. At the time Michaels was interviewed, Arbitron surveys showed that the average time spent listening to radio by consumers twelve years old and older had dropped 9 percent since deregulation. The young especially were tuning out: teenage listeners were down 11 percent, and listeners between the ages of eighteen and twenty-four had declined 10 percent. From 1998 to 2008, the average share of Americans listening to radio at any given time declined 14 percent.

Indeed, the real story was not that radio stations were trying to give listeners what they wanted so much as fretting about chasing them off with new, unfamiliar music. In this environment, taking chances on unproven artists supported by underfunded independent labels was considered bad business.

Clear Channel's Michaels argued that listeners didn't want adventuresome music chosen for reasons of taste; they wanted familiarity. His argument wasn't particularly new; corporations had always put making a buck ahead of aesthetics. But now that philosophy was integral to the corporate culture. "We all have nostalgia for the way things were, but radio is experiencing the same kind of consolidation that every other business has seen," Michaels said. "I love to visit small towns and eat at the mom-and-pop restaurants. But more and more it's getting harder to do, because there are a million choices and the chain restaurants are nudging out the mom-and-pop places. There are people, including me, who think that's bad. But people want to eat at the chain restaurant for some reason."

A handful of locally owned stations, such as WMPS in Memphis, were hanging tough by reviving some of the adventurousness and eclecticism of FM radio's free-form golden age in the seventies. WMPS's playlist blended Ben Harper, R.E.M., and Ani DiFranco with hard-core country acts (Rodney Crowell), Tex-Mex roots groups (Los Super Seven), and independent local artists.

"We play records based on gut instinct," said WMPS program director Alexandra Inzer, an adventurer marooned in an ocean of Clear Channel vanilla. "The problem with radio today is that corporations have paid a tremendous amount to buy these properties, so they can't afford to take a risk, which makes for really boring radio. Our approach is risky, and our audience is smaller because of it. But the ones who do like it stick with us. They have the station on for long periods because they're not going to hear the same songs over and over."

A similar philosophy prevailed at locally owned WWCD, an alternative rock station in Columbus, Ohio, that worked records by indie artists and local rockers into its rotation in a town where rigorously programmed playlists by Clear Channel and Infinity stations predominated.

"This conglomeration thing has totally ruined our industry," said WWCD program director Andy Davis. "I think people are listening to radio less and disappointed more when they do listen. We are fortunate to be owned by a local guy who loves music, who has a passion for new and progressive sounds.

But always lingering in the back of my mind is that the next quarter could be our last, because there aren't many of us left."

Indeed, no comment summarized commercial radio's attitude toward music more succinctly than one made by Clear Channel chairman Lowry Mays to *Fortune* magazine in 2003.

"We're not in the business of providing news and information," he said. "We're not in the business of providing well-researched music. We're simply in the business of selling our customers products."

Panos Panay

Rethinking Music: The Future of Making Money as a Performing Musician

I. Introduction

If you take to heart what's been written in the press about the "music business" of the past 10 years, you may quickly conclude that there's not much hope left for 21st-century performers.

The record business is in free fall, with U.S. sales and licensing revenues plummeting by half in the past decade.[1] Rampant piracy and a disinterested and disaffected public have savaged reliable artist income from record sales. Young consumers are reportedly turning their backs on emerging artists, preferring to "steal" music rather than pay for it. (According to a recent study by the University of Hertfordshire, 61% of consumers aged 14–24 admit to illegally downloading music.[2]) Radiohead is giving away its albums, previously reliable high sellers like Bruce Springsteen and U2 have peaked commercially, and, for the first time since the SoundScan era began in 1991, the number one selling album on the Billboard Top 200 charts sold just 40,000 units (Amos Lee with "Mission Bell"; by contrast, in its heyday in 2000, 'N Sync sold over 2.4 million units with "No Strings Attached").

At first glance, things don't look much better on the live music side. The world's largest concert promoter, Live Nation, is bleeding money, reporting that its 2010 fourth quarter revenue declined by 2%; ticket sales were down by 10%; cash flow dropped 15%; and quarterly losses more than doubled to $86 million.[3] More than 40% of its ticket inventory remained unsold last summer.[4] And, if you take a quick look at the average age of touring concert performers—with the one exception being Lady Gaga—you'd be forgiven if you thought that the conceit business' better days are behind it. This is the list of the highest-grossing 10 tours of the last 10 years: Rolling Stones, U2, AC/DC, Madonna, U2 (again), The Police, Celine Dion, Cher, Bruce Springsteen, Bon Jovi.[5] (No, the last ever concert tour did not take place in 1986.)

And radio? Don't ask. Although 2010 provided an unexpected bright spot with a slight revenue uptick, listenership is down, audiences are more and more fragmented, advertisers are, accordingly, harder to attract, and, if you ask most listeners, radio has stopped being their primary source of new music discovery and its pop culture relevance is quickly evaporating.

A closer look, however, reveals that the music business is not so much imploding as—like any other industry that has been around for more than a dozen years—it is *evolving*. Consumer tastes are changing, and record labels and radio are no longer the cultural arbitrators they once were. Music listeners are moving away from the mass-produced music consumption habits of the broadcast media to the more tailored and personalized experiences of the social media age. Just as importantly, artists are migrating away from the mass-market revenue model of the broadcast era to the *mass of niches* model of the new, Internet era. They are not antagonizing their customers (as the record industry did with its lawsuits), but they are collaborating and dialoguing with them in new and, sometimes, surprising ways.

As the founder of Sonicbids, the leading matchmaking site for bands and people who book or license music, with a membership of 300,000 bands and 25,000 music promoters, I have a front row seat to all these changes and shifts. I launched the site almost exactly 10 years ago out of my apartment with the express mission of empowering a new class of artists (we call it the *Artistic Middle Class*) by helping every band get a gig and by giving artists the tools they need to develop a sustainable audience.

Perhaps what's been most amazing has been the way that the music performer community has adjusted to all of these changes both by seizing opportunities that did not exist a few years ago as well as by adapting to the new landscape of the industry—and by adopting and co-opting revenue generating ideas from other industries and applying them to their trade. Far from dying, the music business is alive and ever resourceful in finding new ways of making money and evolving.

II. The New Live Music Business (Live Performance Revenue)

Yes, the traditional concert business is having a hard time adjusting to the new realities of less disposable consumer incomes, smaller (or non-existent) record label tour funding, lack of sustainable new megastars and the aging demographic of its best sellers. But "live music" is not just what's performed in stadiums and arenas—and it doesn't always entail a show that involves a consumer buying a ticket.

Last year on Sonicbids, nearly 80,000 gigs were booked between artists and promoters that would traditionally fall "under the radar." (Internal estimates put the total number of U.S. live gigs at close to 8 million). This is a vibrant and expanding list of people that are taking advantage of new tools such as Sonicbids to bring live music to their consumers—and often not as the "end product," but as a means to another experience. This includes bars, coffee houses, art galleries, cruise ships, wineries, amusement parks, breweries, restaurants, cinema lobbies, ski resorts, corporate retreats, museums, colleges, street fairs, and countless others. It's a nearly $10 billion market that's expanding at a rate of 11% a year.[6] You just won't read about it in any mainstream press.

According to the National Association of Campus Activities, U.S. colleges eager to entertain their student bodies with live music spend nearly $250 million each year. Most of this goes to artists that generally earn less than $3,000 per show (read: members of the middle class).[7] The UK Performing Rights Society (PRS) has recently published a study that shows that the live music festival sector is the most quickly growing sector of the music business. This is also evident by the fact that even in the worst recession in a generation, festivals such as Coachella, South By Southwest, and Bonnaroo have been routinely selling out. The oft-derided wedding band market has grown. Nearly 83% of Sonicbids' bands indicate that they make at least part of their annual income from playing private events such as weddings and increasingly do so by playing original music instead of "cover" songs.

The live music business is not dead. It's simply fragmenting, evolving, becoming more organic, less mass produced, and more homegrown.

III. Consumer Brands: The New Arts Patrons (Sponsorship and Marketing Revenue)

As long as there's been art, there have been wealthy patrons that have sponsored artists. Many of the world's classic masters would have never seen their work produced had it not been for some rich family who funded their creativity. Van Gogh, Mozart, Da Vinci—all had wealthy backers.

In the modern music business, these patrons were once major record labels that plucked artists from obscurity and made them into mass-consumed mega stars. Labels funded artists' time in the studio (production), paid money to distribute their records in retail stores (distribution), paid money for promotion through outlets like radio and TV (promotion), and hired managers, agents, and publishers to help maximize each artist's income potential (professional connections). In return, they kept the lion's share of each artist's income and held the keys to the kingdom called "viable music career."

With the advent of the Internet and the **shift of consumer tastes from mass to niche,** labels have experienced a steady erosion of their incomes over the past eight years. Consequently they have ceased playing the traditional role of art patron for up and coming musical artists.

In their place—as both art patrons as well as popular taste curators—major (and niche) consumer brands have stepped in and figured out that **music can help them sell whatever product they produce** (coffee, electronics, carbonated beverages, clothing, video games, hand bags, financial services, insurance, etc.). In North America alone total sponsorship spending by consumer brands for such marketing programs was projected to exceed $1 billion in 2010, almost double what it was six years earlier.[8]

Even more promising for emerging artists, there's been a steady shift of this sponsorship money in recent years towards more "niche" artists who do not yet have an entrenched public image like, say, Taylor Swift or Lady Gaga. Why? Because more and more companies are realizing that the **coveted young consumers coming of age today demand authenticity from the brands they will endorse—a trait most associated with independent, non-major** label artists. It doesn't hurt that these artists tend to be less expensive and carry less PR risks than artists with large public profiles. Given that social media is the venue that most young consumers are spending their time on, marketers are eager to engage these customers on this turf, and no one knows social media marketing better than emerging artists—their careers literally depend on it.

In the past couple of years, large consumer brands ranging from Diesel, Converse, Gap, Ford, and Levis to more niche ones like Midas, Zippo, Jagermeister, and JanSport have all spent millions creating programs that use emerging music as the primary marketing means of their wares to social media. Just as importantly, artists are showing an increased eagerness to work with these brands to get their music out to the public—a sharp contrast to the cries of "sell out" that accompanied such acts in the '70s, '80s, and all through the '90s.

Could it be that these brands with all of their marketing muscle and deep pockets are becoming the new record labels? I think so.

IV. Fan as Collaborator (Fan-Generated and Merchandise Revenue)

I was talking with a friend of mine from MTV recently, and we were chatting about how MTV no longer plays music videos. He turned and said something that never occurred to me: "No one who watches MTV today complains about music videos because no one under the age of 30 even remembers MTV playing music videos. People today turn to MTV to watch *Jersey Shore* and *Skins and 16 & Pregnant* and discover new music through these programs. MTV does not age with its audience, it adapts to its audience which is forever the young." I think the same way about "music piracy." The music industry is trying to age its morals with its original audience when our paradigm should shift to the new audience's preferred ways of engagement with music.

Much fuss has been made by the industry about the "new music fan." The 16-year-old who refuses to pay for music, who routinely downloads gigabytes of "illegal" music, the one who spends hours and hours on bit torrent sites—the music thief, the pirate, the one who if you can't educate through public service announcements, you go after with a legal sledge hammer and sue them out of existence.

But the music fan that most emerging artists see is not an antagonist. They're a collaborator. Over the past two years, more and more artists like Amanda Palmer, Kristin Hersch, and Kat Parsons are using fan-funding sites to finance their records, tours, and other marketing activities. Even in 2001, eighties rockers Marillion funded their album *Anoraknophobia* with 12,674 pre-orders from fans.[9] More recently, Jill Sobule raised some $80,000 from about 500 fans to record her album *California Years*.[10]

Sites like Pledge Music and Kickstarter and even on-demand merchandise sites like Zazzle and Café Press are helping artists raise money not in the form of donations, but by selling album credits, unique experiences, exclusive concert tickets, one-of-a-kind merchandise, and more. These are not acts of charity, but acts of collaboration, co-creation, and co-development. Very much the way that young, urban consumers are turning to Community Supported Agriculture programs that help support local farmers, young music fans are supporting their favorite artists not necessarily by buying records and downloading "legal" music, but by contributing to these artists in very different ways.

The new music consumer's relationship with music is not declining. It's changing. And smart artists are taking advantage of it and leading the way in finding ways to monetize it.

V. And Music Licensing for All (Licensing and Performing Rights Revenue)

Each year, MTV contributes to the market for emerging artists by integrating them into its programing. True, MTV pays little for this content, but having your song aired in a program like Jersey Shore that reaches over 8 million viewers a week can reap all kinds of benefits—not to mention lucrative performing rights revenues. ASCAP alone has distributed over $2.5 billion in performance rights revenue to its members over the last three years.[11] At Sonicbids, last year we identified over $4 million in unclaimed royalties that we distributed to some 10,000 of artist members through SoundExchange, the non-profit performance royalties collection agency.

More encouragingly, even large advertisers like Coca Cola, Dell, JC Penney, and Chevrolet are turning to new artists to find and license music for their commercials. (Sonicbids artist Temper Trap's song "Sweet Disposition" is the featured song in the Diet Coke commercials aired during the recent Academy Awards broadcast.)

And this does not stop at advertising. Recent licensees of up-and-coming artists without major label affiliations include video game publishers like Electronic Arts and Activision; toy companies like Fisher-Price and Mattel; specialized music broadcast companies like Cinema Sounds who broadcasts music in 15,000 US movie theater lobbies; airlines like Delta Airlines and Virgin who are looking for unique content for their seatback channels; and movie studios like Paramount and Universal.

Music consumption is not curtailed. It's shifting venues from the record store to your TV set—or your next elevator ride.

VI. The New Entrepreneurs (Advertising and Subscriptions Revenue)

In the last two years, companies like Pandora, Spotify, Rdio, MOG, and countless others have raised over $200 million from investors with the promise of generating money primarily by offering music listening for free in exchange for advertising and subscription revenue.[12]

Early numbers are encouraging: According to *Digital Music News*, Spotify has over 650,000 paid subscribers, approximately four percent of its total listener base.[13] Pandora has over 80 million listeners and just filed for its initial public offering expecting to raise some $100 million.[14] and even companies like Shazam boast a user base of more than 100 million.[15]

These are early days of course, and it's still unclear how much of this revenue will find its way back to the actual performer and what form that revenue will take. (Regional legislation surrounding this matter is very much evolving and varying by continent and country.) One thing is inevitable: whatever industry attracts money and talent (sadly, that is no longer the record business), inevitably will succeed. And there's a lot of money and a lot of people betting that the model of online, ad supported radio will succeed. I would not bet against it.

Amidst all the noise, we tend to forget that the modern music business has only existed for less than 60 years, propelled in earnest first by Frank Sinatra, taken to the next level by Elvis Presley and then the Beatles, and culminating in the mega stadium tours of the '70s and '80s and the blockbuster record sellers of the '90s.

In most industries, it is rare that a new form of innovation and revenue generation will completely supplant the incumbents. In the transportation business, for example, ships, railroads, automobiles, and airlines all happily coexist. The same holds in the entertainment business with theater, radio, film, TV, and now the Internet all overlapping. In each of these examples, there have been clear losers (the horse and buggy for example, or the VCR and soon the DVD player), but the basic, underlying need for, respectively, movement and entertainment has ushered in new innovations by new breeds of entrepreneurs that led to the creation of new sub-industries and, very importantly, new ways of wealth creation.

The music business is at a similar moment and has a similar opportunity for reinvention.

Endnotes

1. David Goldman, *Music's Lost Decade: Sales Cut in Half,* CNNMONEY.COM (Feb. 3, 2010), http://money.cnn.com/2010/02/02/news/companies/napster_music_industry/.

2. Press Release, University of Hertfordshire, What does the MySpace Generation really want? (June 17, 2008), *available at* www.herts.ac.uk/news-and-events/latest-news/MySpace-Generation.cfm.

3. Ben Sisario, *Weak Ticket Sales Contribute to Large Loss for Live Nation,* N.Y. TIMES, Feb. 28, 2011, at B8, *available at* www.nytimes.com/2011/03/01/business/media/011ive.html.

4. Ray Waddell, *Live Nation Drops Service Fees for June,* BILLBOARD.BIZ (June 1, 2010), www.billboard.biz/bbbiz/content_display/industry/news/e3i9a9ec43069ab4f97ca78c8feOf683797.

5. *List of Highest-Grossing Concert Tours,* WIKIPEDIA (April 4, 2011), http://en.wikipedia.org/wiki/List_of_highest-grossing_concert_tours.

6. Sonicbids Corporation internal research compiled from number from sources including the U.S. Census Bureau, the American Federation of Musicians, The PRS, National Association of Campus Activies, and others.

7. NATIONAL ASSOCIATION OF CAMPUS ACTIVITIES, NACA SELF STUDY (Jan. 7, 2011).

8. Damian Kulash Jr., *The New Rock-Star Paradigm,* THE WALL STREET JOURNAL (Dec. 17, 2010) at D1, *available at* http://online.wsj.com/article/SB10001424052748703727804576017592259031536.html.

9. *Anoraknaphobia,* MARILLION.COM, http://marillion.com/music/albums/anorak.htm (Last visisted April 6, 2011).

10. James Reed, *Lighters Down, Checkbooks Up,* THE BOSTON GLOBE (April 12, 2010) at Living Arts 1, *available at* www.boston.com/ae/music/articles/2009/04/12/lighters_down_checkbooks_up.

11. Press Release, American Society of Composers, Authors, and Publishers, ASCAP 2010 Financial Results Reflect the Challenging Music Licensing Environment (March 31, 2011), *available at* www.ascap.com/press/2011/0331_Financial_Results.aspx.

12. Spotify recently raised $100 million. Michael Arrington, *DST About to Lead Huge Spotify Funding,* TECHCRUNCH (Feb. 20, 2011), http://techcrunch.com/2011/02/20/dst-about-to-lead-huge-spotify-funding/. In June 2010 Pandora raised an unspecified fifth round of funding on top of an existing $56.3 million. David Kaplan, *Pandora Raises Its Fifth Funding Round,* PAIDCONTENT.ORG (June 2, 2010), http://paidcontent.org/article/419-pandora-raises-its-fifth-funding-round-/. Rdio recently raised $17.5. Robin Wauters, *Exclusive: Social Music Startup Rdio Raises $17.5 Million, Adds Rob Cavallo To Board,* TECHCRUNCH (Feb. 3, 2011), http://techcrunch.com/2011/02/03/exclusive-social-music-startup-rdio-raises-17-5-million-adds-rob-cavallo-to-board/. Last year MOG brought its funding to over $21 million. Paul Bonanos, *MOG Takes in $9.5M More in Advance of Mobile Launch,* GIGAOM (Feb. 25, 2010), http://gigaom.com/2010/02/25/mog-takes-9-5-million-more-in-advance-of-mobile-launch/.

13. Alexandra Osorio, *Spotify's Paying Subscribers Up 160% This Year...,* DIGITAL MUSIC NEWS (Nov. 19, 2010), www.digitalmusicnews.eom/stories/l11910spotify160.

14. Ryan Kim, *Pandora Files for IPO to Keep the Music Playing,* GIGAOM (Feb. 11, 2011), http://gigaom.com/2011/02/11/pandora-files-for-ipo-to-keep-the-music-playing/.

15. Press Release, Shazam, Shazam Surpasses 100 Million Users and Becomes One of World's Leading Discovery Services (Dec. 6, 2010), *available at* www.shazam.com/music/web/newsdetail.html?nid=NEWS20101206124027.

EXPLORING THE ISSUE

Did Consolidation of the Music Industry Hurt Music Distribution?

Critical Thinking and Reflection

1. Have you observed any other media industries that have undergone, or are undergoing tremendous changes in terms of how they conduct business? In addition to the recording industry, you might want to examine the electronic print (e-book) market, and the recent changes to the DVD and video downloading business of Netflix.
2. Interestingly, with less emphasis on mass media and more on individual choice of media, including distribution systems that provide choice (like cable TV), consumers now pay more for media product than they did in the past, when advertising models supported much of a media industry's costs. Do you think that this shift in payment from advertising to consumer payments is good for the consumer, the industry, and the economy?
3. Where are the jobs in the media industries today? Does a person have to be more realistic and open-minded about the potential for a career in any one of the current media industries? We hope that whatever your choices of career are, you should keep your eyes open to the changing business and economic landscape to be ready for the inevitable changes we can expect.

Is There Common Ground?

In recent years, we've seen many businesses fail, or experience downsizing, because of shifting consumer tastes, different distribution systems that use more personal technologies, and industries that are attempting to accommodate these changes. The "mom and pop" stores are being relegated to history, and even big box retailers are making choices about what products to have available, and which to eliminate. It's hard to find a traditional "music" store in many communities, and big box retailers like WalMart carry only products that support the founder's ideology. "Hit" records are almost a rare commodity now, as the music industry focuses on "micro-hits" and local distribution. Cloud technology is now heralded as the way we will store all of our media content—particularly music—in the virtual cloud, only to download it on demand, wherever we are. These changes hit the music industry quickly, and we've seen evidence that other media industries are also struggling to find the best methods of meeting consumer choice. Netflix mounted an alternative distribution form called Quickster, which promised to download digital content direct to someone's home computer or Internet TV, only to rescind the program weeks after implementation because consumers began to cancel their subscriptions rather than pay for two services that basically duplicated the same end result—the accessing of movies through Netflix. These business models and others will continue to be challenged in the future, and we will probably see many firms come and go. Who would have thought that such dynamos as Blockbuster Video, or Borders Bookstores would go bankrupt? These examples show that in the business world of media, we have to expect massive changes in the future.

Additional Resources

Billboard magazine is a trade magazine for the radio, recording, and music industries:

www.info.com/billboards%20magazine?cb=23&cmp=4619&golid=
CNrTopCKgKwCFYSK4Aod61DvVw

The Web site for the Recording Industry Association of America (RIAA) is:

www.riaa.com/

The Electronic Frontier Foundation has taken a perspective on piracy:

www.eff.org/deeplinks/2011/03/It-s-time-recording-
industry-stop-blaming-piracy

The Web site, Good Technology has an interesting animated feature that allows you to see the demise of the recording industry over 30 years, as portrayed on a computer graphic:

www.good.is/post/intermission-watch-the-recording-
industry-s-demise-in-30-seconds/

ISSUE 14

Should Newspapers Shut Down Their Presses?

YES: Clay Shirky, from "Newspapers and Thinking the Unthinkable," www.shirky.com/weblog/2009/03/newspapers-and-thinking-the-unthinkable/

NO: Paul Farhi, from "A Bright Future for Newspapers," *American Journalism Review* (June/July 2005)

Learning Outcomes

After reading this issue, you should be able to:

- Identify the changes that threaten the newspaper business model.
- Compare and contrast alternative funding models for the press.
- Evaluate the importance of the unique competitive advantages of newspapers.

ISSUE SUMMARY

YES: Clay Shirky argues that the old economies of newspapers are destroyed in the digital age. This is a revolution similar to that which occurred with the invention of the printing press. No one knows what the future will hold, but we can only hope that journalism is not lost with the demise of newspapers.

NO: All news media are facing challenges in these difficult economic times. Paul Farhi, a *Washington Post* staff writer, argues that newspapers have unique competitive advantages that should assure that the worst case won't happen.

Are newspapers dying? The press is filled with reports of calamity. The *Rocky Mountain News*, a daily Denver newspaper, shut down in February 2009. *The Christian Science Monitor* ceased daily print publication in March 2009,

moving to an online daily offering. *The State of the News Media 2009* (www
.stateofthemedia.org/2009) reports a drop from 49.3 billion in advertising revenue in 2006 to 38 billion in 2008—a decline of 23 percent. These losses come
from loss of classifieds to online competitors such as craigslist and the loss
of lucrative employment, auto, and retail advertising. Yet despite these dire
figures, the majority of newspapers remain profitable—although not nearly as
profitable as previously. High debt loads are one cause of financial problems
for some papers. But the longer-term issue is whether the traditional business
model of printed newspapers delivered to homes will continue to be viable.

At one level, the question is simple. Which is the better idea: to print
papers using expensive ink and paper and to transport them daily to people's homes at substantial delivery costs, or to put that information online for
virtually no reproduction or distribution costs? Clay Shirky thinks the unthinkable in his blog. Newspapers anticipated the transformational nature of the
Internet, but they could not find a business model to profit from it. Would it
be walled content, micropayments, nonprofit status? Shirky compares this to
the revolution wrought by the printing press. What happens now will be as
chaotic and unanticipated as the events following Gutenberg's invention.

Farhi does not see such a bleak future. Certainly circulation is down,
advertising has dropped, and a heavy debt load threatens some newspaper
companies. But Farhi challenges the reader to compare the newspaper to other
traditional media, which are experiencing similar problems. And new media
are not the panacea, failing even now to advance a profitable business plan for
news. Newspapers carry an important tradition of localism and public service,
and typically field the largest reporting staffs within their area. They have a
tradition of profitability fueled by attractive numbers, the demographics of
their readers, and the commitment of those readers to the product. Are newspapers troubled? Yes, but they have every resource to respond to the current
situation and continue into the coming decades.

The economics of this prediction haven't changed, according to Alan
Mutter, a self-styled Newsosaur who explains "why it would be suicidal for
any reasonably profitable publisher to stop its presses." (See "Why Newspapers Can't Stop the Presses," *Reflections of a Newsosaur*, February 1–4, 2009:
newsosaur.blogspot.com/2009/02/why-newspapers-cant-stop-presses.html.) He offers
a complex economic analysis of the flaws in plans to stop the presses. Because
newspapers generate about 90 percent of revenue from print advertising,
he argues that transitioning to Web-only would produce at best 10 percent of
the cash generated by the print-online model. From such drastic reductions in
revenue, the only option would be to drastically reduce the remaining major
expense center—the newsroom. His analysis challenges easy assumptions that
the move to Web-only papers would be easy and would generate savings to
cancel lost revenue.

If news content is available online, will we be willing to pay for it? The
outlook seems dim: We are used to free access to information online. One suggestion is micropayments, which would require the payment of small amounts
of money to read content online. Some have dubbed it an iTunes or PayPal
model. Free access to some stories or to limited content would be available; to

follow the story in more depth a small amount would be charged for access. For more information, see the Nieman Journalism Lab Web site, which defines their efforts as a collaborative attempt to figure out how quality journalism can survive and thrive in the Internet age. Go to www.niemanlab.org and search for "Micropayments for news: The Holy Grail or just a dangerous delusion?" Spend some time checking out the many other issues that are discussed.

Related to micropayments are suggestions about the use of walled or paid content. Generally speaking, this would involve purchasing a subscription that would allow access to any material behind the wall. *The Wall Street Journal* and *The New York Times* have been somewhat successful with this model. The PBS Mediashift site discusses many aspects of changing media in the digital age. Go to www.pbs.org/mediashift and search for "The Great Debate on Micropayments and Paid Content." Again, it is worth spending some time looking at the variety of topics discussed. For journalism and mass communication majors, there is an excellent section on education. A related suggestion is that readers may be willing to give up the printed paper if they can receive that material on a portable reading device such as a Kindle or an iPad. This retains the portability of a paper and still requires readers to subscribe. There are a number of studies in progress, examining reader responses to news on these devices. See *The New York Times* for an interesting article on whether the Kindle can save newspapers at www.nytimes.com (type "Can a supersize Kindle save newpapers" in their search area).

Reorganizing newspapers into nonprofit corporations is being widely discussed. It remains a controversial suggestion with significant concerns about the independence of newspapers in this organizational configuration. Go to www.newyorker.com to read Steve Coll's blog on "Nonprofit Newspapers." Coll argues that nonprofit status can be the future because it will allow the independent journalism that commercial pressure does not support. Guensburg in *American Journalism Review* (February/March 2008) examines both sides of the "Nonprofit News" argument.

You will notice that several issues are related in this volume. Issue 8 asks how journalistic practice will change in the digital age. The selections in this issue ask us to consider dramatic changes in how newspapers will operate. All share a similar concern with the future of newspapers and journalism in the digital age. Before you delve into these selections, ask yourself a question that is truly unthinkable to all of the authors in the issues noted above: If newspapers collapse, would quality journalism die?

YES

Clay Shirky

Newspapers and Thinking the Unthinkable

Back in 1993, the Knight-Ridder newspaper chain began investigating piracy of Dave Barry's popular column, which was published by *The Miami Herald* and syndicated widely. In the course of tracking down the sources of unlicensed distribution, they found many things, including the copying of his column to alt.fan.dave_barry on usenet; a 2000-person strong mailing list also reading pirated versions; and a teenager in the Midwest who was doing some of the copying himself, because he loved Barry's work so much he wanted everybody to be able to read it.

One of the people I was hanging around with online back then was Gordy Thompson, who managed internet services at *The New York Times:* I remember Thompson saying something to the effect of "When a 14 year old kid can blow up your business in his spare time, not because he hates you but because he loves you, then you got a problem." I think about that conversation a lot these days.

The problem newspapers face isn't that they didn't see the internet coming. They not only saw it miles off; they figured out early on that they needed a plan to deal with it, and during the early 90s they came up with not just one plan but several. One was to partner with companies like America Online, a fast-growing subscription service that was less chaotic than the open internet. Another plan was to educate the public about the behaviors required of them by copyright law. New payment models such as micropayments were proposed. Alternatively, they could pursue the profit margins enjoyed by radio and TV, if they became purely ad-supported. Still another plan was to convince tech firms to make their hardware and software less capable of sharing, or to partner with the businesses running data networks to achieve the same goal. Then there was the nuclear option: sue copyright infringers directly, making an example of them.

As these ideas were articulated, there was intense debate about the merits of various scenarios. Would DRM or walled gardens work better? Shouldn't we try a carrot-and-stick approach, with education *and* prosecution? And so on. In all this conversation, there was one scenario that was widely regarded as unthinkable, a scenario that didn't get much discussion in the nation's newsrooms, for the obvious reason.

The unthinkable scenario unfolded something like this: The ability to share content wouldn't shrink; it would grow. Walled gardens would prove unpopular. Digital advertising would reduce inefficiencies, and therefore profits. Dislike of micropayments would prevent widespread use. People would resist being educated to act against their own desires. Old habits of advertisers and readers would not transfer online. Even ferocious litigation would be inadequate to constrain massive, sustained law-breaking. (Prohibition redux.) Hardware and software vendors would not regard copyright holders as allies, nor would they regard customers as enemies. DRM's requirement that the attacker be allowed to decode the content would be an insuperable flaw. And, per Thompson, suing people who love something so much they want to share it would piss them off.

Revolutions create a curious inversion of perception. In ordinary times, people who do no more than describe the world around them are seen as pragmatists, while those who imagine fabulous alternative futures are viewed as radicals. The last couple of decades haven't been ordinary, however. Inside the papers, the pragmatists were the ones simply looking out the window and noticing that the real world was increasingly resembling the unthinkable scenario. These people were treated as if they were barking mad. Meanwhile the people spinning visions of popular walled gardens and enthusiastic micropayment adoption, visions unsupported by reality, were regarded not as charlatans but saviors.

When reality is labeled unthinkable, it creates a kind of sickness in an industry. Leadership becomes faith-based, while employees who have the temerity to suggest that what seems to be happening is in fact happening are herded into Innovation Departments, where they can be ignored *en masse*. This shunting aside of the realists in favor of the fabulists has different effects on different industries at different times. One of the effects on the newspapers is that many of their most passionate defenders are unable, even now, to plan for a world in which the industry they knew is visibly going away.

❧❦❧

The curious thing about the various plans hatched in the '90s is that they were, at base, all the same plan: "Here's how we're going to preserve the old forms of organization in a world of cheap perfect copies!" The details differed, but the core assumption behind all imagined outcomes (save the unthinkable one) was that the organizational form of the newspaper, as a general-purpose vehicle for publishing a variety of news and opinion, was basically sound, and only needed a digital facelift. As a result, the conversation has degenerated into the enthusiastic grasping at straws, pursued by skeptical responses.

"*The Wall Street Journal* has a paywall, so we can too!" (Financial information is one of the few kinds of information whose recipients don't want to share.) "Micropayments work for iTunes, so they will work for us!" (Micropayments work only where the provider can avoid competitive business models.) "*The New York Times* should charge for content!" (They've tried, with QPass and later TimesSelect.) *"Cook's Illustrated* and *Consumer Reports* are doing fine on subscriptions!" (Those publications forgo ad revenues; users are paying not just for content but for unimpeachability.) "We'll form a cartel!" (. . . and hand a competitive advantage to every ad-supported media firm in the world.)

Round and round this goes, with the people committed to saving newspapers demanding to know "If the old model is broken, what will work in its place?" To which the answer is: Nothing. Nothing will work. There is no general model for newspapers to replace the one the internet just broke.

With the old economics destroyed, organizational forms perfected for industrial production have to be replaced with structures optimized for digital data. It makes increasingly less sense even to talk about a publishing industry, because the core problem publishing solves—the incredible difficulty, complexity, and expense of making something available to the public—has stopped being a problem.

Elizabeth Eisenstein's magisterial treatment of Gutenberg's invention, *The Printing Press as an Agent of Change*, opens with a recounting of her research into the early history of the printing press. She was able to find many descriptions of life in the early 1400s, the era before movable type. Literacy was limited, the Catholic Church was the pan-European political force, Mass was in Latin, and the average book was the Bible. She was also able to find endless descriptions of life in the late 1500s, after Gutenberg's invention had started to spread. Literacy was on the rise, as were books written in contemporary languages, Copernicus had published his epochal work on astronomy, and Martin Luther's use of the press to reform the Church was upending both religious and political stability.

What Eisenstein focused on, though, was how many historians ignored the transition from one era to the other. To describe the world before or after the spread of print was child's play; those dates were safely distanced from upheaval. But what was happening in 1500? The hard question Eisenstein's book asks is "How did we get from the world before the printing press to the world after it? What was the revolution *itself* like?"

Chaotic, as it turns out. The Bible was translated into local languages; was this an educational boon or the work of the devil? Erotic novels appeared, prompting the same set of questions. Copies of Aristotle and Galen circulated widely, but direct encounter with the relevant texts revealed that the two sources clashed, tarnishing faith in the Ancients. As novelty spread, old institutions seemed exhausted while new ones seemed untrustworthy; as a result, people almost literally didn't know what to think. If you can't trust Aristotle, who can you trust?

During the wrenching transition to print, experiments were only revealed in retrospect to be turning points. Aldus Manutius, the Venetian printer and publisher, invented the smaller *octavo* volume along with italic type. What seemed like a minor change—take a book and shrink it—was in retrospect a key innovation in the democratization of the printed word. As books became cheaper, more portable, and therefore more desirable, they expanded the market for all publishers, heightening the value of literacy still further.

That is what real revolutions are like. The old stuff gets broken faster than the new stuff is put in its place. The importance of any given experiment isn't apparent at the moment it appears; big changes stall, small changes spread. Even the revolutionaries can't predict what will happen. Agreements on all sides that core institutions must be protected are rendered meaningless by the very people doing the agreeing. (Luther and the Church both insisted, for years, that whatever else happened, no one was talking about a schism.) Ancient social bargains, once disrupted, can neither be mended nor quickly replaced, since any such bargain takes decades to solidify.

And so it is today. When someone demands to know how we are going to replace newspapers, they are really demanding to be told that we are not living through a revolution. They are demanding to be told that old systems won't break before new systems are in place. They are demanding to be told that ancient social bargains aren't in peril, that core institutions will be spared, that new methods of spreading information will improve previous practice rather than upending it. They are demanding to be lied to.

There are fewer and fewer people who can convincingly tell such a lie.

⋅◈⋅

If you want to know why newspapers are in such trouble, the most salient fact is this: Printing presses are terrifically expensive to set up and to run. This bit of economics, normal since Gutenberg, limits competition while creating positive returns to scale for the press owner, a happy pair of economic effects that feed on each other. In a notional town with two perfectly balanced newspapers, one paper would eventually generate some small advantage—a breaking story, a key interview—at which point both advertisers and readers would come to prefer it, however slightly. That paper would in turn find it easier to capture the next dollar of advertising, at lower expense, than the competition. This would increase its dominance, which would further deepen those preferences, repeat chorus. The end result is either geographic or demographic segmentation among papers, or one paper holding a monopoly on the local mainstream audience.

For a long time, longer than anyone in the newspaper business has been alive in fact, print journalism has been intertwined with these economics. The expense of printing created an environment where Wal-Mart was willing to subsidize the Baghdad bureau. This wasn't because of any deep link between advertising and reporting, nor was it about any real desire on the part of Wal-Mart to have their marketing budget go to international correspondents. It was just an accident. Advertisers had little choice other than to have their money used that way, since they didn't really have any other vehicle for display ads.

The old difficulties and costs of printing forced everyone doing it into a similar set of organizational models; it was this similarity that made us regard

Daily Racing Form and *L'Osservatore Romano* as being in the same business. That the relationship between advertisers, publishers, and journalists has been ratified by a century of cultural practice doesn't make it any less accidental.

The competition-deflecting effects of printing cost got destroyed by the internet, where everyone pays for the infrastructure, and then everyone gets to use it. And when Wal-Mart, and the local Maytag dealer, and the law firm hiring a secretary, and that kid down the block selling his bike, were all able to use that infrastructure to get out of their old relationship with the publisher, they did. They'd never really signed up to fund the Baghdad bureau anyway.

⋖⊙⋗

Print media does much of society's heavy journalistic lifting, from flooding the zone—covering every angle of a huge story—to the daily grind of attending the City Council meeting, just in case. This coverage creates benefits even for people who aren't newspaper readers, because the work of print journalists is used by everyone from politicians to district attorneys to talk radio hosts to bloggers. The newspaper people often note that newspapers benefit society as a whole. This is true, but irrelevant to the problem at hand; "You're gonna miss us when we're gone!" has never been much of a business model. So who covers all that news if some significant fraction of the currently employed newspaper people lose their jobs?

I don't know. Nobody knows. We're collectively living through 1500, when it's easier to see what's broken than what will replace it. The internet turns 40 this fall. Access by the general public is less than half that age. Web use, as a normal part of life for a majority of the developed world, is less than half *that* age. We just got here. Even the revolutionaries can't predict what will happen.

Imagine, in 1996, asking some net-savvy soul to expound on the potential of craigslist, then a year old and not yet incorporated. The answer you'd almost certainly have gotten would be extrapolation: "Mailing lists can be powerful tools," "Social effects are intertwining with digital networks," blah blah blah. What no one would have told you, could have told you, was what actually happened: craigslist became a critical piece of infrastructure. Not the idea of craigslist, or the business model, or even the software driving it. Craigslist itself spread to cover hundreds of cities and has become a part of public consciousness about what is now possible. Experiments are only revealed in retrospect to be turning points.

In craigslist's gradual shift from 'interesting if minor' to 'essential and transformative,' there is one possible answer to the question "If the old model is broken, what will work in its place?" The answer is: Nothing will work, but everything might. Now is the time for experiments, lots and lots of experiments, each of which will seem as minor at launch as craigslist did, as Wikipedia did, as *octavo* volumes did.

Journalism has always been subsidized. Sometimes it's been Wal-Mart and the kid with the bike. Sometimes it's been Richard Mellon Scaife. Increasingly, it's you and me, donating our time. The list of models that are obviously working today, like *Consumer Reports* and NPR, like ProPublica and WikiLeaks, can't be expanded to cover any general case, but then nothing is going to cover the general case.

Society doesn't need newspapers. What we need is journalism. For a century, the imperatives to strengthen journalism and to strengthen newspapers have been so tightly wound as to be indistinguishable. That's been a fine accident to have, but when that accident stops, as it is stopping before our eyes, we're going to need lots of other ways to strengthen journalism instead.

When we shift our attention from 'save newspapers' to 'save society,' the imperative changes from 'preserve the current institutions' to 'do whatever works.' And what works today isn't the same as what used to work.

We don't know who the Aldus Manutius of the current age is. It could be Craig Newmark, or Caterina Fake. It could be Martin Nisenholtz, or Emily Bell. It could be some 19 year old kid few of us have heard of, working on something we won't recognize as vital until a decade hence. Any experiment, though, designed to provide new models for journalism is going to be an improvement over hiding from the real, especially in a year when, for many papers, the unthinkable future is already in the past.

For the next few decades, journalism will be made up of overlapping special cases. Many of these models will rely on amateurs as researchers and writers. Many of these models will rely on sponsorship or grants or endowments instead of revenues. Many of these models will rely on excitable 14 year olds distributing the results. Many of these models will fail. No one experiment is going to replace what we are now losing with the demise of news on paper, but over time, the collection of new experiments that do work might give us the journalism we need.

Paul Farhi    **NO**

A Bright Future for Newspapers

Philip Meyer, who has studied the newspaper industry for three decades, can see the darkness at the end of the tunnel. If present readership trends continue indefinitely, says the University of North Carolina professor, the last daily newspaper reader will check out in 2044. October 2044, to be exact. "I use that as an attention-getting device," says Meyer, whose latest book, "The Vanishing Newspaper: Saving Journalism in the Information Age," spells out the bad news in elaborate detail. "It's shocking, but that's what the numbers say."

It's not hard to understand how we could get from here to there. The media have been covering the bad news about newspapers for years. To see and read these accounts is to encounter an industry that seems on the verge of crisis, and possibly on the edge of the abyss. "In many U.S. markets, the dominant paper is a fading enterprise," wrote Slate media critic Jack Shafer this spring. "In the long run, no newspaper is safe from electronic technologies." *Barron's Online* columnist Howard R. Gold put it this way recently: "A crisis of confidence has combined with a technological revolution and structural economic change to create what can only be described as a perfect storm. . . . [P]rint's business model is imploding as younger readers turn toward free tabloids and electronic media to get news." *The Washington Post* was more succinct: "The venerable newspaper is in trouble," it declared in a long feature story in February.

Wait a second. Newspapers, which predate the founding of the American republic, are "imploding," "in trouble" and staring at oblivion? Is the future really so bleak?

To be certain, all is not as well as it once was at the average daily. Circulation, which has been on an orderly downward trajectory for two decades, has lately shown signs of free fall. (Daily newspaper circulation dropped 1.9 percent in the last year, according to the Audit Bureau of Circulations numbers.) Young readers are scarce, newsroom budgets are tight, and the competition remains unrelenting. Newspapers have wounded themselves with a series of credibility-shredding scandals and screwups—from Jayson Blair's and Jack Kelley's fictions to Judith Miller's mistaken WMD stories to last year's Enron-style circulation-inflation mess. The Internet, with its vastness, its vibrancy and its immediacy, does seem poised to blow away the snoozy old newspaper.

From *American Journalism Review*, June/July 2005. Copyright © 2006 by the Philip Merrill College of Journalism at the University of Maryland, College Park, MD 20742-7111. Reprinted with permission.

And yet all of this misses a bigger, more positive picture. Media accounts of the rise and fall of newspapers are greatly exaggerated, if not flat wrong. The case for the survival of the daily paper is at least as compelling as the one for its much-reported demise. Considering the hurricane of change that is buffeting all segments of the news media these days, I'd argue that no part of the business is as firmly anchored as the average daily newspaper. Rather than accepting their own mortality, newspapers may have the best chance of any of the old media to survive in a new-media world.

All of the pessimistic assessments of the newspaper industry's future invite a simple rejoinder: Compared with what? Since all traditional media—newspapers, magazines, radio, TV, etc.—are gradually losing readers, listeners and viewers, assessing any single medium in isolation provides a flawed and distorted picture. Compared with the rest of the media industry, newspapers are doing no worse, and in some respects quite a bit better, than the competition, including the Internet.

Let's take a quick tour.

Cable TV news? Except for the surge in interest late last year due to the presidential election, the three news channels—Fox News Channel, CNN and MSNBC—likely would have experienced their third no-growth year in a row.

In any case, the audience trends in cable news aren't promising. For one thing, cable news viewing is subject to extreme volatility—people come and go, driven to the set by the big breaking stories but paying only sporadic attention the rest of the time. More important, cable and the all-news networks it carries are at saturation. Cable's audience grew during the last decade partly as a result of expanded distribution—as more households could receive Fox News or CNN, more people watched. However, the wiring of America is all but complete now. So cable companies have had to look for new ways to grow, and they're doing so by expanding the number of channels available to their existing household customers. This can only mean more audience fragmentation, as viewers click around their new digital channels. Since new viewers aren't rushing to watch the all-news channels (and the audience for cable news is small to begin with—between 2 million and 3 million people at a time), the only way a network can grow is by cannibalizing the other guy's audience. Hardly a vibrant scenario.

The broadcast networks and local stations? They've been shedding viewers for years. It's not just the networks' prime time entertainment schedules that have been faltering; sports, soap operas, talk shows and game shows have been, too. Over the past two decades, the networks' news programming has lost viewers at a much faster pace than newspapers have been losing their readers. The Big Three still command the attention of roughly 29 million people each weeknight—but that's down 10 million, or 26 percent, from as recently as the mid-1990s.

Unlike cable, the broadcast networks still have a massive audience, and thus have further to fall. But TV networks are hypersensitive to even small movements in the Nielsen numbers these days. It's easy to lament, but not hard to understand, ABC's deliberations over the fate of "Nightline." In the past decade, the program has lost almost 40 percent of its audience (it still averages a respectable 3.8 million viewers per night). Journalists may shudder at the possible cancellation of "Nightline," but competence and prestige are no longer guarantees of survival on network TV.

Radio? Long ago, in a quainter, slower America, radio was a significant source of news and information. But since deregulation and consolidation, hundreds of commercial stations have dropped news, even the most rudimentary rip-and-read kind. The audience for all-news radio has remained relatively stable (and in the case of stations carrying NPR programming has actually grown). But conventional over-the-air radio seems to be in about the same position now as broadcast television was a couple of decades ago—on the verge of huge change. New technologies—satellite radio, multichannel digital terrestrial radio, podcasting, even enhanced cell phones—are already starting to chip away at radio's car-bound audience.

Magazines? They're also losing their claim on the ever-shortening attention span of Americans (a Pew Research Center for the People & the Press survey reports that only a quarter of Americans said they read a magazine "yesterday," down from a third that reported the same thing in 1994). Magazines have always lived in a world of ferocious competition and fragmentation—they're easy to start and can be tailored for readers interested in almost any subject. But the magazine industry is, in many respects, among the least economically healthy segments of the media. Consider: There were nearly one-third fewer titles being published in 2004 than there were in 1999, according to the National Directory of Magazines.

The most interesting and complicated case is the New News Media. Despite the hype, the Internet isn't swallowing everything in its path. A mere 2 percent of the people surveyed by Pew last year said the Internet was their only regular news source. The appetite for news from the Internet is growing, but it's just one part of a varied diet. The average person gets news from a variety of sources—some online, some from TV or radio, some from newspapers and magazines, Pew's figures show. The Internet is actually a small part of that; the average amount of time spent reading the news online was just seven minutes a day last year. No question Internet advertising is growing rapidly, but from a base of almost nothing just a few years ago.

Unlike TV, which created instant and sustained riches, Internet news pioneers are still grasping for a sustainable business model 10 or so years into the online era. Only a few news Web sites earn their keep—and prominent on this list are the online versions of print-and-ink newspapers. This is not to say that the Internet, with its speed and near-zero distribution costs, won't someday dominate news delivery. It could, but it's still hard to see how that day will come about. Will people pay for content online, or is the free model an established fact of life? If it is, will there be enough advertising, at high enough prices, to support as many reporters and editors as now staff even a small newspaper? Will general one-stop, online newspapers amass enough visitors (and enough geographically concentrated visitors at that) to attract lost print subscribers and local advertising? And with people spending relatively few minutes a day on news sites, will anyone be sitting still long enough to see an online ad in the first place?

A couple of aspects of the changing media landscape plainly seem hyped, or maybe just misreported. One is that young people don't read newspapers. They don't, to a shocking degree (just 23 percent of people under 30 said they had read a newspaper the day before they were interviewed, according to the Pew survey). But here's the other part of the picture: The same survey says young people aren't very interested in news from any source, electronic or print. The time spent watching or reading the news by adults under 30 has dropped by about 16 percent in the past decade. The advent of online news hasn't helped reverse the trend.

The major fear in the newspaper industry is that today's young people won't grow into the next generation of readers. That's a reasonable concern, but the evidence suggests it's far too narrowly focused. If young people are less interested in consuming news of any kind, isn't this a problem for news organizations of all types, including those on the Web? Some of the "young reader" problem is self-correcting; people tend to become more interested in the world around them as they buy houses, pay taxes, raise families and generally settle down. Some of these people will probably read the paper, someday. Where will the rest seek news and information (if they go anywhere at all)? How about the Internet? If that is the case, newspapers are as well positioned as anyone at the moment to offer the most comprehensive package of daily local news and features on the Web. Forget paper and ink; journalists (and publishers) have to be ready to deliver the goods via whatever delivery system "end users" want it in.

The other piece of misinformation is the kind spread by the blogosphere about the blogosphere. Despite their role in fanning a few important stories (such as Dan Rather's flawed "60 Minutes II" report on President Bush's National Guard service), bloggers seem at best a part of the news media's future, not the future itself. At the moment, most people have never even heard of blogs. Fifty-six percent of all adults polled by CNN/USA Today/Gallup said in February that they had no knowledge of blogs, and fewer than a third (32 percent) said they were very or somewhat familiar with them. For all their self-infatuation and all their (often useful) criticism of the Old Media, many bloggers would be out of business without the traditional media. Blogs draw their lifeblood from the raw material served up each day by conventional news organizations.

So how do newspapers fit into this dynamic cosmos? Nicely, I'd say. Consider just a few unique competitive advantages that newspapers (still) enjoy:

- **Monopoly status.** A hundred-plus years of competition have left most American cities with just one newspaper. This is, by far, a newspaper's biggest competitive advantage and the source of even the lowliest daily's fat profits.
- **Newsgathering power.** Local newspapers typically still have the largest reporting staffs in town of any single news outlet, print or electronic. This (coupled with wire sources) enables a newspaper to produce the broadest range of daily news and features of any single news outlet. In a world of specialty, there's still great value and convenience in such a general package. Think of the retail analogy: Some

people prefer shopping at boutiques and specialty stores, but lots of people still patronize supermarkets and department stores.

- **Localism.** Readers will always want to know about the schools, government, businesses, taxes, entertainment and teams closest to home. No news organization is better equipped or staffed to supply this information than a newspaper.
- **The best customers.** Newspapers typically beat their direct competition in both the quantity of customers (i.e., readers) and their quality (i.e., demographics). Even with declining circulation, this advantage remains relatively stable. As traditional newspaper advertisers—airlines, retailers, banks, auto dealers, etc.—undergo their own transformation, newspaper advertising remains one of the most efficient ways to reach relatively large numbers of educated, affluent people. Young people may not read the newspaper much, but in strictly business terms, this is somewhat irrelevant. Advertisers already know this. They buy newspaper space to sell goods and services aimed at an older, more moneyed crowd.
- **Lots of attention.** Newspapers no longer play the central role in people's daily lives they once did, but they are far from irrelevant. Some 42 percent of adults surveyed by the Pew researchers in 2004 reported that they had read a newspaper "yesterday" (a figure that rose slightly over 2002). With the exception of local TV news, no other news source reaches so many people on a given day.
- **Brand-name recognition.** Newspapers big and small have spent millions of dollars over the years reminding people what they do. This has created a vast but hard-to-measure reservoir of goodwill for newspapers and represents a major strategic advantage over, say, the latest shopper startup or flashy Web site. It partly explains why, even today, no one has been able to create a local news site that outdraws the newspaper's own on the Internet (and Microsoft and America Online have tried).
- **Historic profitability.** Thanks to all of the above, newspaper companies enjoy profit margins unmatched not just by most other news media but by most other industries. Industrywide, newspapers reaped about 23 cents of profit for every dollar they took in last year, according to Merrill Lynch analyst Lauren Rich Fine. Newspaper revenues and profits are rising even as readers are deserting. This could be because newspapers are raising prices while skimping on long-term investment in their plants and people—harvesting the assets," in business speak.

Of course, the newspaper industry's high profitability cuts both ways, as many newsroom managers know. The need to maintain those margins to satisfy the short-term demands of stockholders and Wall Street analysts compels some companies to cut back on hiring, newsgathering and the size of the newshole. This can create its own vicious cycle: As the amount of news shrinks thanks to the pursuit of higher profits, readers despair and depart, thereby undermining the basis for higher profits.

Washington Post Associate Editor Robert G. Kaiser, the coauthor (with Post Executive Editor Leonard Downie Jr.) of "The News About the News: American Journalism in Peril," calls the huge profit margins enjoyed by newspapers both arbitrary and pernicious. Once newspapers began regularly achieving these profit levels in the early 1980s, Kaiser says, many publishers became unwilling to settle for anything less and began shortchanging their newsrooms in the drive to achieve them.

"The question we need to ask is, 'What's an appropriate profit for a newspaper?'" says Kaiser. "If you went to a newspaper publishers' meeting in 1975 and told them their papers could make 15 percent profits, they would have been overjoyed. Now, the standard is 20 percent, 30 percent. Why? Because it's possible, for no other reason."

But the thing about obscenely high profits is they're a whole lot better than no profit at all. For newspapers, they can be the seed that provides tomorrow's harvest. Wisely reinvested, today's profits could prevent the day Philip Meyer believes is coming. To be fair, many newspaper companies aren't sitting still. They've beefed up their Web offerings and expanded their Internet "footprint" by buying independent sites (see "Dotcom Bloom," June/July 2005). Dow Jones recently purchased MarketWatch.com, *The New York Times* nabbed About.com, and the Washington Post Co. bought *Slate* from Microsoft. Major industry players also are embracing ethnic media (primarily Spanish-language) and niche publications like real-estate shoppers. The hottest single publishing market of the moment may be the battle for young readers (see "Hip—and Happening," April/May 2005). In Dallas, the *Morning News* started *Quick*, an easy-to-read freebie. In Chicago, both the *Tribune* and the *Sun-Times* have similar papers. *The Washington Post* launched *Express*, beating to the punch a new tabloid called *The Washington Examiner,* which is delivered free to mostly affluent families and is not aimed squarely at the young. Critics can argue about the quality of these papers, but their existence does say something about the prospects for print. *The Examiner,* for one, is the brainchild of billionaire Philip Anschutz, who has revived the moribund *San Francisco Examiner* and registered the *Examiner* trademark in some 70 cities nationwide. While the extent of Anschutz's publishing ambitions remain a mystery, his moves raise a larger question: Why does a billionaire think investing in newspapers is a good idea right now? Similarly, executives at fast-growing Lee Enterprises see newspapers as a growth industry (see "Lee Who?" June/July 2005).

Ultimately, some in the industry believe newspapers will have to rethink much of what they do to survive. A recent white paper by the Newspaper Association of America suggested, among other things, publishing smaller editions some days of the week and charging higher subscription fees to offset ad losses. Kaiser says it's a lot simpler than that. The best defense, he says, is a great offense. Put more money back into the newsroom and build up the journalistic firepower—and the community credibility—that many newspapers have been frittering away for years.

He'll get no argument from Phil Meyer on this. The premise of Meyer's most recent book is that high-quality journalism—accurate, clear and in-depth—strongly correlates with, if it doesn't create, market success (see Books, February/March 2005). He worries, however, that even quality may not be enough to save newspapers. Meyer sketches a "tipping point" scenario that would hasten the end—the day when a paper's slide is so prolonged and deep that a critical mass of advertisers concludes it's no longer worth supporting it. Maybe. But the mistake the newspapers-are-dead crowd makes is believing that trend lines continue in the same direction forever. It pays to remember that new communications media rarely eliminate the old ones; the old simply adapt to accommodate the new. So movies didn't eliminate novels and TV didn't eliminate movies or radio.

It could be just as likely, therefore, that the worst case doesn't happen. Maybe newspapers will find stability and equilibrium with a core of loyal, demographically attractive readers. Old habits do die hard. In a world of ever-expanding choice, many people—pressed for time and seeking the trusted and familiar—may just stick with what they already know and respect.

Without doubt, it will take skill, vision and creativity for newspapers to survive. But I'd bet on success sooner than I'd bet on failure. It may be that newspapers are dinosaurs. But then again, dinosaurs walked the earth for millions of years.

EXPLORING THE ISSUE

Should Newspapers Shut Down Their Presses?

Critical Thinking and Reflection

1. What are the major factors that threaten the business model of newspapers today? Can newspapers be dying despite the number of newspapers that remain profitable?
2. What is the possibility that alternative funding models might save newspapers?
3. Why are people willing to pay for a newspaper subscription, but resistant to paying for news that is delivered digitally?
4. Would the demise of newspapers negatively influence local economies?

Is There Common Ground?

Are newspapers the buggy whip company of the digital age or are they the IBM who transformed themselves from copiers to information management? You will find passionate advocates for traditional newspapers, those ready for a digital only product, and every point in between. What about you? Would it matter if newspapers were no longer produced in the physical form they currently take? I would miss having a morning newspaper at my door. Others would not. But presses and delivery are expensive, especially when there is another model without those costs. The common wisdom is that newspapers will continue for at least another decade or two, until presses wear out and would be replaced and/or distribution costs become too high.

Make no mistake, all this is not just about what form the "paper" will take. It is about the business model that will support itself. Right now most newspapers and magazines are taking melded approach, continuing the print version but experimenting always with a digital version. What will work? Will people pay for content? Can a vital web or app product recapture lost revenue that can support the printed copy? That and many other models are at the core of the common ground that is being explored on a daily basis. Many are promising; none has, as of yet, solved the problem. But a search for common ground motivates them all.

Additional Resources

The State of the News Media (2010)

An annual Pew Report on news media, including print, broadcast, and online outlets, a very valuable tool to trace changes in the economic health of these industries. It is available online and best found by searching the report title mentioned above.

Joseph Epstein, "Are Newspapers Doomed?"*Commentary* (January, 2008)

Epstein reminds us that issues of readership retention in newspapers were grave, even before the recent economic downturn.

Robert W. McChesney and John Nichols, *The Death and Life of American Journalism: The Media Revolution That Will Begin the World Again* (AK Press, 2010)

The authors argue that journalism is essential in a democratic society, but that the decline of commercial journalism cannot be reversed. They examine various models of support for journalism and call for the government to subsidize a free press.

Paul McCaffrey (ed.), *The News and its Future* (HW Wilson, 2010)

This book is a collection of essays on journalism of the future. At its core, it asks if new journalism is capable of upholding the principles and obligations of journalism in a democratic society.

ISSUE 15

Do New Business Models Result in Greater Consumer Choice of Products and Ideas?

YES: **Chris Anderson**, from "The Long Tail: How Technology Is Turning Mass Markets into Millions of Niches," in *The Long Tail: Why the Future of Business Is Selling Less of More* (Hyperion, 2006)

NO: **Kathryn C. Montgomery**, from "Social Marketing in the New Millennium," in *Generation Digital: Politics, Commerce, and Childhood in the Age of the Internet* (MIT Press, 2007)

Learning Outcomes

After reading this issue, you should be able to:

- Describe the difference between legacy and digital business models for the music industry.
- Define niche and mass markets.
- Contrast public service announcements and edutainment.

ISSUE SUMMARY

YES: Chris Anderson, an editor of *Wired* magazine, writes of the decline of the mass market and the rise of niche markets. He claims that the future of business, particularly in book, music, and DVD sales, will shift toward selling a wider range of media to audiences that have much broader interests.

NO: Professor Kathryn Montgomery looks at the cooperative relationships between social interest groups and media content providers, to better understand how themes with social objectives permeate media content.

The online world fosters the creation of business models that were unthinkable only a generation ago. Industrialization shaped a system for the production of goods that centralized populations, produced affordable goods,

326

and created complex distribution systems. In the transition from agricultural to industrial societies, families went from producing goods that could be sold or bartered to working for salaries that allowed the purchase of goods and services. The invention of the printing press is a case study of a similar transformative process. Gutenberg famously produced Bibles, contributing to transformative change in religion. As printing presses evolved into the publishing industry, books became our first mass medium. Investment cost of production was enormous (printing presses are expensive) and the financial risk to the publisher was high if the book did not sell. This remains the model of traditional media through today. Barriers to entry are high (e.g., television stations are expensive) as are the risks involved in attracting large audiences.

This business model has changed in the digital age. At minimum, the online world has become an adjunct to traditional media; many worry that online will ultimately replace traditional media entirely. To return to our example about the publishing industry, many worry that print will be replaced by digital versions read on digital tablets. Vartan Gregorian, President of the Carnegie Corporation, contemplates the demise of the physical book, and considers the loss that would entail in his essay, "The Book and the Library in an Age of Technology." (Search the carnegie.org site for the essay.) Business models are all about money. Mass media moved from a sale/subscription model to an advertising model in the twentieth century. In the advertising model, mass media aggregates audiences and sells them to advertisers. Although sales/subscription models remain important (newspaper and magazine circulation, cable charges), advertising is a major revenue source for all legacy mass media. With easy distribution and no copy costs, how will digital media transform our traditional information and entertainment media? "What is the business model?" is the question on the minds of all media CEOs.

But to focus only on how this medium transforms previous media misses the larger revolution in the business world. One revolution is the explosion of resources for aggregating public knowledge in accessible ways. Wikipedia is a well-known example. This is a collaborative product, created by individuals who volunteer their expertise. Consider apps such as Yelp that use geopositioning for locating local businesses paired with consumer reviews of these firms. What an intriguing business model: people freely giving their input and thereby creating valuable goods and services. Is Facebook an example of this? Are charitable transmedia experiences, such as Conspiracy for Good, a similar one?

In this issue, we explore how the business models of legacy industries have been changing over the years. The YES and NO selections provide different scenarios for the consumer; Chris Anderson examines how consumer choice can keep the legacy recording industry profitable, and Kathryn Montgomery addresses the relationships behind the scenes to better understand why some television content seems to promote particular ideals. Both authors look to legacy industries and document how more digitally oriented migrations of content target specific audiences.

Many people flippantly say, "The media only give us what we want," but the complex nature of media industries actually reframes that statement so that a more accurate assessment might be that the media give us what we're willing to take. The various business models in media respond to the pressure from other forms of media and new distribution channels. As Anderson writes, "The sales data and trends from [these] services and others like them show that the emerging digital economy is going to be radically different from today's mass market." The social-marketing campaigns studied by Montgomery show that multiplatform media content geared to teens has resulted in "public education strategies [that] have been evolved into highly sophisticated interactive campaigns, often employing the same tools of the trade that advertisers use to promote brands to young people."

Chris Anderson discusses how legacy industries can successfully adapt their business models to online sales, and actually increase their profits by selling less of a wider range of products to niche audiences. It's probably not too surprising that Chris Anderson is an editor of *Wired* magazine, which often makes predictions about the future of media, consumerism, and new technology. His most recent book, *Free: The Future of a Radical Price* (Hyperion, 2009), extends the metaphor of the Long Tail to examine how free products on the Internet (including media) could be the new economic model for our future. If he's right, the legacy industries will undoubtedly look toward greater diversification and divestiture, or, they may crumble.

Kathryn Montgomery takes a different approach, but discusses how nonprofit companies influence social campaigns. The partnership between MTV and the Kaiser Family Foundation's "Fight for Your Rights: Protect Yourself" program is typical of partnerships that take into consideration the vulnerability of children and teens. Kathryn Montgomery explores how nonprofit organizations have been collaborating with the creators of primetime TV and soap operas to influence teens' attitudes and behaviors. While she does not reference "product placement" or "product enhancement" as direct marketing tools that are being used, she does chronicle how attitudes toward sex, pregnancy, drug abuse, and smoking can use similar techniques to get the teen audiences' attention and promote particular values. The term "edutainment" or "entertainment-education" refers to this practice of inserting educational materials or plot lines into entertainment shows for the purpose of educating audiences. Social marketing, a broader term, is now an emerging field, though it has roots back to the 1970s when health care industry professionals sought to use traditional marketing strategies to influences attitudes and behaviors. Over the years, these strategies have resulted in anti-smoking campaigns, anti-drinking, anti-drug use, and health and wellness campaigns. Today, however, social networking, especially the use of Twitter, has become a method of immediate, direct marking to the consumer.

Both of these selections demonstrate that media business is always experiencing change—whether it is a migration to a different distribution form of music or the behind-the-scenes cooperative ventures that influence social norms and mores. Together they raise questions about media businesses that either drive consumer expectations or respond to consumer demand, as well as pose situations that make us think about our relationship to the products and images we see in media. Both of the ideas supported by these authors demonstrate how complicated media business is and how the history of media images and products continually changes with the distribution forms and content available at any given time.

YES

Chris Anderson

The Long Tail: How Technology Is Turning Mass Markets into Millions of Niches

In 1988, a British mountain climber named Joe Simpson wrote a book called *Touching the Void,* a harrowing account of near death in the Peruvian Andes. Though reviews for the book were good, it was only a modest success, and soon was largely forgotten. Then, a decade later, a strange thing happened. Jon Krakauer's *Into Thin Air,* another book about a mountain-climbing tragedy, became a publishing sensation. Suddenly, *Touching the Void* started to sell again.

Booksellers began promoting it next to their *Into Thin Air* displays, and sales continued to rise. In early 2004, IFC Films released a docu-drama of the story, to good reviews. Shortly thereafter, HarperCollins released a revised paperback, which spent fourteen weeks on the *New York Times* best-seller list. By mid-2004, *Touching the Void* was outselling *Into Thin Air* more than two to one.

What happened? Online word of mouth. When *Into Thin Air* first came out, a few readers wrote reviews on Amazon.com that pointed out the similarities with the then lesser-known *Touching the Void,* which they praised effusively. Other shoppers read those reviews, checked out the older book, and added it to their shopping carts. Pretty soon the online bookseller's software noted the patterns in buying behavior—"Readers who bought *Into Thin Air* also bought *Touching the Void*"—and started recommending the two as a pair. People took the suggestion, agreed wholeheartedly, wrote more rhapsodic reviews. More sales, more algorithm-fueled recommendations—and a powerful positive feedback loop kicked in.

Particularly notable is that when Krakauer's book hit shelves, Simpson's was nearly out of print. A decade ago readers of Krakauer would never even have learned about Simpson's book—and if they had, they wouldn't have been able to find it. Online booksellers changed that. By combining infinite shelf space with real-time information about buying trends and public opinion, they created the entire *Touching the Void* phenomenon. The result: rising demand for an obscure book.

This is not just a virtue of online booksellers; it is an example of an entirely new economic model for the media and entertainment industries, one just beginning to show its power. Unlimited selection is revealing truths about *what* con-

From *The Long Tail: Why the Future of Business Is Selling Less of More,* (Hyperion, 2006), pp. 15–20, 22–26 (excerpts). Copyright © 2006 by Chris Anderson. Reprinted by permission of Hyperion Books, and by permission of Random House Business Books/Random House Group Ltd. All rights reserved.

sumers want and *how* they want to get it in service after service—from DVDs at the rental-by-mail firm Netflix to songs in the iTunes Music Store and Rhapsody. People are going deep into the catalog, down the long, long list of available titles, far past what's available at Blockbuster Video and Tower Records. And the more they find, the more they like. As they wander farther from the beaten path, they discover their taste is not as mainstream as they thought (or as they had been led to believe by marketing, a hit-centric culture, and simply a lack of alternatives).

The sales data and trends from these services and others like them show that the emerging digital entertainment economy is going to be radically different from today's mass market. If the twentieth-century entertainment industry was about *hits*, the twenty-first will be equally about *niches*.

For too long we've been suffering the tyranny of lowest-common-denominator fare, subjected to brain-dead summer blockbusters and manufactured pop. Why? Economics. Many of our assumptions about popular taste are actually artifacts of poor supply-and-demand matching—a market response to inefficient distribution.

The main problem, if that's the word, is that we live in the physical world, and until recently, most of our entertainment media did, too. That world puts dramatic limitations on our entertainment.

The Tyranny of Locality

The curse of traditional retail is the need to find local audiences. An average movie theater will not show a film unless it can attract at least 1,500 people over a two-week run. That's essentially the rent for a screen. An average record store needs to sell at least four copies of a CD per year to make it worth carrying; that's the rent for a half inch of shelf space. And so on, for DVD rental shops, video-game stores, booksellers, and newsstands.

In each case, retailers will carry only content that can generate sufficient demand to earn its keep. However, each can pull from only a limited local population—perhaps a ten-mile radius for a typical movie theater, less than that for music and bookstores, and even less (just a mile or two) for video rental shops. It's not enough for a great documentary to have a potential national audience of half a million; what matters is how much of an audience it has in the northern part of Rockville, Maryland, or among the mall shoppers of Walnut Creek, California.

There is plenty of great entertainment with potentially large, even rapturous, national audiences that cannot clear the local retailer bar. For instance, *The Triplets of Belleville*, a critically acclaimed film that was nominated for the best animated feature Oscar in 2004, opened on just six screens nationwide. An even more striking example is the plight of Bollywood in America. Each year, India's film industry produces more than eight hundred feature films. There are an estimated 1.7 million Indians living in the United States. Yet the top-rated Hindi-language film, *Lagaan: Once Upon a Time in India,* opened on just two screens in the States. Moreover, it was one of only a handful of Indian films that managed to get *any* U.S. distribution at all that year. In the tyranny of geography, an audience spread too thinly is the same as no audience at all.

Another constraint of the physical world is physics itself. The radio spectrum can carry only so many stations, and a coaxial cable only so many TV channels. And, of course, there are only twenty-four hours of programming a day. The curse of broadcast technologies is that they are profligate users of limited resources. The result is yet another instance of having to aggregate large audiences in one geographic area—another high bar above which only a fraction of potential content rises. . . .

However, most of us want more than just the hits. Everyone's taste departs from the mainstream somewhere. The more we explore alternatives, the more we're drawn to them. Unfortunately, in recent decades, such alternatives have been relegated to the fringes by pumped-up marketing vehicles built to order by industries that desperately needed them. . . .

This is the world of *scarcity*. Now, with online distribution and retail, we are entering a world of *abundance*. The differences are profound.

For a better look at the world of abundance, let's return to online music retailer Rhapsody. A subscription-based streaming service owned by RealNetworks, Rhapsody currently offers more than 1.5 million tracks. . . .

So although there are millions of tracks in the collective catalogs of all the labels, America's largest music retailer, Wal-Mart, cuts off its inventory pretty close to the Head. It carries about 4,500 unique CD titles. On Rhapsody, the top 4,500 albums account for the top 25,000 tracks. . . . In Wal-Mart's inventory, . . . the top 200 albums account for more than 90 percent of the sales.

Focusing on the hits certainly seems to make sense. That's the lion's share of the market, after all. Anything after the top 5,000 or 10,000 tracks appears to rank pretty close to zero. Why bother with those losers at the bottom? . . .

What's extraordinary is that virtually every single one of those tracks will sell. From the perspective of a store like Wal-Mart, the music industry stops at less than 60,000 tracks. However, for online retailers like Rhapsody the market is seemingly never-ending. Not only is every one of Rhapsody's top 60,000 tracks streamed at least once each month, but the same is true for its top 100,000, top 200,000, and top 400,000—even its top 600,000, top 900,000, and beyond. As fast as Rhapsody adds tracks to its library, those songs find an audience, even if it's just a handful of people every month, somewhere in the world.

This is the Long Tail.

You can find *everything* out here in the Long Tail. There's the back catalog, older albums still fondly remembered by longtime fans or rediscovered by new ones. There are live tracks, B-sides, remixes, even (gasp) covers. There are niches by the thousands, genres within genres within genres (imagine an entire Tower Records store devoted to eighties hair bands or ambient dub). There are foreign bands, once priced out of reach on a shelf in the import aisle, and obscure bands on even more obscure labels—many of which don't have the distribution clout to get into Tower at all.

Oh sure, there's also a lot of crap here in the Long Tail. But then again, there's an awful lot of crap hiding between the radio tracks on hit albums, too. People have to skip over it on CDs, but they can more easily avoid it online, where the best individual songs can be cherry-picked (with the help of personalized recommendations) from those whole albums. So, unlike the CD—where each crap track costs perhaps one-twelfth of a $15 album price—all of the crap tracks online just sit harmlessly on some server, ignored by a marketplace that evaluates songs on their own merit.

What's truly amazing about the Long Tail is the sheer size of it. Again, if you combine enough of the non-hits, you've actually established a market that rivals the hits. Take books: The average Borders carries around 100,000 titles. Yet about a quarter of Amazon's book sales come from *outside* its top 100,000 titles. Consider the implication: If the Amazon statistics are any guide, the market for books that are not even sold in the average bookstore is already a third the size of the existing market—and what's more, it's growing quickly. If these growth trends continue, the potential book market may actually be half again as big as it appears to be, if only we can get over the economics of scarcity. Venture capitalist and former music industry consultant Kevin Laws puts it this way: "The biggest money is in the smallest sales." . . .

When you think about it, most successful Internet businesses are capitalizing on the Long Tail in one way or another. Google, for instance, makes most of its money not from huge corporate advertisers, but from small ones (the Long Tail of advertising). EBay is mostly Tail as well—niche products from collector cars to tricked-out golf clubs. By overcoming the limitations of geography and scale, companies like these have not only expanded existing markets, but more important, they've also discovered entirely new ones. Moreover, in each case those new markets that lie *outside* the reach of the physical retailer have proven to be far bigger than anyone expected—and they're only getting bigger.

In fact, as these companies offered more and more (simply because they *could*), they found that demand actually followed supply. The act of vastly increasing choice seemed to unlock demand for that choice. Whether it was latent demand for niche goods that was already there or the creation of new demand, we don't yet know. But what we do know is that with the companies for which we have the most complete data—Netflix, Amazon, and Rhapsody—sales of products *not offered* by their bricks-and-mortar competitors amounted to between a quarter and nearly half of total revenues—and that percentage is rising each year. In other words, the *fastest-growing* part of their businesses is sales of products that aren't available in traditional, physical retail stores at all.

These infinite-shelf-space businesses have effectively learned a lesson in new math: A very, very big number (the products in the Tail) multiplied by a relatively small number (the sales of each) is still equal to a very, very big number. And, again, that very, very big number is only getting bigger.

What's more, these millions of fringe sales are an efficient, cost-effective business. With no shelf space to pay for—and in the case of purely digital services like iTunes, no manufacturing costs and hardly any distribution fees—a niche product sold is just another sale, with the same (or better) margins as a hit. For the first time in history, hits and niches are on equal economic footing, both just entries in a database called up on demand, both equally worthy of being carried. Suddenly, popularity no longer has a monopoly on profitability. . . .

The Hidden Majority

One way to think of the difference between yesterday's limited choice and today's abundance is as if our culture were an ocean and the only features above the surface were islands of hits. There's a music island composed of hit albums, a movie island of blockbusters, an archipelago of popular TV shows, and so on.

Think of the waterline as being the economic threshold for that category, the amount of sales necessary to satisfy the distribution channels. The islands represent the products that are popular enough to be above that line, and thus profitable enough to be offered through distribution channels with scarce capacity, which is to say the shelf space demands of most major retailers. Scan the cultural horizon and what stands out are these peaks of popularity rising above the waves.

However, islands are, of course, just the tips of vast undersea mountains. When the cost of distribution falls, it's like the water level falling in the ocean. All of a sudden things are revealed that were previously hidden. And there's much, much more under the current waterline than above it. What we're now starting to see, as online retailers begin to capitalize on their extraordinary economic efficiencies, is the shape of a massive mountain of choice emerging where before there was just a peak.

More than 99 percent of music albums on the market today are not available in Wal-Mart. Of the more than 200,000 films, TV shows, documentaries, and other video that have been released commercially, the average Blockbuster carries just 3,000. Same for any other leading retailer and practically any other commodity—from books to kitchen fittings. The vast majority of products are *not* available at a store near you. By necessity, the economics of traditional, hit-driven retail limit choice.

When you can dramatically lower the costs of connecting supply and demand, it changes not just the numbers, but the entire nature of the market. This is not just a quantitative change, but a qualitative one, too. Bringing niches within reach reveals latent demand for noncommercial content. Then, as demand shifts toward the niches, the economics of providing them improve further, and so on, creating a positive feedback loop that will transform entire industries—and the culture—for decades to come.

 **NO**

Social Marketing in the New Millennium

When it premiered on MTV in 1992, *The Real World* generated mixed reviews from TV critics. A cross between a soap opera and a documentary, the show recruited seven people in their twenties and set them up in a plush apartment, where their lives were videotaped, day and night, for the next four months. The edited footage, with its steamy sex and raunchy language, was then set to a rock soundtrack featuring the latest hot music groups. "This is not reality as we know it," wrote Ginny Holbert in the *Chicago Sun-Times*, "but a highly artificial setup designed to turn ordinary life into an extended music video." Despite its obviously contrived nature, the show's success helped usher in a new genre of "reality programming" that by the end of the decade had begun to dominate programming schedules. With no union writers to pay, these shows—*Big Brother, Survivor, American Idol,* and the like—proved cheap to produce as well as highly popular with younger demographics.

By 2002, *The Real World* had become one of MTV's staple shows, selecting a fresh new cast of young people each year to act out their lives before millions of television viewers. Among the seven strangers thrown together that season—this time in a posh Las Vegas apartment—was Trishelle, a young woman from the rural town of Cutoff, Louisiana. Within the first few episodes, she succumbed to several serious temptations. She fell for a married man, got drunk, and had sex, all against her better judgment. She even kissed another girl, even though she was not gay. In angst, she called home to confide in her stepsister, only to have her father lambaste her for what he saw as sinfulness. Then, on top of everything else, her period was late.

It took Trishelle three episodes to get up the courage to take a pregnancy test. To her great relief, it turned out negative, but before the series ended that year, MTV turned the pregnancy scare into an educational opportunity. "Have you ever been late?" the show's Web site asked MTV's young viewers. "If so, you're not alone. To find out how to prevent being late or what to do if you are, click here." The next link provided a toll-free number for Planned Parenthood, advice on birth-control methods, and a hotline for access to emergency contraception. Viewers also were invited to take part in an online talk show with Trishelle, other cast members, and a representative of Planned Parenthood, who was on hand to answer questions about pregnancy prevention, sexually transmitted diseases (STDs), and communication strategies for dealing with sex partners.

From *Generation Digital: Politics, Commerce, and Childhood in the Age of the Internet* by Kathryn C. Montgomery (MIT Press, 2007), pp. 141–153 (excerpt; notes omitted). Copyright © 2007 by Massachusetts Institute of Technology. Reprinted by permission of MIT Press.

These efforts were part of the multimillion dollar public-education initiative Fight for Your Rights: Protect Yourself. A partnership between MTV and the Kaiser Family Foundation, the project's goal was to educate young people about sexual health and to promote safe sex. Because the campaign targeted teens and young adults through their own media, it was able to address sensitive sexual themes and controversial topics that might have sparked an outcry if they were more visible to the public.

For decades, youth have been the target of hundreds of "social marketing" campaigns, aimed at such vexing problems as teen pregnancy, drug abuse, and smoking. Over the years, nonprofit groups and government agencies have produced public-service advertising messages aimed at teens and young adults, often enlisting popular celebrities to promote pro-social messages in television spots, billboards, and magazine ads. In the new fragmented digital-media universe, these public-education strategies have evolved into highly sophisticated interactive campaigns, often employing the same tools of the trade that advertisers use to promote brands to young people. Just as marketers follow youth through the new digital landscape, closely tracking their every move, and inserting sales pitches into every possible venue, social marketers have crafted their campaigns to mesh with the media habits and journeys of teens and young adults. With the growth of the Internet and the proliferation of teen TV, public-health and social-issue organizations are able to incorporate their messages throughout the youth media culture, reaching their demographic targets with precision. Interactive media also make it possible to engage young people as never before, enlisting them in the campaigns, and encouraging them to spread the word among their peers. Sometimes these efforts generate controversy over their unorthodox methods and edgy messages. But much of the time they operate freely within the confines of a youth media world where adults seldom venture, addressing topics in a frank and direct manner that would be taboo in the mainstream media.

Sex Ed in the Digital Age

In August 1996, less than a month before the Democratic National Convention, President Clinton signed the Personal Responsibility and Work Opportunity Reconciliation Act of 1996 (commonly called the Welfare Reform Act), fulfilling a campaign promise he had made in 1992 to "end welfare as we know it." The landmark law eliminated more than sixty years of federally guaranteed assistance to the poor and enabled states to develop their own programs to move people from welfare to work. The legislation triggered a fiery debate in the midst of this election year. Clinton's support for the law prompted outcries from liberal groups, including the Children's Defense Fund and the National Organization for Women, who charged the White House with abandoning the Democratic Party's long-standing commitment to women, children, and the poor.

Among the law's new federal mandates was a little-known provision that had been pushed by conservative groups and slipped into the legislation at the last minute, requiring that $50 million a year be made available to the states to fund "abstinence-only" sex education. The new program, to be administered through schools, public agencies, and community organizations, was designed to deliver a clear and consistent message to young people: abstaining from sexual activity was the "only certain way" to avoid pregnancy and sexually transmitted diseases; the "expected standard" for sexual activity was "a monogamous relationship within the context of marriage"; and extramarital or premarital sex was likely to be "psychologically and physically harmful." Since passage of the law, abstinence-only programs grew in the nation's schools. A 2002 survey found that 23 percent of high school sex-education programs were teaching abstinence-only curricula, compared to only 2 percent in 1988.

But by the 1990s, neither schools nor parents held the exclusive franchise on sex education. The mass media already were eclipsing these traditional institutions. A national survey in 1997 found that more than half of high school boys and girls were learning about birth control, contraception, or pregnancy prevention from television, while two thirds of the girls and 40 percent of the boys had learned about these topics from magazines. Scholars studying the impact of television on teens found that messages in entertainment programming could affect attitudes, expectations, and behavior. Since the 1970s, a handful of nonprofit organizations had been collaborating with the creators of prime-time TV and soap operas to insert dialogue and storylines into programming, in order to educate youth about birth control, drunk driving, and other social issues. Over the years these efforts grew into an entire infrastructure of "entertainment-education" initiatives, part of the landscape of the television industry.

Advocates for Youth was one of the pioneers in the entertainment-education movement, establishing a Los Angeles office in the 1970s to encourage producers and writers to incorporate messages about birth control, abortion, and sexually transmitted diseases into their TV programs. By the mid-1990s, the group's Media Project was an established presence in the entertainment community, conducting informational workshops, consulting on scripts, and handing out awards for responsible and "balanced" depictions of sex. After passage of the abstinence-only legislation, Advocates for Youth's work in Hollywood became a key component in its political fight against the law. The group argued that young people had a right to a full spectrum of sexual information, including lifestyle options, birth control, abortion, and sexually transmitted diseases. By collaborating with creators of popular TV programs, the Media Project sought to communicate directly to teens, circumventing the restrictive curricula that many schools adopted in the wake of the new law.

With the growing number of entertainment programs created exclusively for teenagers, the project found a stable of willing and eager producers with whom to forge partnerships, developing ongoing storylines and characters that could help educate the loyal teen following. Project staff worked closely with producers of popular teen shows such as *Dawson's Creek* and *Felicity* to develop episodes dealing with teen sexual health and date rape. The project's Web site featured detailed lists of specific program episodes that the group felt had done a good job of dealing with sexual issues. "Whether dealing with sexual abuse, contraception, or unplanned pregnancy or portraying strong parent-child communication or peer pressure resistance, the producers and writers of these programs have a right to be proud." The list included dozens of news and entertainment shows, with synopses of the episodes, as well as the ratings figures. For example, in a 2003 episode of *The Gilmore Girls* on the WB network, "Paris confides to Rory that she had sex for the first time, leading to a conversation about how the right time is different for everyone." The project commended a 2003 episode of *The Simpsons* in which Homer and Marge separate and Homer moves in with two gay guys, learning "to be more accepting of gays and lesbians." On ABC's *All My Children*, "JR gives Jamie a condom in preparation for him 'getting lucky' at a party." Among the shows to receive the Media Project's SHINE Awards (for Sexual Health IN Entertainment) were: *Any Day Now, Sunset Beach, ER, The West Wing, Popular, Dawson's Creek, Will & Grace, Dateline NBC, That 70s Show,* and *Moesha.*

But addressing matters of sex in the context of prime-time television can be tricky business. Conservative media watchdog groups keep a close watch on television programs, taking their complaints to the government. In 2002, a storyline about oral sex (on which Advocates for Youth had consulted) was featured in the Fox Television series *Boston Public.* Aired at 8:00 p.m., the program sparked an outcry from fifteen conservative groups, including Focus on the Family, Christian Coalition, and the American Family Association. The organizations petitioned the FCC to enforce its rules governing indecent content on television and radio. Though the commission levied no fines against the network, the steady drumbeat for government intervention into sexual content on television would grow.

While continuing to work with TV producers, Advocates for Youth also turned to the Internet, using its Web site not just as an educational vehicle, but also as an organizing tool in the fight against the abstinence-only policy. "End Censorship in America's Schools," students were urged. "Join other youth activists in the My Voice Counts! Campaign, as they raise their voices about the need for honest sex education in communities in the U.S. and abroad." As more and more young people were going online to seek out resources and support for a range of health issues, those with limited knowledge of such matters at home or school now had unprecedented access to a wealth of information about sexual behavior, sexual lifestyles, and sexual health. Dozens of sites were set up to provide discussion forums on sexual issues, access to experts and community resources, as well as opportunities to be involved in the policy debate about sex education. At the Live Teen Forum page of . . . created by the American Social Health Association, teenagers could communicate directly with a health specialist about their own sexual-health concerns, through e-mail or a toll-free phone number. Rutgers University's Network for Family Life Education created . . . which quickly became a popular source of lively discussion and information among teens. The site included polls, surveys, and other interactive components to enable teenagers to voice their opinions on sex, sexually transmitted disease, and sex education policies. Sex, etc. also offered a downloadable "Teen Guide to Changing Your School's Sex Ed," with detailed instructions about building a local coalition, staging a community forum, drafting resolutions, and working with the press.

Youth seeking information and support about sexual-identity issues could find a new world online. "For homosexual teenagers with computer access," wrote Jennifer Egan in the *New York Times* magazine, "the Internet has, quite simply, revolutionized the experience of growing up gay." For those "with the inhospitable families and towns in which many find themselves marooned," she explained, "there exists a parallel online community—real people like them in cyberspace with whom they can chat, exchange messages, and even engage in (online) sex." Outproud.org, a Web site created by the National Coalition for Gay, Lesbian, Bisexual & Transgender Youth was one of hundreds of resources in this "parallel online community." It was set up "to help queer youth become happy, successful, confident and vital gay, lesbian and bisexual adults." The site offered "outreach and support to queer teens just coming to terms with their sexual orientation and to those contemplating coming out." Youth could find fact sheets and statistical information "to help make your case why supporting gay, lesbian, bisexual and transgender youth is important to your school." A Coming Out Archives provided a fully search-able database of hundreds of personal narratives, designed to "provide you with the benefit of the experiences of the millions of others who have found the right words on their own journeys. Sometimes things go well, sometimes they don't—whatever the results, they're here for you to see." Youth were also invited to share their own coming out stories on the Web site.

The explosion of new media technologies has created both opportunities and challenges for health educators. The Internet and cable television can be used to circumvent the mainstream media, providing a relatively unfet-tered arena for addressing otherwise taboo topics. However, with the grow-ing number of media available to teenagers, there is no guarantee that certain health messages will reach most or all teens. Media researchers have found that individual teenagers are customizing their own "sexual media diets," selecting from a growing menu of available TV programs, Web sites, music, and movies to suit their own needs, tastes, and desires for sexual information.

"I Want My MTV!"

Executives at the Henry J. Kaiser Family Foundation took these trends into account when designing their public-education campaign on sexual health in the late 1990s. As Vicky Rideout, vice president and director of Kaiser's Pro-gram for the Study of Entertainment Media and Health, explained, the foun-dation's strategy was to "surround youth with a variety of messages in many different forms and styles." With assets of more than a half billion dollars, the Kaiser Foundation was in a particularly unique and powerful position to carry out its goal. The California-based philanthropic organization functions mainly as an "operating foundation," which means that, rather than just giving out grants to nonprofits, it can design its own large-scale public-education and research initiatives, often in partnership with other influential organizations. The foundation has been particularly effective at commanding the attention of the media, promoting widespread coverage of its research on such topics as health-care policy, women's health, HIV/AIDS, and minority health.

Because television still plays a central role in the media diets of teens, part of Kaiser's effort has been aimed at the Hollywood creative community. The foundation followed the lead of other entertainment-education projects to encourage the television industry to use its programs as a way to educate youth about sexual-health issues. But with more resources than many nonprofits, the foundation has been able to develop a more comprehensive initiative for influencing entertainment television, combining its work to influence the producers of popular prime-time series with formal research that assessed the impact of its efforts on both the viewers and the programming. Foundation staff worked regularly with the producers of the NBC prime-time series *ER*, helping them insert storylines on a variety of health-related issues, including episodes that dealt with emergency contraception and sexually transmitted diseases. Follow-up surveys of viewers of these programs showed that the depictions helped increase awareness of the issues, prompted discussions among friends and family members, and in some cases helped people make decisions about their own health care. For several years, Kaiser underwrote Advocates for Youth's Media Project in Los Angeles. The foundation also has tracked the sexual content of entertainment television programming, conducting biennial studies to measure levels and kinds of sexual activity, in addition to depictions of "safe-sex" practices.

To reach its target audience more directly, Kaiser partnered with popular teen magazines such as *Teen People, TM*, and *Seventeen*, working with editors to develop special features on sexual-health issues and reader surveys about sexual behavior. The foundation's most ambitious effort for reaching young people is through its partnership with MTV. Launched in 1981, MTV is the number-one cable network among 12–24-year-olds, and the network has become "nearly synonymous with youth." Its global reach (in 2006) includes more than 400 million subscribers in more than 164 countries.

Sexual issues are front and center in the lives of the MTV Generation. The proportion of sexually active girls age 15–19 rose from 47 percent in 1982 to 55 percent by 1990. Although rates of teen pregnancy declined somewhat since the high point in 1990, more than one million pregnancies still occurred in teenagers between ages 15 and 19, with nearly 30,000 in girls under 15. And a quarter of sexually active teenagers contracted a sexually transmitted disease every year. As far as teens are concerned, explained MTV's Jaime Uzeta, director of strategic partnerships and public affairs, sexual health is "public health #1." For many social critics, however, MTV was part of the problem. Since the cable channel began, its 24/7 stream of graphic sexual images had sparked protests from parents groups and conservative Christians. But for Kaiser, the pervasive sex on the cable network created an opportunity. Since MTV already was promoting sexual activity, it could be persuaded, with some financial incentives, to add responsible messages to the mix.

For years, nonprofit organizations seeking to use the mass media for their social-marketing campaigns often relied on the goodwill of the television networks and local stations (and encouragement by federal regulators) to provide free airtime. But many public-service announcements (PSAs) have been buried in the wee hours before dawn. With deregulation of the broadcasting industry in the 1980s, the number of PSAs that networks and stations were willing to run at all declined sharply. Many nonprofits turned to paid advertising to get their messages on at a desirable time. But the TV industry still was reluctant to air controversial PSAs. This was especially true with sexual issues.

The Kaiser Foundation's strategy with MTV was a deliberate departure from traditional public-service campaigns. The foundation entered into a business relationship with the cable channel, offering financial and organizational support to sweeten the deal. This arrangement became the model for Kaiser's other media efforts over the years. "Kaiser has approached its entertainment media partnerships as business propositions with a philanthropic purpose," foundation executives explained. Kaiser crafts its agreements in "formal memoranda of understanding," offering an appealing package to its media partners that includes support for: "issues research; briefings for writers and producers, and other media staff; substantive guidance on message development; and funds to support program production and the creation of information resources for consumers." In return for this financial commitment from the foundation, media companies contribute "creative and communications expertise; on-air programming on the issues addressed by the campaign; and guaranteed placement of the PSAs and other content to reach target audiences." Kaiser's campaigns are "undertaken in much the same way that any commercial product would be marketed—by using the best creative teams to help develop compelling messages for the target audience and securing commitments that ensure that they are seen on the right television shows in the right time slots." Kaiser's "product" is not "sneakers or beer" however, but "awareness and prevention."

The Be Safe campaign was launched in 1997 with a series of hip PSAs, a toll-free hotline, and the booklet "It's Your (Sex) Life," offering detailed advice and information about how to avoid getting sexually transmitted diseases. In the first six months, 150,000 viewers called the hotline, and more than 100,000 of them requested a copy of the Kaiser booklet. By 2002, the effort had been "rebranded" under MTV's existing Fight for Your Rights pro-social initiative with a new tag line added: Protect Yourself. Fight for Your Rights: Protect Yourself soon became a recognizable brand on its own, woven throughout the TV schedule and Web site on the popular youth network. The campaign themes and messages became a pervasive presence on MTV, appearing in PSAs, interactive Web features, and print materials, as well as on-the-ground, grassroots activities. The Kaiser Foundation spent $440,000 on its partnership with MTV in its initial year.

Though carefully framed as a public-health initiative, the campaign was not without controversy. In 1998, Christian right-to-life group Rock for Life, a division of the American Life League, attacked the Kaiser/MTV campaign for promoting sexual behavior among teens. "MTV has no business teaching kids about sexual relationships and promoting abortion," the group charged. "MTV is trying to take over the role of the parents and families and teach deadly values to kids under the disguise of looking out for their welfare." The group charged that by sending out informational materials directly to teens on abortion and contraception, it was attempting to undermine parents.

Despite these initial complaints, the campaign not only continued, but also expanded. During the first five and a half years, more than sixty public-service ads were produced, airing more than 4,600 times. The videos were much edgier, realistic, and graphic than anything that could run on broadcast television. Through research, the campaign also was able to identify specific subsegments of the MTV audience, tailoring PSAs to gays and lesbians, Latinos, females, and African Americans. One of the ads, for example, featured an inner-city Latino rocker speaking directly to the camera, trying to convince himself that he would know if he had a sexually transmitted disease. "If I was feeling weak, or had a rash downstairs—I'd definitely know something," he assures himself. But the voice-over announcer warns: "Most people with STDs show no symptoms at all. Get perspective. Get tested. For more information go to Fight for Your Rights @ MTV.com."

Programming on MTV is an integrated multimedia effort, employing cross-platform promotion strategies that have become standard operating procedure for entertainment-media companies in the digital era. The network takes full advantage of the multitasking media habits of youth to extend the reach of its brand and ensure maximum exposure and ongoing relationships with its viewers. These same strategies were central to the Fight for Your Rights: Protect Yourself campaign. Branded sexual-health messages were woven throughout the MTV franchise. Through interactive media, teens could discuss sex and sexual-health issues candidly with experts as well as peers, without fear of parental interference. Public-service advertising and TV programs featured links to the special Web site created for the campaign, itsyoursexlife.com, where viewers could access a wealth of online resources, including: "e-PSAs"; a searchable nationwide database of HIV- and STD-testing facilities; an interactive guide to sexual health; a sexual-health news site; monthly features that provide the latest information about HIV/AIDS and other topics; and 24-hour message boards where viewers could meet and discuss sexual-health-related issues in an ongoing dialogue. Through a toll-free hotline run by the Kaiser Foundation, teens could receive the free "Sex Life" booklet, and be "connected immediately to a live operator at the CDC's National HIV/AIDS or STD hot lines or to their local Planned Parenthood clinic."

In keeping with MTV's edgy, rebellious-youth image, the campaign encouraged its viewers to become engaged in sexual politics. The project's Web site featured a Take Action section, where MTV's other partners, including Advocates for Youth, offered opportunities to become involved in grassroots efforts. "Find out where you can be trained as a peer educator, learn how to take political action both locally and nationally, and get inspired by checking out what other young activists are doing," the Web site urged. But Kaiser was careful to distance itself from these overtly political aspects of the initiative, frequently pointing out that it neither engaged in nor funded advocacy. In its report "Reaching the MTV Generation," for example, among the specials listed as part of the campaign were several MTV broadcasts that directly took on the controversial policies around abstinence-only education. One was the 2002 MTV/*Time* magazine special "Sex in the Classroom." The program dealt with abstinence-only and comprehensive sex-ed curricula in the nation's schools, and it included sections where "students, educators, and experts speak out." Though the foundation listed this broadcast among the campaign's programmatic accomplishments, it noted that the special was "produced independently of the Foundation, but aired as part of the Fight for Your Rights campaign."

Dozens of TV programs were produced dealing with sexuality and sexual-health issues. During the 2002–2003 season, the network's documentary series *True Life* featured several episodes with sexual themes. In the episode "I Need Sex RX," camera crews followed several young people as they visited doctors and health-care centers, providing an up-close-and-personal view of one woman having her first gynecological exam and another getting tested for HIV. "It Could Be You" featured two young HIV-positive women on a road-trip around the country, meeting up with others who had tested positive for the disease. The special *9 Things You Need to Know before You're Good to Go* featured R&B/hip-hop star Tweet offering practical advice on how to have sex without getting an STD. The documentary *Dangerous Liaisons* examined the consequences of mixing drugs and alcohol with sex. And on *Live Loveline,* comedian Adam Carolla and MTV's sex doctor, Drew Pinsky, answered studio-audience and call-in questions about STDs. *MTV News* ran stories about teen pregnancy, STDs, HIV/AIDS, and other sexual-health issues. During the 2000 presidential election, the MTV special *Choose or Lose: Sex Laws* addressed such hot political issues as abortion, sex-ed policy, gay rights, and age of consent. The network's global reach enabled it to stage live, large-scale, international media events. The 2001 broadcast of *Staying Alive* 3, a special about young people and HIV/AIDS, aired in 150 countries, including South Africa, Kazakhstan, Russia, and China.

On-air specials frequently were coordinated with "offline" community events, in partnership with local chapters of Planned Parenthood and other sexual-health groups. Youth also could take part in live, online "e-discussions" about the TV programs on the MTV Web site. To kick off the 2002 campaign, MTV broadcast a live one-hour special called the "National Sex Quiz," promoting it in advance both on the air and online: "When it comes to sex, everybody thinks they know the score. You know everything you need to know . . . right? You sure? Prove it: Take MTV's 21-question pop quiz on sex and health, and then tune in to our live special on April 20 to find out if you know as much as you think (and get schooled if you don't!)." More than 700,000 viewers participated in the event, according to MTV executives. Inserts on "safer sex" were distributed in MTV's "Party to Go" CDs, as well as the *Real World* video, reaching 117,000 individuals. As part of MTV's 1998 Campus Invasion concert tour, "sexual information" tents were set up at thirty different colleges and universities around the country, staffed by college health counselors who distributed free literature and condoms.

But while TV specials and Web-site materials can offer fairly straightforward information on sexual health, incorporating the campaign's themes into unscripted reality shows sometimes can result in a muddled and confused message. With its rotating stable of eager young participants, *The Real World* has been a hotbed of topical issues confronting teens and young adults, making it a natural venue for pro-social messages. Over the years, the show has featured young people dealing with a variety of problems, including AIDS, sexual identity, and alcohol abuse. According to Kaiser executives, sexual-health themes have been "placed" in the popular series. Since it is a reality show, however, the issue cannot be written into scripts. Rather, when characters confront sexual issues on the show, the incidents can be linked to a more deliberate pro-social message.

So, when Trishelle went through her pregnancy scare, MTV put the young woman on an "online talk show," where she could debrief with her *Real World* viewers, accompanied by an expert to provide additional health information. But as Trishelle answered questions, it became clear that the fishbowl nature of the show itself may have contributed to her problem. When asked by the moderator why they did not use a condom when they had sex, Trishelle replied: "I think the first time we had sex it wasn't planned. And . . . the fact we had cameras on us, no one wanted to get up and get a condom. Then the camera crews would know that we were definitely having sex." The Planned Parenthood representative quickly intervened with her own advice: "The good news is most people don't have cameras on them when they're having sex. It's still a good idea to have condoms nearby if there's any chance you'll get involved in sexual behavior." After hearing the Planned Parenthood expert reel off a long list of birth control methods, the moderator asked Trishelle: "Did you consider going on the birth control pill?" The young woman replied that she had planned to go on the pill, but because she had to make a hasty move to Las Vegas in order to be on the show, she was having trouble getting her prescription transferred.

The *Real World* incident underscored what some media critics see as a contradiction in the Kaiser/MTV initiative. The highly popular youth network is a perfect venue for reaching the audience that Kaiser seeks to influence, but embedding socially responsible messages into a channel known for its titillating and graphic sexual content may send a double message to young people. "It's tremendously ironic," Bob Thompson, director of Syracuse University's Center for the Study of Popular Television, commented to the press. "The campaign is working with a network whose programming features exactly the opposite messages." But Kaiser officials counter that teens and young adults already are heavy viewers of MTV, "so the bottom line is, are they better off with this information included or without it?" Kaiser's Vicky Rideout told the press. "And the answer is that those who get our materials are more likely to see a doctor, talk to their parents and use birth control as a result."

Whether one agrees with the approach or not, the campaign's message appears to have gotten through. According to research released by the Kaiser Foundation, "a majority (52%) of all 16–24-year-olds in the country say they have seen sexual health ads on MTV, and a third (32%) say they have seen full-length shows." The research also found that "nearly two-thirds (63%)" of those who saw the campaign personally learned from it, and many told researchers they had become more cautious and careful in their own sexual behaviors, as a result of paying attention to the campaign. The campaign has won numerous awards, including an Emmy and a Peabody award in 2004. . . .

EXPLORING THE ISSUE

Do New Business Models Result in Greater Consumer Choice of Products and Ideas?

Critical Thinking and Reflection

1. Can existing legacy systems adapt and participate in the new digital age?
2. Do the new offerings of the digital age add new and valuable choices for consumers?
3. How can non-media businesses benefit from using capabilities made available by the digital age?
4. What are the implications for business of the perception that Internet-based information is free?
5. What are the implications for public service activities in the digital age?

Is There Common Ground?

In present circumstances, media organizations are frantically looking for ways in which this disruptive technology can be harnessed to their legacy media business models. The entire field of information, entertainment, and distribution are galvanized by the changes that are occurring since the World Wide Web debuted in the 1990s. For most nonmedia businesses, the Web does not threaten their basic functions and can instead be viewed as a useful tool for better communications and often for less costly management of information distribution, communication with suppliers and end users, and product distribution (Netflix anyone?). For entrepreneurs everywhere, the Web is a business opportunity. Who could have ever dreamed that some of the more valuable corporations on the planet would be Apple, Facebook, and Google? What other products, services, and business plans will emerge?

Additional Resources

John Battelle, *The Search: How Google and Its Rivals Rewrote the Rules of Business and Transformed Our Culture* (Nicholas Brearley Publishing, 2005)

Part of an emerging literature on e-commerce, Batelle provides a comprehensive analysis of Google's rise and power.

James Marcus, *Amazonia: Five Years at the Epicenter of the Dot.com Juggernaut* (New Pr, 2004)

An entertaining story of the founding of Amazon and its slow rise before finally becoming a profitable company.

Chel Holtz and John C. Havens, *Tactical Transparency: How Leaders Can Leverage Social Media to Maximize Value and Build Their Brand* (Jossey-Bass, 2009)

Books on social marketing are beginning to appear. As the title suggests, this is an effort to alert businesses to the value and function of social media in marketing their products and their brand.

Clay Skirky, *Cognitive Surplus* (Penguin, 2010)

Subtitled *Creativity and Generosity in a Connected Age*, Shirky explores the phenomenon of people freely donating their time, creativity, and expertise to create information and services online. This book is full of interesting examples of how social and informational products and projects have been accomplished through the freely-given time of participants.

Internet References . . .

IFPI Music Market Statistics

IFPI (International Federation of the Phonographic Industry) is an industry association. As part of their services, the statistics section provides a "comprehensive range of global industry statistics." The goals of this association are to promote the value of recorded music, safeguard the rights of record producers, and expand the commercial uses of recorded music.

www.ifpi.org/content/section_statistics/index.html

Center for the Digital Future

Maintained by the University of Southern California, the Center for the Digital Future is a research and policy institute seeking to maximize the positive potential of the mass media and our rapidly evolving communication technologies.

www.digitalcenter.org

Electronic Frontier Foundation

Electronic Frontier Foundation is a nonprofit civil liberties organization working to protect free expression and access to public resources and information online and to promote responsibility in the new media.

www.eff.org

Yahoo International

The Yahoo service can access a number of countries, provide information about the media systems, and list media programming.

http://dir.yahoo.com/Regional/Countries/

The Media Lab

MIT's Media Lab allows you to glimpse the many ways that researchers are thinking about the digital media future. Look at the research groups listed in the research section of the Web site, and then visit the group Web sites of the ones that interest you.

www.media.mit.edu

Pew Internet and American Life Project

An outstanding source for up-to-date reports on issues of Internet use and its integration into American society. Those interested in research can download surveys and data for secondary analysis.

www.pewinternet.org

Life in the Digital Age

*P*redictions of a world that is increasingly reliant upon media and communication technologies have generally provided either utopian or dystopian visions about what our lives will be like in the future. New media distribution technologies present new options for traditional ways of doing things. Not too many years ago, people were talking about the possibility of an information superhighway. Today, people talk about Facebook and Twitter. Although we are still learning how electronic communication may change our lives and the ways we work and communicate, many questions have not changed. Will new ways of communication change the way individuals interact? Will we find ways to protect the individual in this arena? Will the weakest members of society be protected? Will the decision making of citizens change? Will everyone have access to the services and technologies that enable more immediate information exchange? What will new technologies mean to us as individuals as we live in the information age?

- Are Youth Indifferent to News and Politics?
- Are Online Services Responsible for an Increase in Bullying and Harassment?
- Are People Better Informed in the Information Society?

ISSUE 16

Are Youth Indifferent to News and Politics?

YES: David T. Z. Mindich, from "Journalism and Citizenship: Making the Connection," *Nieman Reports* (Winter 2008)

NO: Pew Internet & American Life Project, from *The Internet and Civic Engagement* (September 2009), www.pewinternet.org

---

Learning Outcomes

After reading this issue, you should be able to:

- Evaluate whether an informed citizenry is necessary for democracy.
- Analyze the connections between an informed public and engaged citizens.
- Discuss if there are new forms of engagement emerging in the digital age.
- Debate whether these differences are generational in nature.

ISSUE SUMMARY

YES: Author and professor David T. Z. Mindich addresses the sobering facts of why youth do not follow the news. He links this with low voter turnout, a widening knowledge gap between younger and older citizens, and a lack of trust in news media. The author of *Tuned Out: Why Americans Under 40 Don't Follow the News*, Mindich explores the essential link between news and information and being an informed and engaged citizen.

NO: The Pew Internet & American Life Project released *The Internet and Civic Engagement* in 2009. This report examined whether the Internet could change long-established patterns of civic and political involvement. Based on a sample of more than 2,000 adults, the project found that new forms of civic engagement based on the Internet, blogs, and social media have the potential to alter long-standing patterns of information and engagement of younger voters.

Criticism of the younger generation is certainly not new. Contemporary media, popular books, and even government officials decry the failures of the millennial generation of young adults. Millennials are described as digital natives who are comfortable with multitasking and resourceful in the digital world. They are decried as feeling entitled and unaccustomed to punching a time clock. Yet baby boomer bosses also marvel at the chaotic energy that can produce innovative outcomes through seemingly inexplicable processes.

The perceived indifference of youth and young adults to news and civic and political engagement is seen by Mindich as a deepening and crucial flaw in younger generations. Newspapers have long operated on the assumption that as young adults settle into adulthood, they will begin subscribing to newspapers. Increasingly, that is not happening. In this age of multiplatform journalism, the percentage of adults who subscribe to the newspaper is diminishing significantly, contributing to the difficulties faced by newspaper companies at this time. Similarly, political engagement has been the province of older voters. Was the election of 2008 a turning point? This was an election where slightly more than half of all voters under 30 cast ballots, an historic election that put an African American in the White House as Mindich notes. These numbers were stunning, but not reflective of youth voting patterns in general where it is not unusual for under-30 voters to be about 19 percent of the voting public in an election. Mindich is deeply concerned that the linkage between an informed citizenry and political and civic engagement has been broken in contemporary society. If this is true, it is our democracy that will pay the price.

These confusing trends should not obscure the improved youth voter turnout of 2004 and 2008. Youth voter turnout in 2004 was higher than usual at 49 percent. It rose to 51 percent in the 2008 presidential election. Two million more young people ages 18–29 voted in 2008 than in 2004. Turnout in the 2008 election was diverse with black turnout at an historic high of 58 percent, compared to 52 percent for white youth, 41 percent for Hispanic, and 43 percent for Asian youth. Nonetheless, these figures remain lower than the overall turnout across the population for both elections, with a 63.8 percent in 2004 and a 63.6 percent in 2008 turnout (Pew Report: Dissecting the 2008 Electorate).

When the Internet burst upon the world stage, many felt that its ease of communication and grassroots foundation would lead to social change. One potential benefit was allowing the public to participate directly in the great debates of our time, wresting control of communications from corporations and politicians. Information is now widely available online, but ironically open access to the Web and the sheer volume of information available has made evaluating what you find difficult. *The Pew Report on Internet and Civic Engagement* asks what tools are being used by Americans to engage with the political system and are these tools bringing new voices into the process. They found many vestiges of older patterns remaining. Online or offline, those with higher education and income tend to participate more in political activities. Yet certain forms of online political engagement were dominated by younger citizens. Whether these activities will evolve into more extensive involvement is unknown. Still it provides a hint of the ways in which contemporary digital media may provide the tools of engagement to younger generations.

Many are concerned about the level of what Zukin, Keeter, Andolina, Jenkins, and Carpini call citizen engagement. In their book, *A New Engagement?* (2006), they challenge the notion of youth apathy. They explore ways in which different forms of participation are being created that may reverse declining electoral participation. They would argue that the terms civic engagement and political engagement should not be confused. Our selections talk most about political engagement at the national and local level. Civic engagement certainly refers to political engagement, but it also implicates the many ways that individuals work to promote their community. These range widely from serving meals at the homeless shelter and cleaning up local parks to running for the local school board or participating in creating a charter school in your area. While many laud the levels of civic engagement in today's college-bound students, cynics note that community involvement is important in college admission decisions.

Fostering a lack of engagement, some feel that the education system has failed to produce appropriate levels of civic knowledge. CIRCLE (The Center for Information & Research on Civic Learning and Engagement) conducts research on the civic and political engagement of young Americans. They provide data online from their research, such as the proportion of youth versus older turnout in the 2010 election by state. They are also involved in civics education projects and studies.

Although the link between youth and news has always been tenuous, are their aspects of journalism at fault? Michael Schudson lists seven things that news can do for democracy, in his book *Why Democracies Need an Unlovable Press* (Polity Press, 2008), including information, investigation, analysis, creating social empathy, facilitating a public forum, mobilization, and publicizing a representative democracy. He argues that journalistic obsession with facts and events is the unlovely side of this goal, but is the job of journalists who "get in the face of power." In so doing, they keep democracy from grave danger. In the selection, Schudson contends that some of the behaviors that have made journalists so unpopular are exactly what is needed to make it effective. He explains how story selection is kept unpredictable by an event orientation toward reporting, journalists' inherent skepticism about politicians, and how they relish confrontation and their outsider status. Are these foundations that must be retained if journalism is again to be trusted the very behaviors that turn younger generations away from news?

Mindich argues that the link between information and engagement is essential in a democratic society. The report by Pew Internet and American Life Project asks if engagement is being promoted by the Internet and social media; they do not examine traditional media, but assume that engagement both presupposes and creates informed citizens. Whatever the direction of the link between information and engagement, as you read these selections you may want to consider the ways in which you—democracy's next generation—can fulfill the obligations of citizenship.

YES

David T. Z. Mindich

Journalism and Citizenship: Making the Connection

"Not only do citizens benefit from good journalism, but also journalism gets a boost from having engaged, news-hungry citizens."

My book, *Tuned Out: Why Americans Under 40 Don't Follow the News*, published in 2004, opened with a depressing fact: More people watched the 2003 finale of "American Idol" (38 million) than the second Bush vs. Gore presidential debate (37.6 million). Among young viewers, these numbers were even more lopsided. In all, 24 million votes were cast, mainly by young people, for "American Idol" contestants Ruben Studdard and Clay Aiken. Even though we know that some of these votes were by minors (and they were allowed to vote multiple times), it is sobering to remember that fewer than six million (22 percent) of 18- to 24-year-olds voted in the 2006 midterm elections; this means that for every one of these young people who voted, four of their peers stayed home.

Fast forward to the 2008 elections, in which 66 million watched the second presidential debate, and even more watched the vice presidential one. Millions of young people participated in the primaries and caucuses—in a greater percentage than seen in decades. In the general election, 18- to 29-year-olds increased their share of the electorate from 17 percent in the past two elections to 18 percent this year. Still, little more than half of all eligible voters under 30 cast ballots in the general election, according to an early estimate by the Center for Information and Research on Civic Learning and Engagement.

But does this modest upsurge in voting among young people mean that the 30-year widening knowledge gap between them and their elders is being narrowed? Some long-term trends are discouraging:

- Only around 20 percent of today's 20-somethings and 30 percent of 30-somethings read a newspaper every day, way down from decades past. Why should we care? Because studies show that the news habit needs to be cultivated early. The 30-something non-news reader is likely to one day become a 50-something non-news reader.

- Television news viewership is no better: The median viewer age of TV news has risen from 50 to around 60 in the past decade. Although CNN, "The Daily Show With Jon Stewart," and "The Colbert Report" have seen recent upticks in young viewers, long-term trends for television news watching are down.
- An August 2008 report by the Pew Research Center for the People & the Press, found that an engaged minority of Americans are "integrators," people who use both the Internet and traditional sources to get a lot of their news. But while more and more people are logging onto news Web sites—and sharing what they find with one another—until very recently none of this activity had closed the political knowledge gap. There is, of course, a minority of young people—always was and always will be—who use whatever the current medium is to gain a deep knowledge of news and politics. But for too many, Facebook, MySpace, YouTube, and other digital media seem to serve as more of a distraction from civic and political news than as a way to inform.
- In "The Age of Indifference," an important study from the summer of 1990, it was revealed that young Americans from the 1940s to the 1970s were nearly as informed as their elders about current events; this knowledge gap began widening in the 1970s. A decade later, Pew asked Americans if they happen to know the presidential candidate who sponsored campaign finance reform. Only about nine percent of 18–34 year olds knew it was John McCain, far fewer than their elders. A question about Wesley Clark in 2004 showed that young Americans were far less likely than their elders to know that he was a general.

The one exception to these dire numbers is a recent Pew poll published in July that asked respondents to identify McCain and Obama's stances on abortion and withdrawal from Iraq. For the first time in years, 18- to 29-year-olds seemed to know slightly more than their elders about the candidates and these issues. But a closer examination must give us pause. The poll asked whether the candidates are "pro-choice" or "pro-life," a yes or no question. If respondents were totally devoid of knowledge, we could expect a 50 percent accuracy rate. In the poll, only 52 percent and 45 percent of Americans of all ages knew that, respectively, Obama is pro-choice and McCain is pro-life. A flipped coin would do basically as well as the poll respondents. That young people in one poll marginally beat a flipped coin, and the rest of us didn't, is no cause for celebration.

Two recent books, Mark Bauerlein's "The Dumbest Generation" and Rick Shenkman's "Just How Stupid Are We?" seek to plumb the depths of our dumbness. We do, after all, live in a nation in which many of us believed that Saddam Hussein had a role in the 9/11 attacks years after the Bush administration had to pull back from that claim. Still, after conducting research during the past five years—studies that involved speaking with hundreds of young people about their news habits (and lack thereof)—I don't find that today's young people are "stupid" or "dumb." Quite the contrary, I find them to be just as idealistic, thoughtful and intelligent as their parents and grandparents were (and are). And while they're not dumb, most Americans, particularly those under 40, do have what Michael X. Delli Carpini and Scott Keeter once called a "thin" citizenship; this means they only follow the outlines of democracy and, in many cases, don't bother to engage at all. Most young people I talked with during my research couldn't name even one Supreme Court justice or any of the countries in Bush's "Axis of Evil."

The News Habit

A thin citizenship is good for no one. When we don't pay attention, we fall for slogans and get swayed by lofty rhetoric with little regard for policy differences and voting records. Deep citizenship lets us hold leaders accountable by engaging in a deliberative process that goes deeper.

"The role of the press," said the late James W. Carey, a journalism professor, when he addressed a journalism educators' conference in 1978, "is simply to make sure that in the short run we don't get screwed, and it does this best not by treating us as consumers of news, but by encouraging the conditions of public discourse and life." Carey argued that cultivating a deep citizenship is part of a journalist's responsibility. If Carey was indicating that the business part of this equation should not be considered as paramount, it's important for us to recognize that muscular citizens are good for business, too. Not only do citizens benefit from good journalism, but also journalism gets a boost from having engaged, news-hungry citizens.

There are plenty of things that we, as a society, can do to reverse the 30-year trend. I met with poor, black, middle-school students in New Orleans in 2001 who were all reading *The New York Times* online. Why? Because their sixth grade teacher made them. As eighth graders, these kids were still getting the e-mail alerts from the Times. After speaking with them, I concluded that if you assign it, they will read it. In other words, kids who are asked to follow the news often keep up the habit on their own.

This experience—and others like it—have convinced me of the value there would be in news organizations and media companies connecting more actively with schools and with students. While many of us worry about journalists who take on such a public role, there is nothing partisan or unseemly, and certainly no conflict of interest, when journalists try to get kids to follow the news.

Colleges can do their part, too. Imagine what a news and civics portion of the SAT would do to engage college-bound students. Or the effect of a single question on the Common Application: "What have you done to effect political change in your community?" There is a group—the Student Voices Project, sponsored by the University of Pennsylvania's Annenberg School—in which educators, politicians and journalists work together to help students change their communities, and it appears to be effective.

Rebuilding Trust

News organizations can do a lot to improve their product, too, yet most are doing nearly everything wrong. At my former employer, CNN, "Nancy Grace" and "Showbiz Tonight" have been added to the Headline News lineup during the past few years—with a concomitant loss of hard news. When I met CNN President Jonathan Klein at a conference a couple of years ago, I shared with him my view that this kind of programming is a mistake.

I used this example: What if I decided to pander to my students by bringing mixed drinks to class? Most students would object for two reasons: they'd rightly be suspicious of my ability to mix drinks well and, although some would enjoy the party atmosphere, most, I believe, regard my class as a refuge from dorm parties. Similarly, CNN is not a good place for entertainment; for starters, its entertainment isn't as much fun as "Fear Factor" and "Desperate Housewives" but, more importantly, CNN should be a refuge, a place we turn to for elevated conversation, to become politically informed, and to engage in a process that holds the powerful accountable.

Some find The Daily Show to be an example of how entertainment debases news. But watch it and immediately its flashes of intelligence, its analysis, and its ability and willingness to hold leaders accountable are apparent. It's no coincidence, then, that some of the more serious and politically engaged news junkies watch The Daily Show; it shares many, though certainly not all, of the best values and practices of journalism.

What I've come to understand is that part of why young people don't follow the news is that many of them no longer trust those bringing the news to them, especially commercial outlets. My research shows this is due to four factors, which conspire to make many young people deeply suspicious of corporate media.

1. Young people are deeply—and rightly—suspicious of the rising sensationalism in the media.
2. Attacks from the right have labeled, unfairly, I believe, the mainstream press as being left wing.
3. Because many on the left criticize the press for its failure to ask tough questions in the months leading up to the Iraq War, a lot of young people don't realize there were a number of hard-hitting reports and editorials.
4. Well meaning "media literacy" educators have sought to make young people aware of the dangers of media, in general, without helping them to see the benefits of journalism, in particular.

What is the best antidote to their mistrust?

Perhaps it is coverage like that which happened in the aftermath of Hurricane Katrina, when journalists pushed back against power. Not surprisingly, they also saw their credibility (and ratings) shoot up. After Anderson Cooper's role in that coverage, CNN tried to make him more touchy-feely, but then wisely abandoned that tack to push the idea that Cooper and CNN are "holding them accountable" and "keeping them honest." In my journalism and mass communication classes, I assign hard-hitting journalism—Seymour Hersh's Abu Ghraib story, Dana Priest and Anne Hull's Walter Reed investigation, and James Risen and Eric Lichtblau's reporting on domestic spying—and I find my students often are shocked by how important journalism can be.

Despite our present economic difficulties, we live in a hopeful time, with the national zeitgeist certainly more political than it has been in years. Some of my students tell me that their lunchtime conversations are becoming more political, and conversation is certainly part of the solution to lack of civic and political engagement. My research and that of others show that young adults—even schoolchildren—seek out political news when they know that their elders and their peers care about politics. With the blossoming of this youthful interest, now is a perfect time for those who see a need to strengthen the connection between journalism and citizenship to act.

**Pew Internet &
American Life Project**

 **NO**

The Internet and Civic Engagement

Like many technical innovations, the internet was greeted enthusiastically by those who thought it would "change everything" when it comes to democratic governance. Among its predicted salutary effects is the capacity of the internet to permit ordinary citizens to short-circuit political elites and deal directly with one another and public officials; to foster deliberation, enhance trust, and create community; and—of special interest to us—to facilitate political participation.

Other observers have been doubtful about the expected benefits, pointing out that every technological advance has been greeted with the inflated expectations that faster transportation and easier communication will beget citizen empowerment and civic renewal. This insight leads to the more cautious assessment that, rather than revolutionizing democratic politics, it would end up being more of the same and reinforcing established political patterns and familiar political elites. Even more sober were those who feared that, far from cultivating social capital, the internet would foster undemocratic tendencies: greater political fragmentation, "hacktivism," and incivility.

For a variety of reasons, the internet might be expected to raise participation: The interactive capacities of the internet allow certain forms of political activity to be conducted more easily; vast amounts of political information available on the internet could have the effect of lowering the costs of acquiring political knowledge and stimulating political interest; the capacities of the internet facilitate mobilization to take political action. However, it is widely known that, with respect to a variety of politically relevant characteristics, political activists are different from the public at large. And more participation does not necessarily mean that participants are socially and economically more diverse. For one thing, internet access is far from universal among American adults, a phenomenon widely known as the "digital divide," and the contours of the digital divide reflect in certain ways the shape of participatory input. Moreover, access to the internet does not necessarily mean use of the internet for political activity. Therefore, it seems important to investigate the extent to which online political and civic activities ameliorate, reflect, or even exaggerate the long-standing tendencies in offline political activity.

Young Adults Are More Likely to Engage in "New" Forms of Online Civic Engagement

The proportion within each age group who take part in the following activities

	18–24	25–34	35–44	45–54	55–64	65+	Difference between 65+ age group and 18–24 age group
	%	%	%	%	%	%	%
Two or more offline political activities	18	26	30	28	33	26	+8
Among all adults							
Two or more online political activities	16	20	21	21	22	10	−6
Make political use of social network sites	29	15	5	3	3	1	−28
Post political content online	30	17	11	7	7	3	−27
Among internet users							
Two or more online political activities	18	23	24	26	30	27	+9
Make political use of social network sites	33	17	6	4	4	2	−31
Post political content online	34	19	12	9	10	8	−26
Among home broadband users							
Two or more online political activities	21	25	29	31	35	35	+14
Make political use of social network sites	35	18	7	5	5	4	−31
Post political content online	40	21	14	9	10	9	−31

Pew Internet & American Life Project August 2008 Survey. Respondents in the 2+ online/offline activities category include who did two or more of the following: contacting a government official (via email or via phone/letter; signing a petition (online or on paper); sending a letter to the editor (via email or US Postal Service); making a political contribution (online or offline); and communicating with a civic/political group (using digital tools or non-digital tools). Margin of error is ±2% based on all adults (n=2,251), ±3% based on internet users (n=1,655) and ±3% based on home broadband users (n=1,246). Margin of error for subgroups is higher

There are several ways in which digital tools might facilitate political participation. For one thing, several forms of political activity—including making donations, forming a group of like-minded people, contacting public officials, and registering to vote—are simply easier on the internet. Because activity can be undertaken any time of day or night from any locale with a computer and an internet connection, the costs of taking part are reduced. The capacities of the internet are also suited to facilitate the process of the formation of political groups. By making it so cheap to communicate with a large number of potential supporters, the internet reduces the costs of getting a group off the ground. The internet reduces almost to zero the additional costs of seeking to organize many rather than few potential adherents even if they are widely scattered geographically.

Perhaps as important in fostering political activity directly is the wealth of political information available to those who have access to the internet. Just about every offline source of political information is now on the Web, usually without charge: governments at all levels along with such visible public officials as members of the House and Senate, governors, and mayors of large cities; candidates for public office, political parties and organizations; print sources of political news including newspapers, wire services, newsmagazines as well as broadcast news sources that mix print material with audio and video clips. In addition, indigenous to the internet are various potentially politicizing experiences. For example, online conversations, often about political subjects, in a variety of internet venues are in most ways analogous to the political discussions that routinely take place over the dinner table or at the water cooler but have the capacity to bring together large numbers of participants spread over vast distances.

The third mechanism by which the internet might enhance political activity follows directly from its capacity to communicate with large numbers of geographically dispersed people at little cost. Candidates, parties, and political organizations do not simply use the internet as a way of disseminating information, they also use its capabilities to communicate with adherents and sympathizers and to recruit them to take political action—either on or offline. . . .

Political and civic involvement have long been dominated by those with high levels of income and education, leading some advocates to hope that internet-based engagement might alter this pattern. However, a new report by the Pew Research Center's Internet & American Life Project shows that the internet is not changing the fundamental socio-economic character of civic engagement in America. When it comes to online activities such as contributing money, contacting a government official or signing an online petition, the wealthy and well-educated continue to lead the way.

Still, there are hints that the new forms of civic engagement anchored in blogs and social networking sites could alter long-standing patterns. Some 19% of internet users have posted material online about political or social issues or used a social networking site for some form of civic or political engagement. And this group of activists is disproportionately young. . . .

Whether they take place on the internet or off, traditional political activities remain the domain of those with high levels of income and education.

Contrary to the hopes of some advocates, the internet is not changing the socio-economic character of civic engagement in America. Just as in offline civic life, the well-to-do and well-educated are more likely than those less well off to participate in online political activities such as emailing a government official, signing an online petition or making a political contribution.

In part, these disparities result from differences in internet access—those who are lower on the socio-economic ladder are less likely to go online or to have broadband access at home, making it impossible for them to engage in online political activity. Yet even within the online population there is a strong positive relationship between socio-economic status and most of the measures of internet-based political engagement we reviewed.

At the same time, because younger Americans are more likely than their elders to be internet users, the participation gap between relatively unengaged young and much more engaged middle-aged adults that ordinarily typifies offline political activity is less pronounced when it comes to political participation online. Nevertheless, within any age group, there is still a strong correlation between socio-economic status and online political and civic engagement.

There are hints that forms of civic engagement anchored in blogs and social networking sites could alter long-standing patterns that are based on socio-economic status.

In our August 2008 survey we found that 33% of internet users had a profile on a social networking site and that 31% of these social network members had engaged in activities with a civic or political focus—for example, joining a political group, or signing up as a "friend" of a candidate—on a social networking site. That works out to 10% of all internet users who have used a social networking site for some sort of political or civic engagement. In addition, 15% of internet users have gone online to add to the political discussion by posting comments on a website or blog about a political or social issue, posting pictures or video content online related to a political or social issue, or using their blog to explore political or social issues.

Taken together, just under one in five internet users (19%) have posted material about political or social issues or a used a social networking site for some form of civic or political engagement. This works out to 14% of all adults—whether or not they are internet users. A deeper analysis of this online participatory class suggests that it is not inevitable that those with high levels of income and education are the most active in civic and political affairs. In contrast to traditional acts of political participation—whether undertaken online or offline—forms of engagement that use blogs or online social network sites are not characterized by such a strong association with socio-economic stratification.

In part, this circumstance results from the very high levels of online engagement by young adults. Some 37% of internet users aged 18–29 use blogs or social networking sites as a venue for political or civic involvement, compared to 17% of online 30–49 year olds, 12% of 50–64 year olds and 10% of internet users over 65. It is difficult to measure socio-economic status for the youngest adults, those under 25—many of whom are still students. This group is, in fact, the least affluent and well educated age group in the survey. When we look at age groups separately, we find by and large that the association between income and education and online engagement re-emerges—although this association is somewhat less pronounced than for other forms of online political activism. . . .

These forms of online political engagement are, quite simply, the domain of the young.

What is most unambiguous is that posting material about political or social issues on the Web and using social networking sites politically are forms of online engagement that are dominated by the young—especially the youngest adults. Recall that, when it comes to the online political activities discussed earlier, within the population as a whole, the youngest adults (those 18 to 24) are less likely than other age groups to take part in online political activities and more likely to do so than those aged 65 and over. This pattern is largely a function of the extraordinarily high rates of internet use by young adults—90% of whom go online. When we look just at internet users, 18-to-24 year olds are actually the least likely of all age groups to take part in such online political acts as emailing a public official or making an online political donation.

In contrast, civic involvement on social network sites and blogs exhibits a much different pattern. Whether we are looking at the population as a whole or only at those who are online, these modes of online civic engagement decline steadily with age—with the youngest adults much more likely than their elders either to make political use of social networking sites or to post material about political or social issues. Among internet users, just 18% of 18-to-24 year olds engage in two or more acts of political participation online based on the activities identified in the previous chapter, but fully 33% make political use of social networking sites, and 34% post political material on the Web.

Put another way, those under age 35 represent 28% of the respondents in our survey but make up fully 72% of those who make political use of social networking sites, and 55% of those who post comments or visual material about politics on the Web. The youngest members of this group—those under age 25—constitute just 10% of our survey respondents but make up 40% of those who make political use of social networking sites and 29% of those who post comments or visual material about politics online.

It is noteworthy that neither political involvement on social networking sites nor posting material about political or social issues on the Web is strongly associated with socio-economic status. For the scale of online political activity we presented earlier, the difference between the lowest and highest income groups was 27%. For political use of social networking sites on the other hand, the difference is 3% and, for posting political content online, the difference is 5%. . . .

Compared to income and education, the relationship between age and these political activities is somewhat more complex. For offline political participation, young adults (those ages 18–24) are the group that is least likely to take part. In contrast, when it comes to online political activity, for the population as a whole, the participatory deficit of young adults is less pronounced, and it is seniors who are the least active group. This relationship, however, is largely a function of very high rates of internet use among young adults. When we consider just the internet users within each age cohort, young adults are again the least likely group to engage in political acts online, and the relatively small group of internet users who are 65 and over are quite active. In other words, the under representation of the young with respect to political participation over the internet is related to their greater likelihood to be internet users and not necessarily to any innate propensity to use the internet politically once online. . . .

When we look at the relationship of age and education to contacting a government official, we see patterns similar to what we saw earlier for over-all online and offline civic involvement. Education is highly correlated with both online and offline government contact—even among internet users. With respect to age, the relative likelihood of young adults to email a government official is largely a function of their high rates of internet use: within the online population, those aged 65 and older are roughly three times more likely to contact a government official via email as are those aged 18 to 24 (35% vs. 13%).

However, we must be cautious before concluding that these rapidly evolving, internet-based forms of political engagement will disrupt the long-standing association between education or income and various forms of political involvement. Assessing the strength of the relationship between socio-economic status and either political involvement on social networking sites or posting material about political or social issues on the Web is complicated by the fact that these forms of engagement are the province of the youngest citizens—for whom measuring socio-economic status (SES) is problematic. Because many of them are still in school or are just setting out in the work force, the 18-to-24 year olds who constitute such a disproportionate share of those who engage in these forms of internet use have not yet come to rest in terms of level of income or education and are, in fact, the least affluent and least well-educated group in the survey. Thirty-four percent are in the lowest income category, and 62% have not graduated from high school. The analogous figures for their immediate elders, those who are 25 to 34, are markedly different: 16% and 36% respectively. And, unlike the elderly, who also have relatively low levels of income and education, and the youngest adults are likely to see improvements in their educational attainment and income in the near future.

Unfortunately the relatively small number of 18–24 year olds in our survey prevents us from conducting a detailed analysis of this subgroup. However, we can gain some insight into the relationship among age, socio-economic status and these forms of internet-based engagement by isolating those under the age of 30 and comparing different subgroups within this cohort.

Considering those under thirty, we see familiar patterns for the association between online political activity and both education and income. Furthermore, when it comes to political engagement on social networking sites or posting political content online, similar patterns emerge for income but not for education. What is most striking, however, is the strong relationship between being a student and these measures of online political engagement. Among those under thirty, students are much more likely than those who are not in school both to make political use of a social networking site and to post political material online. Thirty-nine percent of the students, but only 16% of the non-students, make political use of social networking sites. The analogous figures for posting political information online are 39% and 15% respectively.

Hence, we must watch carefully to see whether these new modes of online political engagement will act as a trip wire interrupting the usual patterns of stratification of political involvement by income and education. We will have to see whether the fascinating patterns that have emerged in this survey—one that was conducted during a particular and in many ways atypical presidential campaign—will recur though time. What is more, we will have to see whether the internet continues to evolve politically, offering still more possibilities for political engagement and participation.

Will the students who have embraced the political possibilities of the internet so much more fully than their elders continue to act as early political adopters or will they be locked into their youthful technological experiences only to be trumped by a succeeding generation in the vanguard of the political uses of the Web? Furthermore, will these forms of internet-based political engagement which entail opportunities for political expression and communication among large numbers of dispersed people foster the forms of political participation that involve attempts to influence political outcomes?

EXPLORING THE ISSUE

Are Youth Indifferent to News and Politics?

Critical Thinking and Reflection

1. Do you believe an informed citizenry is necessary for democracy?
2. Is the linkage between news and citizen engagement broken? Can the Internet fix it?
3. Are there emerging forms and directions for political and civic engagement?
4. Are the differences generational in scope and influence?

Is there Common Ground?

There is always finger pointing when a social ill is identified. The resources mentioned below can be helpful for you in clarifying your own position on this issue. In this, as in all of the issues in this volume, it is important to think about this issue in abstract and general terms, and then to also consider how it operates in your own social circle. Are you informed? Are your friends? What sources do you use? How much does political discussion matter? Are you and your friends politically engaged? Finally, you are encouraged to compare your conclusions from your general impression with the reality in which you operate. The contrast is always illuminating.

Additional Resources

Pew Research Center Online at http://pewresearch.org

Check out the News IQ quiz, found on the right-hand column along with a number of other interesting quizzes, that allows you to assess your level of political knowledge and compare your results to a national sample. The Pew Internet and American Life Project at www.pewinternet.org offers many reports on uses and consequences of Internet and online activities for American life, including political concerns.

Russell Dalton, *The Good Citizen: How a Younger Generation is Reshaping American Politics* (CQ Press, 2008)

Russell Dalton uses a new set of national public opinion surveys to show how Americans are changing their views on what good citizenship means. Trends in participation, tolerance, and policy priorities reflect a younger generation that is more engaged, more tolerant, and more supportive of social justice. https://pod51004.outlook.com/owa/redir.aspx?C=p_77YJlqDEmt1oi8cyaYqOWe_7yE Vc4IeJ05Ujm5KEN8MQggmOjShGk1nE7MJSI4TDcLO4hUdTc.&URL=http%3a%2f

%2fwww.amazon.com%2fGood-Citizen-Generation-Reshaping-American%2fdp%2f1
604265566%2fref%3dsr_1_3%3fs%3dbooks%26ie%3dUTF8%26qid%3d131696902
7%26sr%3d1-3

J. Pasek, K. Kenski, D. Romer, and K. Jamieson, "America's Youth and Community Engagement" in *Communication Research* (SAGE Publications, June, 2006)

This interesting article explores how media use is related to civic activity and political awareness in 14–22–year olds.

Barb Palser. "Beneath the Tattoos," *American Journalism Review* (Summer, 2010)

In a brief op-ed piece Palser takes issue with the label of indifference that has been attached to the Millennials, pointing to their extraordinary levels of social and civic consciousness.

L.R. Sherrod and J. Lauckhardt, "The Development of Citizenship," in *The Handbook of Adolescent Psychology* (Wiley, 2009)

The authors offer an extensive analysis of the study of civic engagement. Topics include definition, conceptualization, socialization, and factors and programs that promote civic engagement.

ISSUE 17

Are Online Services Responsible for an Increase in Bullying and Harassment?

YES: **Penny A. Leisring**, from "Stalking Made Easy: How Information and Communication Technologies Are Influencing the Way People Monitor and Harass One Another," in Sharon Kleinman, ed., *The Culture of Efficiency* (Peter Lang, 2009)

NO: **Amanda Lenhart**, from "Cyberbullying and Online Teens," Pew Internet & American Life Project (June 27, 2007)

Learning Outcomes
After reading this issue, you should be able to:
• Understand the ways by which technologies contribute to bullying and harassing behavior.
• Understand that a great deal of bullying and online harassment may be unintentional.
• Evaluate your own behaviors as well as the behavior of others to become more critical about what types of information can be classified as bullying, or contributing to a hostile environment.
• Apply some common sense approaches toward thinking about how technologies influence the communication process.
• Conclude with a better understanding of what constitutes unwanted or inappropriate behavior online, and consider whether personal communication technologies contribute to an unwanted effect of online communication.

ISSUE SUMMARY

YES: Penny Leisring discusses negative effects of using online technology to cyberstalk or harass someone. Use of social networking, e-mail, GPS systems, cell phone spamming, and caller ID all can be used to create a threatening or hostile environment for those people who use them for antisocial purposes. The author also addresses the situations that lend themselves most often to these undesirable uses of communication technology, such as in the break-up of romantic relationships, abusive relationships, or just plain hostile behaviors and interactions.

NO: Amanda Lenhart reports the findings of a Pew Internet & American Life Project that investigated the likelihood of teen harassment and cyberbullying and finds that the most likely candidates to experience online abuse are girls between the ages of 15 and 17, though the reported statistics for all teens of both genders are disturbing. However, Amanda Lenhart reports that, still, more teens report being bullied offline than online.

As the selections in this issue show, human behavior sometimes changes when technology is introduced. If we are to successfully adopt social networking and other forms of online communication, we need to continue to pay attention to the deleterious effects that may result. Only by critically examining the social use of social media can we retain positive social behaviors that are necessary for socialization and survival in a more fully technologized world.

Online services are a wonderful way to communicate with others inexpensively and in real time, but the substitution of face-to-face communication often brings problems too. In this issue, we explore the phenomenon of online communication from the perspective of technology that actually causes potential problems for the senders and receivers of messages that would otherwise be monitored by face-to-face communication, including nonverbal cues, gestures, and the presence of the body.

Parents and educators have become very concerned about the use of online technologies that exacerbate antisocial childhood behavior. When greater use of e-mail, social networks, and other forms of online communication is used to harass or bully someone, the children who are the victims often fear telling parents or teachers because they are afraid that their access to the technology might be curbed.

There have been many tragic situations in which an impressionable youth has been bullied, harassed, or intimidated to such a degree that he or she experiences physical and mental problems. Perhaps one of the most well publicized tragedies is that of the young Megan Meier, a socially awkward 15-year-old who was the victim of a hoax that created so much distress for her that she committed suicide. The situation involved an adult's creation of a fictitious boy who romantically flirted with Megan, and then broke up with her online and told her that she was such a loser that she would be better off dead. The adult was indicted of computer fraud and in 2009 was acquitted. In the meantime, the "Megan Meier Cyberbullying Prevention Act (H.R., 1966)" has been introduced in the U.S. House of Representatives, which would make it a crime to knowingly transmit communication "intended to coerce, intimidate, harass, or cause substantial emotional distress to another person, using means to support severe, repeated, and hostile behavior."

Cyberbullying and online harassment are also increasing in the workplace, as more personal interactions take place on social networks, and companies are now dealing with the creation of policies that prohibit the creation of a hostile workplace. Harassment is now viewed as an act of discrimination that can be viewed as a part of the Civil Rights Act of 1964. Lewd remarks, offensive jokes, and unwanted physical contact are some of the ways in which a hostile work environment can be created, but the use of e-mail for images, jokes, and even gossip and rumors can also target an individual and fall into the category of cyberbullying and harassment.

While discourse about the impact of technology has moved far beyond the debate of the "positive" and "negative" qualities and characteristics of some communication forms, the distancing of activities beyond the interpersonal realm is increasingly viewed as an alienating effect of technology. As we live, work, and play more and more online, we need to become aware of how easy it is to let the technology do the work, and how easy it is to exercise those qualities that make us civil human beings in the increasingly technologized world.

The selections in this issue demonstrate how new problems emerge as we move from "mass" media to more personally produced and consumed media. Can technology be an excuse for bad behavior? We have been working to understand "media literacy" for many years now, but should we also think about the need to discuss "technological literacy"? Familiarity with immediate two-way communication forms is not likely to change in the near future, but we might expect to start seeing the impact of interactive media as we use more technology for a wide variety of purposes. Like many of the issues in this edition of *Taking Sides*, we are asked to consider the appropriate role of technology in communication. The technologies themselves do not induce bad behavior, but become tools for bad behavior in the hands of people who don't think critically about the relationship of media, social life, and personal behavior.

We do know that bullies, for the most part, exhibit similar behaviors in face-to-face communication and in online situations. Bullies like to control situations and watch other people being humiliated. For some reason, bullies tend to want to embarrass other people, though if they became the targets of other bullies, it's hard to predict how they might react. Online bullies hide behind their computer screens and cell phones, and can make themselves appear to be just bystanders, or cogs in the transmission of messages.

Forwarding messages, spamming, and blocking information are typical ways of creating an uncomfortable situation for someone else. Often these behaviors show up as other compulsions or obsessive behaviors too. Recent studies about children and teen behavior in Britain shows that cyberbullying is on the rise, and the insidious ways of using the Internet (especially social networks), and cell phones is the primary means of creating a hostile environment. Often the humiliating situations are recorded by cell phone and posted to YouTube or another video-sharing site; in some cases these humiliating records have gone viral on the Internet, taking the victim's identity to a global arena.

Personal communication technologies give us the illusion of personal choice and personal use, but in many ways, they can also be used as tools for communicating messages of a much broader concern. Cameras on cell phones, for example, are often banned in locker rooms, public restrooms, and places where customers might be trying on clothes—because some recorded messages have violated reasonable expectations of privacy in these environments.

YES

Penny A. Leisring

Stalking Made Easy: How Information and Communication Technologies Are Influencing the Way People Monitor and Harass One Another

Your phone rings and obscene callers are on the line. Strangers show up repeatedly in the middle of the night at your door wanting to force themselves on you sexually. This is what happened to the victim in the first case prosecuted under California's cyberstalking law. Randi Barber was being cyberstalked by a man from her church, Gary Dellapenta, who was posting things about her on the Internet. After Barber rejected Dellapenta's romantic overtures, Dellapenta posed as Barber in Internet chat rooms and announced that she had fantasies about men raping her. He posted her home address and phone number online and urged men to show up at her home in the middle of the night. He even told them how to break into her apartment and bypass her home security system. Dellapenta told the men that her refusals were part of her fantasy but that she really wanted the men to force themselves on her. Six men showed up at her home. Barber was traumatized. She lost 35 pounds, lost her job, and moved out of her home. Dellapenta was sentenced to six years in prison for stalking and for soliciting others to commit rape.

This case illustrates one way that people use the Internet to stalk and harass others. Information and communication technologies such as computers, cell phones, and BlackBerry-like devices are making stalkers more efficient. Remarkably, a "stalker's home page" exists on the Internet, containing information and Web links for people interested in stalking others. Cyberstalking is "easier and less risky" to engage in than more traditional offline forms of stalking. Stalking with technology—cyberstalking—is common, especially among college students. Most cyberstalking is perpetrated by someone who knows the victim, and often cyberstalking, like other forms of stalking, is perpetrated by an ex-partner after a romantic relationship ends. Some ex-partners hope to rekindle the relationship. Computer-mediated communication may "promote a false sense of intimacy and misunderstanding of intentions." If a person's messages are responded to, their hope and behavior may persist or increase. According to Brian Spitzberg's review of offline stalking methods, stalking often lasts for almost two years. Paul Bocij suggests that cyberstalking typically lasts about four months.

All 50 states in the U.S. have laws against stalking, and the Federal Violence Against Women Act now includes cyberstalking. Stalkers have used a variety of methods to monitor and harass their victims, including phone calls, in-person contact, and surveillance methods. The Internet has expanded stalking methods, and now people can stalk others anonymously or pseud-onymously. Cyberstalkers may send repeated e-mails, chat requests, or text messages, or they may make repeated cell phone calls to the victim. Some monitor the victim's activities by reading the victim's e-mails; online "away messages," which sometimes reveal the current location and behavior of the victim; and postings to social networking Web sites, such as MySpace and Facebook. Some perpetrators use global positioning system (GPS) devices to track their target's physical location, and they may even use computer spyware to monitor their victim's Web activity or computer keystrokes. When victims discover these activities, it can lead to tremendous fear and distress, especially for female victims. . . .

Types of Stalking with Technology

The ways in which information and communication technologies are being used to stalk and harass others are numerous. Cindy Southworth and Sarah Tucker have provided an excellent review of many cyberstalking methods. Stalkers may use cell phones to repeatedly call or send text messages to their victims. Fax machines may be used to send messages and the header on faxes may reveal the location of a victim, if she sends a fax to the stalker. Stalkers may use computers to send e-mail or instant messages to the victim or to post information about the victim on Web pages, bulletin boards, or blogs (Web logs). Spoofing is another technique used by cyberstalkers, which involves imper-sonating the victim online. Some stalkers have used anonymous re-mailers, e-mail forwarding services that mask the originating address of e-mail messages so that the sender cannot be traced. Others have spammed victims by sending hundreds of e-mail messages to clog up the victim's e-mail inbox or have signed the victim up for numerous online mailing lists so that the victim is flooded each day with e-mail. Some cyberstalkers purposely e-mail the victim files containing computer viruses. Some stalkers send pornography to their victims. Some even enlist third parties to stalk their victims, which Paul Bocij refers to as "stalking by proxy."

The Internet with its search engines and databases is also used to collect information for the purpose of monitoring or tracking victims. Vanessa Bufis, Penny Leisring, and Jessica Brinkmann found that many college students view the online "away messages" of their ex-partners. In these messages, people often reveal what they are doing and where they are located. Many college students also acknowledged checking their ex-partners' pages on social networking sites for information.

Perpetrators who are the former romantic partners of their victims may know their victims' passwords and personal identification numbers, which they could use to gain access to the victims' e-mail and voice mail accounts. One stalker accessed his victim's e-mail account and, impersonating the victim, sent threatening messages to himself that he took to the police. Technologies used by deaf individuals such as teletypewriters (TTY) and telecommunication devices for the deaf (TTD) record and save transcripts of all phone conversations, which makes it easy for stalkers to monitor victims' communications if they have access to the victims' devices. Such systems have also been used to impersonate victims. One perpetrator, pretending to be his victim, made a call to a prosecutor using the victim's TTY. The call indicated that the victim would commit suicide if charges against the perpetrator were not dropped. When help arrived it became apparent that the victim had been sleeping and had not made the call.

Stalkers sometimes resort to even more extreme measures, such as installing keystroke loggers or spyware on computers or cell phones belonging to their victims. Keystroke loggers require that the perpetrator have physical access to the victim's computer. Once installed, all keys pressed on the victim's computer are recorded, giving a perpetrator access to a lot of information, including confidential passwords. Spyware, which can be installed remotely, allows the perpetrator to track Web sites visited and e-mails sent and received by the victim. According to Bruce Gross, some spyware allows the user to access all files on the victim's computer and will search for passwords. Spyware is sometimes configured to reinstall itself if it is deleted. Small cameras can be remotely installed and activated that would allow the perpetrator to actually see inside the victim's home. Mapping sites like Google Earth (Atkinson et al., 2007) and GPS devices are used to track victims' physical locations. In addition, some new Caller Identification (ID) systems show the caller's address as well as phone number. Thus, if the victim calls the perpetrator, the victim's address will be revealed. . . .

A National Violence Against Women (NVAW) survey in the late 1990s did not assess cyberstalking, but it found that 8 percent of women and 2 percent of men were stalked by offline methods. The stalking definition used in the NVAW survey required a high level of victim fear. If the definition required that the victims be only somewhat or a little frightened by the behavior, then the stalking rates from that national sample rise considerably to 12 percent for women and 4 percent for men. According to a review by Lorraine Sheridan and her colleagues, the lifetime prevalence of stalking for women is 12 to 16 percent and for men is 4 to 7 percent. This means that approximately 1 in 6 women and approximately 1 in 14 men will be stalked in their lifetime. . . .

Studies have found that more women than men are stalked using offline methods, but at least one study has found that cyberstalking may affect more men than women and one study by Jerry Finn assessing cyberstalking/online harassment in a college sample found no gender differences. Finn's data collected in 2002 indicated that 58 percent of his sample had received unwanted pornography via e-mail or instant messenger, and between 10 and 15 percent of the sample reported that they had repeatedly received e-mails or instant messages that threatened, insulted, or harassed. Fourteen percent of the sample received such messages even after they told the sender to stop sending messages. Sexual minority students were more likely than heterosexual students to receive repeated threatening, insulting, or harassing e-mails from strangers or people that they barely knew. Finn hypothesized that this may be due to the increased harassment faced by gay, lesbian, bisexual, and transgendered individuals in the offline world.

Post-Intimate Stalking and Intimate Partner Violence

Stalking is most often perpetrated by current or former romantic partners. In his review, Brian Spitzberg finds that approximately 50 percent of stalking stems from prior romantic relationships, 25 percent is perpetrated by strangers, and 25 percent is perpetrated by acquaintances. Much stalking occurs after a romantic relationship ends, and the person who was rejected is typically the one to engage in stalking behavior. Keith Davis and his colleagues found that anger and jealousy after a romantic relationship dissolves are associated with post-breakup stalking. They also found that expressions of love are highly correlated with stalking, which supports the assertion that many people stalk their ex-partners in hopes of reuniting. Stalking may be referred to, in this context, as "unwanted pursuit."

Post-intimate relationship stalking seems to be more likely when a relationship has been abusive. T. K. Logan, Carl Leukefeld, and Bob Walker found that college students who had been stalked had higher rates of physical and emotional abuse within their relationship than students who had not been stalked. Jennifer Becker and Penny Leisring also found in a college sample that physical abuse within a relationship was associated with post-breakup unwanted pursuit behaviors. Mindy Mechanic, Terri Weaver, and Patricia Resick, in their study of battered women, found that dominance and isolation within a relationship were associated with stalking behaviors perpetrated against women. Jennifer Langhinrichsen-Rohling found that about 25 percent of sheltered battered women acknowledged engaging in stalking and unwanted pursuit behaviors toward their abusive partners during separations. Most of the stalking was bi-directional in nature. In other words, many of the male partners were also engaging in stalking and unwanted pursuit behaviors.

Partner violence does not necessarily end after a breakup, and stalkers have been known to engage in physical and psychological aggression toward their ex-partners. In a study by Karl Roberts, 35 percent of the college women who had been stalked were victims of violence during the stalking. T. K. Logan, Lisa Shannon, and Jennifer Cole surveyed women who had restraining orders against violent partners or ex-partners and found that the women who had been stalked by their partners or ex-partners experienced more violations of restraining orders and more severe abuse than the victimized women who had not been stalked. Stalking has been characterized as a "severe form of emotional/psychological abuse." Stalking and psychological aggression seem to have similar antecedents, such as a need for control, anxious attachment, and harsh parental discipline.

Characteristics of Stalkers

What do we know about stalkers? Most of the research examining the characteristics of stalkers has focused on those who perpetrate stalking using traditional offline methods, and few studies have focused exclusively on cyberstalkers. However, since many cyberstalkers engage in offline methods of stalking in addition to using technology to stalk their victims, the research examining offline stalkers is likely relevant. Paul Bocij asserts that almost a third of cyberstalkers use offline stalking methods in addition to using technology.

Domestic violence perpetrators and stalkers seem to share many of the same traits. A history of childhood abuse and disrupted attachment are common among stalkers and batterers. Some stalkers and batterers also appear to have borderline personality disorder traits. Borderline personality disorder is characterized by an intense fear of abandonment, impulsivity, emotional instability, and unstable interpersonal relationships. Thus, when people with borderline personality disorder traits are rejected by their intimate partners, they may have extreme difficulty handling the loss, and they may persistently and inappropriately attempt to reconnect and avoid abandonment. . . . Jealousy and a need for control are also characteristics shared by domestic violence perpetrators and stalkers.

We know very little about the characteristics of cyberstalkers in particular. The gender distribution of cyberstalking may be different than that of offline stalking; equal rates of cyberstalking seem to be found across genders, at least in college populations. Cyberstalking can be so easy to perpetrate from the comfort of home that cyberstalkers may have less psychopathology than offline stalkers. This is a hypothesis worthy of study. Paul Bocij points out that not all cyberstalkers (or offline stalkers) have psychological disorders. Stephen Morewitz hypothesizes that cyberstalkers may have higher socioeconomic status than offline stalkers, as reflected in their access to the Internet and other means for electronically mediated communication, such as cell phones and BlackBerry-like handheld devices. He points out, however, that this potential difference is likely to diminish as free e-mail and Internet access become even more widespread.

Information regarding treatment for cyberstalkers is needed. Oliver Howes discussed a case in which a 32-year-old woman was treated for compulsively sending text messages to her ex-boyfriend after he ended the relationship. She was spending four hours per day sending text messages and was treated with the antidepressant Trazodone and with behavior modification. The behavior modification component of treatment involved monitoring the patient's behavior, using relaxation methods, and scheduling time for sending messages with increased intervals between messages. The patient's compulsive texting gradually ceased. While the improvement for the woman in this case study is encouraging, it should be noted that without a control group we cannot know for certain whether improvement was due to the specific treatment utilized. Controlled trials of treatment for cyberstalkers are clearly warranted.

Effects on Victims

Offline stalking and cyberstalking can have various effects on victims ranging from mild annoyance to severe fear and psychological maladjustment. Symptoms of depression, drug use, and posttraumatic stress disorder have been found among stalking victims. . . . In Michele Pathé and Paul Mullen's clinical sample, they found that 24 percent of stalking victims experienced suicidal thoughts or attempted suicide. Kathleen Basile and her colleagues found in a nationally representative sample of the U.S. that stalking was associated with posttraumatic stress symptoms even after controlling for other types of violence perpetrated by the stalker. T. K. Logan and Jennifer Cole found stalking to be associated with anxiety symptoms over and above other forms of intimate partner violence in their sample of women who had obtained restraining orders against their violent partners. Karen Abrams and Gail Robinson suggest that women stalked by ex-partners may experience low self-esteem and guilt over their choice of romantic partners. Some victims may turn to substances as a way of coping with their victimization. Sheryl Pimlott-Kubiak and Lilia Cortina found that men and women who had been stalked had higher levels of prescription and illegal drug use than non-victims. Pathé and Mullen found that stalking victims reported increased smoking and drinking as a result of their victimization.

In addition to psychological consequences, some stalking victims also receive physical injuries. Women stalked by intimate partners or ex-partners are over four times more likely to be physically injured than women stalked by others. Over 80 percent of women who are stalked by an intimate partner have also been physically assaulted by that partner. Acquaintances, as well as intimate partners, can physically harm their stalking victims. Amy Boyer was shot and killed in 1999 by a cyberstalker, Liam Youens, who was able to locate her work address online. Boyer's former schoolmate, Youens had posted his plans to murder her online. Youens claimed he had been in love with her for years. He committed suicide right after killing her.

Many stalking victims report that they have taken precautions and have changed their routines as a result of being stalked. Some victims move and change jobs. Jayne Hitchcock bought a gun for self-protection after she was cyberstalked and her phone number and address had been posted online by the perpetrator. . . .

Preventative Measures and Steps to Take if Cyberstalked

There are various things that can be done to reduce the odds of being a victim of cyberstalking. For example, everyone should periodically conduct an Internet search to see what information about them is available online for all to see. If they find information that they would like removed, they should contact the Web master of the site where the information is located. People should use extreme caution when posting information about themselves, considering the public nature of information on the Internet. Emily Spence-Diehl argues that people should only post information that they would be comfortable having on the front page of their local newspaper. Thus, college students should utilize privacy functions on social networking Web sites like Facebook and MySpace so that they can control who has access to the material they post. They should think twice about posting any personal information on these sites. If college students do not want their ex-partner to know, for example, that they are now dating someone new, then they should refrain from posting such information or pictures with their new partner on social networking Web sites.

To avoid file corruption due to computer viruses sent by stalkers, backing up files on a scheduled basis is recommended. Computer users should also check for and regularly install updates to their operating systems to maximize security. Computer passwords and personal identification numbers (PINs) should be changed regularly, too. Bruce Arnold urges computer users to choose Internet service providers based on professionalism rather than lowest cost. He also recommends that people be cautious about including their cell phone numbers in e-mail signature files.

Once people determine that they are being stalked, there are many concrete steps they can take. Jerry Finn and Mary Banach and Sharon Miceli, Shannon Santana, and Bonnie Fisher list numerous resources that provide information and assistance to stalking victims, including the Working to Halt Online Abuse Web site, www.haltabuse.org. As soon as a person feels uncomfortable with the behavior of a potential stalker, sending a clear statement to the perpetrator that the behavior is unwanted is crucial. J. Reid Meloy recommends that a third party, such as an attorney, spouse, or mental health professional, contact the perpetrator once a pattern of behavior has been established. According to Meloy, the third party should alert the perpetrator that the behavior is unwanted and that the police will be contacted if the behavior continues. If a stalker continues to contact the victim after being told to stop, then the offense becomes "aggravated stalking." Avoiding further contact with the perpetrator will be critical because contact may serve to reinforce or encourage the stalking behavior.

The victim should retain and print all "cyber-evidence," such as e-mails, facsimiles, instant messages, and Web postings. If the software being used does not lend itself easily to printing the communication, then a screen capture utility should be used to document the cyberstalking behavior. Cyber-evidence will enable the victim to make a stronger case against the stalker if police and judicial involvement is warranted. However, most stalking police reports do not lead to arrests, and restraining orders are not necessarily effective; one review found they were violated 40 percent of the time and that they were thought to have intensified the stalking 20 percent of the time. Victims and their advocates should be aware that certain acts by the victim, such as filing a restraining order or threatening to contact authorities, may lead to retaliation or violence by the stalker. Bocij recommends contacting the police if one receives a threat that they believe someone will act on.

Victims should take steps to privatize any personal information about them on the Internet and should block e-mail and instant messages from perpetrators. They should consider contacting the Internet service providers used by their stalkers to request that stalkers' memberships be canceled. A complaint to the Internet service provider or re-mailer will often cause e-mail harassment or "e-mail bombing" to stop. Victims can also change their user-names, their e-mail and instant messaging addresses, and their e-mail pro-viders. Louise Ellison suggests that women use a male or a gender neutral username. Victims can also use encryption software so that only intended recipients can read sent messages. They should also make sure that none of the security codes or accounts that they have (for example, health insurance) use their social security number as the identification number. Antivirus software and a firewall program should be utilized. . . .

Amanda Lenhart

 # NO

Cyberbullying and Online Teens

About one third (32%) of all teenagers who use the internet say they have been targets of a range of annoying and potentially menacing online activities—such as receiving threatening messages; having their private emails or text messages forwarded without consent; having an embarrassing picture posted without permission; or having rumors about them spread online. . . .

Depending on the circumstances, these harassing or "cyberbullying" behaviors may be truly threatening, merely annoying or relatively benign. But several patterns are clear: girls are more likely than boys to be targets; and teens who share their identities and thoughts online are more likely to be targets than are those who lead less active online lives.

Of all the online harassment asked about, the greatest number of teens told us that they had had a private communication forwarded or publicly posted without their permission. One in 6 teens (15%) told us someone had forwarded or posted communication they assumed was private. About 13% of teens told us that someone had spread a rumor about them online, and another 13% said that someone had sent them a threatening or aggressive email, IM or text message. Some 6% of online teens told us that someone had posted an embarrassing picture of them without their permission.

Yet when asked where they thought bullying happened most often to teens their age, the majority of teens, 67%, said that bullying and harassment happens more *offline than online. Less than one in three teens (29%) said that they thought that bullying was more likely to happen online, and three percent said they thought it happened both online and offline equally.*

These results come from a nationally-representative phone survey of 935 teenagers by the Pew Internet & American Life Project.

In focus groups conducted by the Project about the issue, one 16-year-old girl casually described how she and her classmates bullied a fellow student: "There's one MySpace from my school this year. There's this boy in my anatomy class who everybody hates. He's like the smart kid in class. Everybody's jealous. They all want to be smart. He always wants to work in our group and I hate it. And we started this thing, some girl in my class started this I Hate [Name] MySpace thing. So everybody in school goes on it to comment bad things about this boy."

The Gender Gap

Girls are more likely than boys to say that they have ever experienced cyberbullying—38% of online girls report being bullied, compared with 26% of online boys. Older girls in particular are more likely to report being bullied than any other age and gender group, with 41% of online girls ages 15 to 17 reporting these experiences. Teens who use social network sites like MySpace and Facebook and teens who use the internet daily are also more likely to say that they have been cyberbullied. Nearly 4 in 10 social network users (39%) have been cyberbullied in some way, compared with 22% of online teens who do not use social networks. . . .

Fewer Communications Are Private Anymore

The rumor mill speeds up.

A bit more than one in eight or 13% of teens said that someone had spread a rumor about them online. A girl in middle school told us: "I know a lot of times online someone will say something about one person and it'll spread and then the next day in school, I know there's like one of my friends, something happened online and people started saying she said something that she never said, and the next day we came into school and no one would talk to her and everyone's ignoring her. And she had no idea what was going on. Then someone sent her the whole conversation between these two people."

Girls are more likely to report someone spreading rumors about them than boys, with 16% of girls reporting rumor-spreading compared with 9% of boys. Social network users are more likely than those who do not use social networks to report that someone had spread a rumor about them (16% vs. 8%). . . .

Older Girls Receive More Online Threats

One in eight online teens (13%) reported that someone had sent them a threatening or aggressive email, instant message or text message. One fifteen-year-old boy in a focus group admitted, "I played a prank on someone but it wasn't serious. I told them I was going to come take them from their house and kill them and throw them in the woods. It's the best prank because it's like 'oh my god, I'm calling the police' and I was like 'I'm just kidding, I was just messing with you.' She got so scared though."

Older teens, particularly 15- to 17-year-old girls, are more like to report that they have received a threatening email or message. Overall, 9% of online teens ages 12–14 say they have been threatened via email, IM or text, while 16% of online teens ages 15–17 report similar harassment.

Among older girls, 19% have received threatening or aggressive email, IMs or text messages. Social network users are more likely than those who do not use social networks to report that someone had sent them a threatening or aggressive email (16% vs. 8%).

Um, I Swear That Is Not Me

Fewer teens, some 6%, reported that someone had posted an embarrassing picture of them online without their permission. Not surprisingly, given the number of photos posted on social networking websites, users of those sites are more likely to report that someone had posted embarrassing pictures of them online without their permission—9% of social network users reported this, compared with just 2% of those who do not use social networking sites. Similarly, teens who post photos themselves are more likely to report that someone has posted an embarrassing photo of them without their permission. One 17-year-old boy explained "I'm not a big fan of MySpace. Well, I got in trouble from one of them at my school. I had one and they [other friends] put a bad picture up there [on her page] and I got in a little trouble at school. . . . Some girl just put up like pictures of us on New Year's Eve and the Dean saw it."

Intense Internet Users Are Bullied More

Online teens who have created content for the internet—for instance, by authoring blogs, uploading photos, sharing artwork or helping others build websites—are more likely to report cyberbullying and harassment than their peers. Content creators are also more likely to use social networks—places to create and display and receive feedback on content creations, and social network users are also more likely to be cyberbullied. . . .

Bullying Happens More Often Offline

Two-thirds of all teens (67%) said that bullying and harassment happens more *offline* than online. Fewer than one in three teens (29%) said that they thought that bullying was more likely to happen online, and 3% said they thought it happened both online and offline equally.

Girls are a bit more likely than boys to say that bullying happens more online (33% of girls vs. 25% of boys), though overall, both boys and girls say that kids their age are more likely to be harassed offline. White teens are a bit more likely than African-American teens to think that bullying is more of a problem online—32% of white teens said bullying happens more often online, while 18% of African-American teens said the same. Teens who have online profiles are just as likely as those who do not to say that bullying happens more often offline.

Teens who have been cyberbullied are more likely than their peers who have not been bullied to say that they believe bullying happens online more than offline. However, the majority of bullied teens say that bullying is more likely to happen offline than online. More than 7 in 10 (71%) of teens who have not experienced bullying believe it happens more often offline, while 57% of teens who have been cyberbullied themselves say bullying happens more offline.

Why Do Teens Bully Online?

In our focus groups, we asked teens about online experiences they had with bullying and harassment. In some cases what we heard was that adolescent cruelty had simply moved from the school yard, the locker room, the bathroom wall and the phone onto the internet. The simplicity of being able to replicate and quickly transmit digital content makes bullying quite easy. "Just copy and paste whatever somebody says," a middle school girl explains as she describes online bullying tactics. "You have to watch what you say," counsels another middle school girl. "If that person's at their house and if you say something about them and you don't know they're there or if you think that person's your friend and you trust them and you're like, 'Oh, well, she's really being annoying,' she could copy and paste and send it to [anyone]." Another middle school girl describes how the manipulation of digital materials can be used to hurt someone. "Like I was in a fight with a girl and she printed out our conversation, changed some things that I said, and brought it into school, so I looked like a terrible person."

Some teens suggested that it is the mediated nature of the communication that contributes to bullying, insulating teens from the consequences of their actions. One high school boy responded to the question whether he had heard of cyberbullying: "I've heard of it and experienced it. People think they are a million times stronger because they can hide behind their computer monitor. Also known as 'e-thugs.' Basically I just ignored the person and went along with my own civilized business." A middle school girl described "stuff starting online for no reason."

Intolerance also sparks online bullying incidents, as a middle school girl related in a focus group. "I have this one friend and he's gay and his account got hacked and someone put all these really homophobic stuff on there and posted like a mass bulletin of like some guy with his head smashed open like run over by a car. It was really gruesome and disgusting."

Bullying has entered the digital age. The impulses behind it are the same, but the effect is magnified. In the past, the materials of bullying would have been whispered, shouted or passed around. Now, with a few clicks, a photo, video or a conversation can be shared with hundreds via email or millions through a website, online profile or blog posting.

Methodology

This report draws on two main research project methodologies—a telephone survey of teens and parents, and a series of focus group discussions with teens. The Parents & Teens 2006 Survey sponsored by the Pew Internet and American Life Project obtained telephone interviews with a nationally representative call-back sample of 935 teens age 12 to 17 years old and their parents living in continental United States telephone households. The telephone sample was pulled from previous Pew Internet Project surveys fielded in 2004, 2005, and 2006. Households with a child age 18 or younger were called back and screened to find 12- to 17-year-olds. The survey was conducted by Princeton

Survey Research Associates International. The interviews were done in English by Princeton Data Source, LLC, from October 23 to November 19, 2006. Statistical results are weighted to correct known demographic discrepancies. The margin of sampling error for the complete set of weighted data is ±3.7%. The response rate for the full survey is 46% of the previously interviewed households.

A total of 7 focus groups were conducted with youth in June 2006. Three of the groups were conducted in an East Coast city and three were conducted in a Midwestern city. One focus group was conducted online, with high schoolers and a mix of boys and girls. The other six groups were single gender, and interviewed 7th and 8th graders, 9th and 10th graders and 11th and 12th graders, one each of boys and girls for each grade group. . . .

EXPLORING THE ISSUE

Are Online Services Responsible for an Increase in Bullying and Harassment?

Critical Thinking and Reflection

1. Have you, or someone you care about, ever experienced face-to-face or online bullying? How powerless does it make you feel?
2. Sometimes, social cues in online communication are misunderstood, such as when someone uses all capitals to send a message, and the receiver thinks they are being flamed. The unintentional uses of technology and digital communication can be as harmful as other forms of direct hostility or harassment.
3. Critically thinking about the consequences of online behavior can go a long way toward preventing an unintentional hostile situation, but could some form of online "politeness" or "suggested behaviors" help guide people who are new to this way of communicating?
4. Think about the intimacy in online communication. Most people use personal technologies in the home, or in an intimate setting, and because messages are transmitted with the speed of a keystroke, most messages may be emotional, rather than objective. We need to develop a more even-handed approach to thinking about our online behavior.
5. Similarly, people receive the message we send in very intimate settings. How does that influence their vulnerability to a message?

Is there Common Ground?

One of the problems with life in the digital age is that things seem to be changing faster and faster. Our ability to keep up with developing appropriate modes of communication is often somewhat challenged by the speed with which the technologies allow us to send messages. We all probably know that thinking before we act is a good rule of thumb, but in instant communication, we tend to react first, rather than think first.

Additional Resources

The problem of online harassment and cyberbullying has become so prevalent in our society that even the FCC has begun to take a stand on identifying and defining social behaviors online:

www.fcc.gov/search/results/cyberbullying

There are many groups available on the Internet to help parents and teachers deal with children and cyberbullying. The group "Stop Cyberbullying Now" presents information for children and teens from 7 to 17:

www.stopcyberbullying.org/index2.html

The National Crime Prevention Council has sponsored a contest to involve children and teens in creating messages to raise awareness of cyberbullying:

www.ncpc.org/newsroom/current-campaigns/cyberbullying/

The Web site of Ars Technica explains the impact of the Megan Meier Cyberbullying Prevention Act:

http://arstechnica.com/tech-policy/news/2009/05

The Pew Internet & American Life Project has also produced a report called "Social Isolation and New Technology," in which they report on social isolation that sometimes results from more use of social technology and social systems on the Internet:

www.pewinternet.org/

ISSUE 18

Are People Better Informed in the Information Society?

YES: Linda A. Jackson, Alexander von Eye, Frank A. Biocca, Gretchen Barbatsis, Yong Zhao, and Hiram E. Fitzgerald, from "Does Home Internet Use Influence the Academic Performance of Low-Income Children?" *Developmental Psychology* (vol. 42, no. 3, 2006)

NO: Mark Bauerlein, from *The Dumbest Generation: How the Digital Age Stupefies Young Americans and Jeopardizes Our Future* (Tarcher/Penguin, 2008)

Learning Outcomes

After reading this issue, you should be able to:

- Discuss the benefits and challenges of being a digital native.
- Discuss whether technology can replace traditional education.
- Compare and contrast Internet homes with non-Internet homes, whether rich or poor.
- Evaluate the effectiveness of Bauerlein's argument linking the digital age and being dumb.

ISSUE SUMMARY

YES: Linda Jackson et al. conducted a 16-month survey of Internet use by youth age 10–18 in low-income homes. They found that youth who used the Internet more had higher scores on standardized tests of reading achievement and higher GPAs. This work supports the optimism surrounding the Internet as a tool to level the educational playing field.

NO: Mark Bauerlein finds the hopes for better-educated youth in the digital age to be an empty promise. Youth spend much of their leisure time in front of computer and television screens, but the information age has failed to produce a well-informed, thoughtful public. Instead we have a nation of know-nothings who don't read, follow politics, or vote—and who can't compete internationally.

Many people feel that as we move toward a more technologically oriented lifestyle, we, as a nation, and as participants in the new information society, are inevitably moving toward a better quality of life. It almost seems logical that better technology is the result of moving from more primitive forms of communicating to more sophisticated, faster, and efficient means. But an age-old question is whether the ability to communicate equals a quality communication experience. Without a doubt, messages that can be sent, retrieved, and enhanced may all appear to be technological breakthroughs and positive transactions. But there is another side to this scenario in which we must address whether an excess of information truly informs.

In this issue, we examine two selections that ask whether the Internet and other digital technologies have created a better-informed society. Jackson and her colleagues demonstrate the potential of the Internet to enhance educational outcomes for low-income children. Bauerlein is troubled by the poorly educated youth of this generation. Although they are dubbed digital natives, he argues that this is a dumb generation, unable to perform the intellectual work needed for the future of the United States. How can you reconcile these two selections? Both contain factual material. Can both be true?

Jackson et al. were involved in an extensive longitudinal study of Internet use in low-income homes. Their findings were complex, but one conclusion is inescapable: The Internet showed the potential to enhance academic achievement. The introduction to this article tells us that other studies have been equivocal. Issues for you to judge are whether this study seems valid and reliable. Are you convinced that their finding is "inescapable"? If not, what other research questions would you pose? If you are convinced that this conclusion is correct, then how could the outcome for a generation of digital natives be so poor?

The Information Highway and the Digital Age stimulated hopes for a generation able to multitask, plumb the depths of digital information, and create a sophisticated synthesis. The ability to communicate across platforms should be almost inbred, with most everyone able to capture and stream audio and video, create Web sites, post their creations to YouTube, and use sophisticated hardware and software to easily accomplish these tasks. Yet the chapter titles in Bauerlein's book are a litany of accusation: knowledge deficits, the new bibliophobes, online learning, and nonlearning are a few titles. The culprit is the digital age.

Despite the number or sources and technologies available, people are not better educated or more informed today. His statistics are frightening. If Bauerlein is correct, there is much evidence to support the idea that as time goes by, the public's knowledge of basic civics and politics becomes even weaker. If this is the scenario of the future, we must question whether the information society represents a better world, or a world in which we have lost much of what we already had.

Another perspective adds additional concerns to this debate. Marshall McLuhan and his colleague Harold Innis wrote about forms of communication. Innis wrote about time and space-bound communication forms and the influence these types of communication had on society. McLuhan applied these notions to electronic media, famously stating that "the medium is the message." His reflections on "hot" and "cold" media led him to posit that the medium influences the neurological processing, that in fact the medium influences the brain. This radical notion that our forms of communication can actually create neurological changes is termed technological determinism. Nicholas Carr writes on this tradition in his book, *The Shallows*. He argues that there are neurological effects of the Internet that shortchange our brain power, impeding comprehension and attention and thereby limiting our ability to concentrate and immerse ourselves in our work. See reference in Additional Resources.

It is interesting to note that virtually every new form of technology, especially media, has been greeted with a mixed sense of optimism and pessimism. New technologies challenge us to think of new practices, new values, and new structures. Sometimes the combination of those elements suggest comfort, ease, and security—other times the threat to what we already know can be a disconcerting feeling of change, without control. We might be able to look back at the evolution of media and think that the variety of content available is great, but it would also be possible to see how our media forms have changed in negative ways too. Your parents were of the generation who knew free television and radio—when media in the airwaves was delivered to the home without a hefty cable bill. Today, unless you live in a part of the country where broadcast signals can still be received in your home, you may not have any choice in your delivery service or the charges affixed by your program provider.

The YES and NO selections ask the reader to make real decisions about how they feel about new technologies and the quality of our lives. The author Neil Postman wrote about predicting what our future would be like in his book, *Amusing Ourselves to Death* (Penguin, 1985). Postman recalled earlier authors, like George Orwell, who, in 1949, wrote a futuristic book called *1984* (Harcourt, Brace), and Aldous Huxley, who, in 1932, wrote *Brave New World* (London, Chatto, & Windus). Each of these authors focused on the most common form of media available to them—print media in the form of their book—and each dealt with the future in a different way. Orwell foretold of a time in which people couldn't read because they had no books. Huxley's world envisioned a world with books, but the people chose not to read. We ask you, our readers—does a new, improved Internet help transfer and store information that helps you lead a better informed way of life?

YES

Linda A. Jackson et al.

Does Home Internet Use Influence the Academic Performance of Low-Income Children?

Decades of research has focused on the issue of whether using computers facilitates learning, typically measured as school performance. After reviewing dozens of studies of school learning with computer-based technology, including five meta-analytic reviews, Roschelle and colleagues came to the less-than-satisfying conclusion that the findings are inconclusive. For example, one meta-analytic review of over 500 studies (kindergarten through twelfth-grade students) found positive effects of computer tutoring applications on achievement test scores. However, other uses of the computer, such as simulations and enrichment applications, had no effects. Still other findings suggest that the benefits of computer-based instruction are clearer for mathematics and science than they are for other subjects. For example, a study by the Educational Testing Service found that using computers to engage higher-order thinking skills was related to better school performance in mathematics by fourth and eighth graders.

Roschelle et al. offered three explanations for the equivocal findings with respect to computer-based instruction and school performance. First, variability in hardware and software among schools participating in the research may explain the equivocal findings. Second, the failure of schools to accompany technology use with concurrent reforms in the other areas, such as curriculum and teacher professional development, may explain the failure to find beneficial effects of technology use on academic performance. Third, the lack of rigorous, structured longitudinal studies may explain the failure to find positive effects of computer-based instruction, as well as information technology use in general, on academic performance. Rochelle and colleagues suggest that positive effects are most likely to emerge when technology is used to support the four fundamentals of learning: active engagement, participation in groups, frequent interaction and feedback, and connections to real-world contexts.

Subrahmanyam and colleagues reviewed the research on computer use and cognitive skills, focusing on a broad array of cognitive competencies but particularly on visual intelligence skills, such as spatial skills and iconic and image representation skills. These authors conclude that computer use does contribute to cognitive skills, specifically to visual skills. For example, playing certain types of computer games, namely action games that involve rapid movement, imagery, intense interaction, and multiple activities occurring simultaneously, improves visual intelligence skills. As the authors point out, these skills "provide 'training wheels' for computer literacy" and are "especially useful in the fields of science and technology, where proficiency in manipulating images on a screen is increasingly important." However, they also note that, "computer game playing can enhance a particular skill only if the game uses that skill and if the child's initial skill level has matured to a certain level." Moreover, ". . . much of the existing research on computer games has measured effects only immediately after playing, and thus does not address questions about the cumulative impact of interactive games on learning."

Other findings point to a relationship between technology use and academic performance, although causal relationships have been difficult to establish. Several studies show that the presence of educational resources in the home, including computers, is a strong predictor of academic success in mathematics and science. Having a home computer has been associated with higher test scores in reading, even after controlling for family income and other factors related to reading test scores. Still other findings indicate that participating in a networked community of learners improves educational outcomes for at-risk children. Some researchers have even suggested that recent nationwide increases in nonverbal intelligence test scores may be attributable to "exposure to the proliferation of imagery in electronic technology."

Overall, whether using computer-based technology contributes to children's academic performance remains uncertain. Available evidence suggests that having a home computer is linked to somewhat better academic performance, although most studies fail to control for factors that covary with having a home computer (e.g., parental income and education). The effects of computer-based school and after-school activities are unclear, although favorable effects have been observed under some circumstances (e.g., when a supportive learning environment exists; Project TELL, 1990–1997). Even more uncertain is whether using the Internet at home has positive or negative effects on academic performance, such as school grades and standardized tests of achievement. Overall, based on evidence of positive effects of using computer-based technology on academic performance, the following hypothesis was formulated:

Hypothesis 1. Greater home Internet use will be associated with better academic performance in the months that follow than will less home Internet use.

Also of interest in the HomeNetToo project was the frequency and nature of low-income children's home Internet use.[1] Numerous surveys have attempted to measure the frequency of children's Internet use—the length of time children spend online. Estimates vary widely, depending on how Internet

---

[1]A variety of motivation, affective, and cognitive antecedents and consequences of home Internet use were assessed in surveys completed at pretrial, 1 month, 3 months, 9 months, and posttrial (i.e., 16 months).

use is measured (e.g., self-report, automatically recorded), the ages of children sampled, when data were collected (i.e., year of the study), and how Internet use is defined (e.g., length of time online, frequency of use). At one extreme are estimates that children spend approximately 1 hour a day online. At the other extreme are estimates that children spend only 3 hours a week using the Internet. These findings contrast with popular opinion that America's children are spending a great deal of time online.

Other research examined the nature of children's Internet use—what they actually do when they go online. Once again, findings vary, depending on the same factors that influence estimates of the frequency of Internet use as previously discussed (e.g., ages of children sampled). Some studies find that children's primary use of the Internet is for schoolwork, specifically searching the Web for information needed for school projects. The second most common use of the Internet is to communicate with peers using e-mail, instant messaging, and chat rooms. However, the extent of children's Internet use for communication is unclear, in part, because few studies have recorded actual use (versus self-reported use) and, in part, because studies are so few.

Gross, using the diary report of upper-middle-class adolescents, found that the extent to which the Internet was used for communication was dependent on the number of acquaintances, family, and friends online. Communication was the number one use of the Internet in Gross's study, a finding that has appeared consistently in more recent studies using upper-middle-class adolescents. Less clear is whether this finding was true in 2000 for poor adolescents and whether it was or still is true of younger children. Conceivably, younger children may use the Internet more for information gathering than they do for communication.

Based on the limited research available about the frequency and nature of children's Internet use, the following hypotheses were formulated:

Hypothesis 2. Children will spend between 3 hours weekly and 1 hour daily using the Internet at home.

Hypothesis 3. The Internet will more often be used for information than for communication.

Another interest of the HomeNetToo project is the relationship between children's sociodemographic characteristics and their Internet use. Previous research on these relationships has focused almost exclusively on adults. Findings for adults indicate race and age differences in Internet use.[2] African Americans use the Internet less than do European Americans; younger adults use the Internet more than do older adults. Gender differences in Internet use, though prevalent globally, have decreased dramatically in the United States. In 1995, approximately 95% of Internet users were men and boys. By 2002, one half

---

[2]Although socioeconomic status has consistently been related to Internet use, our sample was intentionally homogeneous with regard to this factor.

of all users were woman and girls. Researchers have attributed this gender shift to the proliferation of Internet communication tools that have attracted women and girls to it. In support of this view, studies indicate that women are more likely than men are to use the Internet for communication.

Whether sociodemographic characteristics influence children's Internet use is unclear from existing research. Race differences in children's Internet use have not been examined, especially when access to the Internet is not an issue (i.e., within socioeconomic groups). Among teens, some evidence suggests that African Americans use the Internet less than do European Americans. Some additional evidence asserts that older children use the Internet more than do younger children, especially for communicating with peers. Studies of gender and children's Internet use are sparse, and findings are mixed. One study found gender parity in all Internet activities except the number of Web sites visited: boys (ages 8 to 13) visited more Web sites than did girls the same age. Another study found that, although teenage girls used the Internet less than did teenage boys, they were more likely than boys were to use e-mail (56% of the girls versus 43% of the boys). Based on existing research, the following hypotheses were formulated:

> *Hypothesis 4.* African-American children and younger children will use the Internet less than will European American children and older children, respectively.

> *Hypothesis 5.* Girls will use the Internet's communication tools (e.g., e-mail) more than will boys; boys will use the Internet's information tools (e.g., Web pages) more than will girls.

We also explored relationships among age, Internet use, and academic performance. Two questions were of particular interest. First, does age influence the nature of Internet use such that younger participants use the Internet more for information whereas older participants (i.e., adolescents) use it more for communication? Second, are the effects of Internet use on academic performance, if any, similar across the age range considered in this research (i.e., age 10 to 18 years)? Alternatively, does any evidence exist of a developmentally "sensitive" period during which Internet use has the greatest impact on academic performance?

Methods

Participants and Procedures

Participants in the HomeNetToo project were 140 children residing in a midsize urban community in the Midwestern United States. Demographic characteristics of adult participants are described elsewhere. Participants were recruited at meetings held at the children's middle school and at the Black Child and Family Institute, Lansing, MI. Requirements for participation were that the child be eligible for the federally subsidized school lunch program, that the family have a working telephone line for the previous 6 months, and that the family never had home Internet access. Participants agreed to have their Internet use automatically and continuously recorded, to complete surveys at multiple points during the project, and to participate in home visits. In exchange, the households received home computers, Internet access, and in-home technical support during the Internet recording period (i.e., 16 months). At the end of the project, participants kept their computers and were assisted in locating inexpensive Internet service.

As indicated earlier, children were primarily African American (83%), primarily boys (58%), and primarily living in single-parent households (75%) in which the median annual income was $15,000 or less (49%). Average age was 13.8 years (*SD* = 1.95), median age was 13 years, and modal age was 12 years. Ages ranged from 10 to 18 years, although nearly three-quarters of participants (71%) were between 12 and 14 years of age.

Measures

Internet use.   Four measures of Internet use that were automatically and continuously recorded for 16 months for each participant are considered in this report.[3] The measures are time online (minutes per day), number of sessions (logins per day), number of domains visited (per day), and number of e-mails sent (per day). Some examples of domains visited by participants are www.anygivensunday.net (entertainment), www.senate.gov (government information), and www.kcts.org (news and current events). Internet use measures were divided into five time periods, three corresponding to survey administration points plus half-year and 1-year points. The time periods were: Time 1 (1 to 3 months), Time 2 (4 to 6 months), Time 3 (7 to 9 months), Time 4 (10 to 12 months), and Time 5 (13 to 16 months). Latent linear growth curve analysis was used to evaluate time-related changes in Internet use and academic performance.

Academic performance.   Participants' grade point averages (GPAs) and scores on the Michigan Educational Assessment Program (MEAP) tests of reading and mathematics achievement were obtained directly from the local school district (with parental permission). MEAP tests are standardized tests of known (high) reliability that Michigan educators use to inform decisions regarding educational policy and expenditures. GPAs were obtained for Fall 2000 (the semester before the project began), Spring 2001 (after 6 months of project participation), Fall 2001 (after 1 year of project participation), and Spring 2002 (the semester the project ended [April 2002]). MEAP scores were obtained for 2001 (for tests taken after 5 months of project participation) and 2002 (for tests taken 1 month after the 16-month project ended).

---

[3]A total of 20 measures of Internet use were recorded for each participant.

Results

Academic Performance and Internet Use

Descriptive statistics for measures of percentile ranks on the MEAP tests of reading and mathematics achievement are presented in Table 1. *Hypothesis 1* states that greater Internet use will be associated with better academic performance in the months that follow. Several steps were taken to evaluate this hypothesis.

First, race, age, and gender differences in Internet use and academic performance were examined to determine whether any of these sociodemographic characteristics needed to be controlled in the analyses to predict academic performance from each measure of Internet use (in separate analyses). Second, stepwise regression analyses were used to predict academic performance from Internet use during the preceding time period. Third, latent linear growth curve analysis was used to model relationships between Internet use and academic performance.

Consistent with *Hypothesis 4,* African-American children and younger children used the Internet less than did European American children and older children, respectively. However, no gender differences in Internet use were noted, contrary to *Hypothesis 5.* Additional analyses indicated that African-American children had lower GPAs and standardized test scores than did European American children ($ps < .05$) but that age and gender were unrelated to academic performance. Thus only race was controlled in the analyses to predict academic performance from Internet use.

Regression analyses were used to predict GPA from Internet use during the preceding time period. . . .

Results of these analyses indicated that, after controlling for race (step 1), Internet use did not predict GPA obtained after the first 6 months of the project. However, Internet use did predict GPA obtained after 1 year of home Internet access, and at the end of the 16-month trial. More Internet sessions were associated with higher GPAs.

Table 1

Percentile Ranks on Standardized Tests of Academic Achievement

	2001			2002		
	N	Mean	SD	N	Mean	SD
Reading Comprehension	95	31.85	28.03	75	35.03	29.72
Reading Total Score	95	31.93	28.55	74	33.65	28.34
Mathematics Comprehension	80	32.45	25.69	50	33.60	23.30
Mathematics Total Score	91	29.15	24.85	73	30.53	25.82

Note. Tests were the Michigan Educational Assessment Program (MEAP) tests.

To predict performance on standardized tests of academic achievement (i.e., MEAP percentile ranks) in Spring 2001, measures of Internet use during the first 6 months of the project were used. To predict MEAP performance in Spring 2002, measures of Internet use at Time 5 were used.

Results of these regression analyses indicated that Internet use during the first 6 months of the project predicted reading comprehension and total reading scores obtained at the end of that time period. More time online was associated with higher reading comprehension and total reading scores. Similarly, Internet use during the last semester of the project (Time 5) predicted reading comprehension and total reading scores obtained at the end of that semester. More Internet sessions were associated with higher reading scores. Mathematics scores could not be predicted from Internet use, regardless of which time period and which measure of Internet use was considered.

We also examined whether academic performance predicted Internet use rather than the reverse. Support for the latter would undermine a causal role of Internet use in changes in GPA. Children's GPAs for Fall 2000 were used to predict Internet use at Time 1, GPAs for Spring 2001 were used to predict Internet use at Time 3, and GPAs for Fall 2001 were used to predict Internet use at Time 5. In none of these analyses did GPA predict subsequent Internet use. . . .

Thus results of the regression analyses indicate that children who used the Internet more subsequently had higher GPAs and higher scores on standardized tests of reading achievement than did children who used the Internet less. The reverse was not true. Children who had higher GPAs and higher standardized test scores did not subsequently use the Internet more than did children who had lower GPAs and test scores. . . .

Frequency and Nature of Children's Internet Use

According to *Hypothesis 2*, children will spend between 3 hours per week and 7 hours per week (1 hour per day) using the Internet. Averaging across the 16-month trial, HomeNetToo children spent approximately 27 minutes per day online, at the low end of the broad range predicted by *Hypothesis 2*. Children participated in 0.6 sessions per day, suggesting that they did not logon daily, and visited approximately 10 domains per day. Children sent very few e-mail messages (less than one per week). Thus, consistent with *Hypothesis 3*, HomeNetToo children were more likely to use the Internet for information gathering than they did for communication.

Sociodemographic Characteristics and Internet Use

As previously indicated, consistent with *Hypothesis 4*, African-American children and younger children used the Internet less than did European-American children and older children, respectively. Contrary to *Hypothesis 5*, no gender differences were noted in Internet use. Thus girls were no more likely than boys were to use the Internet's communication tools; boys were no more likely than girls were to use the Internet's information tools.

Age effects on Internet for communication versus information purposes were evaluated in regression analyses to predict e-mail use at each time period from participants' age (controlling for race). No effects of age were noted in any of these analyses.

Discussion

Children who used the Internet more had higher GPAs after 1 year and higher scores on standardized tests of reading achievement after 6 months than did children who used it less. Moreover, the benefits of Internet use on academic performance continued throughout the project period. Children who used the Internet more during the last 4 months of the project had higher GPAs and standardized test scores in reading than did children who used it less. Internet use had no effect on standardized test scores of mathematics achievement.

Previous research has produced equivocal findings with respect to the effects of information technology use, specifically computer use, on cognitive outcomes. At best, some evidence suggests a positive relationship between computer game playing and visual spatial skills and between owning a home computer and school performance, although the causal nature of the latter relationship has yet to be established. Whether Internet use contributes to children's academic performance has, until now, never been systematically investigated. Thus, until now, no evidence exists that using the Internet actually improves academic performance, despite optimism surrounding the Internet as a tool to level the educational playing field.

Why did Internet use enhance HomeNetToo children's academic performance, specifically, their reading performance? One possibility is that children who spent more time online were also spending more time reading compared with their unconnected peers. HomeNetToo children logged on primarily to surf the Web. Web pages are heavily text based. Thus, whether searching for information about school-related projects or searching for information about personal interests and hobbies (e.g., rock stars, movies), children who were searching the Web more were reading more, and more time spent reading may account for improved performance on standardized tests of reading and for higher GPAs, which depend heavily on reading skills. The absence of Internet use effects on mathematics performance is consistent with this view. Web pages do not typically engage mathematics skills. New research is needed to establish the mediational role of reading in the relationship between Internet use and academic performance.

Another subject for future research is whether Internet use has a similar positive impact on the academic performance of all children. Children in the HomeNetToo project were performing well below average in school, as measured by both GPAs and standardized tests scores. Possibly, the academic performance benefits of Internet use are limited to children in this performance range. Children whose academic performance is average or above average may not only fail to show similar benefits of Internet use, but may also show decrements in academic performance with more time online. Whatever the results of future research may be, our findings suggest that the implications of the "digital divide" in Internet use may be more serious than was initially believed. One possibility may be that children most likely to benefit from home Internet access—poor children whose academic performance is below average—are the very children least likely to have home Internet access. Additional research is needed to determine whether Internet use has similar, different, or no effect for middle-class and upper-middle-class children and for low-income children with average or above-average performance in school.

Children in the HomeNetToo project used the Internet approximately 30 minutes a day, at the low end of the broad range suggested by previous research. Contrary to popular beliefs, media hype, and some previous research, HomeNetToo children made scant use of the Internet's communication tools. E-mail, instant messaging, and chat room conversations were infrequent activities at the start of the project, and the number of children participating in these activities dropped dramatically by the end of the project. Indeed, after 16 months of home Internet access, only 16% of the children were sending e-mail or participating in chat, and only 25% were instant messaging.

Why did HomeNetToo children make so little use of the Internet's communication tools? One explanation is so obvious as to be easily overlooked. HomeNetToo children were poor. In all likelihood, their friends and extended family members were poor. Poor people do not typically have home Internet access. Moreover, other evidence obtained from parents indicates that children were often forbidden from participating in chat or other activities that involved contact with strangers online. Thus, with no friends and family to e-mail, and with chat activities and conversations with strangers explicitly forbidden, the fact that HomeNetToo children made so little use of the Internet's communication tools is not at all surprising.

Another explanation for children's infrequent use of the Internet's communication tools lies in cultural influences on communication preferences. The majority of the children in the HomeNetToo project were African American (83%). African-American culture is historically an "oral culture." For example, recent evidence indicates that African Americans prefer face-to-face communication to a far greater extent than do European Americans. The impersonal nature of the Internet's typical communication tools (e.g., e-mail) may have discouraged African-American children from using them. Perhaps as communication on the Internet becomes more enriched with oral and visual cues, Internet use may become more appealing to members of other cultures.

Children's sociodemographic characteristics were related to their Internet use. As in previous research, older children used the Internet more than did younger children. No evidence has been found that age influences whether the Internet was used for information or communication purposes or that age influences the benefits of Internet use to academic performance. However, unequal distribution of participants across the age range (10 to 18 years) may have obscured the finding of significant age effects (71% of participants were between 12 and 14 years of age). Nevertheless, our evidence that home Internet use benefits the academic performance of children as young as age 10 suggests that early home access for all children may be critical to leveling the educational playing field.

Extending previous research with adolescents and adults, European-American children in our research used the Internet more than did African-American children. As with age, these findings have implications for educational policy aimed at leveling the educational playing field. Although home Internet use may account for only a small portion of the variance in academic performance, race differences in home Internet use may serve to exacerbate existing race differences in academic performance.

The persistence of race differences in Internet use when access to the technology is not an issue suggests that cultural factors may be contributing to the racial digital divide. Perhaps the culture of the Internet, created primarily by European-American men, is not a welcoming culture for African-American children. Perhaps the design of Web pages, again primarily by European-American men, lacks esthetic appeal for African-American children.

Systematic research is needed to examine whether cultural characteristics and technology design interact to influence technology use and enjoyment. For example, if a preference for oral communication is responsible for race differences in Internet use observed in the HomeNetToo project and other studies, then changes in interface design that accommodate this preference may help reduce or eliminate race difference in use. As Internet technology evolves to support more multimodal, multisensory experiences, it may be better able to accommodate cultural influences on communication and other preferences.

Mark Bauerlein

The Dumbest Generation:
How the Digital Age Stupefies
Young Americans and Jeopardizes
Our Future

When writer Alexandra Robbins returned to Walt Whitman High School in Bethesda, Maryland, ten years after graduating, she discovered an awful trend. The kids were miserable. She remembers her high school years as a grind of study and homework, but lots more, too, including leisure times that allowed for "well-roundedness." Not for Whitman students circa 2005. The teens in *The Overachievers,* Robbins's chronicle of a year spent among them, have only one thing on their minds, SUCCESS, and one thing in their hearts, ANXIETY. Trapped in a mad "culture of over-achieverism," they run a frantic race to earn an A in every class, score 2350 or higher on the SATs, take piano lessons, chalk up AP courses on their transcripts, stay in shape, please their parents, volunteer for outreach programs, and, most of all, win entrance to "HYP" (Harvard-Yale-Princeton).

As graduation approaches, their résumés lengthen and sparkle, but their spirits flag and sicken. One Whitman junior, labeled by Robbins "The Stealth Overachiever," receives a fantastic 2380 (out 2400) on a PSAT test, but instead of rejoicing, he worries that the company administering the practice run "made the diagnostics easier so students would think the class was working."

Audrey, "The Perfectionist," struggles for weeks to complete her tooth-pick bridge, which she and her partner expect will win them a spot in the Physics Olympics. She's one of the Young Democrats, too, and she does catering jobs. Her motivation stands out, and she thinks every other student competes with her personally, so whenever she receives a graded test or paper, "she [turns] it over without looking at it and then [puts] it away, resolving not to check the grade until she [gets] home."

"AP Frank" became a Whitman legend when as a junior he managed a "seven-AP course load that had him studying every afternoon, sleeping during class, and going lunchless." When he scored 1570 on the SAT, his domineering mother screamed in dismay, and her shock subsided only when he retook it and got the perfect 1600.

Julie, "The Superstar," has five AP classes and an internship three times a week at a museum, and she runs cross-country as well. Every evening after dinner she descends to the "homework cave" until bedtime and beyond. She got "only" 1410 on the SAT, though, and she wonders where it will land her next fall.

These kids have descended into a "competitive frenzy," Robbins mourns, and the high school that should open their minds and develop their characters has become a torture zone, a "hotbed for Machiavellian strategy." They bargain and bully and suck up for better grades. They pay tutors and coaches enormous sums to raise their scores a few points and help with the admissions process. Parents hover and query, and they schedule their children down to the minute. Grade inflation only makes it worse, an A- average now a stigma, not an accomplishment. They can't relax, they can't play. It's killing them, throwing sensitive and intelligent teenagers into pathologies of guilt and despair. The professional rat race of yore—men in gray flannel suits climbing the business ladder—has filtered down into the pre-college years, and Robbins's tormented subjects reveal the consequences.

The achievement chase displaces other life questions, and the kids can't seem to escape it. When David Brooks toured Princeton and interviewed students back in 2001, he heard of joyless days and nights with no room for newspapers or politics or dating, just "one skill-enhancing activity to the next." He calls them "Organization Kids" (after the old Organization Man figure of the fifties), students who "have to schedule appointment times for chatting." They've been programmed for success, and a preschool-to-college gauntlet of standardized tests, mounting homework, motivational messages, and extra-curricular tasks has rewarded or punished them at every stage. The system tabulates learning incessantly and ranks students against one another, and the students soon divine its essence: only results matter. Education writer Alfie Kohn summarizes their logical adjustment:

> Consider a school that constantly emphasizes the importance of performance! results! achievement! success! A student who has absorbed that message may find it difficult to get swept away by the process of creating a poem or trying to build a working telescope. He may be so concerned about the results that he's not at all that engaged in the activity that produces those results.

Just get the grades, they tell themselves, ace the test, study, study, study. Assignments become exercises to complete, like doing the dishes, not knowledge to acquire for the rest of their lives. The inner life fades; only the external credits count. After-school hours used to mean sports and comic books and hanging out. Now, they spell homework. As the president of the American Association of School librarians told the *Washington Post,* "When kids are in school now, the stakes are so high, and they have so much homework that it's really hard to find time for pleasure reading" (Strauss). Homework itself has become a plague, as recent titles on the subject show: *The End of Homework: How Homework Disrupts Families, Overburdens Children, and Limits Learning* (Etta Kralovec and John Buell); *The Homework Myth: Why Our Kids Get Too Much of a Bad Thing*

(Alfie Kohn); and *The Case Against Homework: How Homework Is Hurting Our Children and What We Can Do About It* (Sara Bennett and Nancy Kalish).

Parents, teachers, media, and the kids themselves witness the dangers, but the system presses forward. "We believe that reform in homework practices is central to a politics of family and personal liberation," Kralovec and Buell announce, but the momentum is too strong. The overachievement culture, results-obsessed parents, outcomes-based norms . . . they continue to brutalize kids and land concerned observers such as Robbins on the *Today* show. Testing goes on, homework piles up, and competition for spaces in the Ivies was stiffer in 2007 than ever before. A 2006 survey by Pew Research, for instance, found that more than half the adults in the United States (56 percent) think that parents place too little pressure on students, and only 15 percent stated "Too much."

Why?

Because something is wrong with this picture, and most people realize it. They sense what the critics do not, a fundamental error in the vignettes of hyper-studious and overworked kids that we've just seen: they don't tell the truth, not the whole truth about youth in America. For, notwithstanding the poignant tale of suburban D.C. seniors sweating over a calculus quiz, or the image of college students scheduling their friends as if they were CEOs in the middle of a workday, or the lurid complaints about homework, the actual habits of most teenagers and young adults in most schools and colleges in this country display a wholly contrasting problem, but one no less disturbing.

Consider a measure of homework time, this one not taken from a dozen kids on their uneven way to the top, but from 81,499 students. In 110 schools in 26 states—the 2006 *High School Survey of Student Engagement*. When asked how many hours they spent each week "Reading/studying for class," almost all of them, fully 90 percent, came in at a ridiculously low five hours or less, 55 percent at one hour or less. Meanwhile, 31 percent admitted to watching television or playing video games at least six hours per week, 25 percent of them logging six hours minimum surfing and chatting online.

Or check a 2004 report by the University of Michigan Institute for Social Research entitled *Changing Times of American Youth: 1981–2003,* which surveyed more than 2,000 families with children age six to 17 in the home. In 2003, homework time for 15- to 17-year-olds hit only 24 minutes on weekend days, 50 minutes on weekdays. And weekday TV time? More than twice that: one hour, 55 minutes.

Or check a report by the U.S. Department of Education entitled *NAEP 2004 Trends in Academic Progress.* Among other things, the report gathered data on study and reading time for thousands of 17-year-olds in 2004. When asked how many hours they'd spent on homework the day before, the tallies were meager. Fully 26 percent said that they didn't have any homework to do, while 13 percent admitted that they didn't do any of the homework they were supposed to. A little more than one-quarter (28 percent) spent less than an hour, and another 22 percent devoted one to two hours, leaving only 11 percent to pass the two-hour mark.

Or the 2004–05 *State of Our Nation's Youth* report by the Horatio Alger Association, in which 60 percent of teenage students logged 6 hours of homework per week or less.

The better students don't improve with time, either. In the 2006 *National Survey of Student Engagement,* a college counterpart to the *High School Survey of Student Engagement,* seniors in college logged the astonishingly low commitments to "Preparing for class." Almost one out of five (18 percent) stood at one to five hours per week, and 26 percent at six to ten hours per week. College professors estimate that a successful semester requires about 25 hours of out-of-class study per week, but only 11 percent reached that mark. These young adults have graduated from high school, entered college, declared a major, and lasted seven semesters, but their in-class and out-of-class punch cards amount to fewer hours than a part-time job.

And as for the claim that leisure time is disappearing, the Bureau of Labor Statistics issues an annual *American Time Use Survey* that asks up to 21,000 people to record their activities during the day. The categories include work and school and child care, and also leisure hours. For 2005, 15- to 24-year-olds enjoyed a full five and a half hours of free time per day, more than two hours of which they passed in front of the TV.

The findings of these and many other large surveys refute the frantic and partial renditions of youth habits and achievement that all too often make headlines and fill talk shows. Savvier observers guard against the "we're overworking the kids" alarm, people such as Jay Mathews, education reporter at the *Washington Post,* who called Robbins's book a "spreading delusion," and Tom Loveless of the Brookings Institution, whose 2003 report on homework said of the "homework is destroying childhood" argument, "Almost everything in this story is wrong." One correspondent's encounter with a dozen elite students who hunt success can be vivid and touching, but it doesn't jibe with mountains of data that tell contrary stories. The surveys, studies, tests, and testimonials reveal the opposite, that the vast majority of high school and college kids are far less accomplished and engaged, and the classroom pressures much less cumbersome, than popular versions put forth. These depressing accounts issue from government agencies with no ax to grind, from business leaders who just want competent workers, and from foundations that sympathize with the young. While they lack the human drama, they impart more reliable assessments, providing a better baseline for understanding the realities of the young American mentality and forcing us to stop upgrading the adolescent condition beyond its due.

This book is an attempt to consolidate the best and broadest research into a different profile of the rising American mind. It doesn't cover behaviors and values, only the intellect of under-30-year-olds. Their political leanings don't matter, nor do their career ambitions. The manners, music, clothing, speech, sexuality, faith, diversity, depression, criminality, drug use, moral codes, and celebrities of the young spark many books, articles, research papers, and marketing strategies centered on Generation Y (or Generation DotNet, or the Millennials), but not this one. It sticks to one thing, the intellectual condition of young Americans, and describes it with empirical evidence, recording something hard to document but nonetheless insidious happening inside their heads. The information is scattered and underanalyzed, but once collected and compared, it charts a consistent and perilous momentum downward.

It sounds pessimistic, and many people sympathetic to youth pressures may class the chapters to follow as yet another curmudgeonly riff. Older people have complained forever about the derelictions of youth, and the "old fogy" tag puts them on the defensive. Perhaps, though, it is a healthy process in the life story of humanity for older generations to berate the younger, for young and old to relate in a vigorous competitive dialectic, with the energy and optimism of youth vying against the wisdom and realism of elders in a fruitful check of one another's worst tendencies. That's another issue, however. The conclusions here stem from a variety of completed and ongoing research projects, public and private organizations, and university professors and media centers, and they represent different cultural values and varying attitudes toward youth. It is remarkable, then, that they so often reach the same general conclusions. They disclose many trends and consequences in youth experience, but the intellectual one emerges again and again. It's an outcome not as easily noticed as a carload of teens inching down the boulevard rattling store windows with the boom-boom of a hip-hop beat, and the effect runs deeper than brand-name clothing and speech patterns. It touches the core of a young person's mind, the mental storehouse from which he draws when engaging the world. And what the sources reveal, one by one, is that a paradoxical and distressing situation is upon us.

The paradox may be put this way. We have entered the Information Age, traveled the Information Superhighway, spawned a Knowledge Economy, undergone the Digital Revolution, converted manual workers into knowledge workers, and promoted a Creative Class, and we anticipate a Conceptual Age to be. However overhyped those grand social metaphors, they signify a rising premium on knowledge and communications, and everyone from *Wired* magazine to Al Gore to Thomas Friedman to the Task Force on the Future of American Innovation echoes the change. When he announced the American Competitiveness Initiative in February 2006, President Bush directly linked the fate of the U.S. economy "to generating knowledge and tools upon which new technologies are developed." In a *Washington Post* op-ed, Bill Gates asserted, "But if we are to remain competitive, we need a workforce that consists of the world's brightest minds. . . . First, we must demand strong schools so that young Americans enter the workforce with the math, science and problem-solving skills they need to succeed in the knowledge economy."

And yet, while teens and young adults have absorbed digital tools into their daily lives like no other age group, while they have grown up with more knowledge and information readily at hand, taken more classes, built their own Web sites, enjoyed more libraries, bookstores, and museums in their towns and cities . . . in sum, while the world has provided them extraordinary chances to gain knowledge and improve their reading/writing skills, not to mention offering financial incentives to do so, young Americans today are no more learned or skillful than their predecessors, no more knowledgeable, fluent, up-to-date, or inquisitive, except in the materials of youth culture. They don't know any more history or civics, economics or science, literature or current events. They read less on their own, both books and newspapers, and you would have to canvass a lot of college English instructors and employers before you found one who said that they compose better paragraphs. In fact, their technology skills fall well short of the common claim, too, especially when they must apply them to research and workplace tasks.

The world delivers facts and events and art and ideas as never before, but the young American mind hasn't opened. Young Americans' vices have diminished, one must acknowledge, as teens and young adults harbor fewer stereotypes and social prejudices. Also, they regard their parents more highly than they did 25 years ago. They volunteer in strong numbers, and rates of risky behaviors are dropping. Overall conduct trends are moving upward, leading a hard-edged commentator such as Kay Hymowitz to announce in "It's Morning After in America" (2004) that "pragmatic Americans have seen the damage that their decades-long fling with the sexual revolution and the transvaluation of traditional values wrought. And now, without giving up the real gains, they are earnestly knitting up their unraveled culture. It is a moment of tremendous promise." At *TechCentralStation.com*, James Glassman agreed enough to proclaim, "Good News! The Kids Are Alright!" Youth watchers William Strauss and Neil Howe were confident enough to subtitle their book on young Americans *The Next Great Generation* (2000).

And why shouldn't they? Teenagers and young adults mingle in a society of abundance, intellectual as well as material. American youth in the twenty-first century have benefited from a shower of money and goods, a bath of liberties and pleasing self-images, vibrant civic debates, political blogs, old books and masterpieces available online, traveling exhibitions, the History Channel, news feeds . . . and on and on. Never have opportunities for education, learning, political action, and cultural activity been greater. All the ingredients for making an informed and intelligent citizen are in place.

But it hasn't happened. Yes, young Americans are energetic, ambitious, enterprising, and good, but their talents and interests and money thrust them not into books and ideas and history and civics, but into a whole other realm and other consciousness. A different social life and a different mental life have formed among them. Technology has bred it, but the result doesn't tally with the fulsome descriptions of digital empowerment, global awareness, and virtual communities. Instead of opening young American minds to the stores of civilization and science and politics, technology has contracted their horizon to themselves, to the social scene around them. Young people have never been so intensely mindful of and present to one another, so enabled in adolescent contact. Teen images and songs, hot gossip and games, and youth-to-youth communications no longer limited by time or space wrap them up in a generational cocoon reaching all the way into their bedrooms. The autonomy has a cost: the more they attend to themselves, the less they remember the past and envision a future. They have all the advantages of modernity and democracy, but when the gifts of life lead to social joys, not intellectual labor, the minds of the young plateau at age 18. This is happening all around us. The fonts of knowledge are everywhere, but the rising generation is camped in the desert, passing stories, pictures, tunes, and texts back and forth, living off the thrill of peer attention. Meanwhile, their intellects refuse the cultural and civic inheritance that has made us what we are up to now. . . .

A healthy society needs a pipeline of intellectuals, and not just the famous ones. An abiding atmosphere of reflection and forensic should touch many more than the gifted and politically disposed students. Democracy thrives on a knowledgeable citizenry, not just an elite team of thinkers and theorists, and the broader knowledge extends among the populace the more intellectuals it will train. Democracy needs a kind of minor-league system in youth circles to create both major-league sages 20 years later and a critical mass of less accomplished but still learned individuals. Noteworthy intellectual groupings such as liberal anti-communists in the forties, Beats in the fifties, and neo-conservatives in the seventies steered the United States in certain ideological directions. History will remember them. But in every decade labors an army of lesser intellectuals—teachers, journalists, curators, librarians, bookstore managers, diplomats, pundits, amateur historians and collectors, etc., whose work rises or falls on the liberal arts knowledge they bring to it. They don't electrify the world with breakthrough notions. They create neighborhood reading programs for kids, teach eighth-graders about abolition, run county historical societies, cover city council meetings, and host author events. Few of them achieve fame, but they sustain the base forensic that keeps intellectual activity alive across the institution that train generations to come.

Apart from ideological differences and variations in prestige, greater and lesser intellectuals on the Right and Left, speaking on C-SPAN or in rural classrooms, focusing on ancient wars or on the Depression, blogging on Romantic music or on postmodern novels . . . all may unite on one premise: knowledge of history, civics, art, and philosophy promotes personal welfare and national welfare. Intellectuals may quarrel over everything else, but at bottom they believe in the public and private value of liberal education. Columbia professor John Erskine called it "the moral obligation to be intelligent" 90 years ago, and every worker in the knowledge fields agreed. In the heat of intellectual battle, though, they rarely descend to that level of principle and concord. They usually concentrate friends and enemies within the intellectual class, where that conviction goes without saying, and in formulating rejoinders for the marketplace of ideas, they forget that the marketplace itself must be sustained by something else against the forces of anti-intellectualism and anti-knowledge. Intellectuals can and should debate the best and worst books and ideas and personages, and they will scramble to affect policies in formation, but what upholds the entire activity resides beyond their circles. It grows on top of public sentiment, a widespread conviction that knowledge is as fundamental as individual freedoms. For intellectual discourse, high art, historical awareness, and liberal arts curricula to flourish, support must come from outside intellectual clusters. Laypersons, especially the young ones, must get the message: if you ignore the traditions that ground and ennoble our society, you are an incomplete person, and a negligent citizen.

This knowledge principle forms part of the democratic faith, and it survives only as long as a fair portion of the American people embraces it, not just intellectuals and experts. The production of spirited citizens requires more than meditations by academics and strategies by activists, and it transpires not only in classrooms and among advocacy groups. Learning and disputation, books and ideas, must infiltrate leisure time, too, and they should spread well beyond the cerebral cliques. This is why leisure trends among the general population are so important. They log the status of the knowledge principle, and when they focus on under-30-year-olds, they not only reveal today's fashions among the kids but also tomorrow's prospects for civic well-being.

As of 2008, the intellectual future of the United States looks dim. Not the economic future, or the technological, medical, or media future, but the future of civic understanding and liberal education. The social pressures and leisure preferences of young Americans, for all their silliness and brevity, help set the heading of the American mind, and the direction is downward. The seventies joke about college students after late-sixties militance had waned still holds.

> "What do you think of student ignorance and apathy?" the interviewer
> asks the sophomore.
> "I dunno and I don' care"—

It isn't funny anymore. The Dumbest Generation cares little for history books, civic principles, foreign affairs, comparative religions, and serious media and art, and it knows less. Careening through their formative years, they don't catch the knowledge bug, and *tradition* might as well be a foreign word. Other things monopolize their attention—the allure of screens, peer absorption, career goals. They are latter-day Rip Van Winkles, sleeping through the movements of culture and events of history, preferring the company of peers to great books and powerful ideas and momentous happenings. From their ranks will emerge few minds knowledgeable and interested enough to study, explain, and dispute the place and meaning of our nation. Adolescence is always going to be more or less anti-intellectual, of course, and learning has ever struggled against immaturity, but the battle has never proven so uphill. Youth culture and youth society, fabulously autonomized by digital technology, swamp the intellectual pockets holding on against waves of pop culture and teen mores, and the Boomer mentors have lowered the bulwarks to surmountable heights. Among the Millennials, intellectual life can't compete with social life, and if social life has no intellectual content, traditions wither and die. Books can't hold their own with screen images, and without help, high art always loses to low amusement.

The ramifications for the United States are grave. We need a steady stream of rising men and women to replenish the institution, to become strong military leaders and wise political leaders, dedicated journalists and demanding teachers, judges and muckraker scholars and critics and artists. We have the best schools to train them, but social and private environments have eroded. Some of the kids study hard for class, but what else do they learn when they're young? How do they spend the free hours of adolescence? They don't talk with their friends about books, and they don't read them when they're alone. Teachers try to impart knowledge, but students today remember only that which suits their careers or advantages their social lives. For the preparation of powerful officials, wise intellectuals, and responsible citizens, formal schooling and workplace training are not enough. Social life and leisure time play essential roles in the maturing process, and if the knowledge principle disappears, if books, artworks, historical facts, and civic debates—in a word, an intellectual forensic—vacate the scene, then the knowledge young people acquire later on never penetrates to their hearts. The forensic retreats into ever smaller cells, where nerds and bookworms nurture their loves cut off from the world.

Democracy doesn't prosper that way. If tradition survives only in the classroom, limping along in watered-down lessons, if knowledge doesn't animate the young when they're with each other and by themselves, it won't inform their thought and behavior when they're old. The latest social and leisure dispositions of the young are killing the culture, and when they turn 40 years old and realize what they failed to learn in their younger days, it will be too late.

The research compiled in the previous chapters piles gloomy fact on gloomy fact, and it's time to take it seriously. Fewer books are checked out of public libraries and more videos. More kids go to the mall and fewer to the museum. Lunchroom conversations never drift into ideology, but Web photos pass nonstop from handheld to handheld. If parents and teachers and reporters don't see it now, they're blind.

If they don't respond, they're unconscionable. It's time for over-30-year-olds of all kinds to speak out, not just social conservatives who fret over Internet pornography, or political Leftists who want to rouse the youth vote, or traditionalist educators who demand higher standards in the curriculum. Adults everywhere need to align against youth ignorance and apathy, and not fear the "old fogy" tag and recoil from the smirks of the young. The moral poles need to reverse, with the young no longer setting the pace for right conduct and cool thinking. Let's tell the truth. The Dumbest Generation will cease being dumb only when it regards adolescence as an inferior realm of petty strivings and adulthood as a realm of civic, historical, and cultural awareness that puts them in touch with the perennial ideas and struggles. The youth of America occupy a point in history like every other generation did and will, and their time will end. But the effects of their habits will outlast them, and if things do not change they will be remembered as the fortunate ones who were unworthy of the privileges they inherited. They may even be recalled as the generation that lost that great American heritage, forever.

EXPLORING THE ISSUE

Are People Better Informed in the Information Society?

Critical Thinking and Reflection

1. Does the digital divide harm those without access? What is lost? Could anything be gained?
2. How is that a generation can have so much access to information and still be lacking in basic knowledge?
3. What does it mean to be better informed?
4. Has the Internet rewired our brains? Is your generation less able to concentrate and to immerse themselves? Is information being substituted for critical thinking?

Is there Common Ground?

It would be wonderful if we could predict the future with certainty, but unfortunately, even predictions are subject to change. One of the pleasures of science fiction is that there is usually enough evidence in any portrayal of the future that elements of the story appear to be plausible. One chilling, and certainly plausible, idea is that ways of learning and knowing may be changing in the digital world. Perhaps that helps us to better understand how children can profit from having the Internet in their home, but still may fail traditional tests of education. There are many futuristic novels like *1984* and *Brave New World* that, in their day, sent chills down the spines of readers. Today's equivalent of these novels would be a film like *The Matrix*.

To read more accounts of how media and technology can and do affect the quality of our lives by facilitating changes within our major institutions—such as education, government, and through popular culture, we suggest a number of readings from a variety of viewpoints below. As mentioned previously, Neil Postman's classic *Amusing Ourselves to Death* looks at the impact of television on our lives. His thesis is that even news has to be packaged to be entertaining, and the desire to be entertained stretches to other institutions as well, such as schools and within our political arena.

Additional Resources

Neil Postman, *Technopoly* (Knopf Publisher, 1992) and *Building a Bridge to the 18th Century* (Knopf Publisher, 1999)

Both the books deal with the subtle changes we often experience, but never critically question, as we venerate science and technology and exclude very human traits such as morality and common sense.

Don Tapscott, *Grown Up Digital: How the Net Generation Is Changing Your World* (McGraw-Hill, 2008)

Based on extensive survey research of young people, Tapscott describes a community with new ways of thinking, working, and socializing. He discusses how the Net Generation processes information, actively participates in the distribution of entertainment and information, and is the authority on the evolving digital world.

Nicholas Carr, *The Shallows: What the Internet Is Doing to Our Brains* (W.W. Norton, 2011)

Author of the *Atlantic Monthly* article, "Is Google Making Us Stupid," Carr describes in this book the neurological effects of the Internet that short-change our brain power. His primary argument is that the neurological pathways created by Internet use impede comprehension and attention, rewiring our brains for surfing rather than immersion and concentration.

Mark Bauerline, *The Digital Divide: Arguments For and Against Facebook, Google, Texting, and the Age of Social Networking* (Jeremy P. Tarcher/Penguin, 2009)

This edited volume contains essays from some of the most prominent voices writing about social media's role in everyday life. Subjects covered include learning, social life, culture, and political impact.

Contributors to This Volume

EDITORS

ALISON ALEXANDER is professor of telecommunications and senior associate dean at the Grady College of Journalism and Mass Communication at the University of Georgia. She is the past editor of the *Journal of Broadcasting & Electronic Media,* and past president of the Associate for Communication Administration and the Eastern Communication Association. She received her PhD in communication from Ohio State University. She is widely published in the area of media and family, audience research, and media economics.

JARICE HANSON is professor of communication at the University of Massachusetts, Amherst, and the current Verizon Chair in Telecommunications at the School of Communications and Theater, Temple University. She was the founding dean of the School of Communications at Quinnipiac University from 2001 to 2003. She received a BA in speech and performing arts and a BA in English at Northeastern Illinois University in 1976, and she received an MA and a PhD from Northwestern University in Radio-TV-Film in 1977 and 1979, respectively. She is author or editor of 18 books and numerous articles. The most recent books include *24/7: How Cell Phones and the Internet Change the Way We Live, Work and Play* (Praeger, 2007) and *Constructing America's War Culture: Iraq, Media, and Images at Home* (co-edited with Thomas Conroy) (Lexington Books, 2007). She lives in Massachusetts with three furry creatures: Dewey, Xena, and Frank.

AUTHORS

WAJAHAT ALI is a researcher at the Center for American Progress and a researcher for the Center for American Progress Action Fund.

CHRIS ANDERSON is an editor at *Wired* magazine. His most recent book is *Free: The Future of a Radical Price* (Hyperion Books, 2009).

CRAIG A. ANDERSON is a professor in the department of psychology, University of Iowa. He has written extensively on human behavior and violence.

STEPHANIE C. ARDITO is a specialist in the library and information industry. She is currently the president of the Association of Independent Information Professionals, and a principle at Ardito Information & Research, Inc., in Wilmington, Delaware.

GRETCHEN BARBATSIS is a professor of communication in the Department of Telecommunications, Information Studies, and Media at Michigan State University. She also consults widely on telecommunication issues.

MARK BAUERLEIN is a professor of English at Emory University. He recently served as the director, Office of Research and Analysis, at the National Endowment for the Arts. Apart from his scholarly work, he publishes in popular periodicals such as *The Wall Street Journal, The Weekly Standard,* and *The Washington Post.* His latest book, *The Dumbest Generation: How the Digital Age Stupefies Young Americans and Jeopardizes Our Future,* was published in May 2008.

GAL BECKERMAN is a reporter for *Columbia Journalism Review.* He was the New York bureau chief of the *Jerusalem Post* and has been researching and writing a history of the movement to free the Jews from the Soviet Union during the Cold War.

FRANK A. BIOCCA is a professor of telecommunication, information studies and media at Michigan State University in East Lansing, Michigan.

JOHN E. CALFEE is a resident scholar at the American Enterprise Institute in Washington, DC. He is a former Federal Trade Commission economist, and he is the author of *Fear of Persuasion: A New Perspective on Advertising and Regulation* (Agora, 1997).

ELI CLIFTON is a researcher at the Center for American Progress and a national security reporter for the Center for American Progress Action Fund and ThinkProgress.org.

MATTHEW DUSS is a policy analyst at the Center for American Progress and the director of the Center's Middle East Progress.

SHARI L. DWORKIN is an associate professor of behavioral medicine in the Department of Psychiatry at the New York State Psychiatric Institute and Columbia University. Her research centers on how gender inequalities and privileges influence risk for HIV, and on the impact of media on body image.

MICHAEL ERIC DYSON is a noted scholar and cultural critic. A professor at Georgetown University, he is a popular radio and television personality, and has authored 18 books on matters related to race and class.

LEIGH H. EDWARDS is an Associate Professor of English at Florida State University, where she specializes in nineteenth- and twentieth-century literature and popular culture.

ALEXANDER VON EYE is a professor of psychology at Michigan State University, and former Chair of the unit on Developmental Psychology.

LEE FANG is a researcher at the Center for American Progress and an investigative researcher/blogger for the Center for American Progress Action Fund and ThinkProgress.org.

PAUL FARHI is a staff writer for *The Washington Post* who has written extensively on media industries and products.

HIRAM E. FITZGERALD is the associate provost for outreach and engagement at Michigan State University, where he is also a distinguished professor in the Department of Psychology.

JULIA R. FOX is an associate professor of telecommunications at Indiana University–Bloomington. Her research interests include television news coverage and how people process and remember television news messages.

HENRY A. GIROUX holds the Global TV Network Chair in English and Cultural Studies at McMaster University in Canada. A prolific author, his most recent book is *Youth in a Suspect Society: Beyond the Politics of Disposability* (Palgrave Macmillan, 2009).

MALCOLM GLADWELL is a staff writer with *The New Yorker* magazine and author of four best-selling books including *The Tipping Point, Outliers, Blink,* and most recently *What the Dog Saw*. He previously was a reporter with *The Washington Post*.

DINYAR GODREJ is an editor with the *New Internationalist*. Recent books include the *No Nonsense Guide to Climate Change* (2006) and *Peace (Books to Go)* (2005), both published by New Internationalist Publications.

BARRY A. HOLLANDER is an associate professor of journalism at the University of Georgia. His research interests include the political effects of new media and the interaction of religious and political beliefs.

LINDA A. JACKSON is a professor in the Department of Psychology at Michigan State University. She has research interest in the cultural, social, and psychological factors influencing the use and consequences of information technologies.

HENRY JENKINS is the director of the comparative media studies program at MIT. He has co-authored several books, including *Democracy and the New Media* (Cambridge, MIT Press 2003).

ALEX S. JONES is a Pulitzer prize-winning journalist and director of the Joan Shorenstein Center on the Press, Politics and Public Policy at Harvard's John F. Kennedy School of Government, where he is the Laurence

M. Lombard Chair in the Press and Public Policy. He has written for the *New York Times* and was host of NPR's On the Media.

SCOTT KEYES is a researcher at the Center for American Progress and an investigative researcher for ThinkProgress.org at the Center for American Progress Action Fund.

GLORY KOLOEN was a graduate student at Indiana University when she co-authored the selection in this edition. She has since written several articles on politics and the media.

GREG KOT is a music critic who has worked for the *Chicago Tribune.* He also hosts a nationally syndicated rock 'n' roll radio program, *Sound Opinions,* and writes about music on his blog, "Turn It Up."

MARCIA LANDY teaches at the University of Pittsburgh, where she is a Distinguished Service Professor with an appointment in French and Italian.

PENNY A. LEISRING is an associate professor at Quinnipiac University in Hamden, Connecticut. Her work in psychology deals primarily with the prevention and reduction of aggressive behavior in adults and children.

AMANDA LENHART directs the Pew Internet & American Life Project's research on teens, children, and families.

MICHAEL P. LEVINE is the Samuel B. Cummings Jr. Professor of Psychology at Kenyon College, where he teaches and conducts research on abnormal psychology, eating disorders, body image, and the development of personality.

IAN LLOYD is a retired professor of information technology law at the University of Strathclyde, United Kingdom.

DAVID T.Z. MINDICH, a former assignment editor of CNN, is a professor of journalism and mass communication at St. Michael's College. Author of the popular *Tuned Out: Why Americans Under 40 Don's Follow the News,* he lectures to both popular and professional audiences about the issues of journalism and citizenship.

KATHRYN C. MONTGOMERY, PhD is the president and co-founder of the Center for Media Education (CME) in Washington, DC, dedicated to responsible electronic media for children and families. She is also a member of staff at the Center for Social Media (CSM).

SARAH K. MURNEN is professor and chair of the Department of Psychology at Kenyon College. Her research focuses on gender-related issues from a feminist, sociocultural background.

PANOS PANAY is the CEO and Founder of Sonicbids, a matchmaking service that connects emerging musical performers with band promoters, and individuals who license music.

VOLKAN SAHIN teaches in the Department of Child and Family Studies at Weber State University in Ogden, Utah. At the time, he co-authored the selection in this edition, he was a graduate student at Indiana University.

BRIAN SCOGGINS is a Gonzaga University criminal justice graduate.

FAIZ SHAKIR is a vice president at the Center for American Progress and serves as editor-in-chief of ThinkProgress.org. Faiz has previously worked as a research associate for the Democratic National Committee, as a legislative aide to Sen. Bob Graham (D-FL) on the Senate Veterans Affairs Committee, and as a communications aide in the White House Office of National Drug Control Policy.

CLAY SHIRKEY divides his time between consulting, teaching, and writing about the social and economic effects of Internet technologies. He holds a joint appointment at NYU, as an associate arts professor at the Interactive Telecommunications Program (ITP) and as a distinguished writer in Residence in the Journalism Department.

CLAY SHIRKY divides his time between consulting, teaching, and writing on the social and economic effects of Internet technologies. His consulting practice is focused on the rise of decentralized technologies such as peer-to-peer, Web services, and wireless networks. Mr. Shirky has written extensively about the Internet since 1996. Over the years, he has had regular columns in *Business 2.0* and *FEED;* and his writings have appeared in *The New York Times, The Wall Street Journal,* and the *Harvard Business Review.*

KAREN STERNHEIMER teaches in the Sociology Department at the University of Southern California. She is the author of *It's Not the Media: The Truth About Pop Culture's Influence on Children.*

NEIL SWIDEY is a journalist and reporter for the *Boston Globe Magazine* and often writes for the online version of the magazine, Boston.com.

SIVA VAIDHYANATHAN is an associate professor of culture and communication at New York University. He is the author of *Copyrights and Copywrongs: The Rise of Intellectual Property and How It Threatens Creativity* (NYU Press, 2001).

FAYE LINDA WACHS is currently on the faculty of behavioral sciences at California Polytechnic–Pomona. Her research focuses on women's and men's body images, sport, and issues of masculinity.

GEORGIE ANN WEATHERBY is an assistant professor of sociology and criminal justice at Gonzaga University.

YONG ZHAO is currently Presidential Chair and associate dean for Global Education at the College of Education at the University of Oregon. He was previously a distinguished professor of education at Michigan State University.